Federated Learning for Multimedia Data Processing and Security in Industry 5.0

Other related titles:

You may also like

- PBPC064 | Rajput | Intelligent Multimedia Processing and Computer Vision: Techniques and applications
- PBPC061 | Lv | Access Control and Security Monitoring of Multimedia Information Transmission | contracted Jan 2022 (Multimedia Series)
- PBSE030 | Deb | Fortressing Pixels: Information security for images, videos, audio and beyond
- PBPSE029 | Rani | Machine Learning and Deep Learning Driven Techniques Data Security in the Internet of Multimedia Things

We also publish a wide range of books on the following topics:
Computing and Networks
Control, Robotics and Sensors
Electrical Regulations
Electromagnetics and Radar
Energy Engineering
Healthcare Technologies
History and Management of Technology
IET Codes and Guidance
Materials, Circuits and Devices
Model Forms
Nanomaterials and Nanotechnologies
Optics, Photonics and Lasers
Production, Design and Manufacturing
Security
Telecommunications
Transportation

All books are available in print via https://shop.theiet.org or as eBooks via our Digital Library https://digital-library.theiet.org.

IET SECURITY SERIES 66

Federated Learning for Multimedia Data Processing and Security in Industry 5.0

Edited by
Gautam Srivastava and Thippa Reddy Gadekallu

The Institution of Engineering and Technology

About the IET

This book is published by the Institution of Engineering and Technology (The IET).

We inspire, inform, and influence the global engineering community to engineer a better world. As a diverse home across engineering and technology, we share knowledge that helps make better sense of the world, accelerate innovation, and solve the global challenges that matter.

The IET is a not-for-profit organisation. The surplus we make from our books is used to support activities and products for the engineering community and promote the positive role of science, engineering, and technology in the world. This includes education resources and outreach, scholarships and awards, events and courses, publications, professional development and mentoring, and advocacy for governments.

To discover more about the IET please visit https://www.theiet.org/.

About IET books

The IET publishes books across many engineering and technology disciplines. Our authors and editors offer fresh perspectives from universities and industry. Within our subject areas, we have several book series steered by editorial boards made up of leading subject experts.

We peer review each book at the proposal stage to ensure the quality and relevance of our publications.

Get involved

If you are interested in becoming an author, editor, series advisor, or peer reviewer please visit https://www.theiet.org/publishing/publishing-with-iet-books/ or contact author_support@theiet.org.

Discovering our electronic content

All of our books are available online via the IET's Digital Library. Our Digital Library is the home of technical documents, eBooks, conference publications, real-life case studies, and journal articles. To find out more, please visit https://digital-library.theiet.org.

In collaboration with the United Nations and the International Publishers Association, the IET is a Signatory member of the Sustainable Development Goal (SDG) Publishers Compact. The Compact aims to accelerate progress to achieve the SDGs by 2030. Signatories aspire to develop sustainable practices and act as champions of the SDGs during the Decade of Action (2020–30), publishing books and journals that will help inform, develop, and inspire action in that direction.

In line with our sustainable goals, our UK printing partner has FSC accreditation, which is reducing our environmental impact on the planet. We use a print-on-demand model to further reduce our carbon footprint.

Published by The Institution of Engineering and Technology, London, United Kingdom

The Institution of Engineering and Technology (the "**Publisher**") is registered as a Charity in England & Wales (no. 211014) and Scotland (no. SC038698).

First published 2024

The Institution of Engineering and Technology
Futures Place,
Kings Way,
Stevenage,
Herts, SG1 2UA,
United Kingdom

www.theiet.org

British Library Cataloguing in Publication Data

A catalogue record for this product is available from the British Library

ISBN 978-1-83953-757-8 (hardback)
ISBN 978-1-83953-758-5 (PDF)

Typeset in India by MPS Limited

Cover Image: Olemedia/E+ via Getty Images

Gautam Srivastava dedicates this book to Mom, Dad, Andrea, Arjun, and Krishna.

Thippa Reddy Gadekallu dedicates this book to Mom, Dad, Narmada,
and all other family members and friends.

Contents

Foreword

Multimedia (and more generally multimodal data) stands as one of the most demanding and exciting aspects of the information era. The processing of multimedia has been an active research area with applications in secure multimedia content on social networks, digital forensics, digital cinema, education, secured e-voting systems, smart healthcare, automotive applications, the military, finance, insurance, and more. The advent of the Internet of Things (IoT), cyber-physical systems (CPSs), and robotics, as well as personal and wearable devices, now provides many opportunities for the multimedia community to reach out and develop synergies.

Our book series comprehensively defines the current trends and technological aspects of multimedia research with a particular emphasis on interdisciplinary approaches. The authors will review a broad scope to identify challenges, solutions, and new directions. The published books can be used as references by practising engineers, scientists, researchers, practitioners, and technology professionals from academia, government, and Industry working on state-of-the-art multimedia processing and security in Industry 5.0 applications. It will also be useful to senior undergraduate and graduate students, as well as PhD students and Postdoc researchers.

This book focuses on state-of-the-art research, innovations, and future perspectives in federated learning-enabled multimedia applications in Industry 5.0. The authors introduce the role of federated learning, enabling technologies such as digital twins, edge computing and 5G and beyond, cybersecurity aspects, and applications in supply chain management, cobots, and medical-oriented applications. The unique contribution of this volume is to bring together researchers from distinct domains that seldom interact to identify theoretical, technological, and practical solutions.

We hope the readers will find this book of great value in its visionary words.

Dr Amit Kumar Singh, Book Series Editor
Department of Computer Science and Engineering
National Institute of Technology Patna, India

Prof. Stefano Berretti, Book Series Editor
Department of Information Engineering
University of Florence, Italy

Preface

Industry 5.0 is an up-and-coming industrial revolution where people will be working together with smart machines and robots, thereby bringing the human touch and intelligence back to decision-making which was lacking in Industry 4.0. Routine and tough tasks will be carried out by smart machines as well as robots and less reliance will be on humans for decision-making. Industry 4.0 failed to adapt to the demand of mass personalisation. By contrast, Industry 5.0, with effective collaboration between humans and robots, promises to amend this and realise mass personalisation. Some of the challenges that need to be addressed to realise the full potential of the Industry 5.0 era are handling Big Data, preserving the privacy of sensitive data, and near-zero latency for mission-critical applications. Federated learning, which is a recent development in machine learning can be used to address some of these issues. The objective of this book is to present some of the main applications of federated learning to solve known issues in Industry 5.0. The chapters include federated learning for several Industry 5.0 applications such as Healthcare 5.0, digital twins, collaborative robots, communication channels, supply chain management, and blockchain systems. Moreover, some emphasis is given in the book on the security and privacy challenges and solutions that persist with federated learning in Industry 5.0.

Chapter 1 gives an overview of the use of federated learning in 5G networks and beyond in Industry 5.0. Chapter 2, since communication channels are of great importance in Industry 5.0, this chapter looks at optimising communication channels using federated learning in Industry 5.0. Chapter 3 begins discussing federated learning in conjunction with digital twins.

Switching gears, Chapter 4 investigates collaborative intelligence using federated learning in Industry 5.0. Chapters 5 and 6 focus on cybersecurity with one chapter harnessing the power of blockchain whilst the latter using digital twins. The next two chapters focus on the amalgamation of federated learning and blockchain, with Chapter 7 giving an overview of the topic whilst Chapter 8 investigates encryption and decryption techniques in such intertwined systems.

Chapter 9 focuses on supply chain management issues using federated learning. Moving on with other applications in Industry 5.0, Chapter 10 investigates collaborative robots (cobots) in Industry 5.0.

The last three chapters investigate medical applications, with Chapter 11 looking at the use of federated learning in medical education. Next, Chapter 12 focuses on privacy techniques in healthcare systems and finally Chapter 13 looks at securing medical image analysis using federated learning.

The editors would like to thank Brittany Insull and the rest of the IET staff for their editorial assistance and support in producing this important scientific work. Without this collective effort, this book would not have been possible to be completed.

About the editors

Dr Gautam Srivastava (senior member, IEEE) has extensive editorial experience including *IEEE Transactions on Fuzzy Systems*, *IEEE Transactions on Industrial Informatics*, *Computer Standards and Interfaces*, *Applied Stochastic Modeling and Business*, *Information Sciences*, *IEEE Transactions on Computational Social Systems*, *ISA Transactions*, *IEEE Intelligent System*, and *IEEE Sensors*. Dr Srivastava received his BSc from Briar Cliff University in Sioux City, Iowa, USA in 2004, followed by an MSc and PhD from the University of Victoria in Victoria, British Columbia, Canada, in 2006 and 2012, respectively. He then worked for 3 years at the University of Victoria in the Department of Computer Science (Faculty of Engineering), where he was regarded as one of the top undergraduate professors in Computer Science Course Instruction at the University. From there, in 2014, he started a tenure-track position at Brandon University in Brandon, Manitoba, Canada, where he currently is a Full Professor. Dr G (as he is popularly known) is active in research in the fields of Data Mining and Big Data Security and Privacy. During his 10-year academic career, he has published a total of 400 papers in high-impact conferences and journals. He has also given guest lectures at many Taiwan universities in Big Data. He currently has active research projects with other academics in Norway, Taiwan, Singapore, Canada, and the United States.

Thippa Reddy Gadekallu is currently working as a chief engineer at Zhongda Group, Haiyan County, Jiaxing City, Zhejiang Province, China. He is also working as an associate professor in the School of Information Technology and Engineering, Vellore Institute of Technology, India. He obtained his Bachelor's degree in Computer Science and Engineering from Nagarjuna University, India, in 2003, his Master's degree in Computer Science and Engineering from Anna University, Chennai, Tamil Nadu, India in 2011, and his PhD from Vellore Institute of Technology, Vellore, Tamil Nadu, India, in 2017. He has more than 15 years of experience in teaching. He has authored more than 200 international/national publications in reputed journals and conferences. Currently, his areas of research include machine learning, the Internet of Things, deep neural networks, blockchain, and computer vision. He serves as an editor for several publishers, including Springer, Hindawi, Plosone, Scientific Reports (Nature), and Wiley, and has also acted as a guest editor for IEEE, Elsevier, Springer, Hindawi, and MDPI. He was recently recognised as one of the top 2% of scientists in the world, as per the survey conducted by Elsevier in 2021, 2022, and 2023. He was also recognised as a highly cited researcher in the young scientist category by Clarivate (Web of Science) for the period 2017–22 in 2023.

Chapter 1
Federated learning-enabled 5G and beyond for Industry 5.0

Chamitha De Alwis[1]

Abstract

The evolution towards Industry 5.0 will bring smart machines, robots, and collaborative robots, enabling multiple stakeholders to work collaboratively to boost efficiency, productivity, and innovation. These developments will be underpinned by technological advancements in AI and intelligent communication systems. Federated learning is identified as a key enabler of developments toward 5G and beyond, empowering Industry 5.0 by ensuring scalability, data privacy, security, and rights. This chapter explores the evolution of industries and mobile communication technologies toward federated learning-enabled 5G and Beyond for Industry 5.0.

Keywords: Industry 5.0, 5G, Beyond 5G, AI, Federated learning

1.1 Introduction

The dawn of 5G has paved the path toward creating a paradigm shift toward the development of Industry 4.0 that merges communication infrastructure and internet technologies with industries [1]. Owing to the advents of communication technologies, edge computing, and especially AI, Industry 4.0 is expected to evolve toward Industry 5.0 that can enable humans to work alongside robots, smart machines, and collaborative robots (cobots) [2]. Industry 5.0 will have massive numbers of sensors, devices, and interfaces connected with each other to facilitate complete integration with cloud/edge computing, Big Data collection and processing, AI, and ML.

However, developments of Industry 5.0 demand multiple stakeholders, including designers, workers, customers, and suppliers to work collaboratively. This requires AI-based models to be trained by multiple parties. Federated learning (FL)-enabled collaborative machine learning via multiple independent sources [3]. This deviates from the traditional machine learning approach of utilizing a common data set for training a ML model assuming local data samples to be identical. Furthermore,

[1]School of Computer Science and Technology, University of Bedfordshire, United Kingdom

FL can ensure data privacy, security, and rights while utilizing ML for Industry 5.0 applications facilitated by 5G and beyond networks.

The rest of this chapter is organized as follows. Section 1.2 presents the evolution of industries toward Industry 5.0. Furthermore, Section 1.3 presents the evolution of mobile networks while discussing how FL is utilized in 5G and beyond networks. Section 1.4 presents how FL enables 5G and beyond for Industry 5.0, whereas Section 1.5 concludes the chapter.

1.2 Evolution of industries toward Industry 5.0

1.2.1 From Industry 1.0 to Industry 4.0

The beginning of the industrial revolution, known as Industry 1.0, began in the 18th century with the mechanization of production and related activities using various steam-powered engines. This development was followed by Industry 2.0 in the 19th century, which incorporated electricity and assembly lines in factories. The dawn of the 20th century marked the third evolution of industries, Industry 3.0. This development took place because of electronic systems, computers, and information systems.

The present evolution of industries in the beginning of the 21st century, incorporating a plethora of technological advancements, including Internet of Things (IoT), cloud computing, information systems, robots, augmented reality, and AI, is known as Industry 4.0 [4]. The advanced cyber-physical systems in Industry 4.0 enable smart factories and smart manufacturing by connecting sophisticated machinery with large numbers of connected sensors and intelligent systems. These advancements are realized through 5G networks, which facilitate enhanced mobile broadband (peak data rates up to 10 Gbps), massive machine-type communication (supports over 100x more devices per unit area compared to 4G), and ultra-reliable machine-type communication (minimizes the delays up to 1 ms) [2]. In addition, processing large amounts of sensory data is facilitated through cloud computing and emerging multi-access edge computing (MEC) technologies.

1.2.2 Industry 5.0

Industry 5.0 is expected to have people working alongside smart machines and robots [2]. This will develop the connected, autonomous, and efficient Industry 4.0 toward developing a personal and human touch of creativity and customization through cognitive systems facilitating human–robot interactions for next-generation industrial applications. It is envisaged that a massive number of things will be connected harnessing the communication capabilities of 5G and beyond communication networks. Furthermore, these networks are also expected to provide seamless integration of cloud/edge computing, Big Data, small data, and AI capabilities to facilitate future Industry 5.0 applications, such as more intelligent and capable collaborative robots known as cobots. The evolution from Industry 1.0 toward Industry 5.0 is portrayed in Figure 1.1. Furthermore, Industry 5.0 aims to be more human-centric to empower the human workforce and not only considers productivity but also aims

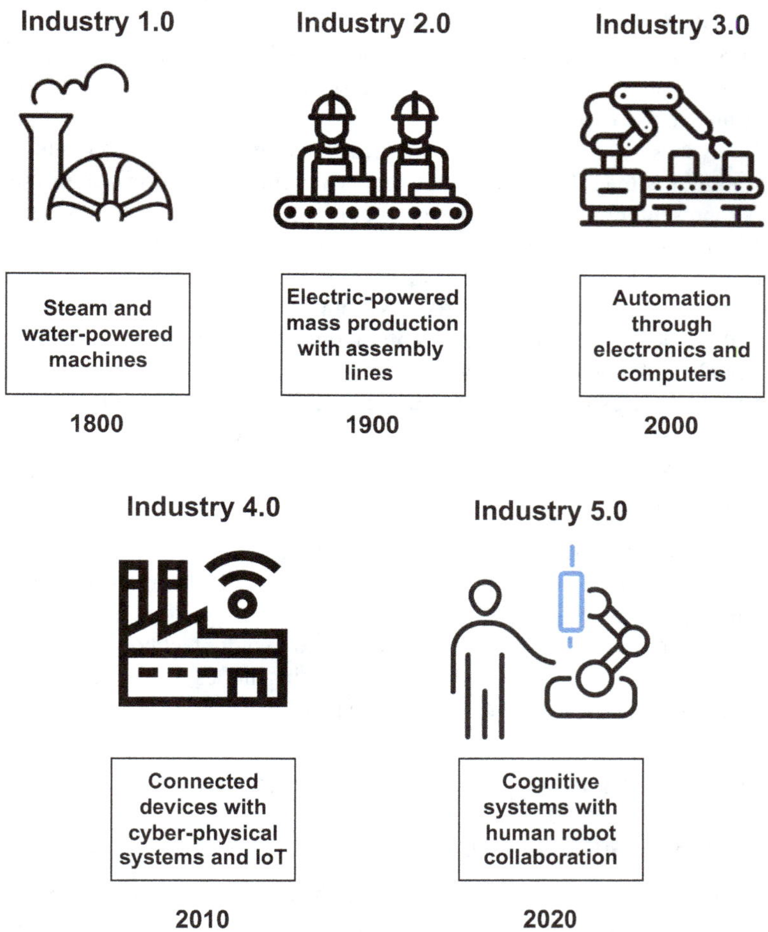

Figure 1.1 Evolution of industries toward Industry 5.0

to be greener to the environment. This would make Industry 5.0 a more sustainable approach to develop and operate industries in the beyond 5G era [5].

1.2.2.1 Industry 5.0 features

Industry 5.0 is envisaged to be equipped with many advanced features [6]. For instance, smart additive manufacturing applies AI and computer vision for better representation of product design. In addition, predictive maintenance allows transparent application of prediction tools where data is systematically processed to define any uncertainties. This allows machines and services to operate in a self-conscious manner. Moreover, cyber-physical cognitive systems utilize cognitive methods for applications, including surveillance, industrial automation, and environment monitoring to achieve better performance. These features will be realized because of network intelligence realized through edge AI capabilities in 5G and beyond networks.

1.2.2.2 Industry 5.0 applications

Industry 5.0 is expected to enable many new applications [6]. One such application is cloud manufacturing, where multiple stakeholders can collaborate to realize efficient and low-cost manufacturing. Cloud manufacturing also allows reliability, cost-effectiveness, and on-demand capabilities by utilizing advanced manufacturing tools. A digital twin (DT) on the other hand is a digital replication of a physical system. DT representation can range from jet engines to large factories. DTs are realized through collecting data from IoT and IIoT devices. Owing to the advancements of AI, ML, and Big Data analytics, DTs can minimize maintenance costs to improve system performance in smart industry environments. On the other hand, cobots are collaborative robots designed to work collaboratively with humans to make humans more capable and efficient. Supply chain management is another feature of Industry 5.0, where industries can efficiently and cost-effectively deliver personalized and customized products and services by identifying the true demand.

1.2.3 FL for Industry 5.0

It is also evident that industrial robots and sensors generate massive amounts of Small Data and Big Data that needs to be processed in real time using AI and ML techniques. However, processing these data centrally at the cloud is not an effective solution. This requires Industry 5.0 applications to explore technologies such as federated learning (FL) that can coordinate computing nodes at the network edge to process Small Data and Big Data in real time [7].

1.3 Federated learning in 5G and beyond networks

1.3.1 Mobile network evolution

Mobile networks have seen five generations in the last four decades, as a new mobile network generation emerges every 10 years [2]. Each generation of mobile networks becomes more capable of empowering humans with better tools and technologies. The zeroth generation (0G) of mobile communication networks only had simple radio communication, whereas the first generation (1G) introduced cellular networks supporting analog voice communication. The second generation (2G) made the transition from analog to digital technologies while supporting simple data services such as short message services. The third generation (3G) provided mobile broadband services, multimedia message services, mobile TV, and video calls, while the fourth generation (4G) provided better mobile broadband services, all-IP communication, and ultra-high-definition streaming.

The advent of 5G offers enhanced mobile broadband (eMBB) delivering peak data rates up to 10 Gbps, ultra-reliable low-latency communication (uRLLC) with delays of 1 ms, and massive machine-type communication (mMTC) supporting over 100× more devices per unit area compared to 4G. In addition, network reliability and availability are expected to be over 99.999% [2]. Furthermore, network hardware is shifting from dedicated devices to softwarized platforms with network softwarization, supporting applications such as virtual reality (VR), augmented reality (AR), mixed reality (MR), autonomous vehicles, Internet of things (IoT), Industry 4.0, multi-access edge computing (MEC), and smart grids [8–11].

Beyond 5G networks, such as 6G networks that are envisaged to be deployed by 2030, are expected to be more capable. 6G is expected to provide extreme data rates (peak data rates of 1 Tbps), extremely low delays (less than 0.1 ms), extreme reliability and availability (in the range of 99.9999%), massive scalability, extreme power efficiency, and extreme mobility [2].

Six key technological directions have been identified toward realizing 6G networks in Ref. [12]. They are intent-based networking (IBN), terahertz (THz) communication, artificial intelligence (AI), distributed ledger technology (DLT), smart devices and gadget-free communication (SDG), and quantum communication (QC), as illustrated in Figure 1.2.

IBN automates business intent deployment in networks [13]. IBN consists of three primary functions. They are intent translation, activation of intents, and assurance. Intent translation function performs the translation of business into policies. These policies can be understood by networks. The activation of intents function performs network-wide deployment of intent policies. This is performed by automating configuration through networking devices. The assurance function is capable of monitoring and analyzing networks to ensure the intent. This is required to be performed through AI technologies.

The THz frequencies are able to provide bandwidths in the range of hundred GHz. The THz frequencies are also suitable to be used in massive multi-input multi-output (MIMO) systems that have a large number of antennas to provide high directionality and interference mitigation [14].

AI is expected to facilitate efficient network optimization and management toward realizing zero-touch network and service management (ZSM) in 6G networks [12]. AI techniques will be leveraged in many aspects of 6G networks, including spectrum sharing, radio resource management, network slicing, and network virtualization.

DLT, blockchain, in particular, is expected to enable secure and distributed storage and operation in 6G networks [2]. Blockchain consists of immutable and timestamped blocks that are linked together using a cryptographic hash. This will enable immutability, nonrepudiation, security, pseudonymity, and decentralized operations in 6G networks.

Over 24 billion devices are expected to be connected to 6G networks by 2030 [2]. Large number of smart devices and gadgets, developed utilizing technologies ranging from extended reality (XR) to holographic telepresence (HT) will enable a plethora of new applications, such as smart cities and Industry 5.0. Gadget-free communication will remove the need for physical devices and provide a user environment through haptics, holograms, and other digital interfaces.

Quantum computing enables massive data rates, fast computing, and strong security in 6G networks. Quantum computing exploits traditional concepts of physics by using photons to process the computation to quantum qubits [15].

When the aforementioned use cases and applications discussed in preceding sections are taken into consideration, it is reasonable to think that AI can be incorporated

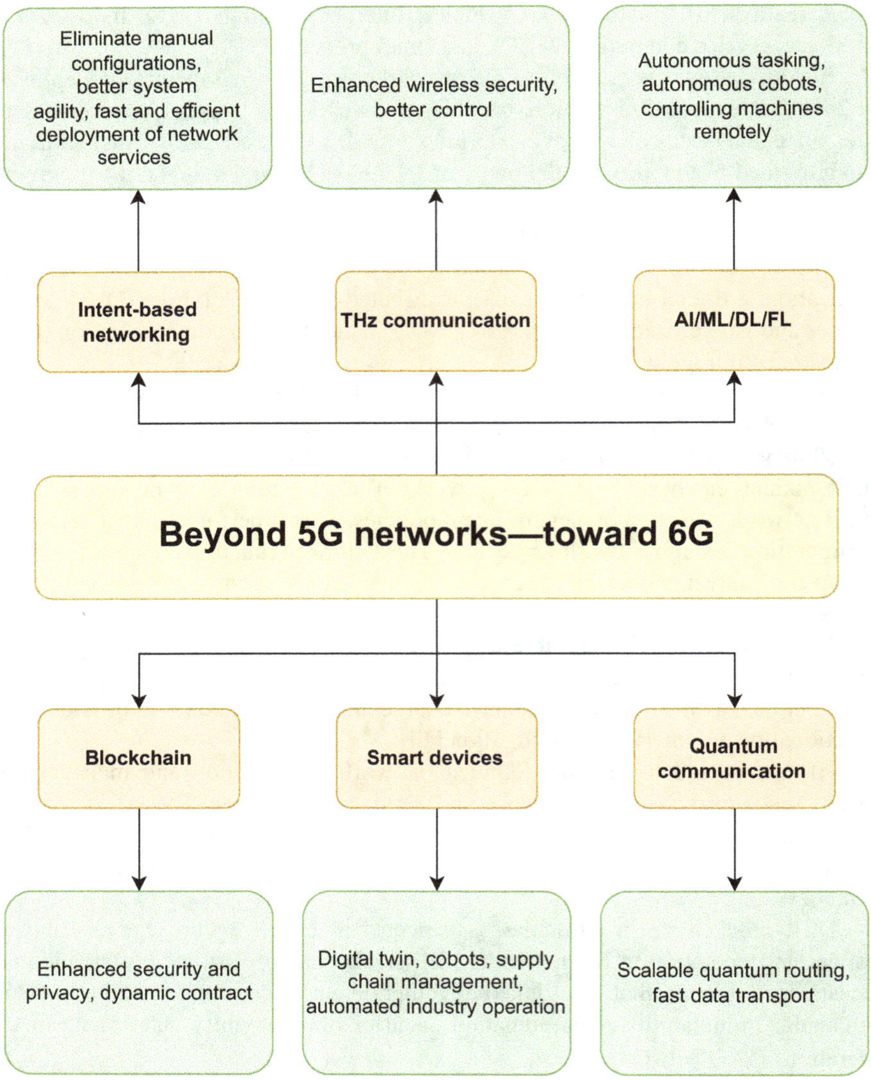

Figure 1.2 Technological directions of beyond 5G networks

into 6G systems on both fronts, i.e., components and applications, in the appropriate manner [2].

Many beyond 5G technologies act as enablers of Industry 5.0. For instance, Internet of Everything (IoE), which will connect people, processes, information, and things, is another beyond 5G technological enabler of Industry 5.0. IoE-generated data needs to be processed efficiently utilizing technologies such as FL to optimize networks and services. Furthermore, efficient Big Data analysis for Industry 5.0 is vital to better understand consumer behavior to optimize products, services, cost, and production efficiency. Blockchain is yet another technology that can facilitate Industry 5.0 by enabling decentralized and distributed management, transparency and accountability, and smart contracts. On the other hand, edge computing can enable data processing at the network edge while minimizing communication overheads. What is more, technologies such as eXtended Reality (XR) also act as enabling Industry 5.0 and its applications to design advanced training, DT operation, and collaborative working.

1.3.2 Federated learning in beyond 5G networks

The advents of AI and ML enable computer systems to learn by identifying data patterns using statistical models and algorithms. This has enabled many new applications and services that can make intelligent decisions.

The expansion of mobile networks has also significantly increased the complexity of networks. The evolution toward 5G and beyond will also expand the networks to terrestrial, aerial, satellite, underground, marine, and space. This demands the usage of intelligent technologies to resolve challenges including the design and operation of complex air interface, spectrum and network resource utilization, network orchestration, signal processing, network programmability, network monitoring, and network security [16]. Therefore, to enable hyper-intelligent networks, AI solutions should be deeply integrated into network design and operation. Therefore, many AI technologies including machine learning, deep learning, federated learning, and computational intelligent are being investigated toward realizing 5G and beyond networks in the coming decade.

For instance, radio systems can be designed to be re-configurable and adaptable through an end-to-end learning design [2]. Furthermore, deep convolutional neural networks can be used to achieve better performance in classification accuracy and inference time compared to ML-based approaches [17]. Moreover, swarm intelligence has shown better performance in handling non-linear channel models in visible light communication (VLC) [18]. Furthermore, deep reinforcement learning is used to enhance data security by maximizing the minimum secrecy rate in an intelligent reflecting surface (IRS)-enabled multi-user multi-eavesdropper network [19]. What is more, AI will enable many pivotal network functions, including automatic network conflict avoidance and intelligent network optimization. However, utilizing AI-based technologies in mobile networks also has several challenges [2]. For instance, it is a challenge to generate high-quality data sets for training models, explain the operation of underlying networks, and orchestrate networks with massive numbers of IoT devices are some of the key challenges. Furthermore, it is a challenge to explore the capabilities of FL and provide hybrid centralized-distributed AI solutions for IoT applications and services at the network edge.

Future 6G wireless networks will guarantee global coverage and provide services with various QoS satisfaction levels. In this network, storage and computing capabilities are distributed over the whole network, from the central cloud to the MEC server at the network edge and wearable computing devices at the user side. Obviously, AI is a key enabler for hyper-intelligent networking in 6G networks. Explainable AI solutions should be investigated so that the underlying operations of the network can be explained well. Moreover, to exploit the computing capabilities and generated data from massive IoT devices, hybrid centralized-distributed AI solutions are very promising. In particular, the global server, deployed at central clouds and satellites, can be leveraged to build a learning model over multiple regions of the world. As transferring a large amount of data from massive IoT devices to a central server is not efficient and sometimes unavailable, the data can be processed hierarchically, from end devices to edge nodes (e.g., terrestrial and aerial base stations) and global nodes. Moreover, FL is a promising concept to design privacy-preserving solutions.

Federated learning (FL) is emerging as a new AI concept that can collaboratively train a shared learning model. FL allows participating nodes such as smartphones to cooperatively learn a shared prediction model keeping training data locally in the device without sending to central servers. Hence, many devices can contribute toward training the learning model. Each participating device trains a local model and shares the updates with the central federated server, as illustrated in Figure 1.3.

Therefore, with FL, data security and privacy are enhanced as devices only share updates instead of sharing user and device data [20]. Furthermore, as model training happens at the network edge, devices or organizations can adhere to their security and privacy regulations while keeping their data local. Moreover, FL gives real-time results by minimizing communication delays and overheads, as the data need not travel back and forth to a centralized server. This can even happen in the absence of internet connections as the prediction model is already available at the end nodes. Furthermore, FL utilizes the increasing computational capabilities and processing power of mobile devices, IoT devices, and autonomous vehicles to train the local learning model [3]. In addition, FL allows participating nodes, such as smartphones, to cooperatively learn a shared prediction model keeping training data locally in the device without sending to central servers.

FL can be categorized as vertical, horizontal, and hybrid [5]. Vertical FL utilizes distributed servers that can locally train learning algorithms. These locally trained algorithms are aggregated in a centralized server for global coordination. For instance, vertical FL is utilized in industrial applications such as warehouse localization. In this application, robots can perform path planning based on local data sets. The training results can be uploaded to centralized controller for global analysis. Vertical FL is efficient, especially in instances where the computational capability of end devices is limited. Yet, having the centralized server as a single point of failure is a concern considering the overall reliability. On the other hand, horizontal FL analyzes local information and updates dynamic information with each other. This leads to all nodes eventually sharing global information with each other. This reduces the reliability and stability concerns related to vertical FL. However, efficient and secure data sharing between distributed servers remains a challenge in horizontal FL. In line with addressing these concerns, hybrid FL is emerging as a solution to combine vertical and horizontal FL to provide both reliability and efficiency.

The advent of 5G enables many IoT devices to be connected to mobile networks. These devices need to collect and process data using AI and ML to facilitate emerging applications and services. However, conventional approaches to perform AI and

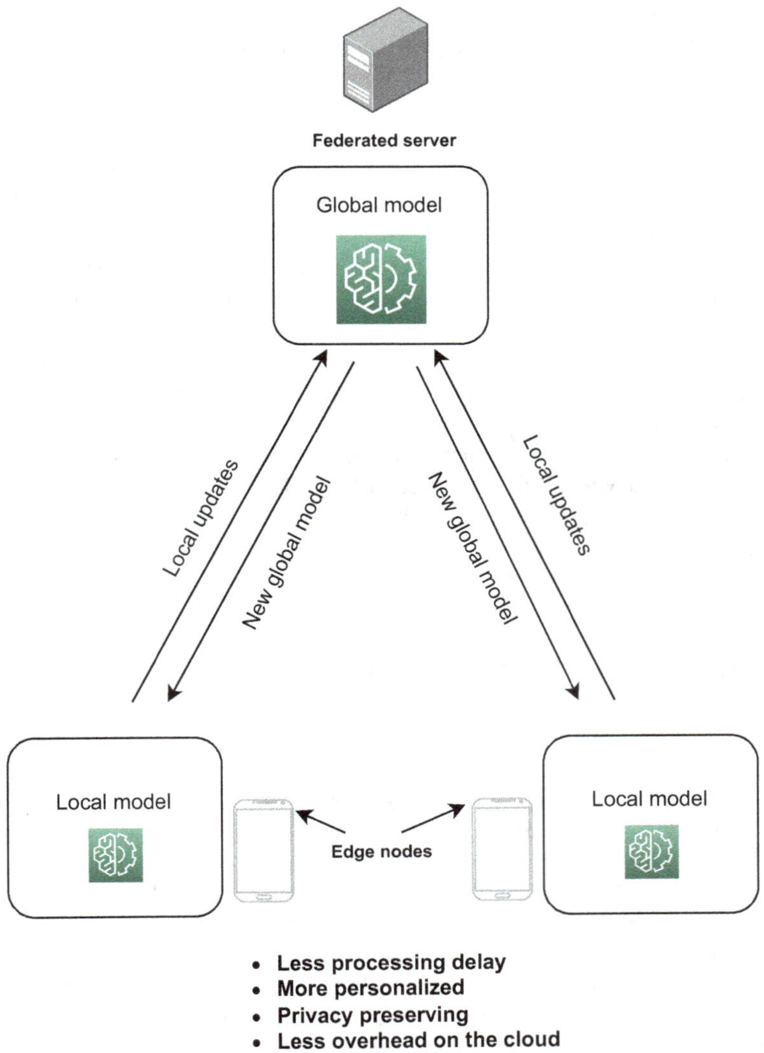

Figure 1.3 Federated learning

ML in a centralized fashion are not suitable as data need to be collected and processed in a distributed fashion to minimize delays and protect privacy. Furthermore, beyond 5G networks are envisioned to have AI and ML as a core component for network operation and function. For instance, AI is expected to be used efficiently to perform tasks, such as waveform detection, signal processing, physical layer network design, and modulation classification [17,21,22].

Therefore, FL is emerging as a promising solution to empower 5G and beyond networks with distributed AI capabilities, enabling the vision for ubiquitous AI in future mobile networks [23]. FL is envisaged to overcome the limitations of centralized AI, such as communication overheads and privacy concerns. In addition, FL offers many benefits for 5G and beyond networks. These include support for heterogeneous data originating from different sources, communication-efficient distributed AI, privacy-protection, and large-scale deployment [24].

Beyond 5G networks are expected to support FL in several methods [20]. One such method is facilitating communication-efficient FL at the system level. This can be achieved through data distribution, device distribution along with distributed computing, and efficient communication methods. Furthermore, communication-efficient FL algorithms are expected to reduce communication costs and facilitate accelerated model training. FL can also be made more secure through robust aggregation to reduce low-quality model updates, robust detection to prevent malicious devices from participating in model training, and reliable reputation management to prevent malicious devices from damaging the global model. On the other hand, techniques such as differential privacy, deep net pruning, and gradient compression can be used to protect the privacy of FL in future networks. Efficient FL training can be realized through methods such as federated parallelization and federated distillation, and efficient inference can be achieved through utilizing techniques including pruning and weight sharing [20].

1.4 Federated learning-enabled 5G and beyond for Industry 5.0

The advent of 5G and beyond technologies is expected to be a key enabler of the envisaged developments toward realizing Industry 5.0. These networks will automatically adapt to the dynamic industry environments toward facilitating the Industrial Internet of Things (IIoT) with human interventions and interaction connecting humans and devices through diverse and heterogeneous networks.

5G and beyond networks are considered to be a key enabler of Industry 5.0. These mobile networks are envisaged to not only provide connectivity but also the joint optimization of computation, caching, control, and intelligence [25]. What is more, the large amount of data generated by many heterogeneous sensors can be processed with AI and ML to make robots more intelligent. Also, 5G and beyond networks can facilitate smart spectrum management, AI-powered mobile edge computing, and smart mobility. Furthermore, AI techniques can be used to optimize mobility predictions, handover management, and energy management in 5G and beyond networks to facilitate Industry 5.0 applications and services.

FL-enabled 5G and beyond networks are expected to become a key enabler of the developments toward realizing many new applications, including, Industry 5.0, as illustrated in Figure 1.4 [26,27]. For instance, beyond 5G networks will advance Software Defined Networking (SDN) and Network Function Virtualization (NFV) in 5G to have pervasive AI and zero-touch network services and management (ZSM). This will make beyond 5G networks to be more flexible and scalable to provide the ultra-fast, hyper-connected, energy-aware networks with better security and privacy, as demanded by Industry 5.0 applications [5]. In line with these developments, IBN will automate the business intent deployment in networks by means of setting up

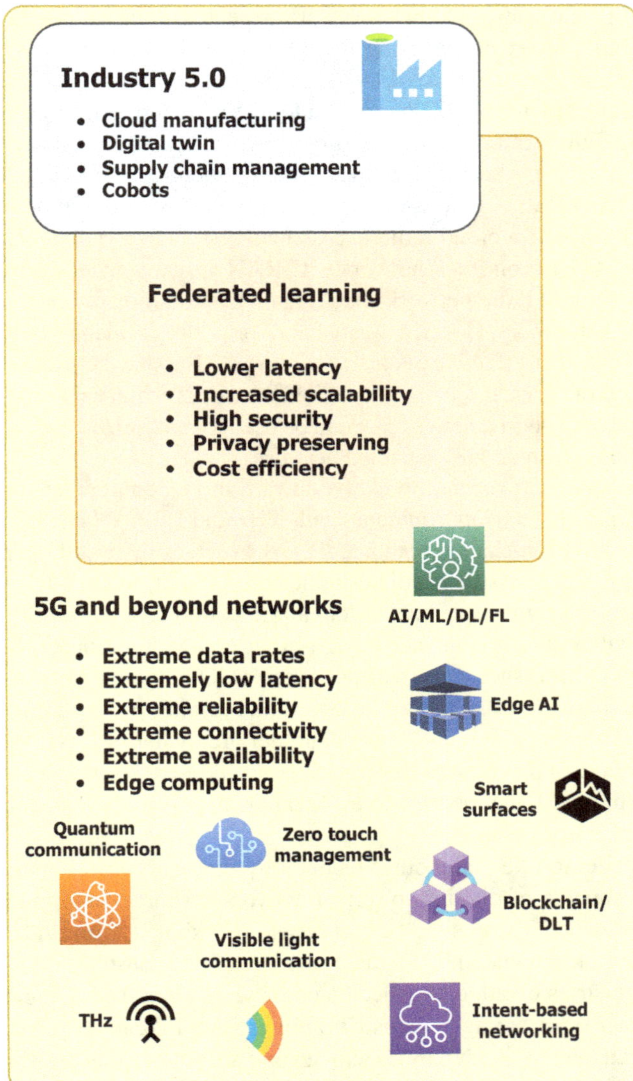

Figure 1.4 Federated learning-enabled 5G and beyond for Industry 5.0

well-defined policies to support Industry 5.0 applications and services [12]. FL can be a promising approach to realize IBN, which in return will be a key facilitator of Industry 5.0 applications and services.

Industry 5.0 applications and services are also envisaged to provide extreme connectivity to many heterogeneous devices and platforms. Toward achieving this objective, the 95 GHz frequency band is released by the Federal Communications Commission to achieve the high data rates envisaged in 5G and beyond networks [5]. Furthermore, 6G networks are expected to provide data rates in the range of terabits per second utilizing the THz band. In addition, low-power wide area network (LPWAN) technologies will also be utilized to connect IIoT devices in an energy-efficient manner. This requires intelligent antennas, transceivers, and signal processing. Furthermore, networks should be controlled dynamically to through ZSM technologies [2]. These capabilities cannot be realized without harnessing the power of AI, specifically FL considering the distributed nature of mobile networks.

The emergence of a cloud radio access network (C-RAN) also enhances ZSM capabilities of 5G beyond 5G networks. C-RAN is capable of coordinating the resource allocation of radio networks banking on the common public radio interface standard [5]. Furthermore, C-RAN is capable of providing scalable resource pooling in an efficient and cost-effective manner. Moreover, AI-assisted C-RAN can improve network quality of service (QoS) with limited network resources. For instance, two-step deep Q-learning-based networking can be used to maximize bandwidth resource utilization efficiency in an NFV-enabled network.

Networks are also expected to evolve toward more complicated and dense network cells in Industry 5.0 environments with THz and LPWAN capable beyond 5G networks. Hence, it is a challenge to handle tasks such as inter-cell interference and handovers. Cell-free massive multiple-input-multiple-output (MIMO) networks in beyond 5G networks will distribute antenna arrays into larger areas by associating IIoT devices with multiple cells instead of a single cell with one antenna array, as per pre-5G networks. Yet, such cell-free massive MIMO networks demand significant intelligence to perform tasks including coordinating multiple cells and performing channel estimation for antennas. This is another area where FL will be utilized to enable 5G and beyond networks toward realizing Industry 5.0 applications and services. Furthermore, FL can be used to evaluate the access point allocation for use in a cell-free network environment.

Network slicing (NS) is another technology emerging in 5G and beyond networks. NS is capable of dividing physical network resources into multiple logical end-to-end networks. These slices can be custom designed to provide diverse network requirements demanded by applications including Industry 5.0 [28]. NS facilitates smart industries by allocating dedicated network slices satisfying different network requirements pertaining to industrial applications. FL can be utilized in the process of efficiently deploying NS in 5G and beyond networks to perform network management for NS, slice management, NS service management, and NS orchestration.

Pervasive AI in 5G and beyond networks can also assist Industry 5.0 applications. Decentralized network automation in 5G and beyond networks will facilitate edge AI to process data locally together with global information. FL will enable edge AI processing to be more efficient, secure, and privacy aware.

It should also be noted that Industry 5.0 will include multiple heterogeneous IIoT devices connected through B5G networks in an industrial environment. These devices will increase the security threats for industrial applications and services. This is even prominent with the emergence of IIoT botnets. AI and ML are identified as a promising approach toward identifying such threats. However, centralized learning models are not ideal for this due to reasons such as lack of up-to-date data sets and centralized techniques for data processing [29]. This can be realized through multi-access edge computing (MEC) and edge intelligence (EI)-enabled FL in beyond 5G mobile networks [12]. Together with MEC and EI, the edge of industrial systems will have better computational capabilities, which can be utilized by FL. Hence, FL can perform collaborative learning in a multi-industrial system without sharing data with centralized servers. This can be a significant advancement toward securing data and privacy in Industry 5.0 applications. For instance, [29] proposes an MEC-based framework that can secure IIoT applications using FL. This algorithm enables multiple MEC platforms to collaboratively tackle IIoT attacks without compromising data security and privacy. Furthermore, to allow MEC nodes to obtain virtual resources from the centralized MEC orchestrator, a noncooperative game is formulated. Through this, the algorithm proposed in Ref. [29] facilitates efficient means to handle IIoT attacks to secure beyond 5G-enabled Industry 5.0 applications.

Furthermore, [30] discusses how to combine AI with edge AI toward defending Industry 5.0 applications and services in 5G and beyond networks from data poisoning attacks in a federated fashion. This method utilizes a defense mechanism for data poisoning attacks and then determines optimal parameters to improve the performance of the federated split learning model to defend against data poisoning attacks. Furthermore, [31] presents a method to further preserve privacy in an FL-enabled environment. This is through the fusion of FL together with blockchain technologies to preserve privacy in Industry 5.0 applications and services. FL protects the privacy of data of various parts operating in an industry while decentralized, and secure storage is achieved through the utilization of a distributed hash table (DHT) at the cloud layer. The seamless connectivity demanded by this method is provided by 5G and beyond networks.

1.5 Conclusion

Industry 5.0 is envisaged to dawn with the advanced communication and computation capabilities realized through 5G and beyond networks. This new generation of industries will have people working alongside smart machines and robots to fuse the efficiency of machines along with the creativity of humans. FL is considered as a significant enabler of 5G and beyond technologies to realize Industry 5.0. Through this chapter, the development of Industries is discussed to identify how FL is a key enabler toward the development of efficient, secure, and privacy-preserving Industry 5.0 applications and services.

References

[1] H. Lasi, P. Fettke, H.-G. Kemper, T. Feld, and M. Hoffmann, "Industry 4.0," *Business & Information Systems Engineering*, vol. 6, pp. 239–242, 2014.

[2] C. De Alwis, A. Kalla, Q.-V. Pham, *et al.*, "Survey on 6g frontiers: Trends, applications, requirements, technologies and future research," *IEEE Open Journal of the Communications Society*, vol. 2, pp. 836–886, 2021.

[3] T. Li, A. K. Sahu, A. Talwalkar, and V. Smith, "Federated learning: Challenges, methods, and future directions," *IEEE Signal Processing Magazine*, vol. 37, no. 3, pp. 50–60, 2020.

[4] S. K. Rao and R. Prasad, "Impact of 5G technologies on Industry 4.0," *Wireless Personal Communications*, vol. 100, pp. 145–159, 2018.

[5] H. R. Chi, C. K. Wu, N.-F. Huang, K. F. Tsang, and A. Radwan, "A survey of network automation for industrial internet-of-things towards Industry 5.0," *IEEE Transactions on Industrial Informatics*, vol. 19, no. 2, pp. 2065–2077, 2022.

[6] C. De Alwis, Q.-V. Pham, and M. Liyanage, *6G Frontiers: Towards Future Wireless Systems*. John Wiley & Sons, 2022.

[7] P. Ranaweera, C. De Alwis, A. D. Jurcut, and M. Liyanage, "Realizing contact-less applications with multi-access edge computing," *ICT Express*, vol. 8, no. 4, pp. 575–587, 2022.

[8] Y. Siriwardhana, C. De Alwis, G. Gür, M. Ylianttila, and M. Liyanage, "The fight against the Covid-19 pandemic with 5G technologies," *IEEE Engineering Management Review*, vol. 48, no. 3, pp. 72–84, 2020.

[9] G. Gür, A. Kalla, C. De Alwis, *et al.*, "Integration of ICN and MEC in 5G and beyond networks: Mutual benefits, use cases, challenges, standardization, and future research," *IEEE Open Journal of the Communications Society*, vol. 3, pp. 1382–1412, 2022.

[10] C. Yapa, C. de Alwis, and M. Liyanage, "Can blockchain strengthen the energy internet?" *Network*, vol. 1, no. 2, pp. 95–115, 2021.

[11] A. Saputhanthri, C. Alwis, and M. Liyanage, "Emergence of blockchain based IoT marketplaces," in *Joint European Conference on Networks and Communications (EuCNC) & 6G Summit*, 2020.

[12] C. De Alwis, P. Kumar, Q.-V. Pham, *et al.*, "Towards 6G: Key technological directions," *ICT Express*, vol. 9, no. 4, pp. 525–533, 2022.

[13] G. M. Karam, M. Gruber, I. Adam, F. Boutigny, Y. Miche, and S. Mukherjee, "The evolution of networks and management in a 6G world: An inventor's view," *IEEE Transactions on Network and Service Management*, vol. 19, no. 4, pp. 5395–5407, 2022.

[14] K. M. S. Huq, S. A. Busari, J. Rodriguez, V. Frascolla, W. Bazzi, and D. C. Sicker, "Terahertz-enabled wireless system for beyond-5G ultra-fast networks: A brief survey," *IEEE Network*, vol. 33, no. 4, pp. 89–95, 2019.

[15] I. B. Djordjevic, "On global quantum communication networking," *Entropy*, vol. 22, no. 8, p. 831, 2020.

[16] Q.-V. Pham, N. T. Nguyen, T. Huynh-The, L. B. Le, K. Lee, and W.-J. Hwang, "Intelligent Radio Signal Processing: A Survey," *arXiv preprint arXiv:2008.08264v2*, 2020.

[17] T. Huynh-The, C.-H. Hua, Q.-V. Pham, and D.-S. Kim, "MCNet: An efficient CNN architecture for robust automatic modulation classification," *IEEE Communications Letters*, vol. 24, no. 4, pp. 811–815, 2020.

[18] Q.-V. Pham, T. Huynh-The, M. Alazab, J. Zhao, and W.-J. Hwang, "Sum-Rate Maximization for UAV-assisted visible light communications using NOMA: Swarm intelligence meets machine learning," *IEEE Internet of Things Journal*, vol. 7, no. 10, pp. 10 375–10 387, 2020.

[19] H. Yang, Z. Xiong, J. Zhao, D. Niyato, L. Xiao, and Q. Wu, "Deep reinforcement learning based intelligent reflecting surface for secure wireless communications," *IEEE Transactions on Wireless Communications*, vol. 20, no. 1, pp. 375–388, 2021.

[20] Y. Liu, X. Yuan, Z. Xiong, J. Kang, X. Wang, and D. Niyato, "Federated Learning for 6G Communications: Challenges, Methods, and Future Directions," *arXiv preprint arXiv:2006.02931*, 2020.

[21] H. Li, K. Ota, and M. Dong, "Learning IoT in edge: Deep learning for the Internet of Things with edge computing," *IEEE Network*, vol. 32, no. 1, pp. 96–101, 2018.

[22] M. Alsenwi, N. H. Tran, M. Bennis, S. R. Pandey, A. K. Bairagi, and C. S. Hong, "Intelligent resource slicing for eMBB and URLLC coexistence in 5G and beyond: A deep reinforcement learning based approach," *IEEE Transactions on Wireless Communications*, vol. 20, no. 7, pp. 4585–4600, 2021.

[23] Y. Xiao, Y. Li, G. Shi, and H. V. Poor, "Optimizing resource-efficiency for federated edge intelligence in IoT networks," in *2020 International Conference on Wireless Communications and Signal Processing (WCSP)*. IEEE, 2020, pp. 86–92.

[24] Y. Xiao, G. Shi, and M. Krunz, "Towards Ubiquitous AI in 6G with Federated Learning," *arXiv preprint arXiv:2004.13563*, 2020.

[25] W. Saad, M. Bennis, and M. Chen, "A vision of 6G wireless systems: Applications, trends, technologies, and open research problems," *IEEE network*, vol. 34, no. 3, pp. 134–142, 2019.

[26] S. Pandya, G. Srivastava, R. Jhaveri, *et al.*, "Federated learning for smart cities: A comprehensive survey," *Sustainable Energy Technologies and Assessments*, vol. 55, p. 102987, 2023.

[27] L. Teng, Y. Qiao, M. Shafiq, *et al.*, "FLPK-BiSeNet: Federated learning based on priori knowledge and bilateral segmentation network for image edge extraction," *IEEE Transactions on Network and Service Management*, vol. 20, no. 2, pp. 1529–1542, 2023.

[28] T. Umagiliya, S. Wijethilaka, C. De Alwis, P. Porambage, and M. Liyanage, "Network slicing strategies for smart industry applications," in *2021 IEEE Conference on Standards for Communications and Networking (CSCN)*. IEEE, 2021, pp. 30–35.

[29] Z. Abou El Houda, B. Brik, A. Ksentini, L. Khoukhi, and M. Guizani, "When federated learning meets game theory: A cooperative framework to secure iiot applications on edge computing," *IEEE Transactions on Industrial Informatics*, vol. 18, no. 11, pp. 7988–7997, 2022.

[30] F. Khan, R. L. Kumar, M. H. Abidi, S. Kadry, H. Alkhalefah, and M. K. Aboudaif, "Federated split learning model for Industry 5.0: A data poisoning defense for edge computing," *Electronics*, vol. 11, no. 15, 2022. [Online]. Available: https://www.mdpi.com/2079-9292/11/15/2393

[31] S. K. Singh, L. T. Yang, and J. H. Park, "FusionFedBlock: Fusion of blockchain and federated learning to preserve privacy in Industry 5.0," *Information Fusion*, vol. 90, pp. 233–240, 2023. [Online]. Available: https://www.sciencedirect.com/science/article/pii/S1566253522001658

Chapter 2

Federated learning for optimized communication in Industry 5.0

Dasari Bhulakshmi[1], *Gokul Yenduri*[2], *Praveen Kumar Reddy Maddikunta*[2], *Celestine Iwendi*[3] *and Thippa Reddy Gadekallu*[4]

Abstract

The rapid advancements in Industry 5.0 necessitate efficient communication optimization techniques to facilitate seamless collaboration between humans and advanced technologies. This chapter explores the potential of federated learning (FL) as a solution to address the challenges faced by current communication optimization techniques in Industry 5.0. FL enables collaborative model training while preserving data privacy by keeping sensitive data decentralized. By leveraging FL, organizations can achieve data efficiency by training models locally on devices or edge servers, reducing the need for extensive data transfer. FL promotes collaboration and knowledge sharing without sharing raw data, fostering collective intelligence. Moreover, FL operates in a decentralized manner, reducing infrastructure costs and enabling efficient communication in distributed environments. The continuous learning capabilities of FL ensure that models stay up-to-date with changing circumstances. By minimizing communication overhead through the sharing of encrypted model parameters or gradients, FL enhances communication efficiency in Industry 5.0. However, challenges related to managing model updates and ensuring fairness should be carefully addressed. This chapter presents FL as a promising approach to optimize communication in Industry 5.0, offering privacy preservation, data efficiency, collaboration, decentralized infrastructure, and continuous learning.

Keywords: Federated learning, Machine learning, Edge computing, Blockchain

[1]School of Computer Science Engineering and Information Systems, Vellore Institute of Technology, Vellore, India
[2]School of Computer Science and Engineering, VIT-AP University, Amaravati, India
[3]School of Creative Technologies, University of Bolton, United Kingdom
[4]Division of Research and Development, Lovely Professional University, Phagwara, India

2.1 Introduction

Industry 5.0 is an emerging concept that relies on Industry 4.0 principles. Industry 5.0 emphasizes the collaboration between humans and several technologies and AI-powered robots to improve the procedures in the workplace. The term Industry 5.0 represents a vision for the future of industrial production [2]. Industry 5.0, the new wave of industrialization, combines human invention with efficient, intelligent, and precise equipment to create efficient resources and user-preferred manufacturing solutions. Potential ideas and technologies should help Industry 5.0 to enhance productivity and offer customized goods quickly [35].

Industry 5.0 has several outperforming characteristics like human-centric nature, collaborative robotics, enabling customization and personalization, and decentralized decision-making. Industry 5.0 recognizes the unique capabilities of humans, like creativity, problem-solving, and adaptability [49]. Industry 5.0 uses these qualities in combination with advanced technologies to drive innovation and improve productivity. Industry 5.0 encourages close interaction between humans and robots, where both work side by side. Collaborative robots (Cobots) play a major role in Industry 5.0, which help humans in tasks that need precision, strength, or repetitive actions. This collaborative approach enhances safety, efficiency, and flexibility in industrial operations. Industry 5.0 aims to enable mass customization and personalized manufacturing [62]. Figure 2.1 discusses FL for optimized communication in Industry 5.0. Industry 5.0 recognizes the need for a skilled workforce that can adapt to technological advancements. By collecting and analyzing data from machines, sensors, and other sources, organizations can gain valuable insights to enhance decision-making, optimize operations, and achieve continuous improvement. It aims to reduce resource consumption, minimize waste generation, and optimize energy efficiency in production processes [37].

Industry 5.0 involves a huge communication between several different sectors and within the sector. In the fast-growing era of Industry 5.0, the delay in communication is not acceptable and it has to be optimized in order to meet the needs of the end users [28].

In addition to the use of modern communication technologies like IoT, AI, and robots in order to improve efficiency and productivity while maintaining effective communication between both humans and machines, Industry 5.0 places a strong emphasis on human–machine collaboration [40]. This provides smooth coordination across diverse services, real-time data sharing, and remote monitoring. In Industry 5.0, communication is essential for enabling easy communication between people and modern technologies. It makes information exchange, real-time data analysis, remote monitoring, and collaboration between multiple manufacturing stages possible. Process optimisation, easier decision-making, and improved efficiency can all be ensured by effective communication [60].

Communication optimization techniques play a crucial role in Industry 5.0, where efficient and reliable communication is vital for seamless connectivity, collaboration, and data exchange. These techniques aim to enhance communication performance, reduce latency, optimize bandwidth usage, ensure data integrity and

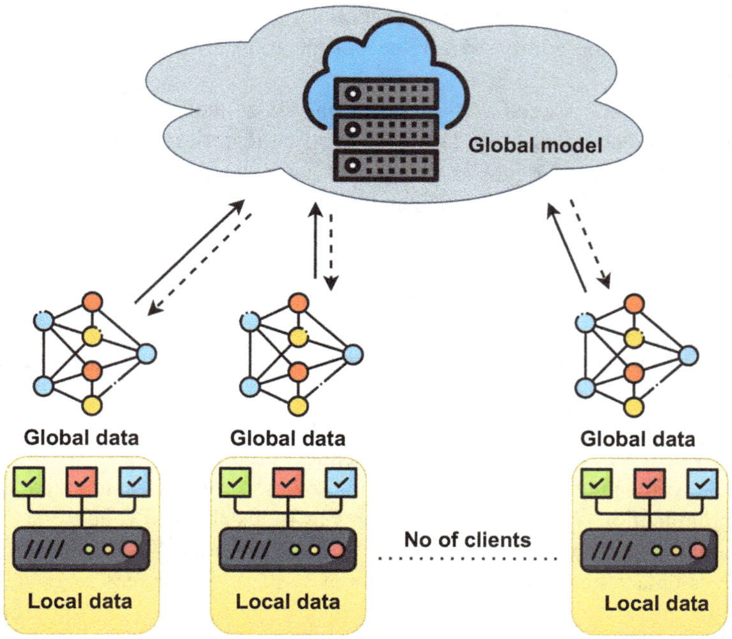

Figure 2.1 FL architecture

security, and support real-time decision-making. Several optimisation techniques are used in Industry 5.0 [51].

Edge computing (EC) is one of the optimisation techniques that bring computational capabilities closer to the data source. This reduces latency and enhances real-time communication. EC enables faster response time and reduced network congestion. It is more useful in time-sensitive applications in Industry 5.0 [13]. 5G networks are one of the other methods that can optimise communication in Industry 5.0. The adoption of 5G networks in Industry 5.0 enables high-speed, low-latency communication, supports real-time data transfer, and also offers improved bandwidth for communication, reduced latency, and higher reliability, enabling faster and more efficient communication between devices [40]. In Industry 5.0, where large volumes of data are generated, compressed data transmission enables efficient communication, and reduces transmission costs. Compression techniques can be applied to various types of data, including sensor data, images, videos, and audio streams. Ensuring data integrity, confidentiality, and security is essential in Industry 5.0. Various advanced technologies like Augmented Reality(AR) and Virtual Reality(VR) provide experiences and enable remote collaboration. They are used for training purposes, troubleshooting, and support workers [12]. These technologies use real-time information and communication and transfer of knowledge between human operators and machines. The implementation of these communication optimisation techniques enables seamless collaboration, data exchange, and decision-making in Industry 5.0 and helps its overall performance success [57].

While Industry 5.0 holds great potential, there are several challenges and issues that need to be addressed for the optimisation techniques to be applied in Industry 5.0.

The integration of several communication-related technologies and systems is found to be more complex [33]. This technology integration might sometimes lead to compatibility issues. Organisations that advanced to Industry 5.0 need to adopt good strategies for efficient data management, and visualisation to prevent bottlenecks in communication. Since communication in Industry 5.0 involves a large amount of exchange of data between several devices there is a major threat to the data. Industry 5.0 needs a few techniques to secure the data [31]. Upgrading communication infrastructure and adopting advanced technologies can involve significant costs. Organisations need to invest in the necessary hardware, software, and network infrastructure to support effective communication in Industry 5.0 [41].

The communication optimisation challenges in Industry 5.0 can be solved by using many different techniques and one such technique is FL.

FL can offer potential solutions to some of the problems associated with current communication optimisation techniques in Industry 5.0. FL addresses privacy concerns by training models collaboratively while keeping data decentralised [23]. It improves data efficiency by allowing local training on devices or edge servers, reducing the need to transfer large amounts of data. FL promotes collaboration and knowledge sharing without sending sensitive data, leveraging collective intelligence. It operates in a decentralised manner, reducing costs and infrastructure requirements [14]. FL supports continuous learning and minimises communication overhead by sharing encrypted model parameters or gradients instead of raw data.

2.1.1 Contributions

The main contributions of this chapter are summarised as follows:

- First, we discuss FL in Industry 5.0 and their importance for optimised communication.
- Second, we examine the motivation to adapt FL for optimised communication in Industry 5.0.
- Third, we examine the existing work and several benefits of FL-based Optimised communication in Industry 5.0.
- Fourth, we discuss Key enabling technologies that help FL for communication optimisation in Industry 5.0.
- Next, we discuss role of FL for communication optimisation in the context of Industry 5.0.
- Finally, we discuss several challenges and open issues in FL for optimised communication in Industry 5.0, as well as future directions.

The rest of this chapter is organised as follows: Section 2.2 discusses the preliminaries and motivation to adapt FL for optimised communication in Industry 5.0, and Section 2.3 discusses existing works in FL and Industry 5.0 for optimised communication. In Section 2.4 of this chapter, benefits of FL-based optimisation in Industry

5.0 are discussed. Key enabling technologies that help FL for communication optimisation in Industry 5.0 are discussed in Section 2.5. In Section 2.6, the role of FL for communication optimisation in the context of Industry 5.0 is discussed. Challenges and open issues, including future directions, are discussed in Section 2.7, Section 2.8, and the conclusion.

2.2 Preliminaries and motivations

This section describes the preliminary concept of federated learning and Industry 5.0 in optimised communication.

2.2.1 Federated learning

FL is a machine learning (ML) technique that allows for the training of models on several devices while maintaining the data on those devices, eliminating the need to transfer the data to one place [58]. The process of FL can be explained in the following steps:

- Local training: Each device computes its model update based on local data.
- Aggregation: Model updates from various devices are aggregated on a central server or a chosen node to form a global model.
- Iteration: The global model is sent back to the devices for further local updates, and the cycle continues until convergence.

2.2.2 Federated learning for Industry 5.0

The decentralised nature of FL aligns perfectly with Industry 5.0. The key advantages of FL in Industry 5.0 are:

- Optimised communication: By only exchanging model updates instead of raw data, the volume of data traffic over the network is substantially reduced.
- Data privacy: Since raw data remains at the source, proprietary information or sensitive data is never exposed.
- Localised decision-making: Devices can make instant decisions based on local updates, supporting real-time adaptations and reactions in industrial settings.

FL preserves privacy, reduces communication costs, and utilises heterogeneous data without sharing information. FL includes several communication optimisation methods.

Different techniques for compression are used to reduce the number of updated models before transmission because communication among edge devices and the centralised server can become a resource [61]. Communication expenses can be greatly decreased by using methods like quantisation, sparsification, and information extraction [18]. The difference between privacy and confidentiality is that a privacy-preserving method adds noise to the model updates earlier than aggregation, making it difficult to retrieve sensitive data about specific data points [59]. This makes sure that the personal information used for training is kept secret, even from the main server [67]. Secure multi-party computation (SMPC) methods are employed during aggregation to defend against possible server-based attacks. These methods add an additional degree of security by enabling the aggregation of model updates without allowing direct access to them [47]. Adaptive communication solutions dynamically change the communication frequency based on variables like communication conditions of use, device availability, or model growth rates rather than simply delivering model updates at predetermined intervals [68]. This avoids unnecessary communication and reduces training time in general.

2.2.3 Industry 5.0

Industry 5.0 can enable the extremely fast transfer of data with reduced latency across communication networks. Real-time data sharing across devices and systems allows for rapid decision-making and optimisation. Industry 5.0 may require decentralised communication methods. These standards can allow safe communication between many devices, sensors, and components, keeping the manufacturing process flexible and robust [20]. IoT devices may be more fully integrated in Industry 5.0, with optimised communication for data gathering, analysis, and feedback loops. FL is being used in Industry 5.0 to train models across industries while protecting data. To enhance growth, manufacturers may refine common models.

Industry 5.0 is an industrial future based on Industry 4.0. It emphasises human–technology collaboration for environmentally responsible and customised development [44]. Optimised communication enables seamless connectivity, current information sharing, and effective decision-making across manufacturing components, enabling Industry 5.0 and optimised communication. Industry 5.0 desires to connect people, devices, technologies, and systems in the production environment. Communication optimises data and information transfer between the manufacturing process's components. The interconnection offers immediate feedback, adapted production, and efficient collaboration among different stakeholders. Data enables Industry 5.0 decision-making and optimisation [48]. Optimised communication improves and protects edge device-central system data exchange. Manufacturers can monitor operations, discover irregularities, and react quickly with this real-time data sharing [65]. Industry 5.0 proposes flexible, on-demand production. Optimised communication allows production system reconfiguration to seamlessly encompass innovative goods or production requirements. Manufacturers may easily update machine and robot instructions, setups, and requirements [19]. In Industry 5.0, humans and cobots combine strengths. Optimised communication allows cobots and humans to interact in real time, making production more secure, simpler, and adaptable.

2.2.4 Motivation to adapt FL for optimised communication in Industry 5.0

FL is an emerging technique that allows several devices or people to learn from one another's data while maintaining the data's decentralisation and security [39]. Distributed ML can improve communication in Industry 5.0, which integrates modern technology with a human-centric approach.

Industry 5.0 emphasises data privacy and data-driven technology. FL maintains data on local machines or servers, preventing the risk of data loss and unauthorised access. Centralised ML transfers and stores data on a single server, causing risks. FL processes data locally, transmitting model updates to the central server [49]. This secures critical data during transmission. Industry aids, as well as infrastructure, create a lot of data. FL allows simultaneous model training over separated devices, which allows easier and more efficient learning than centralised systems. Various devices, detectors, and machines are added to Industry 5.0 systems. In Industry 5.0, communication speed could pose a major issue, especially with irregular access [66]. FL minimises data transfer to a centralised server, optimising communication and decreasing costs.

2.3 Literature review

In this section, discuss FL for optimised communication and Industry 5.0. We focus on FL for optimised communication in Industry 5.0 by different authors, which is studied as a basis for the chapter and understanding.

2.3.1 Existing works

Industry 5.0 and FL are currently new concepts, but several studies and applications focus on Industry 5.0, optimisation, and FL.

In Ref. [66], the authors, proposed a deep learning framework for Industrial IoT applications, with a particular emphasis on communication optimisation through locally trained models on edge devices and model aggregation using multitask learning methods. Additionally, it covers energy management in Industry 5.0 and demonstrates the possibility of working together to train deep neural networks across several robots while upholding data privacy.

In Ref. [5], the authors provided a safe and effective framework for Industry 5.0 while also addressing security and efficiency issues in FL. Additionally, the effort investigates the combination of FL and reinforcement learning in autonomous industrial control systems, facilitating cooperative learning across decentralised control units, optimising system performance while ensuring privacy, and minimising communication overhead.

In Ref. [42], the authors proposed an "FL-Based Approach to Energy Management for Smart Grid in Industry 5.0". In the context of Industry 5.0 and the development of the smart grid, this study is dedicated to improving energy management. It suggests a FL-based strategy that enables remote energy resources to learn in concert with minimal communication overhead and without compromising privacy.

In Ref. [32], the authors proposed a digital twin-based model based on FL that improves the stability of edge-server-to-end-user communication. The trustworthiness, safety, and confidentiality of the system are all improved by using a blockchain-enabled FL architecture. An optimisation challenge of edge association may be broken down into three parts: digital twin association, training the number of batches, and bandwidth assignment. The best approach to solving this issue is to investigate multi-agent reinforcement learning.

2.4 Benefits of FL-based communication optimisation in Industry 5.0

In Industry 5.0, there is a collection of enormous and huge volumes of sensitive data. Ensuring privacy and security is very important in order to gain trust and comply with the rules. Since FL has distributive nature, it can ensure the privacy and security of data [16]. FL ensures that the sensitive data is not shared with any external entity. In Industry 5.0 transmitting large amounts of data to the central location can strain the network bandwidth and introduce latency [1]. Since FL reduces the necessity for the transfer of data by performing local model training, it optimises bandwidth usage and reduces communication delays [11]. Industry 5.0 faces the data heterogeneity problem since it creates data from various different sources. FL addresses this challenge by enabling devices to train the models on local data while aggregating the models to build a global model. Industry 5.0 suffers from the challenge of lack of scalability. The decentralised nature of FL supports scalability and enables real-time responsiveness, making FL a suitable solution for Industry 5.0 [44].

Data sharing and collaboration model training ensure data privacy and security. Industries may share information and insight without sharing raw data, improving ecosystem interaction and decision-making. Individual industries can adjust models to local variables for more accurate and relevant production information. FL supports real-time decision-making and response actions by rapidly aggregating knowledge from multiple sources. The model's changes are done locally, decreasing communication and connection abilities. FL-trained maintenance prediction and quality control models optimise processes and decrease interruptions by predicting problems. Real-time workplace information can optimise communication systems for resource allocation and congestion reduction. Industries can meet security concerns and industry regulations by focusing on data. In Industry 5.0, FL-based optimised communication supports dynamic decision-making, effectiveness, and performance during operations while protecting data privacy and security. By leveraging FL for optimised communication in Industry 5.0, organisations can benefit from privacy-preserving communication, efficient bandwidth usage, real-time responsiveness, distributed knowledge sharing, scalability, adaptability, and collaboration between humans and machines. These advantages contribute to enhanced efficiency, productivity, decision-making, and overall performance in Industry 5.0 environments [56]. Figure 2.3 discusses applications of FL-based optimisation in Industry 5.0

2.5 Key enabling technologies that help FL for communication optimisation in Industry 5.0

FL is an innovative approach to training machine learning models across numerous devices while localising data. Industry 5.0 emphasises integrating human understanding and abilities with smart systems and automation, making communication optimisation important. Some significant enabling technologies exist for FL for Industry 5.0 communication. Figure 2.2 discusses various key enabling technologies that help FL for communication optimisation in Industry 5.0.

2.5.1 Edge computing

Edge computing processes and analyses data at or near the 'edge' of a network instead of transmitting all data to a data centre or cloud. This method decreases latency, enhances real-time decision-making, and saves bandwidth [50]. IoT, autonomous cars, and industrial automation applications that need instantaneous responses benefit from it.

Edge computing will be used in FL to optimise Industry 5.0 communication by addressing many critical difficulties. Edge computing in FL by reducing communication latency and improving real-time decision-making by processing and analysing local data in Industry 5.0 [26]. It allows collaborative model training using data from several edge devices, saving bandwidth and data privacy. Edge computing distributes processing among devices, decreasing single-point failures and improving robustness [4]. It uses inputs from other devices to improve local model accuracy and

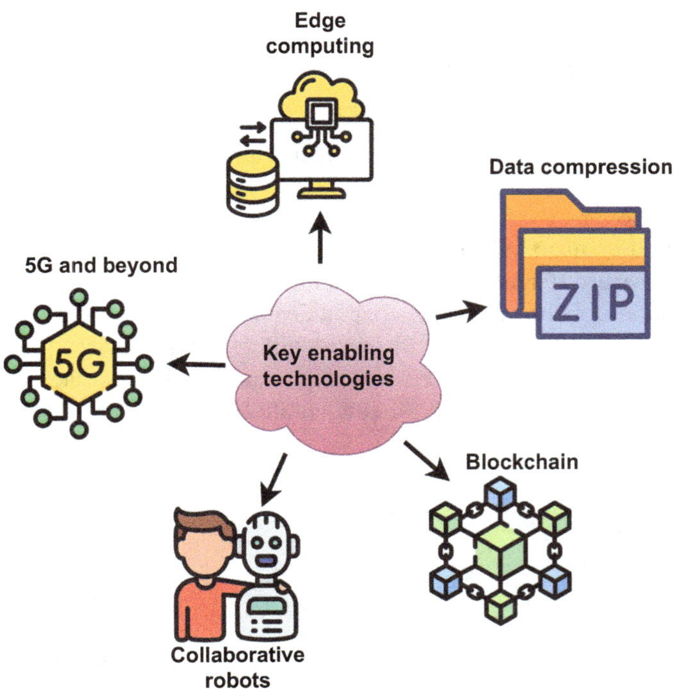

Figure 2.2 Key enabling technologies of FL for communication optimisation in Industry 5.0

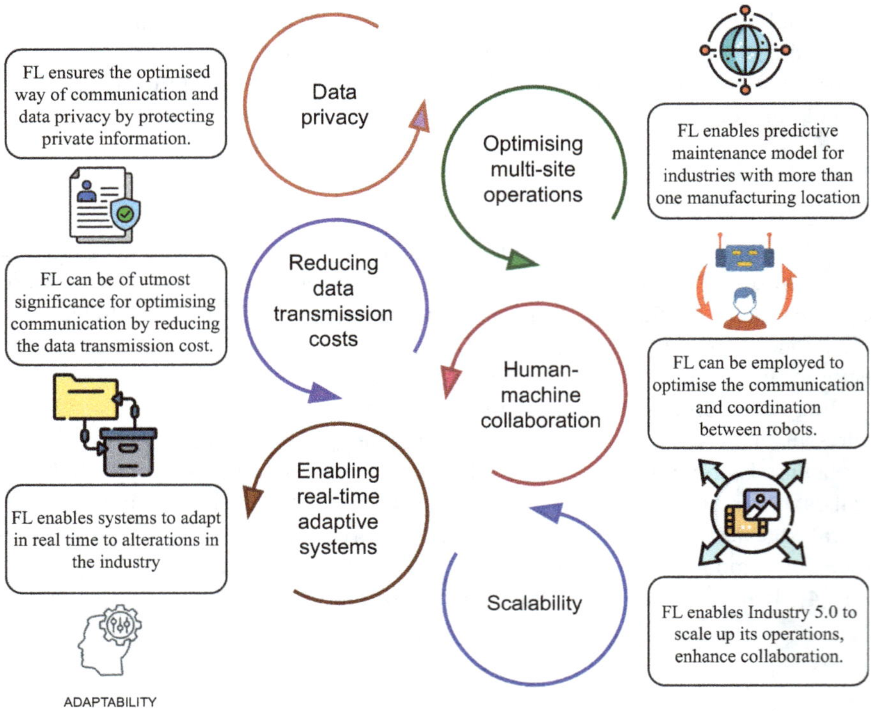

Figure 2.3 Role of FL-based communication optimisation in Industry 5.0

allows customised and localised training, ensuring Industry 5.0 model adaptability and effectiveness.

Edge devices may have a few flaws that restrict computational power, storage, and memory, affecting model complexity and FL outcomes. Edge devices in Industry 5.0 may have different hardware capabilities, making model aggregation and synchronisation difficult. Complex communication protocols and synchronisation procedures are needed to manage FL across different edge devices [28]. Distributing model updates among edge devices improves the attack surface and security risks. Establishing and setting up FL configurations on edge devices takes a lot of resources and time.

2.5.2 5G and beyond

The fifth generation of wireless technology, or 5G, has been designed to offer greater capacity, reduced latency, and higher data speeds than the previous two generations (3G and 4G) [43]. It makes connections more dependable and seamless, which is essential for enabling a variety of applications like Internet of Things (IoT) devices, remote medical treatment, and driverless vehicles.

The term 'beyond 5G' refers to the coming stage in the evolution of wireless technology, often known as 6G or other similar roles. It is projected to build on the strengths of 5G by providing even faster bandwidth, lower latency, and more sophisticated functionality [55]. The features and technologies of the 'beyond 5G' era are now being explored through investigation and development.

5G and beyond will help FL for optimised communication in Industry 5.0, which integrates advanced technology with human collaboration to improve the functioning of industries and relies on 5G and beyond to optimise connectivity [3]. 5G and beyond in FL with effective communication among machine, sensor, and device connections It maintains higher data rates, real-time transmission, and enhanced network dependability with edge computing, which is suitable for industrial applications since it minimises latency and improves real-time processing capabilities. Network splitting enables the creation of specialised virtual networks to meet various communication requirements in Industry 5.0 scenarios [9]. Industrial activities that utilise few resources are made possible by 5G and later technologies, which also allow for efficient device communication and low power.

Technologies like 5G and beyond have many advantages for improving communication in Industry 5.0, but they also possess some drawbacks. 5G and beyond require huge infrastructure expenditures, including base stations and improvements to the network. This may limit some industries, especially smaller ones. 5G adoption is expanding, but certain locations are still uncovered. Accessing these technologies' full benefits in rural areas may be difficult [27]. In certain environments, signal propagation via obstructions may impair 5G and beyond high-frequency bands, decreasing communication dependability. Higher internet rates and device connectivity can increase the consumption of electricity. This may affect Industry 5.0's energy efficiency ambitions. Upgrading or replacing equipment and systems for 5G and beyond may cause compatibility issues and interruptions.

2.5.3 Data compression

Data compression is used to minimise file or stream size while maintaining important data. It's often used to decrease storage space, enhance data transfer, and improve processing [64]. The removal of redundant or repetitive data patterns using compression techniques shrinks the original data. Data compression will be used in FL to optimise communication in Industry 5.0 by addressing the large volumes of data created in industrial processes. Data compression is used in FL to share data among machines, devices, and systems that exchange enormous volumes of data in Industry 5.0 [29]. Compressing data allows faster transmission over a lower bandwidth, preventing network congestion and speeding communication. This is essential for industrial real-time decision-making, process optimisation, and responsive control. Transmission delays, cost savings, energy usage, storage space, and security are reduced by compressed data [38]. It improves system efficiency and responsiveness at the network edge. The main drawback of using data compression in FL to optimise communication in Industry 5.0 is that data loss might come from aggressive data compression. This could decrease model update quality, causing insufficient training performance and model correctness. These activities may increase the cost of resource-constrained devices due to their performance and responsiveness [54].

Implementing compression algorithms for several platforms might be complicated. Information loss may increase with larger compression ratios.

2.5.4 Blockchain

Blockchain is a distributed digital ledger. It securely and transparently records transactions across numerous computers in a chronological chain of blocks. Each block contains transactions and connects to the previous one, creating a tamper-resistant data record [22]. It is often connected with bitcoin, but it is used in supply chain management, healthcare, and more. Blockchain's transparency, security, and efficiency can improve Industry 5.0 communication. Blockchain will be used in FL to make real-time information sharing within the supply chain possible through blockchain technology, improving communication and decreasing delays. Additionally, it improves communication and reduces disagreements by using self-executing smart deals to optimise communication [53]. Collaboration is a key component of Industry 5.0, and blockchain can guarantee safe data sharing. By sharing production information, measurements for quality assurance, and traceability, decentralised manufacturing networks can increase productivity and communication [30]. Additionally, blockchain facilitates the monitoring of maintenance, resource use, and energy consumption, fostering environmentally friendly behaviours and an effective environmental impact on communication. Blockchain's enhanced communication capabilities can be useful for Industry 5.0, but there are some drawbacks as well. Blockchain networks may experience difficulty with adaptability, especially when processing many transactions quickly. This could delay processing and communication. Blockchain networks require a lot of energy for extraction and validation. This environmental impact may concern sustainable industries. Blockchain implementation and management are complicated and demand expertise [17]. This may increase costs and adoption challenges, affecting communication. Blockchain increases data security but raises privacy issues because data cannot be simply wiped. Blockchain and non-blockchain platforms may not communicate well without interoperability.

2.5.5 Collaborative robots

Collaborative robots, which are termed cobots, are robots designed to interact with humans in shared workspaces [21].

Cobots, which are designed for human–machine cooperation, can significantly benefit FL for communication optimisation in Industry 5.0. Cobots, which are equipped with sensors and several processors, can process the data locally that aligns to the principles of FL and ensure the communication efficiency [10]. This approach of cobots not only preserves the sensitive industrial data but also supports real-time adaptability of cobots. The decentralised learning and decision-making, combined with the reduced network traffic from only transmitting essential model updates, ensure scalability and bandwidth efficiency [15]. Thus, in the hyper-connected landscape of Industry 5.0, cobots and FL together forge a path towards cohesive, efficient, and optimised human-machine collaboration.

While cobots integrated with FL offer numerous advantages in communication optimisation for Industry 5.0, several challenges will arise. The merging of FL and cobots is complex, and it is difficult to deal with heterogeneous data across different cobot tasks [45].

2.6 Role of FL for communication optimisation in the context of Industry 5.0

This section discusses different applications of FL-based optimisation in Industry 5.0. Figure 2.4 discusses FL challenges for optimised communication in Industry 5.0.

2.6.1 Data privacy

In the FL environment, only the model updates or gradients are communicated to the central server but not the real data. Several devices in the industrial environment like robotics, sensors, and other machines can acquire the real-time analysis of data without transferring it to the central server [30]. This feature of FL ensures the optimised way of communication and data privacy by protecting private information in different sectors of Industry 5.0.

2.6.2 Reducing data transmission costs

FL involves only the transfer of model weights or gradients, which can be further compressed or quantised. This is in contrast to the traditional method of transmitting vast amounts of raw data. It is possible to speed up the decision-making process by

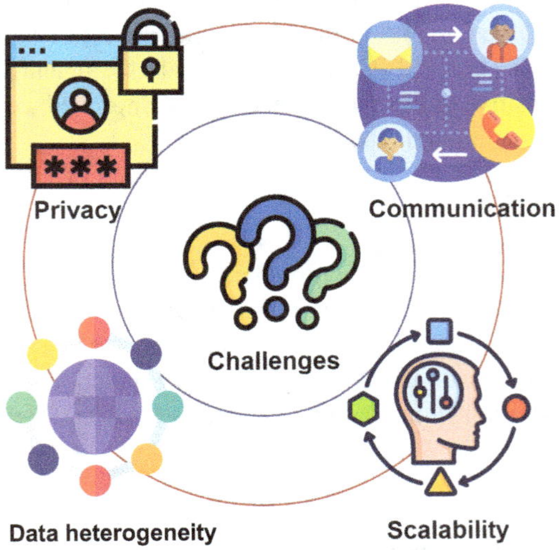

Figure 2.4 FL challenges for optimised communication in Industry 5.0

managing information 'at the edge', or where it is actually produced, and by minimising the amount of data that is transferred [52]. For processes that are time-dependent in Industry 5.0, FL can be of utmost significance for optimising communication by reducing the data transmission cost.

2.6.3 Enabling real-time adaptive systems

As the conditions in the industry change, like a fluctuating demand, change in the quality of the raw material, or failure of a machine, FL allows the system to adapt in real time [25]. Every single node of a network can update based on the local conditions and share the experiences across the large network of Industry 5.0. The machines across the large network can learn from these experiences thereby optimising the communication between several large networks [36]. For example, if one robot develops a more efficient motion pattern, it can share this learning with others.

2.6.4 Optimising multi-site operations

Industries that have more than one manufacturing location or operation may benefit from FL by ensuring that the learning's from one location are applied to the others. This is accomplished without the need to centralise data, which both conforms with regional data standards and brings down the costs of data transmission and communication [24]. By adopting FL, machines located in a variety of locations can contribute data to a centralised predictive maintenance model, improving the model's level of precision and ensuring the reliability and efficiency of the equipment.

2.6.5 Human–machine collaboration

Human-machine collaboration in federated learning can greatly enhance the optimisation of communication in Industry 5.0. Humans can provide domain expertise, curate relevant data, and fine-tune models, while machines handle data processing and model aggregation [8]. This synergy ensures efficient data sharing without centralising sensitive information, leading to improved communication and decision-making in the industrial context.

2.6.6 Scalability

Scalability is crucial in optimising communication for Industry 5.0 through FL. By efficiently distributing computation and training across a network of devices, Federated Learning can handle large datasets and diverse sources of information [63]. This enables Industry 5.0 to scale up its operations, enhance collaboration, and achieve optimised communication while maintaining data privacy and security.

2.6.7 Integrating with other technologies

FL enhances optimised communication by integrating with Industry 5.0 and other technologies such as EC, AI, 5G networks, and the IoT. The data can be processed locally by edge computing, and AI is capable of identifying patterns in the data. The IoT is capable of delivering data streams in real time [34]. FL consequently aggregates the observed information acquired from these various sources, which allows for more effective communication and decision-making while simultaneously protecting users' privacy and reducing latency time.

2.7 Challenges and open issues

FL supports the optimised communication in Industry 5.0 but then several challenges and open issues need to be addressed. These challenges are related to data heterogeneity, privacy and security, scalability, and communication efficiency.

Industry 5.0 deals with large and a variety of data. This data is generated from various devices like sensors, and systems. This leads to heterogeneity in the collected data. Integrating and normalising the heterogeneous data is a greater challenge [26]. Several techniques for preprocessing the data, standardisation, and feature engineering are needed in order to handle these different and heavy loads of data.

Though FL aims in preserving data privacy by performing the training of the local model by keeping the data on the client side, privacy and security concerns are still a point of challenge. There is a need of developing robust techniques for secure model aggregation, and protection against adversarial attacks. Ensuring data confidentiality during communication is very crucial in order to maintain the trust and privacy of data. Industry 5.0 environments have very limited communication bandwidth and less reliable network connectivity [51]. These challenges can be addressed by developing communication protocols, compression techniques, and adaptive strategies. All these techniques are much needed for optimising the communication efficiency of Industry 5.0 networks. In FL, models are trained locally on edge devices or servers, potentially resulting in discrepancies and inconsistencies between models. Ensuring model synchronisation and convergence across the federated network is a challenge. Techniques for efficient model aggregation, handling asynchronous updates, and dealing with variations in local data distributions need to be developed to ensure the consistency and accuracy of models in FL optimisation [6]. Industry 5.0 involves a very large number of devices, sensors, and interconnected systems. The scalability of FL optimisation in very large and dynamic environments is very tough and several techniques for managing the increasing volume of data. Industry 5.0 involves the integration of diverse devices, protocols, and systems from different manufacturers. Achieving interoperability and standardisation in FL optimisation is essential for seamless communication and collaboration between devices and systems [46]. Addressing these challenges and open issues will require further research, technological advancements, and collaborations among industry, academia, and standardisation bodies. By overcoming these obstacles, FL can be effectively applied for optimised communication in Industry 5.0, leading to improved privacy, efficiency, and collaboration between humans and advanced technologies in the industrial context.

2.8 Conclusion

In this chapter, we have explored the details of Industry 5.0 and the current optimisation techniques for communication that are used in Industry 5.0. Later, we also discussed the details of how FL can help in solving the challenges in the communication optimisation in Industry 5.0 [7]. Several applications of FL for optimised communication in the context of Industry 5.0, which emphasises the collaboration between humans and advanced technologies are also discussed in detail. FL offers several benefits in addressing the challenges associated with data privacy, communication efficiency, latency reduction, distributed knowledge sharing, scalability, and adaptability in Industry 5.0. We discussed how FL enables organisations to leverage the power of distributed data while ensuring privacy and data security [42]. By keeping data localised and performing model training on decentralised devices or servers, FL allows for privacy-preserving communication and analysis, addressing concerns regarding data breaches and unauthorised access.

While FL offers significant advantages, there are challenges and open issues that need to be addressed. These include data heterogeneity, privacy and security concerns, model synchronisation, and resource constraints. Overcoming these challenges will require further research, standardisation efforts, and collaboration among stakeholders.

References

[1] Sawsan AbdulRahman, Hanine Tout, Hakima Ould-Slimane, Azzam Mourad, Chamseddine Talhi, and Mohsen Guizani. A survey on federated learning: The journey from centralized to distributed on-site learning and beyond. *IEEE Internet of Things Journal*, 8(7):5476–5497, 2020.

[2] Zakaria Abou El Houda, Bouziane Brik, Adlen Ksentini, Lyes Khoukhi, and Mohsen Guizani. When federated learning meets game theory: A cooperative framework to secure IIoT applications on edge computing. *IEEE Transactions on Industrial Informatics*, 18(11):7988–7997, 2022.

[3] Muhammad Sajjad Akbar, Zawar Hussain, Quan Z Sheng, and Subhas Mukhopadhyay. 6G survey on challenges, requirements, applications, key enabling technologies, use cases, AI integration issues and security aspects. *arXiv preprint arXiv:2206.00868*, 2022.

[4] Rubina Akter, Ahmad Zainudin, and Dong-Seong Kim. Uav-based b5g networks: Blockchain and federated learning technology.

[5] Mamoun Alazab, Swarna Priya RM, M Parimala, Praveen Kumar Reddy Maddikunta, Thippa Reddy Gadekallu, and Quoc-Viet Pham. Federated learning for cybersecurity: Concepts, challenges, and future directions. *IEEE Transactions on Industrial Informatics*, 18(5):3501–3509, 2021.

[6] Omair Rashed Abdulwareth Almanifi, Chee-Onn Chow, Mau-Luen Tham, Joon Huang Chuah, and Jeevan Kanesan. Communication and computation efficiency in federated learning: A survey. *Internet of Things*, page 100742, 2023.

[7] Saeed Haomood Alsamhi, Edward Curry, Ammar Hawbani, Santosh Kumar, Umair Ul Hassan, and Navin Singh Rajput. Dataspace in the sky: A novel decentralized framework to secure drones data sharing in b5g for industry 4.0 toward industry 5.0. 2023.

[8] Joel Alves, Tânia M Lima, and Pedro D Gaspar. Is industry 5.0 a human-centred approach? A systematic review. *Processes*, 11(1):193, 2023.

[9] Alessandro Aveni. Industry 5.0 and industry 4.0 comparative definitions. *Revista Processus de Estudos de Gestão, Jurídicos e Financeiros*, 14(46):01–15, 2023.

[10] Ta Phuong Bac, Do Thu Ha, Kim Duc Tran, and Kim Phuc Tran. Explainable artificial intelligence for cybersecurity in smart manufacturing. In *Artificial Intelligence for Smart Manufacturing: Methods, Applications, and Challenges*, pages 199–223. Springer, 2023.

[11] Bojana Bajic, Nikola Suzic, Slobodan Moraca, Miladin Stefanović, Milos Jovicic, and Aleksandar Rikalovic. Edge computing data optimization for smart quality management: Industry 5.0 perspective. *Sustainability*, 15(7):6032, 2023.

[12] Marcell Balogh, András Földvári, and Pal Varga. Digital twins in industry 5.0: Challenges in modeling and communication. In *NOMS 2023-2023 IEEE/IFIP Network Operations and Management Symposium*, pages 1–6. IEEE, 2023.

[13] Alexander Brecko, Erik Kajati, Jiri Koziorek, and Iveta Zolotova. Federated learning for edge computing: A survey. *Applied Sciences*, 12(18):9124, 2022.

[14] Hao Chen, Shaocheng Huang, Deyou Zhang, Ming Xiao, Mikael Skoglund, and H Vincent Poor. Federated learning over wireless IoT networks with optimized communication and resources. *IEEE Internet of Things Journal*, 9(17):16592–16605, 2022.

[15] K Dasaradharami Reddy, Thippa Reddy Gadekallu, *et al.* A comprehensive survey on federated learning techniques for healthcare informatics. *Computational Intelligence and Neuroscience*, 2023, 2023.

[16] Kapal Dev, Kim Fung Tsang, and Juan Manuel Corchado Rodríguez. Guest editorial: The era of industry 5.0—technologies from no recognizable hm interface to hearty touch personal products. *IEEE Transactions on Industrial Informatics*, 18(8):5432–5434, 2022.

[17] Chandramohan Dhasarathan, Mohammad Kamrul Hasan, Shayla Islam, *et al.* User privacy prevention model using supervised federated learning-based block chain approach for internet of medical things. *CAAI Transactions on Intelligence Technology*, 2023.

[18] Hongchang Gao, My T Thai, and Jie Wu. When decentralized optimization meets federated learning. *IEEE Network*, 2023.

[19] A Shaji George and AS Hovan George. Revolutionizing manufacturing: Exploring the promises and challenges of industry 5.0. *Partners Universal International Innovation Journal*, 1(2):22–38, 2023.

[20] Morteza Ghobakhloo, Mohammad Iranmanesh, Manuel E Morales, Mehrbakhsh Nilashi, and Azlan Amran. Actions and approaches for enabling industry 5.0-driven sustainable industrial transformation: A strategy

roadmap. *Corporate Social Responsibility and Environmental Management*, 30(3):1473–1494, 2023.

[21] Matthias Guertler, Laura Tomidei, Nathalie Sick, *et al.* When is a robot a cobot? Moving beyond manufacturing and arm-based cobot manipulators. *Proceedings of the Design Society*, 3:3889–3898, 2023.

[22] Huaqun Guo and Xingjie Yu. A survey on blockchain technology and its security. *Blockchain: Research and Applications*, 3(2):100067, 2022.

[23] Pengfei Guo, Dong Yang, Ali Hatamizadeh, *et al.* Auto-fedrl: Federated hyperparameter optimization for multi-institutional medical image segmentation. In *European Conference on Computer Vision*, pages 437–455. Springer, 2022.

[24] Sandeep Gupta. An edge-computing based industrial gateway for industry 4.0 using arm trustzone technology. *Journal of Industrial Information Integration*, 33:100441, 2023.

[25] Ahmad Hammoud, Hadi Otrok, Azzam Mourad, and Zbigniew Dziong. On demand fog federations for horizontal federated learning in iov. *IEEE Transactions on Network and Service Management*, 19(3):3062–3075, 2022.

[26] Farzana Islam, Ahmed Shoyeb Raihan, and Imtiaz Ahmed. Winning through collaboration by applying federated learning in manufacturing industry. *arXiv preprint arXiv:2302.13514*, 2023.

[27] Igor Kardush, Sejeong Kim, and Elaine Wong. A techno-economic study of industry 5.0 enterprise deployments for human-to-machine communications. *IEEE Communications Magazine*, 60(12):74–80, 2022.

[28] F Khan, RL Kumar, MH Abidi, S Kadry, H Alkhalefah, and MK Aboudaif. Federated split learning model for industry 5.0: A data poisoning defense for edge computing. *Electronics*, 11:2393, 2022.

[29] Kaushal Kishor. Communication-efficient federated learning. In *Federated Learning for IoT Applications*, pages 135–156. Springer, 2022.

[30] Jiewu Leng, Xiaofeng Zhu, Zhiqiang Huang, *et al.* Manuchain ii: Blockchained smart contract system as the digital twin of decentralized autonomous manufacturing toward resilience in industry 5.0. *IEEE Transactions on Systems, Man, and Cybernetics: Systems*, 2023.

[31] Zihong Li, Yang Hong, Ali Kashif Bashir, Yasser D Al-Otaibi, and Jun Wu. Software-defined GPU-CPU empowered efficient wireless federated learning with embedding communication coding for beyond 5g. *IEEE Open Journal of the Communications Society*, 2023.

[32] Yunlong Lu, Xiaohong Huang, Ke Zhang, Sabita Maharjan, and Yan Zhang. Low-latency federated learning and blockchain for edge association in digital twin empowered 6g networks. *IEEE Transactions on Industrial Informatics*, 17(7):5098–5107, 2020.

[33] Yuqian Lu, Hao Zheng, Saahil Chand, *et al.* Outlook on human-centric manufacturing towards industry 5.0. *Journal of Manufacturing Systems*, 62:612–627, 2022.

[34] Magdalena Maciaszczyk, Zbigniew Makieła, and Radosław Miśkiewicz. Industry 5.0: A new reality, new challenges. In *Innovation in the Digital Economy*, pages 51–61. Routledge, 2023.

[35] Praveen Kumar Reddy Maddikunta, Quoc-Viet Pham, B. Prabadevi, *et al.* Industry 5.0: A survey on enabling technologies and potential applications. *Journal of Industrial Information Integration*, 26:100257, 2022.

[36] Alessandro Massaro. Advanced electronic and optoelectronic sensors, applications, modelling and industry 5.0 perspectives. *Applied Sciences*, 13(7):4582, 2023.

[37] Muhammad Ayzed Mirza, Junsheng Yu, Salman Raza, *et al.* Drl-assisted delay optimized task offloading in automotive-industry 5.0 based VECNs. *Journal of King Saud University-Computer and Information Sciences*, page 101512, 2023.

[38] Nicole Mitchell, Johannes Ballé, Zachary Charles, and Jakub Konečnỳ. Optimizing the communication-accuracy trade-off in federated learning with rate-distortion theory. *arXiv preprint arXiv:2201.02664*, 2022.

[39] Gianfranco E Modoni and Marco Sacco. A human digital-twin-based framework driving human centricity towards industry 5.0. *Sensors*, 23(13):6054, 2023.

[40] Ali Nauman, Marwa Obayya, Mashael M Asiri, *et al.* Minimizing energy consumption for NOMA multi-drone communications in automotive-industry 5.0. *Journal of King Saud University-Computer and Information Sciences*, page 101547, 2023.

[41] Dinh C Nguyen, Ming Ding, Pubudu N Pathirana, Aruna Seneviratne, Jun Li, and H Vincent Poor. Federated learning for internet of things: A comprehensive survey. *IEEE Communications Surveys & Tutorials*, 23(3):1622–1658, 2021.

[42] Sharnil Pandya, Gautam Srivastava, Rutvij Jhaveri, *et al.* Federated learning for smart cities: A comprehensive survey. *Sustainable Energy Technologies and Assessments*, 55:102987, 2023.

[43] Andreas G Papidas and George C Polyzos. Self-organizing networks for 5g and beyond: A view from the top. *Future Internet*, 14(3):95, 2022.

[44] Jakub Pizoń and Arkadiusz Gola. Human–machine relationship—perspective and future roadmap for industry 5.0 solutions. *Machines*, 11(2):203, 2023.

[45] R Raffik, Rithish Ramamoorthy Sathya, V Vaishali, *et al.* Industry 5.0: Enhancing human-robot collaboration through collaborative robots–a review. In *2023 2nd International Conference on Advancements in Electrical, Electronics, Communication, Computing and Automation (ICAECA)*, pages 1–6. IEEE, 2023.

[46] Anichur Rahman, Kamrul Hasan, Dipanjali Kundu, *et al.* On the ICN-IoT with federated learning integration of communication: Concepts, security-privacy issues, applications, and future perspectives. *Future Generation Computer Systems*, 138:61–88, 2023.

[47] Sawsan Abdul Rahman, Hanine Tout, Chamseddine Talhi, and Azzam Mourad. Internet of things intrusion detection: Centralized, on-device, or federated learning? *IEEE Network*, 34(6):310–317, 2020.

[48] Abirami Raja Santhi and Padmakumar Muthuswamy. Industry 5.0 or industry 4.0s? introduction to industry 4.0 and a peek into the prospective industry 5.0

technologies. *International Journal on Interactive Design and Manufacturing (IJIDeM)*, 17(2):947–979, 2023.

[49] Swarna Priya Ramu, Parimala Boopalan, Quoc-Viet Pham, *et al.* Federated learning enabled digital twins for smart cities: Concepts, recent advances, and future directions. *Sustainable Cities and Society*, 79:103663, 2022.

[50] Mohammad Reiss-Mirzaei, Mostafa Ghobaei-Arani, and Leila Esmaeili. A review on the edge caching mechanisms in the mobile edge computing: A social-aware perspective. *Internet of Things*, page 100690, 2023.

[51] Deepti Saraswat, Ashwin Verma, Pronaya Bhattacharya, *et al.* Blockchain-based federated learning in UAVs beyond 5g networks: A solution taxonomy and future directions. *IEEE Access*, 10:33154–33182, 2022.

[52] Satyajeet Rajaram Shinge and Urmila N Shrawankar. Cloud-based cost effective IIoT model towards industry 5.0. *Research Reports on Computer Science*, pages 55–64, 2023.

[53] Sushil Kumar Singh, Laurence T Yang, and Jong Hyuk Park. FusionFedBlock: Fusion of blockchain and federated learning to preserve privacy in industry 5.0. *Information Fusion*, 90:233–240, 2023.

[54] Abla Smahi, Hui Li, Yong Yang, *et al.* BV-ICVs: A privacy-preserving and verifiable federated learning framework for V2X environments using blockchain and zkSNARKs. *Journal of King Saud University-Computer and Information Sciences*, page 101542, 2023.

[55] Charles Ssengonzi, Okuthe P Kogeda, and Thomas O Olwal. A survey of deep reinforcement learning application in 5G and beyond network slicing and virtualization. *Array*, 14:100142, 2022.

[56] D Sudharson, A Bhuvaneshwaran, TR Kalaiarasan, *et al.* A multimodal AI framework for hyper automation in industry 5.0. In *2023 International Conference on Innovative Data Communication Technologies and Application (ICIDCA)*, pages 282–286. IEEE, 2023.

[57] Imran Taj and Umer Farooq. Towards machine learning-based fpga backend flow: Challenges and opportunities. *Electronics*, 12(4):935, 2023.

[58] Prohim Tam, Riccardo Corrado, Chanthol Eang, and Seokhoon Kim. Applicability of deep reinforcement learning for efficient federated learning in massive IoT communications. *Applied Sciences*, 13(5):3083, 2023.

[59] Ha-Vu Tran, Georges Kaddoum, Hany Elgala, Chadi Abou-Rjeily, and Hemani Kaushal. Lightwave power transfer for federated learning-based wireless networks. *IEEE Communications Letters*, 24(7):1472–1476, 2020.

[60] Kalim Ullah, Manal Abdullah Alohali, Muhammad Ibrar ul Haque, *et al.* Hybrid precoding design for secure smart-grid enabled MIMO wireless communications in Industry 5.0. *Journal of King Saud University-Computer and Information Sciences*, 35(7):101579, 2023.

[61] Omar Abdel Wahab, Azzam Mourad, Hadi Otrok, and Tarik Taleb. Federated machine learning: Survey, multi-level classification, desirable criteria and future directions in communication and networking systems. *IEEE Communications Surveys & Tutorials*, 23(2):1342–1397, 2021.

[62] Wei Xian, Kan Yu, Fengling Han, Le Fang, Dehua He, and Qing-Long Han. Advanced manufacturing in Industry 5.0: A survey of key enabling technologies and future trends. *IEEE Transactions on Industrial Informatics*, 2023.

[63] Ranjeet Yadav, Zahid Parwez, R Sree Parimala, U Priya, Sneha Kanwar Rathore, and SSK Deepak. Analysis and prediction of future research trends in the state of Industry 5.0. *Res Militaris*, 13(3):2330–2339, 2023.

[64] Yibo Yang, Stephan Mandt, Lucas Theis, *et al.* An introduction to neural data compression. *Foundations and Trends® in Computer Graphics and Vision*, 15(2):113–200, 2023.

[65] Gokul Yenduri, Gautam Srivastava, Praveen Kumar Reddy Maddikunta, *et al.* Generative pre-trained transformer: A comprehensive review on enabling technologies, potential applications, emerging challenges, and future directions. arXiv preprint arXiv:2305.10435, 2023.

[66] Shah Zeb, Aamir Mahmood, Sunder Ali Khowaja, *et al.* Industry 5.0 is coming: A survey on intelligent nextG wireless networks as technological enablers. arXiv preprint arXiv:2205.09084, 2022.

[67] Chen Zhao, Zhipeng Gao, Qian Wang, Kaile Xiao, Zijia Mo, and M Jamal Deen. Fedsup: A communication-efficient federated learning fatigue driving behaviors supervision approach. *Future Generation Computer Systems*, 138:52–60, 2023.

[68] Zihao Zhao, Yuzhu Mao, Yang Liu, *et al.* Towards efficient communications in federated learning: A contemporary survey. *Journal of the Franklin Institute*, 2023.

Chapter 3

Federated learning enabled digital twins for Industry 5.0: perspectives, challenges, and future directions

Dasaradharami Reddy Kandati[1], Supriya Y[2], Gokul Yenduri[3], Praveen Kumar Reddy Maddikunta[2], Thippa Reddy Gadekallu[4,5] and Abdul Wahid[6]

Abstract

Artificial intelligence (AI) and the Internet of Things (IoT) are continuously enhancing various sectors, including smart healthcare, manufacturing, automobiles, and retail, in Industry 5.0. Digital twins (DTs) are virtual replicas of real-world entities created using AI. The Industrial 5.0 applications based on DTs are still in their early stages, even though DTs have been adopted and used successfully in the manufacturing and industrial sectors. The sharing of sensitive data is limited due to concerns surrounding privacy and trust. The combination of federated learning (FL) and DT has the potential to ensure the confidentiality and reliability of users' data. This chapter addresses how these two novel developments may be combined to promote the widespread usage of both innovations in real time, crucial circumstances, and the simple management of Industry 5.0 applications. Here, we propose a comprehensive overview of the numerous methods that involve FL models being used in DTs to assist efforts toward Industry 5.0. The chapter establishes several key issues as well as recommendations for stepping ahead to improve FL-DT collaboration for future deployments.

Keywords: Industry 5.0, Digital twin, Federated learning, Internet of Things

[1]Department of Computer Science and Engineering, NBKR Institute of Science and Technology, Vidyanagar, India
[2]School of Computer Science Engineering and Information Systems, Vellore Institute of Technology, India
[3]School of Computer Science and Engineering, VIT-AP University, India
[4]Division of Research and Development, Lovely Professional University, Phagwara, India
[5]Zhongda Group, Haiyan County, Jiaxing City, Zhejiang Province, China
[6]School of Computer Science, University of Galway, Ireland

3.1 Introduction

Industry 5.0 has brought in an exciting new era of manufacturing, blending cutting-edge technologies with human-centric methodologies to establish sustainable and cooperative production systems. With the emergence of Industry 1.0 in 1974, the landscape of industrial production has experienced rapid transformation. The first three industrial revolutions occurred over a span of approximately 100 years, whereas the transition from the third revolution to the fourth revolution took only 40 years. The emergence of Industry 1.0 in the 19th century can be attributed to the establishment of mechanical manufacturing plants that utilized water and steam power for their equipment. The concept of electric power and assembly line production brought about the evolution of Industry 2.0 in the year 1870. The focus of Industry 2.0 was primarily on mass production and task allocation, resulting in a significant increase in productivity for manufacturing firms. The concept of Industry 3.0 originated in 1969, encompassing electronics, partial automation, and information technologies [1]. Industry 4.0 focuses on enhancing production efficiency and quality levels while driving innovation and advancing industrial technology development.

Industry 5.0 aims to address the challenges faced by humans in Industry 4.0 by prioritizing the well-being of the workforce throughout the manufacturing process. The concept of Industry 5.0 originated in 2020 through discussions and idea exchanges during two virtual workshops, and it was officially recognized in January 2021 with its formal publication in the document by the European Commission (EC) [2]. Many enterprises are still focused on fully harnessing the potential of the Industry 4.0 era, making Industry 5.0 or 5IR a future-oriented concept for them [3]. Emerging technology is utilized in modern industrial production, with the DT technology effectively integrating interdisciplinary, multi-physics, multi-scale, and multi-probability simulation processes. This integration is achieved by incorporating data from various physical entities and sensor updates. By utilizing simulation technology, DT can collect data from various physical models and generate a digital replica of a real object [4].

Recent advancements in techniques such as cyber-physical systems, high-speed computing, cloud computing, and the internet of things have motivated business organizations to use these advanced technologies in real-world environments. Because of this transformation, businesses may now create digital twins of their goods, tools, and infrastructure in order to test and refine them. These electronic duplicates are referred to as "digital twins" (DTs) [5,6]. To be more precise, DTs are created to serve as an exact duplicate of a real-world component. The distinguishing characteristics of the DTs are as follows:

- The DT and the material entity are constantly and inseparably linked in real time without interruption.
- The DT is capable of self-learning and adapting to its surroundings; it will also direct the educational object in the right direction.
- Machine learning (ML) methods are used to continuously analyze the data, rather than only for a single prediction.
- Periodic information might be continuously monitored and can also be imported into the ML model.

- They deliver resources that are both domain-specific and prioritized on the basis of the industry's immediate requirements.

Combining digitalization with duplication or reflection is not a novel idea. Prior to the introduction of digital twins (DTs), several advanced technologies had already surfaced, such as electronic shadows, semantic virtual factory data models (VFDMs), product avatars, digital product memories, intelligent products, and holons. However, DTs have innovative and unambiguous implementations that make them unique, which improves their acceptance in real time. Table 3.1 illustrates a comparison between DT and currently available technologies [7].

DTs enable the forecasting and prediction using the AI models. In order to predict, huge amount of data needs to be gathered and analyzed. The physical entities in DTs also exchange large amount of data which might be sensitive. This poses to be a greatest challenge in the current trend.

FL is a technology that holds promise in addressing concerns related to data leakage and data breaches. The end users in FL have the ability to train the global model on their local system without the need to share their data with the central server [8]. In the era of Industry 5.0 the combination of DT and FL can be more advantageous when dealing with sensitive data especially in the healthcare sector, education sector, hospitality sector etc.

Recent investigations have examined FL and DT innovations significantly for industrial 5.0-based applications; however, most of the investigations have been conducted independently. When it comes to DTs, there are not many reputable overviews

Table 3.1 Difference between DT and existing technologies

Technology	Difference from DT
Computer simulations	It lacks dynamism and does not have real-time connectivity
ML	It is not a reflection of the physical object
Virtual Model	It was not constructed using IoT components
Modelling in Digital Form	The model's current state is not displayed in real time, and data are exchanged manually
Memory for digital products	It can be regarded as an example of a DT where a particular physical component is monitored, and communication is initiated for exchanging information
Digital Shadows	The data of a physical entity is stored as a duplicate, enabling the one-way transfer of data from the physical entity to the digital object
VFDM	Data synchronization is not real time
Intelligent Products	DT is a development of this technology that avoids cutting-edge approaches like ML, cloud computing, IoT, and big data

outlining potential implementation strategies for areas including the IoT, peripheral technology [9], production in manufacturing [10], and medical treatment [11]. FL utilization in smartphone edge systems [12], medical information systems [13], and other fields are surveyed in detail. Several surveys explore the tools and methods utilized in implementing Industry 5.0 in real time through the use of DTs [4], such as DT-based sustainable intelligent manufacturing [14], DT for smart manufacturing [15], and DT-driven supervised machine learning for developing AI applications in manufacturing [16]. However, there is a lack of extensive research on Industry 5.0 sensing services, adaptive federated learning, and digital twins for the industrial Internet of Things. The studies mentioned, such as the one by [17] on fusion and [18] on adaptive federated learning and digital twins, represent some of the limited existing research in this area. Our study, as presented in Table 3.2, is the first attempt to integrate federated learning and digital twins for Industry 5.0 applications.

Table 3.2 Summary of related surveys

Research Paper	Contributions	Limitations
[9]	Offers a state-of-the-art strategy for edge-based digital twin placement by taking into consideration not just proximity needs but also connections between IoT gadgets set up through the SIoT paradigm	Resources at the network edge are limited and low-latency
[11]	Explain the significance of incorporating digital twins with agents and Multi-Agent Systems (MAS) technologies in the healthcare sector	Trauma management
[12]	Presents an introduction to FL and a wide-ranging analysis of the challenges inherent in its adoption	Communication cost, resource allocation, data privacy and data security
[13]	Provides an extensive review of FL's potential uses in the field of healthcare Informatics	Confidentiality and safety, data heterogeneity, traceability and accountability
[4]	To evaluate the effects that digital twin technology has on industrial production within the framework of Industry 5.0	High inspection pressure, high labor costs, and an inability to find problems in time
[17]	Presents a comprehensive summary of how FL might be integrated with IIoT in terms of data security, allocation of resources, and privacy	Heterogeneous data and the structure is also too complex in nature
Our Survey Paper	Presents an in-depth analysis of FL-enabled DT for Industry 5.0 with important applications, integration challenges, and future research directions	NA

3.1.1 Contributions

The chapter's primary contributions can be summarized as follows:

- We discuss the fundamentals of digital twins, FL, and Industry 5.0. We also discuss the motivations and requirements for integrating FL and DT.
- We examine how federated learning-based decision trees are utilized in various industries, including manufacturing, automotive, retail, and smart healthcare.
- We discuss a few challenges associated with the present studies related to FL and digital twins in Industry 5.0.
- Finally, we discuss the future directions of FL-enabled digital twins for Industry 5.0, like Blockchain, Quantum digital twins, Cognitive digital twins, and 6G and beyond.

3.2 Fundamentals and motivations

This section presents the fundamentals of Industry 5.0, DT, and FL along with the motivations for the integration of DT with FL for Industry 5.0.

3.2.1 Industry 5.0

The emergence of new technologies and changes in the manufacturing paradigms has led to a decline in human and machine interaction. So, the need for maintaining healthy relations between humans and machines in industrial progress led to the evolution of Industry 5.0 [19]. The defining features of Industry 5.0 include its emphasis on human-centricity, sustainability, and resilience. This new era of industry aims to reintegrate humans into the collaborative process and infuse manufactured products with a human touch, all while prioritizing sustainable manufacturing practices. Industry 5.0 is estimated to combine the critical, cognitive thinking of humans with faster and more accurate machines. Industry 5.0 can also increase the quality of the outcomes [20]. The revolution from Industry 1.0 to Industry 5.0 includes many highs and lows. Figure 3.1 shows an illustration of Industrial evolution. The first three industrial revolutions took decades while the last two took very few years to evolve [21]. Each industrial revolution is characterized as follows:

- **Industry 1.0**-Introduction of steam and water power
- **Industry 2.0**-Mass production, assembly lines, electrical energy
- **Industry 3.0**-Robotics, automation and computers
- **Industry 4.0**-Smart systems, IoT, machine learning system
- **Industry 5.0**-Human robot collaboration, cognitive systems

3.2.2 Digital twins

"Digital twins" is the concept that is simply the digital representation of a real thing, is one that has just lately gained popularity [22]. DT consists of three components namely the physical entity, its virtual component, and the data exchange between the device and its counterpart. The physical entities serve as the basis for the DT. The

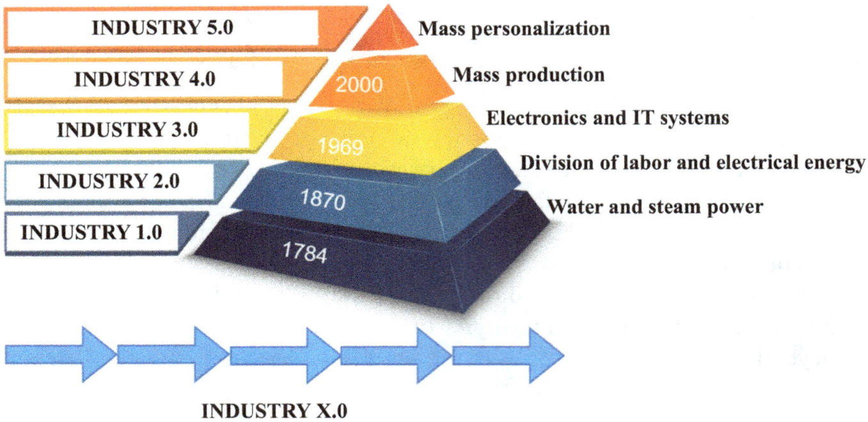

Figure 3.1 Illustration of industrial evolution

physical entities are objectively existing and are capable of at least one independent action [23]. The primary goal of physical entities research is to monitor the functioning of physical entities using various types of sensors in order to collect data on their operational condition [24]. A virtual model is a digital representation of a real object that can depict and explain objects in different dimensions of time and space. The driving force behind DTs is twin data, which usually includes physical, virtual, knowledge-based, and derivative data. Twin data comes in a variety of forms that can help operate virtual models and monitor the state of actual items' operations. [25].

DT has several applications in different sectors like healthcare, smart cities and urban planning, manufacturing, aerospace and Defense, environmental monitoring, and retail and supply Chain. The classification of DTs varies depending on factors such as their creation time, integration level, applications, hierarchy, and maturity level. Various authors use their own terminology when categorizing DTs. Based on the creation time they are classified as digital twin prototype (DTP) and digital twin instance (DTI) [26]. According to the level of integration, they are classified as digital model, digital shadow, and digital twin [27].

3.2.3 Federated learning

FL is a new kind of ML approach that allows training the ML models using data which is distributed across multiple devices without centralizing the data in a single particular location. FL has several entities and characteristics [28]. The following is the description of the entities of FL:

- **Global Server:** Global server is the coordinating entity in FL [29]. It supervises the training procedure, collects model updates, and distributes the revised model to the customers in various allocations [30,31].
- **Participating Devices:** Different devices like smartphones, IoT devices or edge devices have the local data for training. These devices perform training locally with the data that is available at the location.

- **Local Training:** The central server provides the global model, and each client performs training locally on its own data using this model.
- **Model Update:** The next step after the completion of training of global model locally, the clients generate the model update and transfer the update to the central server.
- **Model Aggregation:** The global server collects the model updates from several clients and then performs the aggregation to sum the updates into global model.
- **Model Distribution:** The client is provided with the distributed global model, which is formed by aggregating multiple client models, for further training.
- **Iterative Process:** FL typically follows an iterative process, where multiple rounds of local training, model update, aggregation, and model distribution are performed. The iterations continue until the global model converges or achieves the desired performance level [32].

3.2.4 Motivations to combine FL with DT

Although DT has its own benefits, ensuring data privacy is one area where it falls short since data is transmitted to DT through a variety of physical entities and sensor devices. At FL, the raw sensitive information is not transmitted over the network; instead, only the updates after local training at the edge device are transmitted, protecting data privacy at the end-user level.

Consequently, when FL is linked to a DT, it enables secure communication between DTs and also between the DT and sensors, ensuring privacy protection. The execution of any ML model depends heavily on the system's reaction time because DT technology is widely utilized in the industrial and healthcare sectors. For instance, it is crucial to make a choice and identify irregularities as soon as possible in trauma care. Other motivations for integrating FL with DT include enhancing the accuracy of the data and creating a system with a short reaction time [33]. When FL and DT are combined, the processes of data pre-processing and model training take place directly on the end devices, resulting in enhanced data quality and faster response times. Furthermore, the risk of a data breach can be decreased by merging FL and DT. Additionally, some assaults, like denial of service and man-in-the-middle attacks, can be manageable.

3.3 Core applications

This section describes how FL-based DT is used in the most important areas of Industry 5.0, including production, transportation, retail trade, and smart medicine. Figure 3.2 illustrates numerous applications of FL-based DT.

3.3.1 DTs for production based on FL

Smart manufacturing organizations have been significantly affected by the adverse impact of digital transformation, despite the numerous technological advancements that have enhanced manufacturing and industrial automation in recent years. DT allows manufacturers to design, implement, and certify production processes more

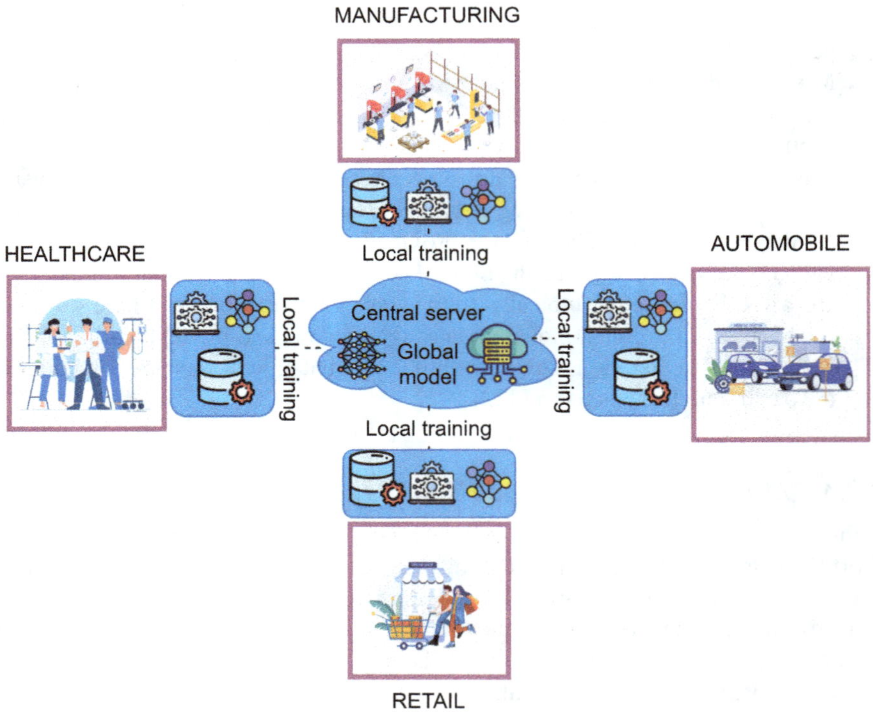

Figure 3.2 Applications of FL for DTs

quickly and efficiently. DT enables manufacturers to solve the challenges associated with supply chain visibility, coordination, and decision-making in the manufacturing process [34]. For industrial IoT (IIoT) decision-making, DTs require large amounts of data, which raises privacy and security concerns as they collect large amounts of data. By establishing suitable prerequisites, the development of novel technologies for data collection and modeling can effectively tackle the challenges posed by privacy protection and big data [35]. The authors of [18] presented a DT framework for IIoT applications in which DTs capture the characteristics of industrial equipment. The utilization of the Deep-Q network aimed to enhance energy efficiency in computing and communication while minimizing the loss function of FL. Clustering nodes and enhancing learning efficiency were used to minimize the straggler effect in their FL architecture [7]. The test results indicated that the proposed model exhibited quicker convergence, a higher rate of learning, and consumed more energy.

3.3.2 The use of FL to create DTs in the automotive industry

DTs utilize sensors, machine learning algorithms, and spatial network display software to deliver high-quality services to intelligent automobile networks. Through learning and upgrading from multiple perspectives, DTs can accurately predict future events based on operational requirements and physical objects. In addition to assessing traffic volume and routes, DTs can predict how many vehicles a country will need for transportation purposes. To ensure the continuous operation of autonomous vehicles equipped with DT, it is necessary for them to transmit driving states and environmental information to servers for updating their DT frameworks [36]. However, the process of data transmission in vehicular networks is made more complex by the presence of adaptive electrical systems and significant co-frequency contamination. Moreover, there is a risk of attackers manipulating the data exchange between vehicles and servers to deceive the vehicle's driving controls. Therefore, it is crucial for automotive networks to maintain the integrity of DT operations.

3.3.3 DTs based on FL for the retail sector

In today's digitally advanced world, customers are driven by innovative ideas, but the products and retail businesses they encounter are failing to meet their expectations. A lengthy, expensive, and risky chain of events begins with design, moves to decision, then production, and ends with sale. A connected network model can be created by retailers using DT. In addition to optimizing retail supply chains, DT also reduces time for consumers and improves their experience. Using DT technology comes with certain disadvantages, such as the risk of security breaches and a general lack of trust, as well as practical challenges like data latency and the handling of large amounts of data. In FL, models are trained without sharing personal information in a privacy-aware manner. The FL server fails to aggregate the global model if some retailers upload unreliable data. Therefore, it is important to find reliable customers in FL. Kang *et al.* [37] proposed using reputation to select trustworthy clients. The deployment of a decentralized consortium blockchain at edge nodes enables the establishment of secure reputation management.

3.3.4 FL-based smart healthcare with DTs

Customers in FL will keep their own copies of the information used for training and will gain knowledge of the shared model, which will allow industrial DT to more effectively aggregate data from various sources. Javaid *et al.* [38] proposed using Industry 5.0 to track the COVID-19 pandemic by integrating DTs with FL. The proposed framework enables the quick sharing of DT status and local strategy. To establish connections between various infection trends and response plans, the FL server oversees the local updates of numerous industrial DTs, and the FL model is trained using multiple Industry 5.0 DT systems. They integrate FL with the industrial DT, which can obtain patterns and knowledge from multiple DTs to establish a global view of pandemic crisis management in Industry 5.0. Furthermore, by combining data from other industries, the proposed approach helps to improve each industry's DT without violating privacy rights.

3.4 Challenges and future directions

The use of digital twins in the context of Industry 4.0 has become widespread due to its ability to accelerate risk assessment, maintenance planning, remote surveillance, and enhance purchasing decisions. However, implementing this technology is not without its difficulties. In this section, we will explore the challenges and potential solutions discussed in the literature, as depicted in Figure 3.3, and also discuss future directions.

3.4.1 Confidentiality and safety of data

The collection of data by DT technology primarily relies on edge devices, which unfortunately are highly vulnerable to various risks like denial of service and SQL injection. The extensive use of data in DT also increases the potential for sensitive information to be exposed, as there is a risk of attacks occurring during the modeling process or when communicating the data.

Security issues will pose a critical challenge during the deployment of Industry 5.0. In addition to integrity, availability, authentication, and auditing, Industry 5.0 will also need to provide access controls [39]. Automation and AI will open up new

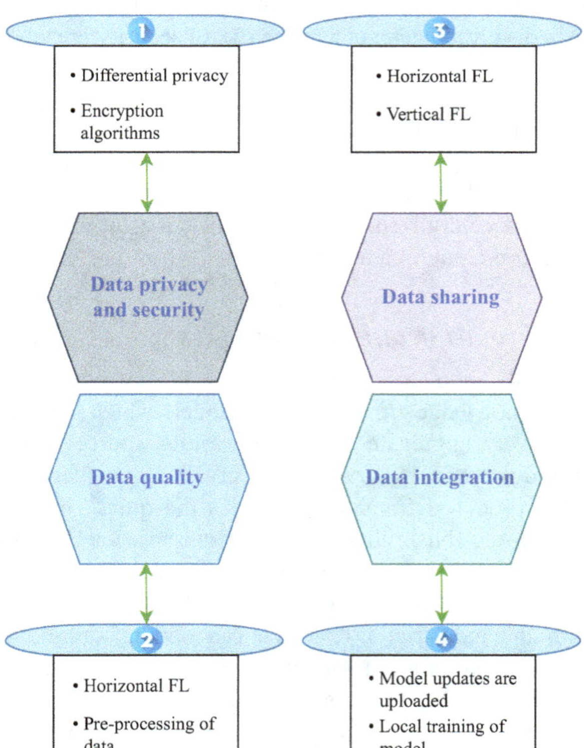

Figure 3.3 Integration of FL and DT: challenges and solutions

threats in Industry 5.0. It is important that AI and ML functions are executed in a trusted manner for security purposes. Data integrity should be preserved in Industry 5.0 applications, especially for training ML models and AI algorithms [40]. Thus, Industry 5.0 stakeholders should safely exchange actual information to train AI models or update models incrementally, as in FL. Moreover, the major applications of Industry 5.0 depend heavily on ICT systems, which will result in emerging safety needs, including the implementation of proactive safety measures [41,42] and the prevention of zero-day attacks [43]. Concerns related to the privacy of data originate from the fact that individuals should be allowed to choose what happens to their information. If user personal information is compromised, users may file a complaint for compensation. Protecting user information [44] is essential for utilizing it to conduct cognitive evaluation in future maintenance without violating their privacy.

Solution: Defining access rights, using secure data transmission methods, fixing the underlying device exposure, and performing frequent safety inspections are all potential solutions to the problem. To generate a unified global model, it is feasible for a copy of DT to be stored on every edge device that performs local training of the model. Since FL and DT only share simulation and performance updates, not actual data, this method of protecting user privacy is a perfect fit for DT. Using this method, sensitive information shared through a network is protected against intrusion. Protecting user information during modifications to the model is an additional potential application of confidentiality protection strategies [45].

3.4.2 Quality of data

DT models get information from instruments that use insecure routes of communication. When training models based on AI, it is important to use high-quality data. It is possible to draw a skewed conclusion if the data being analyzed is full of noise and outliers [46]. In order to achieve Industry 5.0, data from multiple systems, including transportation, urban development, real-world structures, and intelligent collaboration, must be combined. Lacking proper pre-processing, merging data from several sources may lead to inaccurate analysis and decisions [47]. The existence of noise in the information leads to inadequate outcomes.

Solution: When trying to improve the accuracy of the final result, it is best to begin by eliminating noise and outliers from the input data. The information in the DT about the customer's availability may be pre-processed by means of a horizontal FL. In conventional methods, information is gathered and integrated across the different instruments before it is pre-processed. However, when applying the DT with FL method, the information is first processed in each copy of DT and used to train the global models.

3.4.3 Information exchange

The exchange of data necessitates the distribution of data in both a personal and an external setting. The gathering of information from different departments inside an organization is referred to as personal data sharing, while the exchanging of information amongst participants throughout the distribution process is considered external information sharing. Although DT greatly improves flexibility by multiplying the number of electronic versions for every dynamic operation, exchanging information becomes difficult due to privacy concerns and information violations [48]. Regularly, businesses need access to the information stored on local servers for the purposes of data management [49]. Through the use of Industry 5.0, less information has to be transmitted to the server [50]. It is easy to manipulate the data sent through the intelligent smartphone application and the physical devices. Antivirus applications and other security measures can be implemented using edge technologies.

Solution: Combining FL with DT allows for effective information exchange. It would be more efficient if only the necessary components of information needed by the DTs had to be transmitted. To fulfill this objective, vertical FL may be used to focus on the more complex aspects of a subject of interest. Horizontal FL can be utilized when there is a requirement for information regarding specific aspects related to a particular feature.

3.4.4 Data integration

Requiring individuals to possess expert-level knowledge of the specific requirements of each field, integrating data from different domains becomes a challenging task [51]. This is due to the distinct options, circumstances, and optimization strategies that are unique to each stage. Therefore, it is crucial to understand the process's history and future steps in order to produce a constant stream of data. The generation of assessments in various Industry 5.0 application scenarios involves combining data from multiple sources and measurements [52]. The integration process, data variability, information flow, and data sustainability are all challenges that need to be managed in real time. AI methods [53] may be used to manage sophisticated information merging processes.

Solution: User restrictions on access, revision management, and error recognition tools are all useful for addressing security concerns. However, these reliability problems may be solved safely by combining FL and DTs. Integrating the findings from all DTs prevents data breaches since it incorporates just model modifications rather than the data that was originally collected.

3.4.5 Future directions

Our research shows that the DT idea has achieved significant advances in several areas of Industry 5.0, and we conclude that this indicates well for its further growth and development. There are many real-world manufacturing applications for innovation as well. In the future, researchers will need to integrate technological advances across various crucial sectors, including autonomous cars, airplanes, and healthcare, to make Industry 5.0 a reality. Real-time implementation and deployment face significant security and privacy issues. Researchers may continue their research on mechanisms to better include DT and FL for use in applications that depend on real-time constraints. There is a strong potential that the DT technology will be used in all sectors with complex applications in the distant future, which may have an effect on the way people live their lives in the world of reality.

3.4.5.1 Blockchain

Industry 5.0 is expected to benefit significantly from blockchain technology. Decentralized and distributed management platforms can be designed with blockchain by ensuring decentralized reliability [54]. Reliable connections among peers made possible by blockchain technology provide a permanent record of transactions [55–57]. Furthermore, Industry 5.0 applications are able to be transparent and accountable due to the immutable ledger. The Industry 5.0 ecosystem relies heavily on transparency in dispute resolution [58]. Smart contracts will enable security features such as authenticating and automating service-oriented actions in Industry 5.0 applications. Furthermore, a compartmentalized and distributed approach based on blockchains provides a higher level of data and transaction security [59,60]. Blockchain can also be used for data gathering and receiving [61].

3.4.5.2 Quantum digital twins

There are multiple advantages to quantum computing over traditional computing. While classical bits are restricted to assuming one of two possible states, qubits are capable of holding both at once. The term "quantum parallelism" refers to the ability to model a wide variety of states by scaling rapidly with the number of qubits. Information may be scanned with greater efficiency by quantum technology than by conventional database systems. Complex computing operations involving numerous dimensions of data will be completed more quickly. By combining quantum technology with digital twins, it becomes possible to not only mirror reality but also analyze the outcomes of decision-making processes. Transportation businesses often use quantum DT to tell us about the probability and impact of interruptions. So, quantum's primary objective is not simple reflection but rather the management and extraction of maximum value from any number of systems.

3.4.5.3 Cognitive digital twins

The integration of cognitive AI with DTs enhances productivity and improves efficiency in the establishment process. DT uses cognitive methods to examine and recommend structures for current systems or processes. Cognitive twins involve the entity processing thoughts, acquiring input knowledge, independently solving problems, and making decisions. AI is capable of finding solutions to problems, making predictions about the future based on knowledge acquired in the past, and establishing cognitive influence over its twin by employing its own cognitive abilities. DT technology will be able to properly handle unforeseen situations with this next evolution. In all situations, it makes accurate decisions using a combination of human and DT knowledge.

In the future, researchers will need to integrate technological advances across various crucial sectors, including autonomous cars, aeroplanes, and healthcare, to make Industry 5.0 a reality. Real-time implementation and deployment face significant security and privacy issues. Researchers may continue their research on mechanisms to better include DT and FL for use in applications that depend on real-time constraints. There is a strong potential that the DT technology will be used in all sectors with complex applications in the distant future, which may have an effect on the way people live their lives in the world of reality.

3.4.5.4 6G and beyond

In the future, 6G will be able to provide Industry 5.0 with major added-value products and services. Achieving higher latency, better support for high-quality services, extensive IoT infrastructure, and AI capabilities is made possible by 6G and beyond [62]. Providing smart spectrum management, AI-enhanced mobile EC, and smart mobility are all factors that contribute to the efficiency and effectiveness of Industry 5.0 applications [63,64]. The anticipated 6G networks are expected to meet the needs of a smart digital society by providing incredibly fast transmission speeds, minimal latency, high reliability, outstanding energy efficiency, congestion management capabilities, and more, specifically for Industry 5.0 applications. 6G networks will face major challenges in Industry 5.0 in terms of mobility and handover management. There must be numerous transitions since 6G networks are extremely big, unpredictable, and multi-layered [65,66]. Assuring reliable connections is possible with the use of AI-based accessibility forecasting and transition systems [67].

3.5 Conclusion

AI-based approaches, IoT, and FL have all made significant progress in the previous decade, which has ignited the flames of DT's expansion into new domains. DTs have been built and put into use across a wide variety of industries, including production, transportation, retail, and smart health. This chapter presents a review of combining FL and DT for improved management in the Industry 5.0 era. Following that, a discussion on the basics of Industry 5.0, DT, and FL will take place. Next, we addressed the many Industry 5.0-based services where these innovations were adopted, simplified, and enhanced the regulatory framework of Industry 5.0. Finally, we address the distinct problems that exist and act as an obstruction to the use of this combination in real time and life-critical applications of Industry 5.0, and we also address possible solutions to these problems.

References

[1] P. K. R. Maddikunta, Q.-V. Pham, B. Prabadevi, *et al.*, "Industry 5.0: A survey on enabling technologies and potential applications," *Journal of Industrial Information Integration*, vol. 26, p. 100257, 2022.

[2] J. Alves, T. M. Lima, and P. D. Gaspar, "Is industry 5.0 a human-centred approach? a systematic review," *Processes*, vol. 11, no. 1, 2023. [Online]. Available: https://www.mdpi.com/2227-9717/11/1/193

[3] G. Nain, K. Pattanaik, and G. Sharma, "Towards edge computing in intelligent manufacturing: Past, present and future," *Journal of Manufacturing Systems*, vol. 62, pp. 588–611, 2022.

[4] Z. Lv, "Digital twins in industry 5.0," *Research*, vol. 6, p. 0071, 2023.

[5] D. Jones, C. Snider, A. Nassehi, J. Yon, and B. Hicks, "Characterising the digital twin: A systematic literature review," *CIRP Journal of Manufacturing Science and Technology*, vol. 29, pp. 36–52, 2020.

[6] F. Tao, H. Zhang, A. Liu, and A. Y. Nee, "Digital twin in industry: State-of-the-art," *IEEE Transactions on Industrial Informatics*, vol. 15, no. 4, pp. 2405–2415, 2018.

[7] S. P. Ramu, P. Boopalan, Q.-V. Pham, *et al.*, "Federated learning enabled digital twins for smart cities: Concepts, recent advances, and future directions," *Sustainable Cities and Society*, vol. 79, p. 103663, 2022.

[8] Y. Supriya and T. R. Gadekallu, "Particle swarm-based federated learning approach for early detection of forest fires," *Sustainability*, vol. 15, no. 2, 2023. [Online]. Available: https://www.mdpi.com/2071-1050/15/2/964

[9] O. Chukhno, N. Chukhno, G. Araniti, C. Campolo, A. Iera, and A. Molinaro, "Optimal placement of social digital twins in edge IoT networks," *Sensors*, vol. 20, no. 21, p. 6181, 2020.

[10] J. Leng, D. Wang, W. Shen, X. Li, Q. Liu, and X. Chen, "Digital twins-based smart manufacturing system design in industry 4.0: A review," *Journal of Manufacturing Systems*, vol. 60, pp. 119–137, 2021.

[11] A. Croatti, M. Gabellini, S. Montagna, and A. Ricci, "On the integration of agents and digital twins in healthcare," *Journal of Medical Systems*, vol. 44, pp. 1–8, 2020.

[12] W. Y. B. Lim, N. C. Luong, D. T. Hoang, *et al.*, "Federated learning in mobile edge networks: A comprehensive survey," *IEEE Communications Surveys & Tutorials*, vol. 22, no. 3, pp. 2031–2063, 2020.

[13] K. Dasaradharami Reddy, T. R. Gadekallu *et al.*, "A comprehensive survey on federated learning techniques for healthcare informatics," *Computational Intelligence and Neuroscience*, vol. 2023, 2023.

[14] B. He and K.-J. Bai, "Digital twin-based sustainable intelligent manufacturing: A review," *Advances in Manufacturing*, vol. 9, pp. 1–21, 2021.

[15] L. Lattanzi, R. Raffaeli, M. Peruzzini, and M. Pellicciari, "Digital twin for smart manufacturing: A review of concepts towards a practical industrial implementation," *International Journal of Computer Integrated Manufacturing*, vol. 34, no. 6, pp. 567–597, 2021.

[16] K. Alexopoulos, N. Nikolakis, and G. Chryssolouris, "Digital twin-driven supervised machine learning for the development of artificial intelligence applications in manufacturing," *International Journal of Computer Integrated Manufacturing*, vol. 33, no. 5, pp. 429–439, 2020.

[17] P. Boobalan, S. P. Ramu, Q.-V. Pham, *et al.*, "Fusion of federated learning and industrial internet of things: A survey," *Computer Networks*, vol. 212, p. 109048, 2022.

[18] W. Sun, S. Lei, L. Wang, Z. Liu, and Y. Zhang, "Adaptive federated learning and digital twin for industrial internet of things," *IEEE Transactions on Industrial Informatics*, vol. 17, no. 8, pp. 5605–5614, 2020.

[19] P. Coelho, C. Bessa, J. Landeck, and C. Silva, "Industry 5.0: The arising of a concept," *Procedia Computer Science*, vol. 217, pp. 1137–1144, 2023.

[20] A. Raja Santhi and P. Muthuswamy, "Industry 5.0 or industry 4.0 s? Introduction to industry 4.0 and a peek into the prospective industry 5.0 technologies," *International Journal on Interactive Design and Manufacturing (IJIDeM)*, vol. 17, no. 2, pp. 947–979, 2023.

[21] J. Pizoń and A. Gola, "Human–machine relationship—perspective and future roadmap for industry 5.0 solutions," *Machines*, vol. 11, no. 2, p. 203, 2023.

[22] R. Kaul, C. Ossai, A. R. M. Forkan, *et al.*, "The role of ai for developing digital twins in healthcare: The case of cancer care," *Wiley Interdisciplinary Reviews: Data Mining and Knowledge Discovery*, vol. 13, no. 1, p. e1480, 2023.

[23] G. Srivastava, R. H. Jhaveri, S. Bhattacharya, *et al.*, "Xai for cybersecurity: state of the art, challenges, open issues and future directions," arXiv preprint arXiv:2206.03585, 2022.

[24] X. Liu, D. Jiang, B. Tao, *et al.*, "A systematic review of digital twin about physical entities, virtual models, twin data, and applications," *Advanced Engineering Informatics*, vol. 55, p. 101876, 2023.

[25] Y. Wang, Z. Su, S. Guo, M. Dai, T. H. Luan, and Y. Liu, "A survey on digital twins: architecture, enabling technologies, security and privacy, and future prospects," *IEEE Internet of Things Journal*, 2023.

[26] M. Grieves and J. Vickers, "Digital twin: Mitigating unpredictable, undesirable emergent behavior in complex systems," *Transdisciplinary perspectives on complex systems: New findings and approaches*, pp. 85–113, 2017.

[27] W. Kritzinger, M. Karner, G. Traar, J. Henjes, and W. Sihn, "Digital twin in manufacturing: A categorical literature review and classification," *Ifac-PapersOnline*, vol. 51, no. 11, pp. 1016–1022, 2018.

[28] D. R. Kandati and T. R. Gadekallu, "Genetic clustered federated learning for Covid-19 detection," *Electronics*, vol. 11, no. 17, p. 2714, 2022.

[29] S. Pandya, G. Srivastava, R. Jhaveri, *et al.*, "Federated learning for smart cities: A comprehensive survey," *Sustainable Energy Technologies and Assessments*, vol. 55, p. 102987, 2023.

[30] O. A. Wahab, A. Mourad, H. Otrok, and T. Taleb, "Federated machine learning: Survey, multi-level classification, desirable criteria and future directions in communication and networking systems," *IEEE Communications Surveys & Tutorials*, vol. 23, no. 2, pp. 1342–1397, 2021.

[31] S. AbdulRahman, H. Tout, H. Ould-Slimane, A. Mourad, C. Talhi, and M. Guizani, "A survey on federated learning: The journey from centralized to distributed on-site learning and beyond," *IEEE Internet of Things Journal*, vol. 8, no. 7, pp. 5476–5497, 2020.

[32] D. R. Kandati and T. R. Gadekallu, "Federated learning approach for early detection of chest lesion caused by Covid-19 infection using particle swarm optimization," *Electronics*, vol. 12, no. 3, p. 710, 2023.

[33] G. Yenduri, G. Srivastava, P. K. R. Maddikunta, *et al.*, "Generative pre-trained transformer: A comprehensive review on enabling technologies, potential applications, emerging challenges, and future directions," arXiv preprint arXiv:2305.10435, 2023.

[34] G. Srivastava, K. Dasaratha Rami Reddy, G. Yenduri, *et al.*, "Federated learning enabled edge computing security for internet of medical things: Concepts, challenges and open issues," in *Security and Risk Analysis for Intelligent Edge Computing*. Springer, 2023, pp. 67–89.

[35] T. R. Gadekallu, Q.-V. Pham, T. Huynh-The, S. Bhattacharya, P. K. R. Maddikunta, and M. Liyanage, "Federated learning for big data: A survey on opportunities, applications, and future directions," arXiv preprint arXiv:2110.04160, 2021.

[36] S. P. Ramu, G. Srivastava, R. Chengoden, N. Victor, P. K. R. Maddikunta, and T. R. Gadekallu, "The metaverse for cognitive health: A paradigm shift," *IEEE Consumer Electronics Magazine*, 2023.

[37] J. Kang, Z. Xiong, D. Niyato, Y. Zou, Y. Zhang, and M. Guizani, "Reliable federated learning for mobile networks," *IEEE Wireless Communications*, vol. 27, no. 2, pp. 72–80, 2020.

[38] M. Javaid, A. Haleem, R. P. Singh, M. I. U. Haq, A. Raina, and R. Suman, "Industry 5.0: Potential applications in Covid-19," *Journal of Industrial Integration and Management*, vol. 5, no. 04, pp. 507–530, 2020.

[39] P. Porambage, G. Gür, D. P. M. Osorio, M. Liyanage, A. Gurtov, and M. Ylianttila, "The roadmap to 6G security and privacy," *IEEE Open Journal of the Communications Society*, vol. 2, pp. 1094–1122, 2021.

[40] N. Korneev, "Intelligent complex security management system FEC for the industry 5.0," in *IOP Conference Series: Materials Science and Engineering*, vol. 950, no. 1. IOP Publishing, 2020, p. 012016.

[41] Z. Kotianová, "Aspects of safety and security in industry 4.0," *Industry 4.0*, vol. 4, no. 6, pp. 319–321, 2019.

[42] P. Porambage, G. Gür, D. P. M. Osorio, M. Livanage, and M. Ylianttila, "6G security challenges and potential solutions," in *2021 Joint European Conference on Networks and Communications & 6G Summit (EuCNC/6G Summit)*. IEEE, 2021, pp. 622–627.

[43] Y. Siriwardhana, P. Porambage, M. Liyanage, and M. Ylianttila, "AI and 6G security: Opportunities and challenges," in *2021 Joint European Conference on Networks and Communications & 6G Summit (EuCNC/6G Summit)*. IEEE, 2021, pp. 616–621.

[44] E. Pauwels, "The new geopolitics of converging risks: The un and prevention in the era of AI," *United Nations University Centre for Policy Research*, 2019.

[45] Y. Cheng, Y. Liu, T. Chen, and Q. Yang, "Federated learning for privacy-preserving AI," *Communications of the ACM*, vol. 63, no. 12, pp. 33–36, 2020.

[46] A. Gupta, P. Panagiotopoulos, and F. Bowen, "An orchestration approach to smart city data ecosystems," *Technological Forecasting and Social Change*, vol. 153, p. 119929, 2020.

[47] G. T. Reddy, M. P. K. Reddy, K. Lakshmanna, *et al.*, "Analysis of dimensionality reduction techniques on big data," *IEEE Access*, vol. 8, pp. 54 776–54 788, 2020.

[48] A. Hammoud, H. Otrok, A. Mourad, and Z. Dziong, "On demand fog federations for horizontal federated learning in IoV," *IEEE Transactions on Network and Service Management*, vol. 19, no. 3, pp. 3062–3075, 2022.
[49] A. Adel, "Future of industry 5.0 in society: human-centric solutions, challenges and prospective research areas," *Journal of Cloud Computing*, vol. 11, no. 1, pp. 1–15, 2022.
[50] P. Trakadas, P. Simoens, P. Gkonis, *et al.*, "An artificial intelligence-based collaboration approach in industrial IoT manufacturing: Key concepts, architectural extensions and potential applications," *Sensors*, vol. 20, no. 19, p. 5480, 2020.
[51] H.-V. Tran, G. Kaddoum, H. Elgala, C. Abou-Rjeily, and H. Kaushal, "Lightwave power transfer for federated learning-based wireless networks," *IEEE Communications Letters*, vol. 24, no. 7, pp. 1472–1476, 2020.
[52] S. A. Rahman, H. Tout, C. Talhi, and A. Mourad, "Internet of Things intrusion detection: Centralized, on-device, or federated learning?" *IEEE Network*, vol. 34, no. 6, pp. 310–317, 2020.
[53] L. Tan, K. Yu, F. Ming, X. Cheng, and G. Srivastava, "Secure and resilient artificial intelligence of things: a HoneyNet approach for threat detection and situational awareness," *IEEE Consumer Electronics Magazine*, vol. 11, no. 3, pp. 69–78, 2021.
[54] W. Viriyasitavat and D. Hoonsopon, "Blockchain characteristics and consensus in modern business processes," *Journal of Industrial Information Integration*, vol. 13, pp. 32–39, 2019.
[55] N. Deepa, Q.-V. Pham, D. C. Nguyen, *et al.*, "A survey on blockchain for big data: approaches, opportunities, and future directions," *Future Generation Computer Systems*, 2022.
[56] W. Viriyasitavat, L. Da Xu, Z. Bi, and A. Sapsomboon, "Blockchain-based business process management (BPM) framework for service composition in industry 4.0," *Journal of Intelligent Manufacturing*, vol. 31, no. 7, pp. 1737–1748, 2020.
[57] B. Prabadevi, N. Deepa, Q.-V. Pham, *et al.*, "Toward blockchain for edge-of-things: a new paradigm, opportunities, and future directions," *IEEE Internet of Things Magazine*, vol. 4, no. 2, pp. 102–108, 2021.
[58] S. He, W. Ren, T. Zhu, and K.-K. R. Choo, "BoSMoS: A blockchain-based status monitoring system for defending against unauthorized software updating in industrial internet of things," *IEEE Internet of Things Journal*, vol. 7, no. 2, pp. 948–959, 2019.
[59] N. Mohamed and J. Al-Jaroodi, "Applying blockchain in industry 4.0 applications," in *2019 IEEE 9th Annual Computing and Communication Workshop and Conference (CCWC)*. IEEE, 2019, pp. 0852–0858.
[60] L. Da Xu, Y. Lu, and L. Li, "Embedding blockchain technology into IoT for security: A survey," *IEEE Internet of Things Journal*, vol. 8, no. 13, pp. 10452–10473, 2021.

[61] A. V. Barenji, Z. Li, and W. M. Wang, "Blockchain cloud manufacturing: Shop floor and machine level," in *Smart SysTech 2018; European Conference on Smart Objects, Systems and Technologies*. VDE, 2018, pp. 1–6.

[62] M. Z. Chowdhury, M. Shahjalal, S. Ahmed, and Y. M. Jang, "6G wireless communication systems: Applications, requirements, technologies, challenges, and research directions," *IEEE Open Journal of the Communications Society*, vol. 1, pp. 957–975, 2020.

[63] F. Tariq, M. R. Khandaker, K.-K. Wong, M. A. Imran, M. Bennis, and M. Debbah, "A speculative study on 6G," *IEEE Wireless Communications*, vol. 27, no. 4, pp. 118–125, 2020.

[64] Y. Lu and X. Zheng, "6G: A survey on technologies, scenarios, challenges, and the related issues," *Journal of Industrial Information Integration*, vol. 19, p. 100158, 2020.

[65] C. Huang, S. Hu, G. C. Alexandropoulos, *et al.*, "Holographic MIMO surfaces for 6G wireless networks: Opportunities, challenges, and trends," *IEEE Wireless Communications*, vol. 27, no. 5, pp. 118–125, 2020.

[66] C. De Alwis, A. Kalla, Q.-V. Pham, *et al.*, "Survey on 6G frontiers: Trends, applications, requirements, technologies and future research," *IEEE Open Journal of the Communications Society*, vol. 2, pp. 836–886, 2021.

[67] H. Yang, A. Alphones, Z. Xiong, D. Niyato, J. Zhao, and K. Wu, "Artificial-intelligence-enabled intelligent 6G networks," *IEEE Network*, vol. 34, no. 6, pp. 272–280, 2020.

Chapter 4

Collaborative intelligence: federated learning-enabled edge computing in Industry 5.0

M Ramalingam[1], Gokul Yenduri[2], Praveen Kumar Reddy Maddikunta[2], Praveen Kumar Donta[3] and Thippa Reddy Gadekallu[4,5]

Abstract

In the view of Industry 5.0, the collaboration between federated learning (FL) and edge computing has emerged as a captivating paradigm. This article explores the conjunction of federated learning (FL) and edge computing in the context of Industry 5.0, where the smooth integration of advanced manufacturing and IoT technologies is paramount. We investigate the potential of FL as a privacy-preserving and resource-efficient approach for training machine learning models across a distributed network of edge devices. By exploiting the computational capabilities of these devices, Industry 5.0 can help with real-time data analysis and decision-making while reducing latency and conserving bandwidth. This study examines the challenges and prospects of implementing FL at the edge. This includes communication overhead, model aggregation techniques, and security considerations. Through this comprehensive review, we demonstrate the efficiency of federated learning-enabled edge computing in enhancing industrial processes, enhancing supply chains, and making use of a new era of decentralized and intelligent manufacturing.

Keywords: Industry 5.0, Digital twin, Federated learning, Internet of Things

[1]School of Computer Science Engineering and Information Systems, Vellore Institute of Technology, India
[2]School of Computer Science and Engineering, VIT-AP University, India
[3]Distributed Systems Group, TU Wien, Austria
[4]Division of Research and Development, Lovely Professional University, Phagwara, India
[5]Zhongda Group, Haiyan County, Jiaxing City, Zhejiang Province, China

4.1 Introduction

4.1.1 Overview of Industry 5.0

Industry 5.0 is considered to be the fifth industrial revolution, which is described by the use of human-centric, sustainable, and resilient technologies. It builds on the advances of Industry 4.0. The main focus of 4.0 was the automation and digitization of manufacturing processes. It has used technologies such as IoT, big data analytics, and AI to communicate with machines, devices, and systems together [58]. These technologies enable real-time communication, data collection, and instant analysis to improve efficiency, productivity, and decision-making. Industry 4.0 has been proposed to address challenges in the industrial sector such as energy and resource efficiency, urban production, societal needs, and demographic change. To focus on the reduction of resources and energy, it is mandatory to upgrade the manufacturing processes, machinery design, and also plant [27]. Industry 4.0 may not be fully considered as ready for deployment without any challenges. There are also potential drawbacks to be addressed [3]. The increased connectivity of machinery and systems of Industry 4.0 makes them more vulnerable to cyber-attacks [34]. This may lead to the theft of sensitive data, the disruption of the production process, or even physical damage to equipment. Another important challenge is machines and systems become more sophisticated. The processes become completely automated. This could lead to errors in manufacturing for several reasons such as lack of decision-making ability [39], contextual understanding and judgment, flexibility and adaptability, creative thinking, quality control and error handling, data security, interoperability, and ethical and social considerations. Industry 5.0 emphasized human–machine collaboration, where humans and machines work together [28]. This collaboration handles the challenges of 4.0 by leveraging human creativity and problem-solving skills to automation [62]. It also focuses on building secured decentralized systems that give priority to data privacy. It integrates robust cyber-security measures and protocols to protect sensitive information used in industries. The interoperability issue of 4.0 can be managed by proposing open standards and protocols that allow different systems to collaborate and operate together. This proposed method of 5.0 facilitates interoperability, better data exchange, and integration across the industrial ecosystem. With respect to scalability and flexibility, 5.0 seeks to provide scalable and flexible solutions such as modular systems, plug and play devices that can be customized as per the needs of SMEs. This approach enables easy integration that helps smaller organizations adopt and benefit from Industry 5.0 technologies.

4.1.2 Introduction to federated learning

Machine learning contains various learning methods that can be broadly classified into supervised learning, unsupervised learning, and reinforcement learning. Supervised learning means training a model using labeled data, where the input features are connected with known target values [32]. The training model learns to make predictions based on the patterns it recognizes in the labeled data. Unsupervised learning, on the other hand, deals with unlabeled information, where the model aims to discover inherent structures, patterns, or relationships within the training data [10]. It can be utilized for tasks like clustering, dimensionality reduction, or anomaly detection. Reinforcement learning focuses on training an object or person to interact with an environment and learn from feedback in the form of rewards or penalties [48]. The object or person learns to make decisions that maximize its cumulative reward over time. In the context of distributed and privacy-sensitive settings, federated learning evolves as a prominent approach. It allows multiple parties to collaboratively train a shared model without sharing their raw data. It addresses privacy issues by keeping the data on local devices and only transmitting model parameters as updates. It allows distributed learning on edge devices, reduces communication costs, ensures privacy, and improves data security [30]. Federated learning creates possibilities for scalable and privacy-preserving machine learning in decentralized environments, where the power of collective intelligence can be tied together without compromising data privacy. The federated learning process involves the following steps: (1) Initialization: The central FL server initializes a global model and dispenses it to the participating devices. (2) Local Training: Each device carries out model training on its local data using the initial global model. The data remains on the device, ensuring privacy and security. (3) Model update: On completion of local training, the devices generate updated model parameters based on the data of the particular device. These updated parameters represent the knowledge learned on the device. (4) Aggregation: The devices send their updated model parameters to the central FL server, which aggregates and combines the parameters to create a new global model. This global model will have the knowledge obtained from each participating device. Iterative process: Steps 2–4 are repeated for multiple rounds, enabling the model to improve iteratively for better accuracy. These participating devices continue to train on their local data, generate local updates, and send them to the FL server for aggregation.

Privacy of data: Federated learning ensures data privacy by keeping the raw data on local devices. Only model parameters trained on the local device are shared as updates, minimizing the risk of exposing sensitive information.

Reduction in cost of communication: Instead of data transmitted between the federated learning client and the server, only model updates are transmitted [18]. This reduces communication bandwidth requirements, making it suitable for low-bandwidth edge devices.

Distributed learning: Federated learning allows training on distributed data sources, such as edge devices, without the requirement for centralized data collection. This is particularly useful in scenarios where data movement is critical.

Improved security: Federated learning reduces the risk of data breaches or unauthorized access to sensitive information by keeping data decentralized.

Customization and personalization: Federated learning allows models to be trained on personal devices, allowing personalized models that reflect specific user preferences or requirements.

4.1.3 Introduction to edge computing

Edge computing is a distributed computing approach that allows computational power and data storage brought closer to the source of data generation. This is often referred to as the "edge" of the network [9]. In traditional computing approaches, data is sent to a centralized server for analysis and processing. On the other hand, with edge computing, data is processed, analyzed, and stored at or near the edge devices or edge nodes. This approach allows us to cover the major challenges related to centralized computing [15]. By processing data locally at the edge nodes, edge computing allows real-time analysis and response. This also reduces the latency caused by data transfer to a remote storage or computing server. This is predominantly beneficial for time-sensitive applications such as self-autonomous vehicles, industrial automation, computer vision systems, IoUT systems [5], [42], smart cities, and Internet of Things (IoT) devices [24]. Edge devices include devices such as sensors, smartphones, gateways, routers, and edge servers. These devices are capable of performing data pre-processing, filtering, and analysis processes at their end. This reduces the amount of data that needs to be transmitted to the central server [40]. Edge nodes can also be capable of executing applications and algorithms and storing data, allowing localized decision-making and providing offline computing abilities even when connectivity to the central server is intermittent or unavailable.

Edge computing offers various advantages. It reduces network congestion by processing data locally [50]. This is particularly essential in scenarios with limited bandwidth or high data volumes. It helps in improving the scalability of the network. Because, the computational load is shared and distributed across multiple edge devices, easing the load on centralized servers [45]. In addition, edge computing improves data privacy by keeping sensitive information locally, minimizing the need for sending it to external servers. However, edge computing also poses various challenges [52].

Data security and privacy: Sharing data with edge devices introduces a new set of challenges such as security and privacy concerns. Edge devices may have limited security abilities and are vulnerable to cyber-attacks. Confirming data confidentiality, integrity, and availability becomes essential when sharing sensitive data with edge devices.

Bandwidth limitations: Edge nodes usually have limited bandwidth ability compared to centralized computing servers. Transfer of large volumes of data to edge devices can consume the available bandwidth and result in network congestion. This may have an impact on the performance of real-time applications and cause delays in data sharing.

Network latency: Edge computing reduces latency by analyzing and processing data closer to the source of data generation. But, still, data sharing to edge nodes can introduce additional latency. This depends on the network infrastructure and the distance between the data source and edge nodes [38]. This may cause latency issues, affecting real-time or latency-sensitive applications.

Data synchronization and consistency: In distributed edge computing scenarios, confirming data consistency and synchronization across various edge nodes can be challenging. Since data is shared and processed simultaneously across multiple edge nodes, sustaining consistency and avoiding conflicts becomes critical.

Resource constraints: Edge devices have limited computational resources, storage ability, and energy supply. These limitations can question the amount of data that can be effectively processed and stored on edge devices. It may also affect the ability to perform complex analysis or apply machine learning algorithms on the edge.

Heterogeneity and scalability: Edge devices include devices such as sensors, smartphones, gateways, routers, and edge servers [51]. These devices are of varying capabilities, architectures, and operating systems. Managing data sharing and interoperability across different edge nodes becomes complex. More specifically, when scaling the system to accommodate a larger number of edge devices.

Governance and compliance: Sharing data to edge nodes may include compliance with regulatory requirements, industry standards, and data governance policies. Confirming proper data governance, consent management, and adherence to legal and regulatory policies defined by the government or industries can be challenging in edge computing scenarios.

4.2 Understanding FL and edge computing

4.2.1 FL and its benefits in distributed learning scenarios

Distributed learning is a machine learning approach that involves training models across multiple devices or entities instead of depending on a centralized server. In traditional machine learning, data is usually collected and aggregated in a central location for model training. But, in distributed learning, the training process takes place on distributed nodes, such as edge devices, and IoT devices. This distributed decentralized approach proposes several advantages, including privacy preservation, scalability, and the ability to control diverse data sources. Distributed learning permits entities to collaboratively train models while keeping data local. This enables efficient and privacy-conscious machine learning in scenarios with large volume of data or data privacy concerns [53].

Federated Learning offers various benefits in distributed learning scenarios. Here are some key advantages of FL:

FL permits learning models to be trained directly on user devices, such as smartphones or edge devices, without the need to share raw data with a centralized server. This privacy-preserving approach confirms that sensitive user data remains secure and confidential, reducing privacy risks and maintaining data ownership [16]. It stores the data on localized user devices, reducing the need for a large volume of data transfer to a central server. This localization reduces network bandwidth consumption and latency, making FL particularly suitable for scenarios with limited connectivity. It also enables collaboration and knowledge sharing among distributed devices while preserving data privacy. Different devices or organizations can train a global model together by securely exchanging model parameters. This collaboration enables the aggregation of varied insights and improves overall learning performance [31]. FL also offers scalability in distributed learning scenarios [6]. This can be made possible by allowing the participation of a large number of edge devices. The computational load can be distributed across multiple devices, reducing the burden on centralized servers. This decentralized approach allows efficient learning in scenarios with a massive number of devices or data sources [25]. FL also supports energy-efficient learning by reducing the need to transmit large amounts of data to a central server [59]. Local model training at edge devices consumes less energy compared to transmitting data over the network, resulting in lower energy consumption and longer battery life for edge devices. FL is robust to data diversity across different organizations. Models trained through FL can handle variations, heterogeneity, and distributions in data sources. This leads to the development of robust and generalized models that can adapt to various real-world scenarios. FL also addresses regulatory compliance concerns by permitting organizations to maintain control over their data while still benefiting from collaborative learning. It offers a framework for organizations to comply with privacy regulations and data protection laws by reducing the need to share raw data [1].

4.2.2 Edge computing and its role in enabling real-time data processing and analysis

4.2.2.1 Introduction to real-time data processing and its need

Real-time data processing at edge nodes refers to the method of performing data analysis and decision-making close to the data source or point of generation [35]. In the traditional way of computation, data is typically sent to a centralized server for processing and analysis. This introduces latency and may not be suitable for time-sensitive applications like computer vision systems and so on [54]. However, with real-time data processing at edge nodes, data is processed, analyzed, and reacted upon at or near the edge devices. This method brings computational power and analytical intelligence closer to the data source, enabling faster response times, reduced communication latency, and the ability to make immediate, localized decisions [8]. Real-time data processing at edge nodes is predominantly beneficial in applications such as IoT [29], industrial automation [47], autonomous vehicles [20], computer vision systems [11], and remote monitoring [44]. This is because real-time insights and instantaneous actions are critical for operational efficiency, safety, and improved user experiences. By making use of the capabilities of edge computing, real-time data processing at edge nodes enables organizations to leverage data insights and enable near-instantaneous decision-making at the edge of the network.

4.2.2.2 Ability of an edge device and how it helps in real-time data processing

Edge computing has the ability to perform real-time data processing by bringing computational capabilities closer to the source of data generation. Edge computing places computational resources close to the devices or sensors generating the data. This closeness reduces the time and latency associated with transmitting data to a centralized server for processing. By processing data locally at the edge devices, edge computing supports real-time analysis and decision-making abilities without the delays caused by data transfer. Edge devices are equipped with computing power and storage capabilities that allow them to perform data processing tasks [13]. They can execute analysis algorithms, run software applications, and leverage machine learning models directly on the device. This gives the ability to perform immediate processing and analysis of incoming data, enabling real-time insights and actions.

Edge computing is also enabled with filtering and aggregating abilities at the edge devices. As an alternative to transmitting all raw data to a central server, edge devices can pre-process and filter the data locally, sending only relevant required information to the central server. This pre-processing and filtering of data reduce the amount of data that needs to be transmitted to the server, optimizing bandwidth usage and reducing latency. Edge computing enables edge devices with the ability to make localized decisions based on real-time data. By deploying intelligence at the edge, data can be analyzed and decisions can be made without depending on continuous connectivity to a central server. This capability is vital in time-sensitive applications where immediate actions are required. Edge computing is also enabled with real-time data processing ability even in situations with limited network connectivity. Edge devices can continue to perform computations and analysis locally. This can help to ensure uninterrupted operation and immediate response even when there is a loss of network connectivity. This offline processing ability is particularly beneficial in resource-constrained environments. Edge computing also has the ability to perform distributed computing across multiple edge devices. Instead of depending specifically on a centralized server, edge devices can collaborate and share the processing load with the central server. This distributed approach enables scalable real-time data processing, as the computational load is distributed across multiple edge devices of the network.

4.2.3 Potential mutual benefits of integrating FL and edge computing in Industry 5.0

Integrating federated learning with edge computing holds significant value and offers several benefits [7]. Here are some key significance of integrating FL with edge computing:

Enhanced privacy and data security: FL and edge computing together address privacy and data security issues. FL allows training machine learning models locally on edge nodes without the requirement of transferring sensitive data to a central server. This decentralized approach allows data to remain on edge devices, reducing the risk of data leaks and unauthorized access. By keeping data locally, FL mitigates privacy risks associated with transmitting data to the central server.

Reduced bandwidth and latency: Integrating FL with edge computing shrinks the need for transmitting large volumes of data over the network. Only model updates or parameters are exchanged between the edge devices and the central server. This can significantly reduce bandwidth requirements. This reduction in the transfer of data also reduces network congestion and minimizes latency. This enables the edge node to focus more on real-time processing and analysis at the edge. It is predominantly beneficial for time-sensitive applications that require quick responses.

Improved scalability and efficiency: FL powers the computational resources available on edge devices by distributing the model training load across multiple nodes. By integrating FL with edge computing, organizations can increase their machine learning capabilities without depending solely on centralized processing and storage servers. This decentralized approach enhances scalability, as the edge devices as a group contribute to the model training process, resulting in faster training and increased efficiency.

Edge intelligence and autonomy: The integration of FL and edge computing allows edge devices with intelligence and decision-making abilities. They can make autonomous decisions based on the knowledge learned by training models locally on edge devices without relying on continuous connectivity to a central server. This intelligence at the edge level enables real-time data analysis, faster response times, and the ability to operate with intermittent connectivity or even offline.

Flexibility and adaptability: Integration of FL with edge computing enables organizations to adapt to distributed processing. Edge devices can train models based on local data, capturing specific patterns to represent the local data uniquely at the server of their respective locations. This decentralized learning approach allows customized models and applications to be deployed at the edge, accommodating diverse edge computing environments and addressing specific requirements of user contexts.

Energy efficiency: Edge devices often have limited energy resources compared to centralized servers. The energy-efficient model training and inference can be achieved by integrating FL with edge computing. Localized training on edge devices reduces the requirement for data transmission and offloads computational tasks from power-intensive centralized servers. This method optimizes energy consumption and prolongs the battery life of edge devices, making them more sustainable and cost-effective.

The integration of federated learning with edge computing reveals the potential for privacy-preserving, low-latency, scalable, and intelligent edge computing applications. It also allows organizations to leverage the power of machine learning while addressing the challenges related to data security, bandwidth, latency, and scalability in edge-computing scenarios [57].

4.3 Literature review

The authors in [22] have integrated federated learning and edge computing to protect the Industry 5.0 systems from data poisoning attacks. Any unauthorized intruder may feed fabricated training data to distort a model to make biased outputs through a data poisoning attack. This can lead to critical complications in Industry 5.0 systems such as inaccurate prediction and so on. To defend against such types of attacks, the authors have proposed innovative data poisoning defense federated split learning, called DepoisoningFSL for securing edge devices. This proposed work has three stages of learning models to work against data poisoning attacks. The authors have used KNN, random forest, and linear regression for making predictions. The results showed that the proposed work outperformed by offering higher accuracy and a lower error rate than the existing KSSD method. The proposed method increases accuracy by 5% (heart), 14% (diabetes), 7% (IoT Weather), and 1.7% (IoT_GPS_Tracker) for the 25% injection of data poison rate.

The authors in [2] have identified a serious threat to the IIoT botnets deployed within the IIoT systems. This deployment may be a sophisticated tool for the attackers to make an adversarial attack on the IIoT systems which can collapse the prediction system. Machine learning and Deep learning are the widely used effective techniques to detect IIoT attacks. But, building the centralized model and lack of up-to-date datasets are the unresolved challenges in these techniques. The authors identified that edge computing and federated learning can be two complementary technologies that can benefit each other which can secure the IIoT system from IIoT attacks. The authors proposed a multi-access edge computing model framework that makes use of federated learning method called FedGame. FedGame allows multiple MEC domains to securely collaborate to deal with IIoT attacks. This also preserves the privacy of IIoT devices. Fedgame makes use of deep learning in a federated way to enable a multi-access edge computing prediction model while privacy is preserved. On detection of an attack, a non-cooperative game will be established between the multi-access edge nodes to confirm the provisioning of the required virtual resources to deal with the attack.

The authors in [60] have tested federated learning and edge computing combination in intelligent vehicular communications. Vehicular edge computing has exploited computation and communication resources deployed at the edge of vehicular networks. Federated learning integrated vehicular edge computing has been used to meet the increasing demands of AI applications in intelligent vehicular communications. The diversity of the quality of image captured by camera in intelligent vehicles and capability to process the image in vehicular clients has the potential to affect the accuracy and efficiency of federated learning. So, authors have proposed a selective model aggregation approach to share only the fine DNN models from client to server for the contribution of the creation of aggregated models at the server side. Model selection has been done based on the proposed two-dimension contract theory as a distributed framework. This process facilitates communications between the central server and vehicular clients. Here, the privacy of vehicular clients has been preserved, because the vehicle's capabilities, such as processing power, image quality, have not been shared with the central server. This approach can also be used in Industry 5.0 to enhance the communication overhead between FL client and server by sharing only the selected model with the client.

The authors in [61] have proposed an algorithm called EdgeFed, derived from a traditional algorithm of federated learning called FedAvg. It has three main parts: central server, edge devices, and edge servers. The proposed algorithm splits the process of updating the local model, which is completed independently by mobile devices. The outputs of the edge devices are aggregated at the edge server. This separation can help enhance learning efficiency and decrease global communication efficiency. Each iteration contains multiple split training's between the several edge devices and their corresponding edge servers and a global aggregation exchange between the edge servers and a central server. This process split helps to reduce the communication and computational expense of the edge devices compared to the traditional algorithm called "FedAvg."

The authors in [63] have proposed a lightweight and secured federated learning scheme exclusively for edge computing. In the proposed work, the authors used a lightweight two-server secure aggregation protocol. It utilizes two servers to enable secure byzantine robustness and model aggregation. This scheme proposed by the authors helps to protect data privacy and prevents byzantine nodes from influencing the model aggregation on the server side. The proposed scheme has been tested in the LAN environment, and the results show that the proposed lightweight protocol meets the requirements for fidelity, security, and model accuracy when compared with the traditional FedAvg algorithm.

4.4 Applications of FL-enabled edge computing in Industry 5.0

In the world of Industry 5.0, combining federated learning with edge computing carries exciting possibilities for better efficiency and innovation. This powerful combination trains models together and processes data closer to the point of its creation, making quick and smarter decisions possible right wherever needed. In this section, we will explore the different ways federated learning-enabled edge computing can be used in Industry 5.0. This includes smart factories, smart healthcare, effective transportation, and smart grids. We will see how this fusion can change industries and the way we interact with technology. By looking at specific examples, we will also find out the big potential and amazing impact of FL-enabled edge computing in Industry 5.0. Figure 4.1 depicts the possible way of integrating FL with edge computing.

4.4.1 Smart manufacturing

In Industry 5.0, which represents the next phase of industrial evolution, there is a strong focus on integrating the capabilities of humans and machines to attain higher levels of productivity and efficiency. One of the key technologies driving this transformation to enhance each field of Industry 5.0 is edge computing. This edge computing brings computation and storage of data closer to the devices and sensors at the "edge" of the network.

Smart manufacturing, also called Industry 4.0 or the Industrial Internet of Things, refers to the incorporation of advanced technologies and digital systems into manufacturing processes to generate more efficient, automated, and interconnected production systems [21]. It focuses on improving productivity, quality, flexibility, and sustainability in manufacturing-related operations by making use of technologies such as IoT, artificial intelligence (AI), big data analytics, and robotics. This integration of edge computing with federated learning is an innovative machine learning approach that allows multiple edge devices to collaboratively train models while keeping data decentralized. This edge computing can significantly enhance manufacturing processes in Industry 5.0. Here are some ways FL-enabled edge computing can bring improvements:

Data privacy and security: FL integration with edge computing in manufacturing enables the training of machine learning models on local edge devices without sharing sensitive data with the central server. This helps protect intellectual property, trade secrets, and confidential information related to manufacturing while ensuring compliance with data privacy regulations [56].

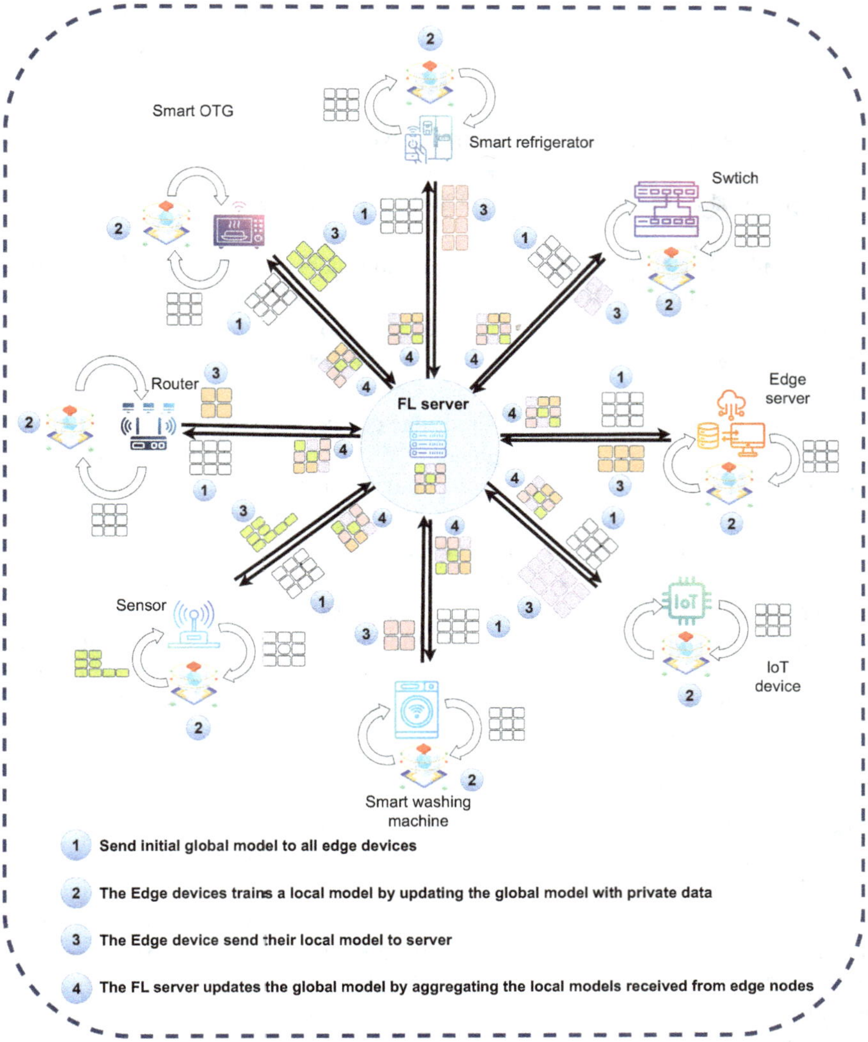

Figure 4.1 Federated learning and edge computing integration

Real-time decision-making: Deployment of machine learning models directly on edge devices enables manufacturing processes to benefit from real-time analytics and decision-making. Edge computing enables the data captured in the field to be analysed instantly by the edge resources. This greatly helps reduce the latency associated with data transmission to the central server. This latency reduction and instant analysis of data enable faster responses and immediate actions for optimizing production and addressing issues.

Connection independence: Edge computing integration with FL greatly reduces dependency on connectivity. The edge resources' ability to perform local computations and training on edge devices over data obtained ensures continued operations even in scenarios where network connectivity is disrupted or latency-sensitive decisions need to be made.

Energy efficiency: By deploying FL at the edge nodes, data obtained does not need to be transmitted to the central server for model training. This reduces the amount of data to be transmitted, which helps with the reduction of energy consumption. This is specifically beneficial for resource-constrained devices and can lead to cost savings.

Scalability and adaptability: Edge computing enables the distributed deployment of machine learning models across a network of edge devices. FL allows these models to be trained together, with updates shared among devices. This decentralized approach makes it easier to scale up the manufacturing system, adapt to changing conditions, and handle the increase in data volumes.

Predictive maintenance: FL-powered edge devices can continuously analyse sensor data from machinery and equipment. This continuous monitoring can detect patterns and anomalies that indicate potential failures. By predicting maintenance needs in real time in advance, manufacturers can improve maintenance schedules, minimize downtime, and reduce costs related to unexpected breakdowns.

Therefore, FL-integrated edge computing brings data privacy, real-time decision-making, connection independence, energy efficiency, scalability, and predictive maintenance capabilities to enhance the manufacturing processes of Industry 5.0. By merging the power of edge devices and collaborative learning, manufacturers can achieve new levels of efficiency, productivity, and agility in manufacturing.

4.4.2 Smart healthcare

Smart healthcare, also known as digital health, refers to the incorporation of advanced technologies and digital solutions into the healthcare industry to enhance the delivery, accessibility, and effectiveness of healthcare services. It includes the use of digital platforms, devices, data analytics, and communication systems to improve patient care, streamline healthcare operations, and allow more personalized and effective healthcare experiences. The integration of federated learning and edge computing in critical, sensitive applications like healthcare can have significant contributions to its advancement [41]. Healthcare is an application where privacy preservation is highly crucial with respect to patient information. Other learning methods have significantly failed to offer privacy because data has to be shared with the server for processing and also to make predictions. However, in the FL case, data need not be shared with the central server for processing. This greatly helps to achieve privacy. Here are some ways FL and edge computing can enhance healthcare services in Industry 5.0:

Privacy-preserving patient data analysis: FL enables healthcare providers and researchers to collaborate and train machine learning models on distributed edge devices. This deployment of machine learning models at edge devices helps bring decision-making ability close to the point of data generation. This preserves patient data privacy as the patient's health information is retained on the local edge device itself [12]. In addition, analysis of patient data can also be done at edge devices. This decentralized approach confirms that sensitive patient information remains on edge devices, securing individual privacy while still benefiting from collective insights.

Real-time patient monitoring: Edge computing allows the deployment of health monitoring devices such as wearable sensors at the point of care. This collects and analyses patient data in real time. By deploying FL on edge devices, it can collaborate to train models that provide personalized insights with respect to patient monitoring, enabling early detection of anomalies and timely interventions.

Efficient diagnostic and treatment support: FL-enabled edge devices can leverage local computational power and train models that improve diagnostic accuracy and treatment planning [36]. By analysing various patient data collected from different healthcare infrastructures, the models can provide more accurate predictions and recommendations to healthcare providers. This can lead to improved patient outcomes and more effective health services.

Telemedicine and remote healthcare: Edge devices equipped with FL abilities can support telemedicine and remote healthcare initiatives. Remote patient data, such as vital signs, medical imaging, or wearable device data, can be processed and analyzed locally on edge devices. This ensures timely and more accurate analysis without the need for extensive data transmission. This allows efficient remote consultations, remote patient monitoring, and personalized healthcare delivery.

Resource optimization and predictive maintenance: By deploying FL on edge devices, it can help monitor medical equipment. Training machine learning models locally on edge devices and FL deployment on them can identify abnormal deviations from the normal operating conditions of edge devices. With respect to hospital management and effective patient healthcare delivery, this can help to predict equipment failures, optimize resource allocation, and proactively schedule maintenance. This helps reduce downtime, decrease disruptions to patient care, and optimize the utilization of healthcare resources.

Edge-assisted emergency response: Edge devices adopted with FL abilities can play a crucial role in emergency response scenarios. They can analyze data from various sources, such as wearable devices, sensors, and patient records, in real time. This can provide timely insights to first responders and emergency medical personnel, facilitating rapid and informed decision-making.

FL integrated with edge computing can enhance healthcare services in Industry 5.0. It can leverage distributed patient data processing, enhanced patient privacy protection, real-time patient health analytics, and improved resource utilization to deliver personalized and efficient healthcare services. These technologies significantly contribute to better patient outcomes, optimized healthcare delivery, and developments in medical research while maintaining high standards of data security and privacy.

4.4.3 Smart transportation

Smart transportation refers to the use of advanced technologies and intelligent systems to enhance the efficiency, safety, sustainability, and overall performance of transportation networks and systems. It encompasses the integration of various technologies, such as Internet of Things, artificial intelligence, big data analytics, and communication systems, to enhance the movement of people and goods, improve infrastructure management, and offer innovative transportation services. Federated learning integrated with edge computing can significantly contribute to the development of smart transportation systems in Industry 5.0. Here are some ways in which FL-enabled edge computing can help provide smart transportation.

Real-time traffic prediction: FL enables edge devices, such as sensors, cameras, and smart vehicles, to collaboratively train models for real-time traffic prediction. By gathering and analyzing data locally, these edge devices can learn patterns and make predictions about crucial applications of transportation such as traffic flow, congestion, and travel times. This analysed information can be used to optimize traffic routing, plan efficient transportation routes, and provide real-time traffic updates to drivers and transportation management systems.

Intelligent traffic signal control: Edge devices installed at traffic intersections can deploy FL to train models for intelligent traffic signal control. By monitoring and analyzing traffic patterns, pedestrian flows, and vehicle density in real time, these edge devices can optimize signal timing, reduce congestion, and improve traffic flow. FL allows collaborative learning across multiple traffic signal intersections without the need for centralized data aggregation.

Autonomous vehicle training and collaboration: FL allows autonomous vehicles to work together and improve their models without sharing sensitive data. Each vehicle can train its initialized local model using its own local data gathered from onboard sensors and share only the model updates, i.e., parameters, with other vehicles. This collaborative learning method allows vehicles to collectively enhance their awareness, decision-making, and control abilities, leading to safer and more efficient autonomous transportation systems.

Intelligent parking management: Federated learning-enabled edge devices, including parking sensors and cameras, can collaboratively learn, predict, and share parking availability in real time. This information can be used to guide drivers to available parking slots, optimize parking space allocation, and decrease traffic congestion triggered by drivers searching for parking.

FL integrated with edge computing in smart transportation systems carries the advantages of local data processing, decreased latency, and enhanced privacy while still allowing for collective intelligence and collaboration. It allows real-time decision-making, improves efficiency, and supports safer and more sustainable transportation solutions.

4.4.4 Smart grids

A smart grid is an advanced and digitally enhanced electrical power grid system that makes use of modern communication, control, and monitoring technologies to improve the efficiency, reliability, and sustainability of electricity consumption, generation, and distribution. It denotes a significant evolution from traditional power grids by adopting various intelligent devices, software, and advanced analytic abilities to optimize the flow of electricity and improve overall grid management. Federated learning-enabled edge computing can play a vital role in enhancing smart grids in Industry 5.0. Here is how federated learning-enabled edge computing can support smart grids in Industry 5.0:

Data privacy: FL permits the collaborative training of machine learning models without the need to share raw data. In the case of smart grids, various edge devices related to the electricity process, such as smart meters, sensors, and controllers, generate massive amounts of sensitive data related to energy consumption, grid performance, and customer behavior. With federated learning, instead of sending this data to the central server, the training of machine learning models can be performed directly on edge devices, ensuring data privacy and reducing the risk of unauthorized access to sensitive information.

Low Latency: Edge computing brings computational power closer to the data source, reducing latency and enabling real-time decision-making. In smart grids, where timely responses are crucial for efficient energy management and grid stability, edge devices can process and analyze data locally, without the need for back-and-forth communication with a central server. This allows for quicker detection of anomalies, prediction of demand, and coordination of distributed energy resources.

Scalability: Federated learning allows distributed learning through multiple edge devices, allowing the models to learn from various data sources. This learning from multiple devices helps maintain a global knowledge base. In the case of smart grids, this means that edge devices deployed in different geographical areas can collaboratively train models to capture local variations in energy usage patterns, weather conditions, and grid characteristics. This scalable approach enables more accurate and localized predictions and optimizations. This leads to increased grid reliability and efficiency in smart grids.

Resilience: Edge computing with federated learning can improve the resilience of smart grids by allowing local decision-making. Traditional grids demand the presence of the central server to make decisions whenever required. These FL-enabled edge computing devices powered by smart grids can control the grids even in the absence of the central server. In case of any network disruptions or server failure situations, edge devices deployed can continue to operate independently, maintaining grid stability and ensuring critical functionalities. Federated learning eases collaborative learning among edge devices, permitting them to collectively adapt and improve their decision-making abilities over time.

Energy efficiency: By performing model training and inference at the edge, FL reduces the necessity for continuous data transmission to the central server. This greatly reduces network bandwidth requirements and the energy consumption associated with data transfer. This leads to improved energy efficiency in smart grid deployments. In addition, edge devices can leverage local computational resources, optimizing energy management techniques and minimizing unnecessary energy usage.

Therefore, federated learning-enabled edge computing offers a distributed and privacy-preserving technique to improve the intelligence and efficiency of smart grids in Industry 5.0. It enables edge devices to collectively learn, adapt, and make informed decisions. This results in more resilient, secure, and sustainable energy systems.

4.4.5 Smart cities and infrastructure management

Smart cities and infrastructure management are vital applications of Industry 5.0 that have huge scope to transform through the integration of federated learning and edge computing [33]. The concept of smart cities has arisen as a transformative vision for urban living, integrating recent technologies to develop highly efficient, sustainable, and organized urban environments. Apart from the confines of mere automation, smart cities represent a holistic paradigm where data-driven intelligence, powered by the Internet of Things, artificial intelligence, and decentralized computing, permits municipalities to enhance resource allocation, public services, and the quality of life of residents [23]. With a strong belief in real-time data analysis, citizen engagement, and responsive infrastructure, smart cities in Industry 5.0 seek to complement technological innovation with urban living, steering to a new era of urbanization where technology catalyzes human well-being, environmental control, and economic growth.

Waste management optimization: Smart bins are the garbage collectors of Industry 5.0. It is equipped with sensors that can monitor waste levels and inform waste collection trucks when they are full. Edge devices deployed in these bins and collection trucks can collaborate through federated learning to optimize waste collection, reduce unnecessary trips, and confirm timely pickups [37]. This can lead to an efficient waste management system, reduced fuel consumption, and cleaner urban environments.

Public safety and security: Smart cities can improve public safety through FL-enabled edge devices. Cameras, sensors, and other surveillance systems deployed in the smart cities can capture data in public spaces. FL-powered models on these devices can analyze this data for real-time threat detection, identifying anomalies and potential security risks [4]. This real-time anticipation can help in identifying the risk in advance and inform the appropriate authorities to take preventive or immediate action on the incident.

Environmental monitoring and pollution control: Edge devices deployed across the city can monitor environmental features like air quality, noise levels, and water quality. FL-enabled models deployed in edge devices can analyze this data on the edge to measure pollution levels and identify trends [17]. This information can help corporation authorities take informed actions to reduce pollution, protect public health, and confirm environmental sustainability.

Infrastructure maintenance and resilience: FL and edge computing can assist in the infrastructure maintenance of a smart city. Sensors deployed in roads, bridges, and other structures can collect data on wear and tear. Through FL models in edge devices, this data can be analyzed locally to predict maintenance demands, assess structural integrity, and prioritize repair needs, confirming the safety and longevity of city infrastructure [49].

The integration of FL and edge computing in smart cities and infrastructure management in Industry 5.0 leads to more efficient resource utilization, enhanced urban planning, improved citizen experiences, and improved sustainability. By allowing localized data processing, collaborative learning, and real-time analysis, this integration of federated learning with edge computing empowers cities to become smarter, safer, and more responsive to the demands of their residents.

4.4.6 *Smart supply chain management*

Supply chain management is a complex and dynamic process of Industry 5.0 that comprises the planning, coordination, movement, execution, and monitoring of all happenings related to goods, services, and information from raw material suppliers to end customers [43]. This includes the entire lifecycle of any product, from sourcing raw materials to manufacturing, distribution, retailing, and after-sales service [46]. In Industry 5.0, supply chain management undergoes substantial advancements because of technological innovations like federated learning and edge computing [26]. FL-enabled edge computing transforms supply chain management by leveraging the following aspects:

Demand forecasting and inventory optimization: Federated learning integrates data from multiple sources at edge locations, such as customer orders, production rates, and inventory levels, to enhance demand forecasting accuracy. Edge devices can analyze real-time data, leading to more accurate demand predictions and improved inventory levels, thus reducing excess inventory costs and minimizing stockouts [55].

Real-time tracking and traceability: Edge devices equipped with sensors can track and trace the movement of goods throughout the supply chain process. Federated learning-enabled models deployed at edge nodes analyze this data locally, providing real-time visibility of the status and location of shipments [19]. This helps to promote transparency in the supply chain, enables timely decision-making, and enhances customer satisfaction.

Supplier collaboration and risk management: Federated learning permits suppliers and partners to collaborate on risk management without sharing sensitive data. Models trained on collected data from various edge sources can predict disruptions, identify possible potential bottlenecks, and estimate the impact of supply chain disturbances, enhancing overall resilience.

In conclusion, federated learning-enabled edge computing transforms supply chain management in Industry 5.0 by allowing real-time insights, enhanced resource utilization, improved transparency, and improved collaboration among stakeholders [14]. This integration leads to a more robust, agile, and effective supply chain ecosystem that can adapt to dynamic market conditions, customer demands, and unforeseen disruptions.

4.5 Challenges and open issues

Data heterogeneity: In Industry 5.0, edge devices generate various types of data, including structured and unstructured data, from diverse sources. Incorporating and processing heterogeneous data for federated learning presents challenges with respect to the preprocessing of data, feature extraction, and data normalization to confirm compatibility and consistency across devices.

Latency and real-time processing: FL-enabled edge computing targets process data and perform machine learning model updates locally at the edge. This can help reduce latency and enhance real-time decision-making. But, ensuring low latency and real-time processing capabilities while maintaining federated learning efficiency and accuracy can be challenging, specifically on resource-constrained edge devices.

Edge device variability: Industry 5.0 consists of a variety of edge devices with varying computational abilities, memory, and energy constraints. Incorporating FL across such a diverse set of edge devices demands efficient algorithms and models that can manage the varying abilities and constraints of different devices.

Network bandwidth and connectivity: FL depends on communication between edge devices and the central server for model updates and aggregation. Restricted network bandwidth and intermittent connectivity in edge scenarios can defer effective FL integration. Efficient data compression methods, adaptive network protocols, and optimization algorithms are required to mitigate these challenges.

Model size and complexity: Traditional machine learning models used in federated learning can be large and complex. This may not be suitable for resource-constrained edge devices. Optimizing model size and reducing complexity to fit the limited computational abilities of edge devices without sacrificing accuracy is a significant challenge in FL-enabled edge computing.

Privacy and security: FL comprises sharing and aggregating data from multiple edge devices, raising worries about data privacy and security. Confirming secure data transmission, protecting sensitive information, and addressing privacy regulations are serious integration challenges. Methods like federated encryption and differential privacy have to be explored to eliminate these concerns.

Scalability and management: Industry 5.0 environments consist of a massive number of edge devices, and handling the FL process at scale becomes complex. Challenges in coordinating model updates, handling device failures, and ensuring consistency across a large number of devices pose scalability and management-related issues that demand efficient coordination methods and distributed algorithms.

Edge infrastructure and deployment: Deploying and managing a device at the edge in Industry 5.0 to support FL demands careful planning and coordination. Identifying edge device placement, managing edge device configurations, and confirming smooth integration with existing industrial systems are critical integration challenges.

Skill and knowledge gap: Federated learning-enabled edge computing demands expertise in both machine learning and edge computing domains. Associating the skill and knowledge gaps among industrial personnel, including engineers and technicians, to effectively integrate federated learning at the edge is crucial for successful integration.

Interoperability and standardization: Industry 5.0 comprises multiple vendors, technologies, and platforms, making interoperability and standardization serious challenges. Launching common standards, protocols, and frameworks for federated learning-enabled edge computing can facilitate smooth integration, data exchange, and collaboration across different industrial systems. Figure 4.2 depicts the integration and open issues of FL and edge computing in Industry 5.0.

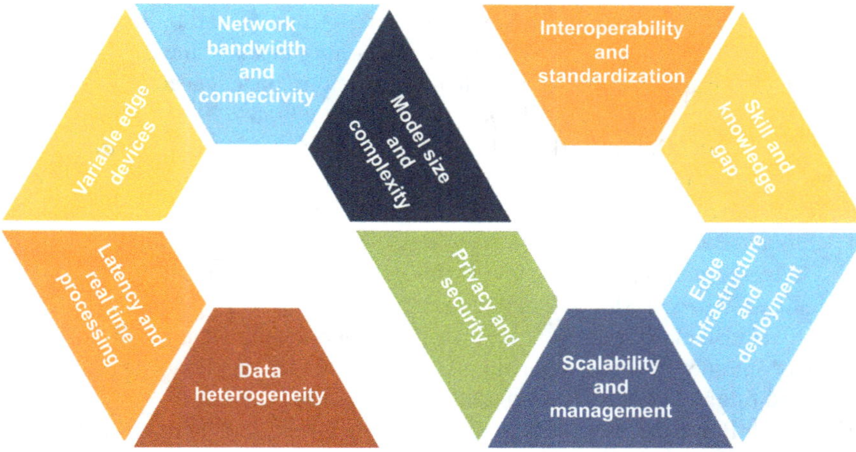

Figure 4.2 Integration challenges and open issues

4.6 Conclusion

In conclusion, this integration of federated learning and edge computing develops as a revolutionary paradigm for Industry 5.0, transforming the landscape of smart manufacturing and industrial automation. By making use of the power of distributed machine learning on edge devices, this integration opens up immense potential for data-driven decision-making, real-time insights, and enhanced operational efficiency. Federated learning's privacy-preserving nature confirms that sensitive data remains localized, guaranteeing compliance with strict industry regulations and raising trust among stakeholders. Furthermore, edge computing's capability to process data at the edge of the network reduces latency and bandwidth requirements, allowing rapid response times which is critical for time-sensitive applications. By collaborative model training and decentralized processing, FL-enabled edge computing permits industries with intelligent, secure, and scalable solutions that drive innovation and propel Industry 5.0 toward a future of adaptive and autonomous processes in various sectors such as manufacturing, healthcare, transportation, and electrical grids. As the transformative journey continues, it is crucial for industry leaders, researchers, and policymakers to hold this synergistic convergence to open up the full potential of Industry 5.0, motivating sustainable growth, improved productivity, and heightened competitiveness in the rapidly evolving industrial landscape.

References

[1] Sawsan AbdulRahman, Hanine Tout, Hakima Ould-Slimane, Azzam Mourad, Chamseddine Talhi, and Mohsen Guizani. A survey on federated learning: The journey from centralized to distributed on-site learning and beyond. *IEEE Internet of Things Journal*, 8(7):5476–5497, 2020.

[2] Zakaria Abou El Houda, Bouziane Brik, Adlen Ksentini, Lyes Khoukhi, and Mohsen Guizani. When federated learning meets game theory: A cooperative framework to secure IIoT applications on edge computing. *IEEE Transactions on Industrial Informatics*, 18(11):7988–7997, 2022.

[3] Chunguang Bai, Patrick Dallasega, Guido Orzes, and Joseph Sarkis. Industry 4.0 technologies assessment: A sustainability perspective. *International Journal of Production Economics*, 229:107776, 2020.

[4] Johan Barthélemy, Nicolas Verstaevel, Hugh Forehead, and Pascal Perez. Edge-computing video analytics for real-time traffic monitoring in a smart city. *Sensors*, 19(9):2048, 2019.

[5] Sweta Bhattacharya, Nancy Victor, Rajeswari Chengoden, *et al.* Blockchain for internet of underwater things: State-of-the-art, applications, challenges, and future directions. *Sustainability*, 14(23):15659, 2022.

[6] Keith Bonawitz, Hubert Eichner, Wolfgang Grieskamp, *et al.* Towards federated learning at scale: System design. *Proceedings of Machine Learning and Systems*, 1:374–388, 2019.

[7] Alexander Brecko, Erik Kajati, Jiri Koziorek, and Iveta Zolotova. Federated learning for edge computing: A survey. *Applied Sciences*, 12(18):9124, 2022.

[8] Hung Cao, Monica Wachowicz, and Sangwhan Cha. Developing an edge computing platform for real-time descriptive analytics. In *2017 IEEE International Conference on Big Data (Big Data)*, pages 4546–4554. IEEE, 2017.

[9] Keyan Cao, Yefan Liu, Gongjie Meng, and Qimeng Sun. An overview on edge computing research. *IEEE Access*, 8:85714–85728, 2020.

[10] M Emre Celebi and Kemal Aydin. *Unsupervised Learning Algorithms*, volume 9. Springer, 2016.

[11] Jiasi Chen and Xukan Ran. Deep learning with edge computing: A review. *Proceedings of the IEEE*, 107(8):1655–1674, 2019.

[12] Liezel Cilliers. Wearable devices in healthcare: Privacy and information security issues. *Health Information Management Journal*, 49(2–3):150–156, 2020.

[13] Chih-Tien Fan, Zong-You Wu, Che-Pin Chang, and Shyan Ming Yuan. Web resource cacheable edge device in fog computing. In *2016 15th International Symposium on Parallel and Distributed Computing (ISPDC)*, pages 432–439. IEEE, 2016.

[14] Guilherme F Frederico. From supply chain 4.0 to supply chain 5.0: Findings from a systematic literature review and research directions. *Logistics*, 5(3):49, 2021.

[15] Pedro Garcia Lopez, Alberto Montresor, Dick Epema, *et al.* Edge-centric computing: Vision and challenges. *ACM SIGCOMM Computer Communication Review*, 45(5):37–42, 2015.

[16] Ahmad Hammoud, Hadi Otrok, Azzam Mourad, and Zbigniew Dziong. On demand fog federations for horizontal federated learning in IoV. *IEEE Transactions on Network and Service Management*, 19(3):3062–3075, 2022.

[17] Zeba Idrees, Zhuo Zou, and Lirong Zheng. Edge computing based IoT architecture for low cost air pollution monitoring systems: A comprehensive system analysis, design considerations and development. *Sensors*, 18(9):3021, 2018.

[18] Celestine Iwendi, Zunera Jalil, *et al.* Keysplitwatermark: Zero watermarking algorithm for software protection against cyber-attacks. *IEEE Access*, 8:72650–72660, 2020.

[19] Arpit Jain and Dharm Singh Jat. Supply chain management using blockchain, iot and edge computing technology. In *Innovative Supply Chain Management via Digitalization and Artificial Intelligence*, pages 87–98. Springer, 2022.

[20] Xiantao Jiang, F Richard Yu, Tian Song, and Victor CM Leung. Intelligent resource allocation for video analytics in blockchain-enabled internet of autonomous vehicles with edge computing. *IEEE Internet of Things Journal*, 9(16):14260–14272, 2020.

[21] Hyoung Seok Kang, Ju Yeon Lee, SangSu Choi, *et al.* Smart manufacturing: Past research, present findings, and future directions. *International Journal of Precision Engineering and Manufacturing-Green Technology*, 3:111–128, 2016.

[22] Firoz Khan, R Lakshmana Kumar, Mustufa Haider Abidi, Seifedine Kadry, Hisham Alkhalefah, and Mohamed K Aboudaif. Federated split learning model for industry 5.0: A data poisoning defense for edge computing. *Electronics*, 11(15):2393, 2022.

[23] Latif U Khan, Ibrar Yaqoob, Nguyen H Tran, SM Ahsan Kazmi, Tri Nguyen Dang, and Choong Seon Hong. Edge-computing-enabled smart cities: A comprehensive survey. *IEEE Internet of Things Journal*, 7(10):10200–10232, 2020.

[24] Wazir Zada Khan, Ejaz Ahmed, Saqib Hakak, Ibrar Yaqoob, and Arif Ahmed. Edge computing: A survey. *Future Generation Computer Systems*, 97:219–235, 2019.

[25] Anusha Lalitha, Shubhanshu Shekhar, Tara Javidi, and Farinaz Koushanfar. Fully decentralized federated learning. In *Third Workshop on Bayesian Deep Learning (NeurIPS)*, volume 2, 2018.

[26] Douglas M Lambert and Martha C Cooper. Issues in supply chain management. *Industrial Marketing Management*, 29(1):65–83, 2000.

[27] Heiner Lasi, Peter Fettke, Hans-Georg Kemper, Thomas Feld, and Michael Hoffmann. Industry 4.0. *Business & Information Systems Engineering*, 6:239–242, 2014.

[28] Jiewu Leng, Weinan Sha, Baicun Wang, *et al.* Industry 5.0: Prospect and retrospect. *Journal of Manufacturing Systems*, 65:279–295, 2022.

[29] He Li, Kaoru Ota, and Mianxiong Dong. Learning IoT in edge: Deep learning for the internet of things with edge computing. *IEEE Network*, 32(1):96–101, 2018.

[30] Li Li, Yuxi Fan, Mike Tse, and Kuo-Yi Lin. A review of applications in federated learning. *Computers & Industrial Engineering*, 149:106854, 2020.

[31] Tian Li, Anit Kumar Sahu, Ameet Talwalkar, and Virginia Smith. Federated learning: Challenges, methods, and future directions. *IEEE Signal Processing Magazine*, 37(3):50–60, 2020.

[32] Bing Liu and Bing Liu. Supervised learning. *Web Data Mining: Exploring Hyperlinks, Contents, and Usage Data*, pages 63–132, 2011.

[33] Zhihan Lv, Dongliang Chen, Ranran Lou, and Qingjun Wang. Intelligent edge computing based on machine learning for smart city. *Future Generation Computer Systems*, 115:90–99, 2021.

[34] Aziz Naanani *et al.* Security in industry 4.0: Cyber-attacks and countermeasures. *Turkish Journal of Computer and Mathematics Education (TURCOMAT)*, 12(10):6504–6512, 2021.

[35] Stefan Nastic, Thomas Rausch, Ognjen Scekic, *et al.* A serverless real-time data analytics platform for edge computing. *IEEE Internet Computing*, 21(4):64–71, 2017.

[36] Dinh C Nguyen, Quoc-Viet Pham, Pubudu N Pathirana, *et al.* Federated learning for smart healthcare: A survey. *ACM Computing Surveys (CSUR)*, 55(3):1–37, 2022.

[37] D Palanikkumar, R Ramesh Kumar, Mehedi Masud, Mrim M Alnfiai, and Mohamed Abouhawwash. Bayes-Q-learning algorithm in edge computing for waste tracking. *Intelligent Automation & Soft Computing*, 36(2):2425–2440, 2023.

[38] Sawsan Abdul Rahman, Hanine Tout, Chamseddine Talhi, and Azzam Mourad. Internet of things intrusion detection: Centralized, on-device, or federated learning? *IEEE Network*, 34(6):310–317, 2020.

[39] Alok Raj, Gourav Dwivedi, Ankit Sharma, Ana Beatriz Lopes de Sousa Jabbour, and Sonu Rajak. Barriers to the adoption of industry 4.0 technologies in the manufacturing sector: An inter-country comparative perspective. *International Journal of Production Economics*, 224:107546, 2020.

[40] G Thippa Reddy, M Praveen Kumar Reddy, Kuruva Lakshmanna, *et al.* Analysis of dimensionality reduction techniques on big data. *Ieee Access*, 8:54776–54788, 2020.

[41] Nicola Rieke, Jonny Hancox, Wenqi Li, *et al.* The future of digital health with federated learning. *NPJ Digital Medicine*, 3(1):119, 2020.

[42] Chemmalar Selvi, Nancy Victor, Rajeswari Chengoden, *et al.* A comprehensive analysis of blockchain applications for securing computer vision systems. arXiv preprint arXiv:2307.06659, 2023.

[43] Weisong Shi and Schahram Dustdar. The promise of edge computing. *Computer*, 49(5):78–81, 2016.

[44] Inés Sittón-Candanedo, Ricardo S Alonso, Juan M Corchado, Sara Rodríguez-González, and Roberto Casado-Vara. A review of edge computing reference architectures and a new global edge proposal. *Future Generation Computer Systems*, 99:278–294, 2019.

[45] Gautam Srivastava, Dasaratha Rami Reddy K, Gokul Yenduri, *et al.* Federated learning enabled edge computing security for internet of medical things:

Concepts, challenges and open issues. In *Security and Risk Analysis for Intelligent Edge Computing*, pages 67–89. Springer, 2023.

[46] Hartmut Stadtler. Supply chain management: An overview. *Supply Chain Management and Advanced Planning: Concepts, Models, Software, and Case Studies*, pages 3–28. Springer Berlin, 2014.

[47] Stevan Stankovski, Gordana Ostojić, Igor Baranovski, Mladen Babić, and Miloš Stanojević. The impact of edge computing on industrial automation. In *2020 19th International Symposium Infoteh-Jahorina (Infoteh)*, pages 1–4. IEEE, 2020.

[48] Richard S Sutton and Andrew G Barto. *Reinforcement learning: An introduction*. MIT press, 2018.

[49] Salman Taherizadeh, Andrew C Jones, Ian Taylor, Zhiming Zhao, and Vlado Stankovski. Monitoring self-adaptive applications within edge computing frameworks: A state-of-the-art review. *Journal of Systems and Software*, 136:19–38, 2018.

[50] Lin Teng, Yulong Qiao, Muhammad Shafiq, *et al.* Flpk-bisenet: Federated learning based on priori knowledge and bilateral segmentation network for image edge extraction. *IEEE Transactions on Network and Service Management*, 2023.

[51] Ha-Vu Tran, Georges Kaddoum, Hany Elgala, Chadi Abou-Rjeily, and Hemani Kaushal. Lightwave power transfer for federated learning-based wireless networks. *IEEE Communications Letters*, 24(7):1472–1476, 2020.

[52] Blesson Varghese, Nan Wang, Sakil Barbhuiya, Peter Kilpatrick, and Dimitrios S Nikolopoulos. Challenges and opportunities in edge computing. In *2016 IEEE International Conference on Smart Cloud (SmartCloud)*, pages 20–26. IEEE, 2016.

[53] Joost Verbraeken, Matthijs Wolting, Jonathan Katzy, Jeroen Kloppenburg, Tim Verbelen, and Jan S Rellermeyer. A survey on distributed machine learning. *ACM Computing Surveys (CSUR)*, 53(2):1–33, 2020.

[54] Omar Abdel Wahab, Azzam Mourad, Hadi Otrok, and Tarik Taleb. Federated machine learning: Survey, multi-level classification, desirable criteria and future directions in communication and networking systems. *IEEE Communications Surveys & Tutorials*, 23(2):1342–1397, 2021.

[55] Hexu Wang, Fei Xie, Qun Duan, Jing Li, *et al.* Federated learning for supply chain demand forecasting. *Mathematical Problems in Engineering*, 2022, 2022.

[56] Kok-Seng Wong and Myung Ho Kim. Privacy protection for data-driven smart manufacturing systems. *International Journal of Web Services Research (IJWSR)*, 14(3):17–32, 2017.

[57] Qi Xia, Winson Ye, Zeyi Tao, Jindi Wu, and Qun Li. A survey of federated learning for edge computing: Research problems and solutions. *High-Confidence Computing*, 1(1):100008, 2021.

[58] Xun Xu, Yuqian Lu, Birgit Vogel-Heuser, and Lihui Wang. Industry 4.0 and industry 5.0—inception, conception and perception. *Journal of Manufacturing Systems*, 61:530–535, 2021.

[59] Zhaohui Yang, Mingzhe Chen, Walid Saad, Choong Seon Hong, and Mohammad Shikh-Bahaei. Energy efficient federated learning over wireless communication networks. *IEEE Transactions on Wireless Communications*, 20(3):1935–1949, 2020.

[60] Dongdong Ye, Rong Yu, Miao Pan, and Zhu Han. Federated learning in vehicular edge computing: A selective model aggregation approach. *IEEE Access*, 8:23920–23935, 2020.

[61] Yunfan Ye, Shen Li, Fang Liu, Yonghao Tang, and Wanting Hu. Edgefed: Optimized federated learning based on edge computing. *IEEE Access*, 8:209191–209198, 2020.

[62] Gokul Yenduri, Gautam Srivastava, Praveen Kumar Reddy Maddikunta, *et al.* Generative pre-trained transformer: A comprehensive review on enabling technologies, potential applications, emerging challenges, and future directions. arXiv preprint arXiv:2305.10435, 2023.

[63] Zhuangzhuang Zhang, Libing Wu, Chuanguo Ma, *et al.* LSFL: A lightweight and secure federated learning scheme for edge computing. *IEEE Transactions on Information Forensics and Security*, 18:365–379, 2023.

Chapter 5

Infusion of federated learning for cybersecurity in Industry 5.0

G. Chemmalar Selvi[1], G. Deepti Raj[1], G. Lakshmi Priya[1], Gokul Yenduri[1], Praveen Kumar Reddy Maddikunta[1], Abdul Rehman Javed[2] and Thippa Reddy Gadekallu[3,4]

Abstract

Industry 5.0, characterized by the convergence of human intelligence and automation creates a new environment for cyberattacks and requires robust security measures. The inherent dangers of Industry 5.0 challenge current cybersecurity solutions and urge the need for cutting-edge methods. Federated learning is one such promising technique that enables collaborative machine learning without centralizing data. However, the introduction of federated learning for cybersecurity in Industry 5.0 raises privacy concerns. In this chapter, we consider several federated learning applications in Industry 5.0 cybersecurity, including malware detection, threat intelligence sharing, intrusion detection systems, and anomaly detection for Industrial Internet of Things (IIoT) systems. We also explore the benefits of federated learning for real-time cybersecurity monitoring. We also discuss federated learning frameworks and algorithms in cybersecurity, as well as secure aggregation methods. Despite its immense potential, Industry 5.0 faces challenges that must be overcome to effectively implement it. This chapter also addresses the ethical and societal implications of adopting federated learning in cybersecurity, as well as challenges related to standardization and interoperability.

Keywords: Federated learning, Cybersecurity attacks, Data security and privacy, Applications of Industry 5.0, Collaborative ML model

[1]School of Computer Science Engineering and Information Systems, Vellore Institute of Technology, India
[2]Department of Cyber Security, Air University, Pakistan
[3]Division of Research and Development, Lovely Professional University, Phagwara, India
[4]Zhongda Group, Haiyan County, Jiaxing City, Zhejiang Province, China

5.1 Introduction

In recent years, the power of machine learning (ML) techniques has shown a wide range of advancement in multi-faceted aspects. This was simply possible because of the following three major contributing factors. The main factor is the abundance of large-scale datasets that grow exponentially from the big data systems. Next, the power of high computational resources like GPUs and TPUs contributes the second most important factor. The recent advances in the deep learning (DL) techniques are another remarkable factor infusing the intelligence of ML models and high-power computational devices. While ML has exhibited high success rate, several domains encounter serious problems in using them to solve the real-time applications. Data privacy, user confidentiality, and computational complexity are the major causes prone to adapting ML models in tackling the real-world problems.

These key challenges of ML are addressed using the advanced concepts of federated learning (FL). FL is a machine learning concept where the training of collaborative ML models is employed over multiple devices without the need for data sharing, except exchanging the model gradients only. Unlike ML, a centralized learning environment, FL leverages the potential to solve data privacy and user confidentiality by learning the collaborative ML models in the distributed and decentralized network. This salient feature enabled the application of FL in several domains such as healthcare [1], mobile networking and edge computing [2], and energy management [3]. FL has a wider range of potential capabilities in the area of cybersecurity [4]. Cybersecurity refers to the collection of practices and technologies, designed to safeguard the digital sensitive data from the unauthorized access or anonymous intruders. The major cybersecurity attacks are distributed denial of service (DDoS), brute force attacks, and IoT-based attacks. For example, FL can greatly help the risk associated with IoT-based attacks. FL enables the model training in the IoT devices connected to the decentralized network without the demand for exposing the sensitive data and eliminating the risk of information tampering during data transmission. This ensures the data security and user privacy concerns. In addition, FL also performs continuous learning from various IoT devices, alleviating the risk of adversarial attacks. FL can therefore address the key challenges of cybersecurity which plays a crucial role in the implementation of Industry 5.0.

The global industrial transformation, Industry 5.0, aims at building smart and interconnected industrial systems. The three key characteristics are human-centricity, sustainability, and resiliency. The power of Industry 5.0 comes into existence by leveraging the enabling technologies such as Internet-of-Things (IoT), big data, cyberphysical systems, edge computing, and artificial intelligence (AI). With the advent of these digital technologies, Industry 5.0 faces a major real-time challenge called data security caused by cybersecurity threats and attacks. In this regard, the fusion of these technologies such as cybersecurity and FL can hold a promising solution to address data security and other serious problems.

This chapter aims to discuss about the real-time challenges faced by Industry 5.0 and how they can be addressed with the help of cybersecurity and FL techniques. The chapter is organized as follows: Section 5.1 is a general introduction related to how Industry 5.0 grew and what are the concerns and challenges before its evolution. Section 5.2 discusses the overview of Industry 5.0, what are the challenges faced due to cybersecurity, what are the current solutions available, why there is an urge for an advanced approach to tackle these cybersecurity challenges, and how FL can resolve Industry 5.0 challenges related to cybersecurity real-time challenges. Section 5.3 highlights the important applications of FL for tackling cybersecurity attacks in Industry 5.0. Section 5.4 explains the existing FL frameworks adopted for the cybersecurity use cases. Section 5.5 presents the challenges and future directions. Finally, the conclusion of this chapter summarizes the potential of the FL concept in addressing the cybersecurity attacks of Industry 5.0 applications.

5.2 Industry 5.0: cybersecurity challenges

5.2.1 Overview of Industry 5.0 and its characteristics

Industry 5.0 is an evolving idea that builds on the innovations of Industry 4.0. It envisions a future where people and technology work together and are fully integrated to increase creativity and productivity. Industry 5.0 seeks to balance automation and human-centricity, taking into account the different characteristics and skills that people bring to their jobs [5]. The key elements of Industry 5.0 are as follows:

A human-centered approach: 1. Industry 5.0 places great emphasis on the value of human skills such as creativity, problem-solving, and competence. We recognize that some tasks are best left to humans, especially those that require empathy, intuition, and complex decisions. Technology is seen as a collaborator and enabler rather than a replacement for human skills [6].

Collaboration and co-creation: 2. Industry 5.0 will foster collaboration and co-creation between humans and technology. It envisions a coexistence situation where machines and humans work together to achieve common goals. This includes smoothly integrating technology into the workplace, enabling real-time communication, and facilitating collaboration using tools such as wearable technology, augmented reality, and virtual reality.

Personalization and individualization: 3. Industry 5.0 focuses on the ability to tailor products and services to each customer's unique needs and preferences. Cutting-edge technologies such as artificial intelligence and machine learning enable businesses to collect and analyze data to deliver personalized experiences and create a unique value proposition for their customers.

Re-skilling and upskilling: 4. Industry 5.0 recognizes the need to continually re-skill and upskill employees as technology advances and job responsibilities change [7]. Employers should invest in training programs to give employees the skills they need to use technology properly. This includes fostering a culture of lifelong learning and giving people the tools they need to adapt to how technology works and the changing demands of work.

Ethical considerations: 5. Industry 5.0 pays close attention to ethical issues related to the introduction of technology. As people and technology become increasingly interconnected, concerns such as privacy, security, openness, and fairness must be addressed. Ethical frameworks and guidelines are important to ensure the proper development and application of technology within Industry 5.0.

Sustainability and social responsibility: 6. Industry 5.0 recognizes the importance of sustainability and social responsibility in business practices. It promotes the use of environmentally friendly technologies, effective resource management, and socially conscious production techniques [8]. In addition to promoting economic progress, Industry 5.0 aims to improve society by addressing environmental and social issues.

In general, Industry 5.0 envisions an era in which technology and people coexist peacefully, promoting innovation, productivity, and social well-being. While making the most of people's individuality, we use technology to develop their strengths and open up new opportunities. Industry 5.0 strives to develop a more holistic and human-centered approach to business and work by prioritizing collaboration, personalization, reskilling, ethics, and sustainability.

5.2.2 Cybersecurity challenges in Industry 5.0

Industry 5.0 brings many benefits and breakthroughs, but it also brings new dangers and threats to cybersecurity [9]. Below are some of the potential cybersecurity issues unique to Industry 5.0 as people and technology become more connected.

Increased attack surface: 1. Industry 5.0 integrates a multitude of technologies into the industrial environment, including IoT devices, robotics, and augmented reality. The number of networked systems and devices is increasing, increasing the attack surface and the number of entry points for hackers.

Data security and privacy concerns: 2. Industry 5.0 will generate vast amounts of data through sensors, connected devices, and collaborative systems. Protecting sensitive data from unauthorized access, security breaches, and theft is becoming increasingly important [10]. Additionally, ensuring privacy compliance when collecting, maintaining, and sharing sensitive data becomes very difficult.

Human–machine interface vulnerabilities: 3. For Industry 5.0 to be successful, the interaction between humans and technology must work smoothly. Cybercriminals can use social engineering tactics and other flaws in human-machine interfaces to trick or manipulate people into giving them access to systems and personal data.

Supply chain attacks: 4. Industry 5.0 requires complex supply networks with many partners and related systems [11]. Cybercriminals can target weak links in the supply chain to gain access to critical systems or inject malicious code, leading to widespread outages and unauthorized access.

Malware and ransomware: 5. The increasing interconnectivity and interdependencies of Industry 5.0 systems make malware and ransomware attacks a serious threat. Malicious software can compromise industrial control systems, causing chaos or encrypting data, causing downtime, financial loss, and potential security risks [12].

Lack of standardization and security by design: 6. As Industry 5.0 evolves, there may be a lack of standardized security practices and protocols across multiple technologies and vendors. Failure to apply security-by-design principles from the start of development can result in vulnerabilities that can be exploited by online criminals.

Insider attacks: 7. The convergence of people and technology in the Industry 5.0 environment increases the potential for insider attacks. Employees and contractors with special access to critical systems are at risk of inadvertently harming others, compromising data, or disrupting operations.

Denial of service (DoS) attacks: 8. Systems in Industry 5.0 are primarily based on continuous connections and real-time data transmission. DoS attacks targeting these systems can cause significant economic damage by slowing, stopping, or disrupting operations and production.

Industry 5.0 requires a comprehensive strategy to address these cybersecurity risks. This includes strong network security, encryption, access controls, regular updates and patches, employee awareness and training programs, incident response plans, and strong partnerships with technology vendors to ensure security by design. It is included. In the changing environment of Industry 5.0, it is critical to prioritize cybersecurity measures to protect your company's critical assets, data, and infrastructure.

5.2.3 Cybersecurity solutions: striving for secure horizons

A number of existing cybersecurity solutions are available to address the challenges in the cybersecurity arena. However, each solution has limitations and often requires a multi-layered strategy to provide complete protection. Below is a list of typical cybersecurity solutions and their shortcomings.

Firewalls: A firewall acts as a barrier between internal and external networks by monitoring and controlling incoming and outgoing network traffic [13]. However, it may not be successful against advanced threats that use encrypted traffic, exploit application bugs, or bypass standard port-based inspection.

Intrusion detection systems (IDS) and intrusion prevention systems (IPS): IDS and IPS systems monitor network traffic to detect suspicious activity and known attack patterns and take appropriate action [14]. However, it may not stop advanced or zero-day attacks that use evasion strategies to avoid detection.

Antivirus/antimalware software: Antivirus software scans documents and computer systems for known malware signatures and unusual activity. Even if you successfully combat identified threats, it can be difficult to identify new or zero-day malware that has not yet been signed.

A security information and event management (SIEM): This system collects and evaluates security event records from numerous sources to detect potential security incidents. However, SIEM solutions can generate a high volume of alerts, which can make it difficult to distinguish between real threats and false positives and respond effectively to real-time situations [15].

Endpoint protection: Endpoint security solutions include individual device security measures such as host-based firewalls, antivirus software, and behavioral tracking. However, it cannot provide complete protection against advanced threats that use multiple attack channels or techniques.

Encryption: Data is encrypted using encryption technology to prevent unauthorized access. However, encryption alone cannot completely solve the cybersecurity problem as hackers can use system bugs and other methods to gain unauthorized access.

Vulnerability management: Vulnerability management solutions scan networks, systems, and applications to find and prioritize security vulnerabilities. However, they require frequent patching and updating, finding and fixing vulnerabilities can be time-consuming and can leave systems vulnerable while fixes are installed [16].

User education and awareness: User awareness of cybersecurity best practices is critical to mitigating the threat of social engineering, phishing scams, and other human vulnerabilities. However, user awareness and training alone cannot ensure security, as attackers are constantly changing their tactics [17].

It is important to remember that no single cybersecurity solution can provide complete protection against all threats. Organizations can improve their cybersecurity posture and mitigate risk more effectively by implementing a combination of solutions, proactive monitoring, incident response plans, frequent updates and patches, and ongoing employee training. Cybersecurity measures also need to be continually evaluated and adapted to combat new threats and vulnerabilities.

5.2.4 Need for advanced approaches to tackle Industry 5.0 cybersecurity challenges

Industry 5.0 poses certain cybersecurity problems that require state-of-the-art solutions to effectively mitigate them. The integration of complex, interconnected technologies increases the attack surface, requiring sophisticated tactics to find and fix bugs. Furthermore, real-time threat detection and response are essential to manage the massive amounts of data generated by Industry 5.0 systems [18]. The growing threat landscape requires improved solutions that can address complex and persistent cyberthreats. Automated solutions to emerging threats are enabled by cutting-edge techniques such as machine learning, artificial intelligence, and behavioral analytics [19]. In addition, Industry 5.0 comes with concerns about data security, human-machine interface flaws, and insider attacks. Addressing these issues requires sophisticated methods such as user behavior analytics, multi-factor authentication, encryption, and secure data storage protocols. Integrating security into automated systems and ensuring resilience against attacks requires sophisticated technology. These techniques include secure coding practices, secure DevOps, and continuous security testing. Ultimately, state-of-the-art practices include disaster recovery plans, redundant systems, and proactive incident response capabilities to make Industry 5.0 environments more resilient and ensure business continuity [20].

5.2.5 Federated learning: securing cybersecurity with collective intelligence

A machine learning technique called federated learning allows multiple units to train a single model together without sharing raw data. Addressing privacy concerns, enabling collaborative threat detection, and enabling real-time monitoring hold great promise for cybersecurity applications [21]. Organizations can train models locally while maintaining privacy and accessing the combined knowledge of many datasets. Aggregated model updates are continuously applied to the global model, enabling real-time adaptation to new threats [22]. Federated learning drives regulatory compliance and data diversity while improving the security, scalability, and agility of cybersecurity systems. Overall, federated learning provides an effective way to leverage the combined intelligence of multiple organizations without compromising data security. Federated learning revolutionizes threat detection and response by enabling collaboration, real-time monitoring, and rich insights, improving model generalization and increasing the overall effectiveness of cybersecurity systems. can do [23].

5.2.5.1 Privacy concerns in federated learning for cybersecurity

While federated learning has advantages for cybersecurity that protect privacy, there are still privacy concerns that need to be addressed [24]. Here are some important privacy considerations in federated learning for cybersecurity:

Data leakage: During the federated learning process, model updates or aggregated data are exchanged between participating units. When sharing or aggregating models, there is the potential for unintended data leakage [25]. Shared model updates can be used by attackers to extract private data and infer patterns, compromising data security.

Attacks based on membership inference: In federated learning, entities add regional models to the overall model. Attackers may attempt membership inference attacks to see if data for a particular entity was used in the model training process. This can reveal sensitive information about the presence or absence of certain data in the training set, compromising privacy [26].

Model inversion attack: A model inversion attack uses information from the model to extrapolate the details of the training dataset [27]. Attackers can recreate parts of your on-premises data or use updated or aggregated models to discover sensitive characteristics, potentially compromising your privacy.

Differential privacy: Various data protection strategies can be used to mitigate data protection concerns in federated learning [28]. Differential privacy seeks to mathematically ensure that an individual's data cannot be distinguished from or associated with model results [29]. To protect private data and avoid data breaches, federated learning must ensure differentiated data protection.

Adversarial participation: Because federated learning requires the participation of many parties, it is possible for an adversary to update the model maliciously or manipulate the training process intentionally [30].

The integrity and privacy of federated learning systems can be compromised by the involvement of adversaries. Addressing these privacy concerns in cybersecurity, federated learning requires effective privacy protection methods and protocols [31]. Some strategies include enhanced authentication and access control controls to prevent unauthorized participation, implementing differentiated data protection methods, secure aggregation of model updates, encryption, and secure transmission of model changes [32]. Additionally, continued research and collaboration among academia, industry, and policymakers are essential to develop privacy-enhancing technologies and establish federated learning best practices in cybersecurity while protecting sensitive data.

5.2.5.2 Challenges of implementing federated learning in Industry 5.0

Implementing federated learning in the context of Industry 5.0 presents various challenges. Federated learning fosters collaboration and offers benefits in terms of data protection, but overcoming these challenges is essential for a successful implementation [33]. Here are the main points in applying federated learning in Industry 5.0:

Data heterogeneity: Industry 5.0 allows different companies to use different data formats, sources, and quality levels [34]. Integrating and harmonizing these heterogeneous datasets to train a single common model can be difficult and time consuming [35]. To successfully address these issues, data preprocessing and standardization solutions must be created.

Network connectivity and bandwidth: Distributed systems, edge devices, and remote locations are commonplace in the context of Industry 5.0 [36]. Ensuring sufficient bandwidth for reliable network access and data transfer during the federated learning process can be difficult. The timely exchange of model updates and the overall effectiveness of federated learning can be adversely affected by limited or inconsistent connectivity [37].

Scalability and resource constraints: Industry 5.0 deployments are massive and involve a wide variety of devices and systems. Coordinating the training and aggregation process across a large number of units, each with limited computational resources, can be difficult. To ensure scalability, you must create effective procedures for resource allocation, task management, and model synchronization.

Security and trust: For federated learning to work, companies need to collaborate and share model changes. It is important to build trust among participating organizations and ensure the safety and integrity of the federated learning process. Strong authentication, access control, and encryption techniques must be implemented to avoid unauthorized access, data breaches, and malicious attacks throughout the collaborative learning process.

Regulatory and compliance requirements: Industry 5.0 operates in regulated industries where privacy and compliance with industry standards are critical. Implementing federated learning while complying with legal and regulatory frameworks such as data protection regulations can be challenging. It is important that federated learning processes comply with legal requirements and protect personal data.

Data imbalance and bias: In federated learning, data can be unevenly distributed across entities, which can lead to data imbalance and bias in the overall model [38]. Addressing data imbalance and mitigating bias when aggregating models is difficult and requires careful algorithm design and monitoring.

Collaborative governance and coordination: Industry 5.0 involves a wide range of stakeholders including businesses, technology companies and government agencies. Establishing a collaborative governance model and coordinating efforts by various stakeholders to draft standards, protocols and rules for federated learning in Industry 5.0 can be difficult and time-consuming.

Overcoming these obstacles will require industry, academia, and policymakers to work together to create standardized frameworks, algorithms, and protocols for federated learning in Industry 5.0. Addressing data heterogeneity, network limitations, scalability, security, compliance, debiasing, and governance issues is critical to successfully adopting and deploying federated learning in Industry 5.0 scenarios.

5.3 Applications of federated learning in cybersecurity

Federated learning (FL) has the potential to bring significant benefits to cybersecurity in Industry 5.0. Here are some of the applications of using federated learning in industry:

5.3.1 Intrusion detection systems (IDS)—network attack detection and prevention

IDS have become a vital line of defense against network threats in the field of cybersecurity. FL, a cutting-edge method that enables cooperative training of IDS models across different organizations or network nodes, is one of the most recent developments in this area. FL protects data privacy while greatly enhancing precision and efficacy by letting each node train a local IDS model using its own network traffic data and then pooling the model updates to produce a thorough global IDS model. Campos *et al.* [39] set out on a mission to exploit the potential of FL for intrusion detection. In this research study, the authors carefully examine the benefits and difficulties of using FL approaches for intrusion detection in IoT contexts. The researchers explain important issues relating to data privacy and cover many components of the evaluation procedure, offering performance evaluation of FL-enabled intrusion detection systems. The crucial scalability problems in extensive IoT installations are also addressed. The researchers investigate a specialized method using a multiclass classifier for identifying various attack types in order to gauge the practicality of FL-enabled IDS in IoT contexts. Their assessment is based on three different settings that were obtained via splitting the ToN_IoT dataset.

The authors of the paper [40] develop a novel IDS system that is especially made to safeguard agricultural IoT systems. The idea of local learning, which preserves data privacy, is at the heart of FELIDS. IoT devices work together to enhance detection models without compromising raw data by exchanging model changes with an aggregation server. FELIDS distinguishes out by outperforming traditional centralized machine learning techniques by utilizing a trifecta of deep learning classifiers: deep neural networks, convolutional neural networks, and recurrent neural networks. The study's conclusions show that FELIDS not only provides exceptional security for the data privacy of IoT devices but also achieves the best level of attack detection accuracy. Finally, a fascinating idea in the framework of Industry 5.0, a futuristic concept that seeks to build an industrial ecosystem that is hyper-connected and data-driven, is brought to light. The paper [41] provides a novel approach that makes use of state-of-the-art elements like fully connected layers, a softmax classifier, bidirectional long short-term memory networks (BiLSTM), bidirectional-gated recurrent unit (Bi-GRU), and complexities and challenges of intrusion detection in Industry 5.0. As a result of the integrated strategy's improved intrusion detection capabilities, Industry 5.0's productivity and efficiency are protected against sophisticated cyberattacks.

5.3.2 Threat intelligence sharing in federated ecosystems

The significance of AI-based systems in Industry 5.0 is explored by [42], especially in the context of the Internet of Things (IoT). Industry 5.0 shows how well intelligent systems and people interact, providing precise production automation with critical thinking abilities. The paradigm also enables quick and inexpensive organizational changes without significant expenditures. The development of Internet of Things (IoT) ecosystems, where networked devices may gather and send data without human involvement, is a result of recent advances in smart devices, wireless communication, and sensor nodes. IoT devices make life more convenient and simple by allowing users to access information even from faraway locations and enabling limitless data reporting. When pre-processing and pertinent information extraction from raw sensed data take place, these devices employ AI-based algorithms for information inference.

5.3.3 Malware detection and prevention/classification

The difficulties of protecting billions of open IoT devices from malware attacks and the demand for effective detection methods are explored. To overcome these issues, cutting-edge technologies like blockchain and federated learning are being implemented. An Android malware detection method called the privacy-preserving federated learning (PPFL) system is discussed [43]. This solution makes it possible for mobile devices to jointly train a classifier without disclosing confidential information, guaranteeing the privacy of app data and locally developed models. The first Android malware detection solution based on privacy-preserving federated learning, experimental findings demonstrate that the PPFL classifier beats a centralized training method. The possibility of federated learning for IoT malware detection is explored in another study effort [44], along with the research's inherent security problems. The suggested approach for identifying malware impacting IoT devices while protecting participant privacy exhibits encouraging results. The method, nevertheless, has trouble responding to hostile attacks. A semi-supervised federated IoT malware detection framework called FedMalDE is introduced [45]. The system reduces privacy issues associated with user data collection by using knowledge transfer techniques to infer labels for user records that are not labeled.

In order to effectively capture various dangerous behaviors, it uses a subgraph aggregated capsule network (SACN), showcasing the efficacy, privacy, and durability of FedMalDE in identifying IoT malware. Furthermore, an overview of integrating FL with IoT is presented [46]. Without disclosing user data, FL's decentralized method enables on-device training and parameter interchange. It goes through FL's uses, research roadblocks, and next plans for improving malware detection in Industry 5.0. This section emphasizes the importance of implementing cutting-edge strategies like federated learning to solve security issues with IoT networks and devices. Federated learning enhances malware detection's accuracy and robustness by working together on a variety of datasets, making it a useful strategy for protecting against emerging threats in Industry 5.0.

5.3.4 Anomaly detection in Industrial Internet of Things (IIoT) systems

The research papers that explore the application of federated learning for anomaly detection in various contexts within the realm of Internet of Things (IoT) and Industrial Internet of Things (IIoT) are discussed in this section. A reliable anomaly detection strategy for IIoT using federated learning is introduced [47]. Effective detection systems are required because anomalies in IIoT devices may represent security and privacy risks. The suggested approach uses deep reinforcement learning (DRL) taught local models in federated learning to create a global anomaly detection model. Due to the fact that FL does not require local datasets, this strategy guarantees privacy protection. The detection accuracy is increased by including the degree of privacy leakage and the action relation in the anomaly detection design. The validation studies demonstrate high throughput, low latency, and precise anomaly detection, which makes it appropriate for a variety of IIoT situations. In order to address privacy issues, a federated learning-based anomaly detection strategy for IoT security is developed [48]. This system preserves data locally on IoT devices and only shares learned weights with the central server. The method uses ensemblers to combine updates from several sources and federated training cycles on gated recurrent units (GRUs) models to maximize the accuracy of the overall machine learning (ML) model. The results of the experiments show that the method is more effective than traditional/centralized machine learning versions at protecting user data privacy and attaining the highest level of accuracy in threat detection for IoT networks.

Architecture for training unsupervised models for network intrusion detection in large, distributed IoT and IIoT deployments is presented [49]. By utilizing federated learning, the architecture enables peer-to-peer collaborative training, hence minimizing difficulties with isolation and network overhead. To address heterogeneity issues in federated learning situations, an unsupervised device clustering technique is incorporated into the pipeline. A testbed containing several simulated IoT/IIoT devices, attackers, and a complicated network topology is used to assess the architecture. The Mirai malware lifecycle and other red-teaming tools that target the simulated devices are used to test the anomaly detection algorithms against actual attacks. In Industry 5.0 systems, federated learning may be used for anomaly detection. Organizations may spot outliers in behavior in real time by training local models on edge devices or local servers. These abnormalities could be signs of hostile or future cyberattacks, allowing for preemptive reaction and mitigation.

5.3.5 Privacy-preserving cybersecurity analysis with federated learning

Federated learning enables organizations to analyze user behavior without compromising privacy. By training models locally on edge devices or servers, organizations can detect anomalies in user behavior and identify potential insider threats or suspicious activities. This approach preserves individual privacy while maintaining a secure environment. In the context of edge-based machine learning, the research article [50] examines the idea of FL and its importance in resolving data privacy and cyber security issues. An overview of the issues with data privacy and cyber security while utilizing centralized classical machine learning methods, particularly in edge computing contexts, is covered. It presents federated learning, a cutting-edge decentralized method that allows collaborative model construction and on-device training without disclosing raw data to central servers. The article discusses FL's possible uses in edge-based machine learning situations with a focus on its use in Industry 4.0 and Industry 5.0 environments.

In conclusion, federated learning has many advantages for the Industry 5.0 cybersecurity landscape, including collaborative threat intelligence, privacy-preserving data sharing, real-time response, robust and diverse models, scalability, resilience to adversarial attacks, and regulatory compliance. Organizations may improve their cybersecurity posture while embracing the cooperation and privacy protection concepts inherent in Industry 5.0 by utilizing federated learning.

5.4 Federated learning frameworks and algorithms for cybersecurity

5.4.1 Overview of existing frameworks

An overview of some well-known cybersecurity frameworks is provided below:

NIST cybersecurity framework (CSF): The NIST CSF is a comprehensive set of guidelines, best practices, and standards for managing and enhancing an organization's cybersecurity risk management process [51]. Developed by the National Institute of Standards and Technology (NIST). It has five main functions: identification, protection, detection, response, and recovery.

ISO/IEC 27001: This well-known Information Security Management System (ISMS) standard was jointly developed by the International Organization for Standardization (ISO) and the International Electrotechnical Commission (IEC). ISO/IEC 27001 provides a systematic method for identifying, managing, and mitigating information security risks within an organization [52].

CIS controls (previously known as SANS critical security controls): Created by the Center for Internet Security (CIS), these controls provide a prioritized list of actions to strengthen your organization's cybersecurity posture. Controls focus on basic security precautions and are updated regularly to reflect new threats.

NIST Special Publication 800-53: NIST's SP 800-53 is another publication that provides an extensive list of security and privacy regulations for government information systems and organizations. Both government and non-government sectors use it extensively.

MITRE ATT&CK (adversarial tactics, techniques, and common knowledge): Developed by the MITRE Corporation, this framework aims to understand and characterize the techniques and strategies used by threat actors in cyberattacks

[53]. It provides detailed information on the many attack vectors, tactics, techniques, and procedures (TTPs) employed by attackers.

COBIT (Control objectives for information and related technologies): COBIT is an IT governance framework that provides a comprehensive set of controls and practices for managing information and technology [54]. COBIT was created by ISACA (Information Systems Audit and Control Association).

OWASP (Open Web Application Security Project): The OWASP framework focuses on application security and provides tools and best practices to help organizations protect their web applications and APIs from common vulnerabilities.

SANS security awareness: To educate employees and users about cybersecurity best practices and potential threats, SANS provides a set of security awareness resources and frameworks.

Cyber kill chain: Originally developed by Lockheed Martin, Cyber kill Chain is a framework that describes the different stages of a cyber attack [55]. This paradigm enables organizations to detect and stop attacks at various points in their lifecycle.

These frameworks provide organizations with guidance on how to strengthen their cybersecurity defenses and align their efforts with widely accepted industry best practices. However, it is important to choose and modify the framework that best suits your organization's specific needs and risk profile. Additionally, maintaining strong protection against future attacks requires staying up-to-date with the changing threat landscape and new innovations in cybersecurity.

5.4.2 Secure aggregation techniques

A "secure aggregation technique" in the field of cybersecurity is a technique that allows the collection and analysis of sensitive data from many sources while protecting the privacy and confidentiality of individual contributors [56]. These methods are particularly important in situations where, for cybersecurity reasons, companies and other parties need to collaborate and share data without disclosing personal information about the source. Here are some common safe aggregation methods.

Homomorphic encryption: This encryption technique allows computations to be performed directly on the encrypted material without first having to decrypt the encrypted material. This technology allows users to encrypt their data before sharing it with others, thus enabling secure data aggregation. Encrypted data is subject to a centralized process, and only users with appropriate privileges can decrypt the results.

Secure multi-party computation (SMPC): This cryptographic protocol allows many parties to jointly compute a function on private inputs without disclosing information about the inputs other than the output [57]. Participants can communicate data via her SMPC protocol as part of secure data aggregation, and the system can calculate aggregated statistics and results without exposing specific data points.

Differential privacy: Before aggregating data, differential privacy introduces noise and random interference to protect user privacy. This prevents the identification of specific individual data points while keeping the aggregate results statistically reliable [58]. Many data protection technologies can be used for secure data aggregation in situations such as sharing threat intelligence or reporting cybersecurity incidents.

Federated learning: A machine learning technique known as federated learning allows multiple parties to train machine learning models together without sharing raw data. Models are trained locally using each participant's data, and only model updates or history are sent to a central server. This method is commonly used in cybersecurity applications to allow organizations to work together to improve their threat detection models without exposing private information.

Secure aggregation protocols: A number of secure aggregation protocols have been proposed in the research community to enable secure data aggregation. These logs are created to reduce the risk of disclosure or data leakage while ensuring that personal data submissions are protected and efficiently aggregated [4].

Secure summation: Under certain circumstances, the safe addition of individual data points can serve as a safe data aggregation method. Strategies such as secure multiparty summation (SMS) and secure aggregation protocols (SAPs) can be used for this.

It is important to keep in mind that choosing the best secure aggregation method depends on the specific use case, the type of data collected, the level of data protection needed, and the computing resources available. It is important to consult cryptography and data protection experts to ensure that the design and implementation of secure aggregation methods are resistant to potential attacks.

5.4.3 Federated learning algorithms for cybersecurity

A machine learning technique called "federated learning" allows multiple entities to train a single model together without sharing raw data. This decentralized strategy is especially important because privacy and confidentiality are very important in cybersecurity. These federated learning approaches and algorithms are commonly used in cybersecurity.

Federated averaging: An important method in federated learning is federated averaging. This involves a large number of clients (devices or entities) training local models based on individual data sets and periodically reporting updates to a central server [59]. Updates are aggregated into a global model by the server and returned to the client. This iterative process continues until convergence.

Secure aggregation: Federated learning uses a privacy-preserving technique, secure aggregation, to protect sensitive data during the model aggregation process. Updates sent from clients to a central server are reliably aggregated and encrypted to protect privacy. Secure aggregation can be achieved using methods such as secure multi-party computation (MPC) and homomorphic encryption [60].

Differential privacy: Federated learning in cybersecurity can take advantage of privacy-enhancing technology, differential privacy. This ensures that private customer data is not exposed during the training process. By introducing noise or using statistical approaches, differential privacy helps protect participant privacy while still providing useful aggregated results [61].

Federated transfer learning: This method combines transfer learning and federated learning strategies. A model trained for one task or domain can be improved for another related task or domain using transfer learning. Federated transfer learning in the context of cybersecurity allows models to learn from data collected across the organization while leveraging expertise acquired in previous tasks and domains [62].

Federated meta-learning: By allowing models to quickly adapt to new clients and tasks, Federated Meta-Learning aims to improve the efficiency and effectiveness of federated learning. The number of training iterations required for convergence is reduced by using a meta-learning approach to learn initialization or prior knowledge that can be transferred to new clients [63].

These are examples of federated learning algorithms and strategies used in cybersecurity to protect sensitive information while leveraging the pooled knowledge of multiple groups. It is important to keep in mind that the topic of federated learning is still evolving, and new improvements and algorithms may be developed in the future.

5.4.4 Real-time cybersecurity monitoring with federated learning

Federated learning is a machine learning approach that allows multiple entities to train a common model together without sharing the original data. It can be applied to real-time cybersecurity monitoring to enhance threat detection while maintaining data confidentiality. Federated learning can help with real-time cybersecurity monitoring using the following methods:

Data privacy: In the cyber security space, companies often have sensitive data that they cannot or do not want to disclose due to data protection issues or regulatory restrictions. These organizations can use federated learning to train models based on their own on-premises data without sharing it with other organizations [64]. Confidentiality of sensitive data is maintained through model updates or simple exchange of aggregated data.

Distributed data and knowledge: Multiple entities, such as separate organizations and devices, maintain their own local datasets that capture the unique characteristics of cybersecurity environments in a federated learning environment. These organizations use their own local data to train their models, making it easier to discover diverse knowledge and insights from different perspectives.

Real-time threat detection: In a real-time cybersecurity monitoring scenario, each participant continuously monitors their network or system for potential threats and anomalies. Federated learning enables collective detection of new threats and patterns quickly in real time [65].

Rapid model iterations: Traditional centralized machine learning models require data collection and centralized processing, which can be slow and slow to respond to emerging threats. Federated learning allows entities to train models autonomously, enabling fast iterations and updates without creating a central bottleneck.

Adaptability and robustness: Federated learning allows models to adapt to local conditions and maintain their effectiveness in different environments. Different entities can train models based on specific network configurations, device categories, and geographic locations, allowing global models to address a wider variety of cybersecurity scenarios [66].

Enhanced security: Federated learning greatly reduces the risks associated with sharing sensitive data. Organizations can keep data within the confines of their network, limiting exposure to external threats and data breaches. Additionally, model updates are securely transmitted and encrypted to protect data privacy.

Overall, federated learning offers a collaborative and privacy-preserving approach to real-time cybersecurity monitoring. It combines the collective knowledge and insights of many organizations while preserving privacy, enabling faster threat detection, increased accuracy, and adaptability in a rapidly evolving cybersecurity environment.

5.5 Future directions and challenges

In Industry 5.0, data sources may differ significantly in terms of volumes, format, structure, and quality. Also, industrial environments may have limited network bandwidth and latency constraints. Building trust and establishing collaborative frameworks will be essential for successful implementation. Adhering to regional and industry-specific regulations will be necessary to navigate legal complexities. Potential vulnerabilities in the communication channels must be addressed to prevent data breaches or model poisoning attacks. Federated learning algorithms must be designed to handle efficiently the above-mentioned challenges. Addressing these challenges and capitalizing on the future directions will drive the adoption of federated learning in Industry 5.0, leading to a more secure and resilient industrial ecosystem. Future directions for federated learning for cybersecurity in Industry 5.0 include the following: (i) using federated learning to improve IoT security; (ii) creating adaptive security mechanisms for continuous learning; (iii) sharing threat intelligence through secure federated learning collaborations; (iv) protecting privacy with privacy-enhancing methods; (v) examining hybrid learning approaches for improved model performance; (vi) promoting cross-industry collaboration. These directions aim to address the unique challenges of Industry 5.0 and foster more effective and resilient cybersecurity measures.

5.6 Conclusion

Federated learning's decentralized and privacy-preserving approach revolutionizes machine learning applications in multiple domains while addressing data privacy, security, and efficiency issues. Industry 5.0 can proactively address evolving cyberthreats while protecting privacy and ownership rights through the power of distributed learning. The convergence of Federated Learning and Industry 5.0 will revolutionize cybersecurity while improving operational efficiency and productivity. Federated learning will allow the industry to coordinate defense strategies by sharing knowledge from distributed data sources as cyberattacks become more complex and interconnected. This collaborative approach will strengthen the industry's resilience to cyberthreats and increase intelligence and adaptability. Federated learning enables Industry 5.0 to build systems to counter cyberattackers and prepare a future of innovations. Our future research direction is to focus on reviewing multiple adversarial attacks to ensure the reliability and security of federated learning models that will shape a secure and interconnected Industry 5.0.

References

[1] Jie Xu, Benjamin S Glicksberg, Chang Su, Peter Walker, Jiang Bian, and Fei Wang. Federated learning for healthcare informatics. *Journal of Healthcare Informatics Research*, 5:1–19, 2021.

[2] Xiaofei Wang, Yiwen Han, Chenyang Wang, Qiyang Zhao, Xu Chen, and Min Chen. In-edge AI: Intelligentizing mobile edge computing, caching and communication by federated learning. *IEEE Network*, 33(5):156–165, 2019.

[3] Zhou Su, Yuntao Wang, Tom H Luan, *et al.* Secure and efficient federated learning for smart grid with edge-cloud collaboration. *IEEE Transactions on Industrial Informatics*, 18(2):1333–1344, 2021.

[4] Mamoun Alazab, Swarna Priya RM, M Parimala, Praveen Kumar Reddy Maddikunta, Thippa Reddy Gadekallu, and Quoc-Viet Pham. Federated learning for cybersecurity: Concepts, challenges, and future directions. *IEEE Transactions on Industrial Informatics*, 18(5):3501–3509, 2021.

[5] Joel Alves, Tânia M Lima, and Pedro D Gaspar. Is industry 5.0 a human-centred approach? A systematic review. *Processes*, 11(1):193, 2023.

[6] Shohin Aheleroff, Huiyue Huang, Xun Xu, and Ray Y Zhong. Toward sustainability and resilience with industry 4.0 and industry 5.0. *Frontiers in Manufacturing Technology*, 2:951643, 2022.

[7] Breda Walsh Shanahan and John Organ. Harnessing the benefits of micro credentials for industry 4.0 and 5.0: Skills training and lifelong learning. *IFAC-PapersOnLine*, 55(39):82–87, 2022.

[8] Paula Fraga-Lamas, Sérgio Ivan Lopes, and Tiago M Fernández-Caramés. Green IoT and edge AI as key technological enablers for a sustainable digital transition towards a smart circular economy: An industry 5.0 use case. *Sensors*, 21(17):5745, 2021.

[9] Daniel Paschek, Caius-Tudor Luminosu, and Elif Ocakci. Industry 5.0 challenges and perspectives for manufacturing systems in the society 5.0. *Sustainability and Innovation in Manufacturing Enterprises: Indicators, Models and Assessment for Industry 5.0*, pages 17–63, 2022.

[10] Diptiben Ghelani, Tan Kian Hua, and Surendra Kumar Reddy Koduru. Cyber security threats, vulnerabilities, and security solutions models in banking. *Authorea Preprints*, 2022.

[11] Huai-Wei Lo. A data-driven decision support system for sustainable supplier evaluation in the industry 5.0 era: A case study for medical equipment manufacturing. *Advanced Engineering Informatics*, 56:101998, 2023.

[12] Rami Ahmad, Raniyah Wazirali, and Tarik Abu-Ain. Machine learning for wireless sensor networks security: An overview of challenges and issues. *Sensors*, 22(13):4730, 2022.

[13] Ashutosh Phatak, Ruturaj Kadikar, K Vijayan, and B Amutha. Performance analysis of firewall based on SDN and openflow. In *2018 International Conference on Communication and Signal Processing (ICCSP)*, pages 0611–0615. IEEE, 2018.

[14] PLS Jayalaxmi, Rahul Saha, Gulshan Kumar, Mauro Conti, and Tai-Hoon Kim. Machine and deep learning solutions for intrusion detection and prevention in IoTs: A survey. *IEEE Access*, 2022.

[15] Mohd Azmi Bin Mustafa Sulaiman, Mohammad Adib Khairuddin, Mohd Rizal Mohd Isa, Mohd Nazri Ismail, Mohd Afizi Mohd Shukran, and Aznida Abu Bakar Sajak. Siem network behaviour monitoring framework using deep learning approach for campus network infrastructure. *International Journal of Electrical and Computer Engineering Systems*, (Special Issue):9–21, 2021.

[16] Steve Furnell. Vulnerability management: not a patch on where we should be? *Network Security*, 2016(4):5–9, 2016.

[17] Hussain Aldawood and Geoffrey Skinner. Analysis and findings of social engineering industry experts explorative interviews: Perspectives on measures, tools, and solutions. *IEEE Access*, 8:67321–67329, 2020.

[18] Praveen Kumar Reddy Maddikunta, Quoc-Viet Pham, B Prabadevi, *et al.* Industry 5.0: A survey on enabling technologies and potential applications. *Journal of Industrial Information Integration*, 26:100257, 2022.

[19] Nisreen Ameen, Sameer Hosany, and Ali Tarhini. Consumer interaction with cutting-edge technologies: Implications for future research. *Computers in Human Behavior*, 120:106761, 2021.

[20] Dmitry Ivanov. The industry 5.0 framework: Viability-based integration of the resilience, sustainability, and human-centricity perspectives. *International Journal of Production Research*, 61(5):1683–1695, 2023.

[21] Zhiyan Chen, Jinxin Liu, Yu Shen, *et al.* Machine learning-enabled IoT security: Open issues and challenges under advanced persistent threats. *ACM Computing Surveys*, 55(5):1–37, 2022.

[22] Gautam Srivastava, Rutvij H Jhaveri, Sweta Bhattacharya, *et al.* Xai for cybersecurity: State of the art, challenges, open issues and future directions. arXiv preprint arXiv:2206.03585, 2022.

[23] William Grant Hatcher and Wei Yu. A survey of deep learning: Platforms, applications and emerging research trends. *IEEE Access*, 6:24411–24432, 2018.

[24] Gokul Yenduri, Gautam Srivastava, Praveen Kumar Reddy Maddikunta, *et al.* Generative pre-trained transformer: A comprehensive review on enabling technologies, potential applications, emerging challenges, and future directions. arXiv preprint arXiv:2305.10435, 2023.

[25] Yunlong Lu, Xiaohong Huang, Yueyue Dai, Sabita Maharjan, and Yan Zhang. Blockchain and federated learning for privacy-preserved data sharing in industrial IoT. *IEEE Transactions on Industrial Informatics*, 16(6):4177–4186, 2019.

[26] Gautam Srivastava, Dasaratha Rami Reddy K, Gokul Yenduri, *et al.* Federated learning enabled edge computing security for internet of medical things: Concepts, challenges and open issues. In *Security and Risk Analysis for Intelligent Edge Computing*, pages 67–89. Springer, 2023.

[27] Fan Mo, Ali Shahin Shamsabadi, Kleomenis Katevas, *et al.* Darknetz: towards model privacy at the edge using trusted execution environments. In *Proceedings of the 18th International Conference on Mobile Systems, Applications, and Services*, pages 161–174, 2020.

[28] Swarna Priya Ramu, Gautam Srivastava, Rajeswari Chengoden, *et al.* The metaverse for cognitive health: A paradigm shift. *IEEE Consumer Electronics Magazine*, 2023.

[29] Zhanglong Ji, Zachary C Lipton, and Charles Elkan. Differential privacy and machine learning: A survey and review. arXiv preprint arXiv:1412.7584, 2014.

[30] Lingjuan Lyu, Han Yu, and Qiang Yang. Threats to federated learning: A survey. arXiv preprint arXiv:2003.02133, 2020.

[31] Sharnil Pandya, Gautam Srivastava, Rutvij Jhaveri, *et al.* Federated learning for smart cities: A comprehensive survey. *Sustainable Energy Technologies and Assessments*, 55:102987, 2023.

[32] Sawsan AbdulRahman, Hanine Tout, Hakima Ould-Slimane, Azzam Mourad, Chamseddine Talhi, and Mohsen Guizani. A survey on federated learning: The journey from centralized to distributed on-site learning and beyond. *IEEE Internet of Things Journal*, 8(7):5476–5497, 2020.

[33] Ahmad Hammoud, Hadi Otrok, Azzam Mourad, and Zbigniew Dziong. On demand fog federations for horizontal federated learning in IoV. *IEEE Transactions on Network and Service Management*, 19(3):3062–3075, 2022.

[34] Ha-Vu Tran, Georges Kaddoum, Hany Elgala, Chadi Abou-Rjeily, and Hemani Kaushal. Lightwave power transfer for federated learning-based wireless networks. *IEEE Communications Letters*, 24(7):1472–1476, 2020.

[35] Catherine Bjerre Collin, Tom Gebhardt, Martin Golebiewski, *et al.* Computational models for clinical applications in personalized medicine—guidelines and recommendations for data integration and model validation. *Journal of Personalized Medicine*, 12(2):166, 2022.

[36] Sawsan Abdul Rahman, Hanine Tout, Chamseddine Talhi, and Azzam Mourad. Internet of things intrusion detection: Centralized, on-device, or federated learning? *IEEE Network*, 34(6):310–317, 2020.

[37] Hassaan Malik, Tayyaba Anees, Ahmad Naeem, Rizwan Ali Naqvi, and Woong-Kee Loh. Blockchain-federated and deep-learning-based ensembling of capsule network with incremental extreme learning machines for classification of covid-19 using CT scans. *Bioengineering*, 10(2):203, 2023.

[38] Chenhao Xu, Youyang Qu, Yong Xiang, and Longxiang Gao. Asynchronous federated learning on heterogeneous devices: A survey. arXiv preprint arXiv:2109.04269, 2021.

[39] Enrique Mármol Campos, Pablo Fernández Saura, Aurora González-Vidal, *et al.* Evaluating federated learning for intrusion detection in internet of things: Review and challenges. *Computer Networks*, 203:108661, 2022.

[40] Othmane Friha, Mohamed Amine Ferrag, Lei Shu, *et al.* Felids: Federated learning-based intrusion detection system for agricultural internet of things. *Journal of Parallel and Distributed Computing*, 165:17–31, 2022.

[41] Danish Javeed, Tianhan Gao, Prabhat Kumar, and Alireza Jolfaei. An explainable and resilient intrusion detection system for industry 5.0. *IEEE Transactions on Consumer Electronics*, 70(1):1342–1350, 2023.

[42] Bhanu Chander, Souvik Pal, Debashis De, and Rajkumar Buyya. Artificial intelligence-based internet of things for industry 5.0. *Artificial Intelligence-based Internet of Things Systems*, pages 3–45, 2022.
[43] Ruei-Hau Hsu, Yi-Cheng Wang, Chun-I Fan, *et al.* A privacy-preserving federated learning system for android malware detection based on edge computing. In *2020 15th Asia Joint Conference on Information Security (AsiaJCIS)*, pages 128–136. IEEE, 2020.
[44] Valerian Rey, Pedro Miguel Sánchez Sánchez, Alberto Huertas Celdrán, and Gérôme Bovet. Federated learning for malware detection in iot devices. *Computer Networks*, 204:108693, 2022.
[45] Xinjun Pei, Xiaoheng Deng, Shengwei Tian, Lan Zhang, and Kaiping Xue. A knowledge transfer-based semi-supervised federated learning for IoT malware detection. *IEEE Transactions on Dependable and Secure Computing*, 2022.
[46] Madumitha Venkatasubramanian, Arash Habibi Lashkari, and Saqib Hakak. IoT malware analysis using federated learning: A comprehensive survey. *IEEE Access*, 2023.
[47] Xiaoding Wang, Sahil Garg, Hui Lin, *et al.* Toward accurate anomaly detection in industrial internet of things using hierarchical federated learning. *IEEE Internet of Things Journal*, 9(10):7110–7119, 2021.
[48] Viraaji Mothukuri, Prachi Khare, Reza M Parizi, Seyedamin Pouriyeh, Ali Dehghantanha, and Gautam Srivastava. Federated-learning-based anomaly detection for IoT security attacks. *IEEE Internet of Things Journal*, 9(4):2545–2554, 2021.
[49] Xabier Sáez-de Cámara, Jose Luis Flores, Cristóbal Arellano, Aitor Urbieta, and Urko Zurutuza. Clustered federated learning architecture for network anomaly detection in large scale heterogeneous IoT networks. *Computers & Security*, 131:103299, 2023.
[50] Jonathan White and Phil Legg. Federated learning: Data privacy and cyber security in edge-based machine learning. In *Data Protection in a Post-Pandemic Society: Laws, Regulations, Best Practices and Recent Solutions*, pages 169–193. Springer, 2023.
[51] Diah Sulistyowati, Fitri Handayani, and Yohan Suryanto. Comparative analysis and design of cybersecurity maturity assessment methodology using NIST CSF, COBIT, ISO/IEC 27002 and PCI DSS. *JOIV: International Journal on Informatics Visualization*, 4(4):225–230, 2020.
[52] Awni Itradat, Sari Sultan, Maram Al-Junaidi, Rawa' Qaffaf, Feda' Mashal, and Fatima Daas. Developing an ISO27001 information security management system for an educational institute: Hashemite university as a case study. *Jordan Journal of Mechanical & Industrial Engineering*, 8(2), 2014.
[53] Wiem Tounsi and Helmi Rais. A survey on technical threat intelligence in the age of sophisticated cyber attacks. *Computers & security*, 72:212–233, 2018.
[54] Steven De Haes, Wim Van Grembergen, Anant Joshi, *et al.* Cobit as a framework for enterprise governance of it. *Enterprise Governance of Information*

Technology: Achieving Alignment and Value in Digital Organizations, pages 125–162, 2020.

[55] Aaron Weathersby and Mark Washington. Extracting network based attack narratives through use of the cyber kill chain: A replication study. *It-Information Technology*, 64(1–2):29–42, 2022.

[56] Al-Huthaifi Rasha, Tianrui Li, Wei Huang, Jin Gu, and Chongshou Li. Federated learning in smart cities: Privacy and security survey. *Information Sciences*, 2023.

[57] Chuan Zhao, Shengnan Zhao, Minghao Zhao, *et al*. Secure multi-party computation: theory, practice and applications. *Information Sciences*, 476:357–372, 2019.

[58] Laraib Javed, Adeel Anjum, Bello Musa Yakubu, Majid Iqbal, Syed Atif Moqurrab, and Gautam Srivastava. Sharechain: Blockchain-enabled model for sharing patient data using federated learning and differential privacy. *Expert Systems*, 40(5):e13131, 2023.

[59] Omar Abdel Wahab, Azzam Mourad, Hadi Otrok, and Tarik Taleb. Federated machine learning: Survey, multi-level classification, desirable criteria and future directions in communication and networking systems. *IEEE Communications Surveys & Tutorials*, 23(2):1342–1397, 2021.

[60] Renuga Kanagavelu, Zengxiang Li, Juniarto Samsudin, *et al*. Two-phase multi-party computation enabled privacy-preserving federated learning. In *2020 20th IEEE/ACM International Symposium on Cluster, Cloud and Internet Computing (CCGRID)*, pages 410–419. IEEE, 2020.

[61] Jong Wook Kim, Kennedy Edemacu, Jong Seon Kim, Yon Dohn Chung, and Beakcheol Jang. A survey of differential privacy-based techniques and their applicability to location-based services. *Computers & Security*, 111:102464, 2021.

[62] Tarek Berghout, Toufik Bentrcia, Mohamed Amine Ferrag, and Mohamed Benbouzid. A heterogeneous federated transfer learning approach with extreme aggregation and speed. *Mathematics*, 10(19):3528, 2022.

[63] Sen Lin, Guang Yang, and Junshan Zhang. A collaborative learning framework via federated meta-learning. In *2020 IEEE 40th International Conference on Distributed Computing Systems (ICDCS)*, pages 289–299. IEEE, 2020.

[64] Christian Fachola, Agustín Tornaría, Paola Bermolen, Germán Capdehourat, Lorena Etcheverry, and María Inés Fariello. Federated learning for data analytics in education. *Data*, 8(2):43, 2023.

[65] Fahad Ahmed KhoKhar, Jamal Hussain Shah, Muhammad Attique Khan, Muhammad Sharif, Usman Tariq, and Seifedine Kadry. A review on federated learning towards image processing. *Computers and Electrical Engineering*, 99:107818, 2022.

[66] Bimal Ghimire and Danda B Rawat. Recent advances on federated learning for cybersecurity and cybersecurity for federated learning for internet of things. *IEEE Internet of Things Journal*, 9(11):8229–8249, 2022.

Chapter 6
Cybersecurity with blockchain for digital twins

Rutvij H. Jhaveri[1] and Ashish Patel[2]

Abstract

A digital twin is an artificial intelligence (AI), machine learning (ML), and Internet of things (IoT)-based digital representation of a physical object, system, or process. Many industries, including medicine, engineering, transportation, aerospace, smart cities, farming, and industry, can benefit significantly from using digital twins. However, with the rise in cyber-attacks and data breaches, safeguarding digital twins has become a top priority. Researchers have proposed using blockchain technology to increase digital twin security to address these challenges. Secure authentication, data privacy, provenance tracking, distributed data storage, interoperability, and an immutable audit trail are just ways blockchain technology improves digital twins. This chapter discusses the current state of blockchain technology's potential to enhance digital twin security in various industries and the research difficulties that lie ahead. The research highlights many significant hurdles that need to be cleared before blockchain-based solutions for digital twin security can be widely adopted.

Keywords: Cyber-attack, Federated learning, Industrial safety, Machine learning, Security

6.1 Introduction

Digital twins are computer models created to impersonate the performance of real-world physical objects, processes, or systems, as shown in Figure 6.1. Sensors, 3D modeling programs, and AI algorithms are only some of the tools used to construct these digital twins. They are finding more and more applications in many fields, including production, medicine, transportation, and building. Due to technological developments and the demand for improved efficiency and cost-effectiveness, the concept of digital twins has acquired substantial support during the past several years.

[1]Department of Computer Science and Engineering, School of Technology, Pandit Deendayal Energy University, India
[2]Department of Computer Engineering, SVM Institute of Technology, India

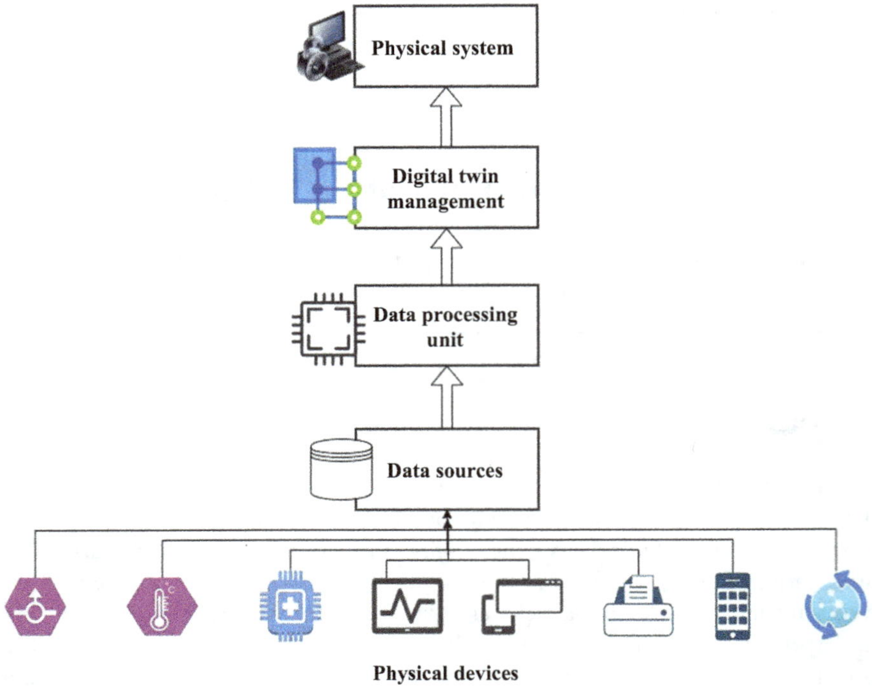

Figure 6.1 Digital twin logical architecture

Digital twins' potential to improve operational efficiency through continuous monitoring, analysis, and feedback is one of its most compelling features. Because of this, firms may enhance their operations, experience less downtime, and increase output [1–3]. In the manufacturing industry, for example, digital twins can be used to model production lines, spot possible bottlenecks, and predict when repairs would be required. Digital twins have applications in healthcare simulation, prediction, and individualization of treatment. The use of digital twins has the potential to impact both efficiency and security significantly. Digital twins can be used to model building plans and spot potential safety risks in the construction industry, for instance, before any physical work is done. This can reduce the likelihood of injuries and save money on treatments. Digital twins can potentially reduce fuel consumption and maintenance costs in the transportation industry by simulating vehicle performance, identifying potential difficulties, and optimizing routes. As a result, digital twins have become an essential resource for boosting productivity, cutting costs, and increasing safety in a wide range of sectors [4–6].

While there are numerous advantages to using digital twins, such as increased efficiency and the ability to perform predictive maintenance, several security concerns must be addressed. Data security, network security, access control through authentication and authorization, cyber-attack protection, privacy preservation, IP protection, and supply chain security are some of the security issues that must be addressed. To overcome these barriers, it is necessary to implement network security measures to safeguard all digital twin data through storage, transport, and access control. Personal information must be protected, and access to digital twins must be strictly regulated. Supply chain security must also be considered to avoid misuse of supply chain vulnerabilities to gain unauthorized access to the digital twin or its data. Strong security protocols must be implemented to protect digital twins from digital damage [7,8].

Blockchain is a distributed, secure, immutable ledger system that enables transparent and tamper-proof data storage and sharing. We can build a reliable approach for overseeing and controlling the real world by integrating blockchain technology and digital twins. Ensuring digital twins are not tampered with or altered in any way is a significant challenge in digital security. The digital twin's history of modifications can be stored in a blockchain ledger that is both immutable and unalterable. A blockchain transaction can be used to record each revision, and once it has been recorded, it cannot be modified or removed. Making sure digital twins are not open to cyber-attacks is another difficulty. Blockchain technology can be utilized to create a trustworthy, decentralized network for keeping an eye on and shielding the digital twin from any potential cyber threats. Using blockchain to store digital twin data makes it considerably more challenging for hackers to access or alter the data. The data from the digital twin can be shared with third parties safely and transparently with the help of blockchain technology. We can ensure that the data is shared only with authorized parties and used only per the agreed-upon terms by using smart contracts on the blockchain to establish the rules and conditions for sharing the data. Thus, we can construct a safe and transparent system for managing and monitoring physical things and systems by integrating digital twins with blockchain technology. This can be especially helpful in sectors where the safety and integrity of physical assets are paramount [9–11]. The security considerations for digital twins that are addressed by blockchain are summarized in Table 6.1.

In the context of extensive and intricate settings, centralizing all data and the execution of model training in a single site may be unfeasible. Federated learning facilitates scalability by decentralizing the training procedure across a network of devices, rendering it well suited for constructing extensive digital twin systems. Federated learning enables edge devices to do localized model updates, hence mitigating the necessity for continuous data transmission to a central server. Reducing latency is essential in applications requiring prompt decision-making or responses, such as autonomous systems, manufacturing, or healthcare.

This chapter investigates the feasibility of using blockchain to strengthen digital twins' security. This section introduces digital twins and their potential uses across multiple sectors. Section 6.2 discusses blockchain technology and its potential as a safety net for digital twins. Section 6.3 discusses the technologies that make blockchain security in digital twins possible. In Section 6.4, we describe how blockchain technology can be used to ensure a digital twin's safety. Current blockchain-based digital twin initiatives are introduced in Section 6.5. In Section 6.6, we discuss some of the open questions about using blockchain technology to ensure the safety of digital twins. In Section 6.7, we sum up our efforts by discussing how blockchain technology might be used to secure digital twins.

Table 6.1 Security aspects addressed by blockchain for digital twin

Security aspect	Description
Data integrity	The blockchain provides a tamper-proof record of every transaction or change made to a digital twin, ensuring that its data remains secure and accurate
Authentication	Blockchain technology can provide strong authentication mechanisms that ensure that only authorized parties can access and interact with the digital twin
Access control	Smart contracts can be used to define access control policies for the digital twin, ensuring that only authorized users can perform certain actions
Transparency	Blockchain technology provides a transparent and auditable record of every transaction made to the digital twin, enabling users to verify its history and authenticity
Immutability	The decentralized nature of the blockchain ensures that the digital twin's data is immutable and cannot be modified without consensus from the network
Privacy	Blockchain technology can provide strong privacy controls that enable users to protect their personal information while still interacting with the digital twin
Resilience	The distributed nature of the blockchain network ensures that the digital twin remains available even in the face of network failures or attacks

6.2 Potential design solutions with blockchain

Incorporating blockchain technology with digital twin systems can address security concerns and improve system reliability, as shown in Figure 6.2. Here, we discuss some of the design choices we made to ensure the integrity of blockchain-based digital twins [12–15].

1. **Immutable records:** Through a distributed ledger, blockchain technology creates immutable records in digital media. Data about a system can be monitored and managed with the help of a digital twin. Data is recorded and maintained in a blockchain-based digital twin system in a decentralized and transparent manner. A distributed ledger called the blockchain uses a network of computer nodes to verify and validate each transaction. When a transaction is recorded on the blockchain, it cannot be modified or removed, making the data secure and unchangeable. Because of this, blockchain technology is an excellent option for digital twin systems since it allows for creating immutable records that can always be relied upon to be true. This is especially crucial in fields

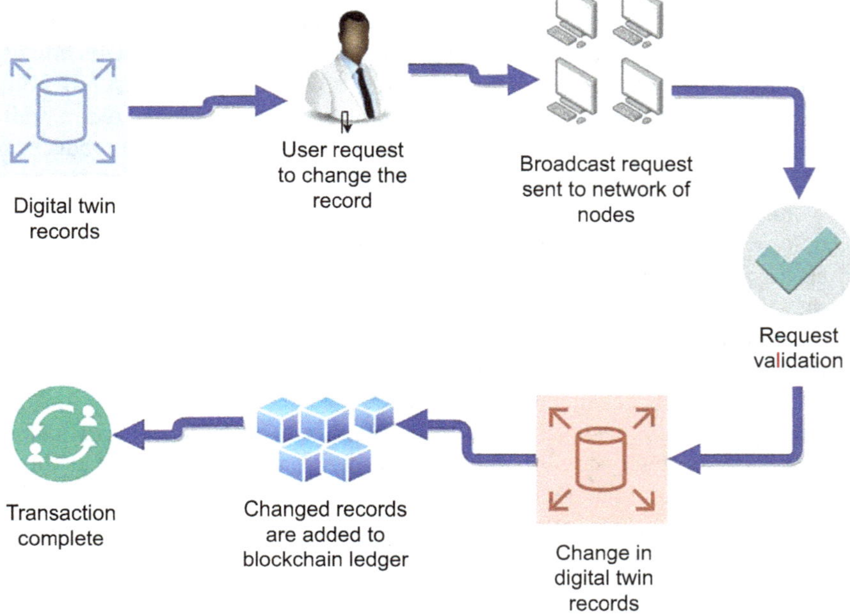

Figure 6.2 Blockchain process for digital twin

where data reliability is fundamental to the entire system's operation. Therefore, digital twin systems can increase trust and reliability by using blockchain technology to produce immutable data recordings that are secure, transparent, and tamper-proof [16,17].

2. **Access control:** Access control in digital twin systems, or deciding who may see and change what is in a digital twin, can be improved with the help of blockchain technology. By removing the need for a centralized authority to govern access, blockchain can produce a decentralized, tamper-proof system that enhances security, transparency, and trust. Users can have complete control over their data with the help of the blockchain's decentralized identity management system. This increases the safety of the digital twin system by allowing users to control who can access their data and how it is used. Smart contracts are another application of blockchain technology. Without the requirement for a central authority, these self-executing contracts can implement access control regulations automatically. There is less room for human error and more room for productivity because of the automatic enforcement of access control rules that can be defined via smart contracts. Access logs created using blockchain technology are immutable and transparent, providing an audit trail of all access operations. Auditing and reviewing immutable access logs improves security and transparency because all requests for and responses to access are documented and cannot be altered. Finally, blockchain technology can be used to design distributed consensus systems that enable concurrency on

access control policies and rules among various parties. This guarantees that decisions on access control are made openly and democratically, with input from all relevant stakeholders. Access control for digital twin systems utilizing blockchain technology can improve security, transparency, and trust [18–20].

3. **Data encryption:** As a distributed ledger, blockchain can be utilized in digital twin technology to encrypt data for storage and management. Data produced by sensors and other devices must be safely communicated and stored for digital twins to function. This information can be encrypted using blockchain technology to make it unalterable and safe. The data integrity is maintained via a cryptographic hash stored in each blockchain block. This is crucial for assuring the correctness and dependability of digital twin technology since it makes it incredibly difficult for any unauthorized entity to alter or manipulate the data. Additionally, blockchain provides a distributed ledger for managing and storing information. Blockchain enables a decentralized network of nodes to store and maintain the encrypted data instead of depending on a central authority to do so. This improves the system's security and resilience by decreasing the likelihood of a single point of failure. For this reason, using blockchain for data encryption in digital twin technology can improve the system's safety, dependability, and robustness [21–23].
4. **Distributed architecture:** Threats to the security of digital twins include but are not limited to, unauthorized access, tampering, and cyber-attacks. Blockchain's distributed ledger technology can improve digital twin safety by keeping track of their ownership, history, and condition in a way that cannot be altered. Blockchain's decentralized design makes it possible to use cryptography and consensus procedures to safeguard digital twins. Since every computer in a blockchain network stores an identical copy of the complete ledger, data manipulation by a single computer is nearly impossible. In addition, the blockchain network's consensus verifies transactions so all nodes acknowledge the same digital twin state. In addition, smart contracts can be used to establish the parameters under which digital twins can be accessed, managed, and transferred from one party to another. Therefore, blockchain's decentralized design can serve as a safe and transparent base for managing digital twins, lowering their risks and protecting the data they contain [24–26].
5. **Audit trails:** By keeping a secure and transparent record of all transactions pertaining to the digital twin, blockchain technology can be utilized to generate audit trails for digital twin data. All digital twin-related transactions are recorded on numerous network nodes using a distributed ledger technology, making data manipulation and tampering extremely difficult. Each purchase is connected to the one before it, forming a chain of acquisitions that leads back to the original data source. Using cryptographic methods, blockchain can verify the data's authenticity, ensuring it has not been altered in any way. The audit trail procedure can be automated with the help of smart contracts, which blockchain technology allows for. As a distributed ledger system, blockchain eliminates the possibility of data modification by a single party. Therefore, blockchain technology is an efficient alternative for producing audit trails because it can give a safe and trustworthy record of all transactions about the digital twin [27–29].

6. **Consensus mechanisms:** Blockchain consensus processes can guarantee the integrity of digital twin data by offering a decentralized and transparent data storage and administration platform. Proof of work (PoW) is a widespread consensus method in blockchains; it forces users to execute complicated calculations to verify transactions and add them to blocks. This procedure guarantees the integrity of the blockchain by making each block immutable once verification is complete. Proof of stake (PoS) is another consensus technique that uses members' stakes in the network to choose who will validate transactions. In addition to being more energy-efficient than PoW, this method can guarantee the precision and dependability of data from digital twins. Smart contracts, another characteristic of blockchain technology, can automate agreements between parties' implementation while facilitating consensus methods. Providing a safe and transparent environment for managing digital twin data and enforcing agreements between various parties can help guarantee the data's accuracy and reliability. As a result, digital twin data can be saved and maintained in an accurate, trustworthy, decentralized, and transparent manner by utilizing blockchain technology and its consensus mechanisms [30–32].

6.3 Enabling technologies

The use of digital twins to enhance the development, operation, and upkeep of complex systems has grown in favor in recent years. The security of digital twins is of essential concern because of their growing use in mission-critical industries like aerospace, defense, and healthcare. Digital twins can be made more secure with the help of blockchain technology, which creates a distributed and tamper-proof ledger for recording transactions. As shown in Figure 6.3, some enabling technologies for blockchain-based digital twin security are as follows.

- **Public Key Infrastructure:** Public Key Infrastructure (PKI) is a critical security mechanism for protecting digital twin data using blockchain. It offers a safe and scalable method of authenticating and authorizing digital twin components using digital certificates and public and private keys [33–35]. The security of digital twins can be improved by integrating PKI with blockchain. Blockchain provides a tamper-evident and decentralized ledger for recording transactions, whereas PKI offers a safe mechanism to authenticate and authorize digital twin components. PKI ensures that only trusted parties have access to and can make changes to the digital twin, making it more secure [36].

Digital certificates are issued by a Certificate Authority (CA), a trustworthy third-party organization used to verify the identity of components of a digital twin. The CA's private key is used to sign the certificate, which may then be checked for validity. The digital certificate is a document that identifies its owner by details such as their public key. The CA has digitally signed it, so its legitimacy may be checked with the CA's public key. Data encryption and decryption are handled by digital twin components using public and private keys. The digital certificate contains the public key, while the digital twin safeguards the private key. When two parts of a digital twin communicate, they can safely exchange their public and private keys. Data is

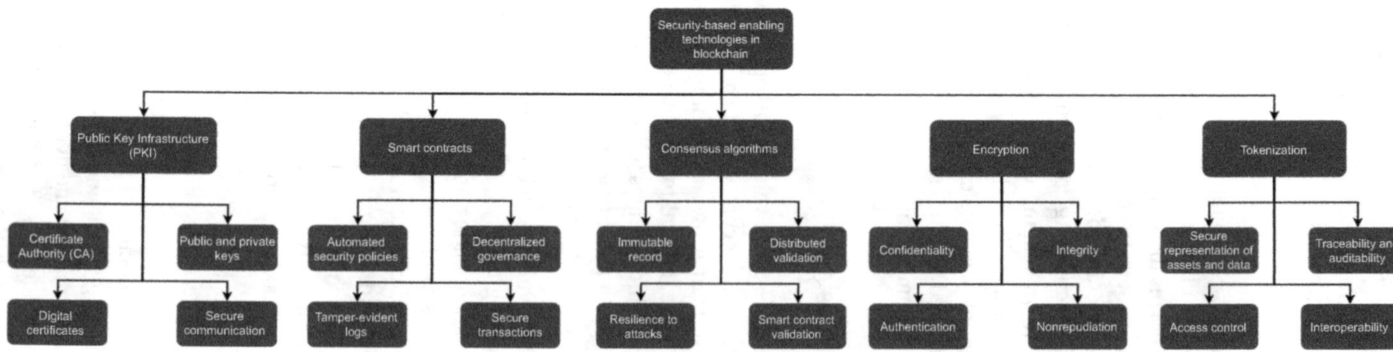

Figure 6.3 Enabling technologies for digital twin with blockchain

encrypted by the initiating digital twin using the recipient's public key and decrypted by the receiver using their private key.

- **Smart contracts:** Security in digital twins using blockchain is greatly enhanced by using smart contracts. Digital twins can employ these autonomous programs, which are self-executing and operate on the blockchain, to enforce security regulations and automate procedures. The digital twin can be protected from unauthorized changes and cyber-attacks using smart contracts, which are programmed to go into effect when specific criteria are met. When it comes to digital twins and blockchain security, smart contracts are essential. They make it possible to execute secure transactions without compromising on the immutability of transaction logs, create decentralized control models, and automate security procedures. The following are some examples of how smart contracts can be used to improve blockchain security in digital twins [37–39].
  (a) Automated security policies: Security measures, such as access restriction, data encryption, and audit logging, can be set to be automatically enforced by smart contracts. This restricts access to the digital twin to just those with permission to make changes, and the blockchain logs all modifications for transparency and audibility.
  (b) Decentralized governance: Smart contracts can be used to design decentralized governance frameworks for digital twins, allowing stakeholders to weigh in on decisions and cast votes on proposed changes. This lessens the likelihood of tyranny of the majority and corruption and guarantees that choices are taken openly and democratically.
  (c) Secure transactions: Transferring ownership of assets, carrying out maintenance duties, and validating sensor data are just a few examples of safe transactions that may be automated with the help of smart contracts in digital twins. This eliminates the potential for mistakes and fraud during the transaction process.
  (d) Tamper-evident logs: Smart contracts can be used to construct tamper-evident logs of all transactions and events in the digital twin. These records are kept on the blockchain and are indelibly immutable, making the digital twin's past completely transparent. This improves safety by making all digital twin operations visible, accountable, and trackable.
- **Consensus algorithms:** Consensus methods help enhance security in a digital twin using blockchain. They are responsible for keeping the blockchain network secure by ensuring that every node in the network uses an identical copy of the digital twin. Distributed consensus algorithms make it hard for intruders to change the digital twin by validating transactions and adding unique blocks to the blockchain. Consensus algorithms are a powerful tool used to increase the level of security in digital twins that use blockchain. They generate an unchangeable sequence of transactions and changes, use a distributed approach to validate the transactions, add new blocks, and prevent attacks and failures. The following discussion shows how consensus algorithms can improve blockchain security in digital twins [40–42].
  (a) Immutable record: Consensus algorithms ensure that all network nodes agree on the same version of the digital twin to prevent tampering.

The mechanism provides increased security by making all digital twin activities transparent, accountable, and traceable by creating an unchangeable record of all transactions and changes.

(b) Distributed validation: Transactions are verified, and new blocks are added to the blockchain via a distributed consensus method. Therefore, it is difficult for a single node to exploit the digital twin, as all nodes in the network must agree on the authenticity of each transaction. This enhances safety by establishing a decentralized system that can resist attacks and malfunctions.

(c) Resilience to attacks: Sybil attacks and other malicious behavior on a blockchain network can be detected and prevented with the help of these algorithms.

(d) Smart contract validation: Before incorporating blockchain, smart contracts can be validated using consensus techniques. This limits potential vulnerabilities by ensuring that only reliable smart contracts are integrated into the digital twin.

- **Encryption:** Encryption is another method that improves security in digital twins using blockchain. It includes using cryptographic techniques to change plaintext data into ciphertext, which can only be deciphered with a secret key. Plaintext data cannot be read without the private key. Encryption provides data confidentiality, integrity, and authenticity in the digital twin, especially when the data is transported across insecure networks. Encryption can improve the safety of digital twins using blockchain in several different ways, some of which are listed below [43–46].

  (a) Confidentiality: The security of sensitive data stored in the digital twin, such as personal information, commercial data, and intellectual property, can be protected with the help of encryption if necessary. It helps to secure data storage and transmission when unauthorized persons try to access it. The encryption process ensures that its confidentiality is maintained.

  (b) Integrity: The data contained in the digital twin can have its integrity safeguarded with the help of encryption, which guarantees that the data has not been altered or otherwise interfered with. Encryption can ensure that data is not altered in storage or transmission by using message authentication codes (MACs) or digital signatures.

  (c) Authentication: Encryption is critical to authenticate the identity of users and devices in the digital twin, ensuring that only authorized users and devices can access the data. Encryption can provide robust authentication and access control if it is combined with techniques such as public-key cryptography and digital certificates.

  (d) Integrity: It is possible to employ encryption to guarantee nonrepudiation, which assures a user cannot deny committing a given action in the digital twin. This can be achieved using decryption. Encryption can offer strong evidence of acts conducted in the digital twin, which is crucial for legal and compliance concerns. This evidence can be provided by using digital signatures and timestamps.

- **Tokenization:** Tokenization is a powerful tool to maintain blockchain safety for digital twins. It permits the representation and transfer of data in a way that is both secure and trackable. It provides control and also guarantees interoperability across various systems. Digital twins benefit from blockchain technology's combined power and safety and several other technologies that enable it. These techniques can be utilized to maintain the security of digital twins, which is essential for ensuring the safety and dependability of critical infrastructure. Tokenization replaces sensitive information with a discrete identifier (a token) that may be safely sent and processed without exposing the original data. Some instances of how tokenization can improve blockchain security for digital twins are presented below [47–49].
  (a) Secure representation of assets and data: Assets and data in the digital twin, such as intellectual property, certificates, and licenses, can be safely represented using tokenization. Tokenization protects sensitive data by replacing it with a digital representation called a token, which only authorized parties can use to access, modify, or transfer the underlying asset or data.
  (b) Traceability and auditability: Assets and data in the digital twin may be tracked and audited using tokenization. Tokenization makes it possible to track and audit the movement of assets and data at any moment by documenting each token transaction on the blockchain. This is crucial for legal and compliance reasons and to prevent fraud and unauthorized access.
  (c) Access control: Access to digital twin assets and data can be tokenized for security. Tokenization restricts access to assets and data transfers to authorized users by issuing unique tokens to each user or set of users. This is crucial for securing personal information and avoiding unauthorized access.
  (d) Interoperability: Tokenization can enable interoperability across different digital twin platforms and systems. Tokenization guarantees the safe movement and processing of assets and data between systems by defining a standard set of tokens for representing various assets and data kinds. This is crucial for maintaining accurate and consistent data in all areas of the digital twin ecosystem.

6.4 Use cases

There are various use cases for security in digital twins with blockchain. Following are some examples:

- Industrial automation: Blockchain technology can protect digital twins used in factory automation [50]. Blockchain can improve security, reliability, and efficiency by providing a transparent platform for operating industrial machinery and facilitating data sharing and collaboration among many parties. For instance, the performance data of a factory machine may be tokenized and safely stored on the blockchain by creating a digital twin of the device. This allows factory managers to track and control the machine's output, identify and neutralize security concerns, and enhance the machine's productivity.

- Real estate: Digital twins in the construction industry can be protected by blockchain technology [51]. Blockchain can improve transparency, security, and efficiency in the real estate industry by providing a decentralized platform for asset management that facilitates data sharing and collaboration among many parties. For instance, a real estate asset's ownership information might be tokenized and safely stored on the blockchain as a digital twin. This helps property agents maintain accurate property ownership and transfer records and prevent fraud.
- Aviation: Blockchain can be used in flight to protect digital twins [52]. Blockchain can improve safety, reliability, and efficiency by making a secure, unchangeable platform for handling aircraft and their parts. It can also make it easier for stakeholders to share data and work together. For example, a digital twin of an airplane can be prepared, and its maintenance data can be tokenized and safely saved on the blockchain. Using this approach, the aviation sector can keep track of planes' maintenance, find and deal with security threats, and improve the planes' performance.
- Identity management: Identity management can use blockchain to keep digital twins safe [53]. Blockchain can improve privacy, security, and interoperability by making a secure, decentralized tool for handling identities. It can also make it easier for stakeholders to share data and work together. For example, a user's identity can be made into a "digital twin," and their personal information can be tokenized and stored safely on the blockchain. The method gives users control over their data, lets them give or take away access to it, and stops identity theft.
- Automotive industry: In the auto business also, blockchain can keep digital twins safe [54]. Blockchain can improve safety and reliability by making a secure and open tool for managing vehicles and their parts. It also helps to improve the efficiency of the production. It can make it easier for different parties to share information and work together. For example, a digital twin of a car can be made, and its maintenance data, performance data, and ownership information can be tokenized and safely saved on the blockchain. This allows car makers and dealerships to track and manage the vehicle's maintenance, deal with security hazards, and improve the vehicle's performance.
- Agriculture: Blockchain can be used in agriculture to keep digital twins safe [55]. Blockchain can improve transparency, traceability, and efficiency by making a secure and transparent platform for managing agricultural goods and their supply lines. It can also allow different stakeholders to share data and work together. For example, a crop can have a digital twin, and its production data can be tokenized and saved safely on the blockchain. This allows farmers and customers to check the crop and its quality.

6.5 Ongoing projects

Following are some of the many ongoing projects related to security in digital twin with blockchain, as presented in Figure 6.4:

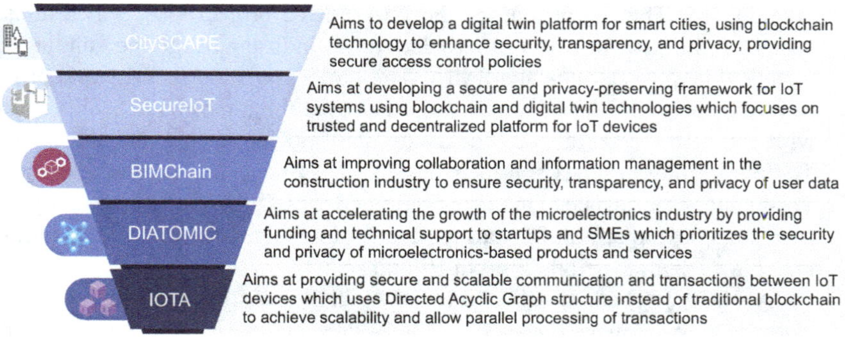

Figure 6.4 Ongoing projects on digital twin with blockchain

- CitySCAPE: The EU is funding the CitySCAPE project [56], which wants to create a digital twin platform for smart cities. This platform will use blockchain technology to improve security, transparency, and privacy. Smart contracts will be used to enforce access control rules on the forum. This will make sure that only authorized users can get to the data. The tool will also provide a straightforward way for data to be shared so that all parties can do so safely and efficiently. The platform will protect user data privacy using advanced cryptographic methods, such as homomorphic encryption and zero-knowledge proofs. The CitySCAPE project aims to create a secure and open platform for smart cities. The technique enables partners to collaborate and share data safely and efficiently while keeping user data private and safe.
- SecureIoT: The SecureIoT project [57] is a European Union-funded project that aims to use blockchain and digital twin technologies to create a safe and private platform for IoT systems. The project's primary goal is to build a trusted, decentralized platform for IoT devices built on blockchain technology and smart contracts called a "digital twin." The platform ensures that data exchange between devices is safe and private by using advanced cryptographic techniques and intelligent contracts to apply access control policies. The SecureIoT platform gives IoT devices a safe and open place to run and helps them deal with security and privacy issues.
- BIMChain: The BIMCHAIN project [58] is a blockchain-based platform that aims to make it easier for people in the construction business to work together and share information. The platform uses blockchain technology to ensure user data is safe, transparent, and private. It gives people a safe and open place to share information, ensuring everyone can access the most recent information. Smart contracts are used to handle tasks like payment and project management on the platform. This lowers the chance of mistakes and data fabrication. It protects user data using advanced encryption methods to keep it private and safe. The platform has a decentralized architecture, which means that data is stored on various nodes across the network. The technique makes it harder for attackers to break into the system.

- DIATOMIC: The EU is funding the DIATOMIC project [59], which aims to speed up the growth of the microelectronics industry by giving funding and technical help to startups and SMEs. The project puts the security and privacy of microelectronics-based goods and services at the top of its list. This is done with a secure, decentralized blockchain platform for storing and sharing data. The platform uses smart contracts to handle payments and data access control. This reduces the chance of mistakes and fraud. The DIATOMIC project provides a safe and open platform for startups and SMEs in the microelectronics industry and allows them to sell their products and services.
- IOTA: IOTA [60] is a distributed ledger system that allows IoT devices to talk to each other and make transactions. IOTA does not use a traditional blockchain. Instead, it has a structure called a directed acyclic graph (DAG) that makes it scalable. It also enables transactions to be processed in parallel. This system also allows IOTA to offer transactions with no fees and many transactions per second. IOTA uses different methods to ensure that transactions are honest and prevent attacks. One of these is a consensus system that eliminates the need for a central coordinator and prevents many digital attacks. In the case of digital twins, IOTA can be used to keep and share data between digital twins and IoT devices in a safe way that protects the data's integrity and privacy.

6.6 Open challenges

Using blockchain to add security to a digital twin is challenging and requires overcoming several technical, social, and economic barriers. To solve these open problems, people from different fields, such as science, business, and law agencies, must work together. New solutions are required to understand these problems and use blockchain to its full potential for security in digital twins. Here are some of the issues that still need to be solved for this technology to reach its full potential [61–63], as shown in Figure 6.5:

First is scalability, a big problem for digital twin settings that want to use blockchain technology. Digital twins make a lot of data that needs to be saved and handled effectively. However, our blockchain systems cannot handle large-scale digital twin use cases, so we must develop new ways to solve this problem. One way to speed up the speed at which transactions are processed is to use off-chain options like sidechains or state channels. Second is interoperability which is problematic when adding blockchain technology to digital twin environments. Most digital twins use different software, hardware, and connection protocols. This makes it hard to make a single system that works for all of them. Interoperability between other systems is essential if you want the digital twin and blockchain communities to be able to share data and information quickly. One way to do this is to use middleware, which can connect different platforms. Security and privacy are other critical issues in digital twin settings; combined with blockchain technology, they become even more problematic. Making sure that data stored on the blockchain and in digital twin environments is private and correct is a big task. Also, the blockchain's openness makes it hard to keep data confidential, so new ways must be uncovered. One way to protect the

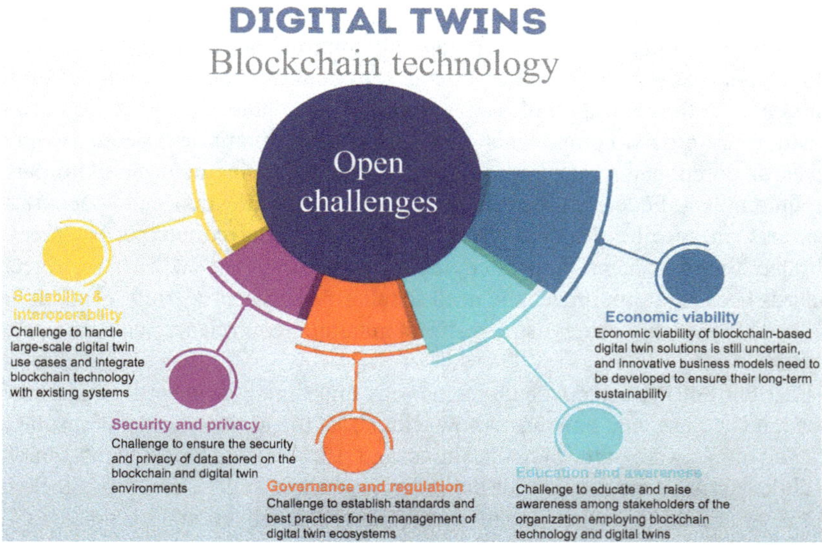

Figure 6.5 Open challenges for digital twins with blockchain technology

data saved on the blockchain and in digital twin environments is to use advanced encryption techniques.

Governing and regulating blockchain and digital twin environments is another challenging task. There needs to be a set of rules and guidelines for how to take care of these ecosystems. Using blockchain to add security to a digital twin requires a lot of infrastructure, hardware, software, and experience. The economic feasibility of blockchain-based digital twin solutions still needs to be clarified, and new business models must be created to ensure they can be used for a long time. Legal systems also need to change to use blockchain technology and digital twins. One way to handle blockchain and digital twin ecosystems is to set up working groups to develop best practices and standards.

Federated learning has the potential to significantly contribute to the integration of digital twins by augmenting their capabilities and effectively tackling several significant obstacles. Digital twins are dependent on the utilization of real-time data obtained from physical systems, which may frequently encompass information that is sensitive or private in nature. Federated learning enables enterprises to conduct model training and updates on distributed devices, without the necessity of data centralization or raw data sharing. This feature guarantees the preservation of confidential data, rendering it appropriate for situations where the utmost importance is placed on data privacy and security. To effectively represent the status of the physical system, it is imperative that digital twins possess precise and accurate models. Federated learning enables the iterative enhancement of these models by integrating fresh input from diverse edge devices. The ability to learn and adapt in real time is of great importance in maintaining the currency and dependability of the digital twin [64–68].

Centralized systems are susceptible to server outages and network connectivity disruptions. Federated learning can potentially improve the resiliency of digital twin deployments by enabling peripheral devices to continue local training and model updates even if the central server is temporarily unavailable. Customization and specialization are crucial components of a digital twin system, as various peripheral devices or components may possess unique characteristics or necessitate particular requirements. Federated learning enables the customization and specialization of models on specific devices, ensuring that the digital counterpart is precisely calibrated to its context. Federated learning is compliant with data protection standards because it minimizes the need for sharing and centralizing sensitive information. This measure can assist firms in maintaining compliance with data privacy legislation.

Last but not least, blockchain technology and digital twin settings are hard to understand and use, and one must know a lot about them. Stakeholders must be educated and more aware of the benefits, limits, and risks of using blockchain technology and digital twins. One way to get the information and skills needed in blockchain technology and digital twins is to offer training and certification programs.

6.7 Conclusions

The combination of blockchain technology and digital twins presents a promising solution for enhancing cybersecurity across a range of industries. Blockchain's ability to create secure and tamper-proof digital records of transactions and activities ensures the integrity and confidentiality of sensitive information in digital twin systems. The immutability of blockchain transactions also provides a critical advantage in preventing cyber-attacks by making it difficult for hackers to alter or corrupt data. Furthermore, the decentralized nature of blockchain technology enables multiple parties to participate in the digital twin system without compromising its security. However, the implementation of blockchain technology for digital twins is not without its challenges. Addressing scalability, interoperability, security, privacy, governance, regulation, economic viability, and stakeholder awareness is necessary to effectively integrate blockchain-based digital twin systems into existing infrastructures. Despite these challenges, the use of blockchain technology in conjunction with digital twins offers a promising approach to meet the growing need for enhanced cybersecurity in our interconnected digital world. Further research and development in this area will likely lead to more widespread adoption of blockchain-based digital twin systems in the future.

6.8 Funding

The author would like to gratefully acknowledge the grant GUJCOST/STI/2021-2022/3922 from the Government of Gujarat, India, and support from Pandit Deendayal Energy University (PDEU) to perform this work.

References

[1] Liu, Mn, Shuiliang Fang, Huiyue Dong, and Cunzhi Xu. "Review of digital twin about concepts, technologies, and industrial applications." *Journal of Manufacturing Systems* 58 (2021): 346–361.

[2] Tao, Fei, Jiangfeng Cheng, Qinglin Qi, Meng Zhang, He Zhang, and Fangyuan Sui. "Digital twin-driven product design, manufacturing and service with big data." *The International Journal of Advanced Manufacturing Technology* 94 (2018): 3563–3576.

[3] Li, Lianhui, Bingbing Lei, and Chunlei Mao. "Digital twin in smart manufacturing." *Journal of Industrial Information Integration* 26 (2022): 100289.

[4] Michalkova, Lucia, Veronika Machova, and Daniel Carter. "Digital twin-based product development and manufacturing processes in virtual space: Data visualization tools and techniques, cloud computing technologies, and cyber-physical production systems." *Economics, Management and Financial Markets* 17(2) (2022): 37–51.

[5] Falekas, Georgios, and Athanasios Karlis. "Digital twin in electrical machine control and predictive maintenance: State-of-the-art and future prospects." *Energies* 14(18) (2021): 5933.

[6] Fuller, Aidan, Zhong Fan, Charles Day, and Chris Barlow. "Digital twin: Enabling technologies, challenges and open research." *IEEE Access* 8 (2020): 108952–108971.

[7] Alcaraz, Cristina, and Javier Lopez. "Digital twin: A comprehensive survey of security threats." *IEEE Communications Surveys & Tutorials* 24(3) (2022):1475–1503.

[8] Alshammari, Kaznah, Thomas Beach, and Yacine Rezgui. "Cybersecurity for digital twins in the built environment: Current research and future directions." *Journal of Information Technology in Construction* 26 (2021): 159–173.

[9] Suhail, Sabah, Rasheed Hussain, Raja Jurdak, *et al.* "Blockchain-based digital twins: Research trends, issues, and future challenges." *ACM Computing Surveys (CSUR)* 54(11s) (2022): 1–34.

[10] Yaqoob, Ibrar, Khaled Salah, Mueen Uddin, Raja Jayaraman, Mohammed Omar, and Muhammad Imran. "Blockchain for digital twins: Recent advances and future research challenges." *IEEE Network* 34(5) (2020): 290–298.

[11] Liu, Xinlai, Yishuo Jiang, Zicheng Wang, Ray Y. Zhong, H. H. Cheung, and George Q. Huang. "imseStudio: Blockchain-enabled secure digital twin platform for service manufacturing." *International Journal of Production Research* 61(12) (2021): 3984–4003.

[12] Sasikumar, A., Subramaniyaswamy Vairavasundaram, Ketan Kotecha, *et al.* "Blockchain-based trust mechanism for digital twin empowered Industrial Internet of Things." *Future Generation Computer Systems* 141 (2023): 16–27.

[13] Tao, Fei, Yongping Zhang, Ying Cheng, *et al.* "Digital twin and blockchain enhanced smart manufacturing service collaboration and management." *Journal of Manufacturing Systems* 62 (2022): 903–914.

[14] Wang, Qin, Xinqi Zhu, Yiyang Ni, Li Gu, and Hongbo Zhu. "Blockchain for the IoT and industrial IoT: A review." *Internet of Things* 10 (2020): 100081.

[15] Putz, Benedikt, Marietheres Dietz, Philip Empl, and Günther Pernul. "Ethertwin: Blockchain-based secure digital twin information management." *Information Processing & Management* 58(1) (2021): 102425.

[16] Gai, Keke, Yue Zhang, Meikang Qiu, and Bhavani Thuraisingham. "Blockchain-enabled service optimizations in supply chain digital twin." *IEEE Transactions on Services Computing* 16(3) (2023): 1673-1685.

[17] Wang, Chenyu, Zhipeng Cai, and Yingshu Li. "Sustainable blockchain-based digital twin management architecture for IoT devices." *IEEE Internet of Things Journal* (2022).

[18] Liu, Jun, Lei Zhang, Chunlin Li, Jingpan Bai, Haibin Lv, and Zhihan Lv. "Blockchain-based secure communication of intelligent transportation digital twins system." *IEEE Transactions on Intelligent Transportation Systems* 23(11) (2022): 22630–22640.

[19] Rahman, Ziaur, Xun Yi, and Ibrahim Khalil. "Blockchain based AI-enabled industry 4.0 CPS protection against advanced persistent threat." *IEEE Internet of Things Journal* 10(8) (2023): 6769–6778.

[20] Di Francesco Maesa, Damiano, Paolo Mori, and Laura Ricci. "Blockchain based access control." In *Distributed Applications and Interoperable Systems: 17th IFIP WG 6.1 International Conference, DAIS 2017, Held as Part of the 12th International Federated Conference on Distributed Computing Techniques, DisCoTec 2017, Neuchâtel, Switzerland, June 19–22, 2017, Proceedings 17*, pp. 206–220. Springer International Publishing, 2017.

[21] Mazzei, Daniele, Giacomo Baldi, Gualtiero Fantoni, *et al.* "A blockchain Tokenizer for industrial IOT trustless applications." *Future Generation Computer Systems* 105 (2020): 432–445.

[22] Putz, Benedikt, Marietheres Dietz, Philip Empl, and Günther Pernul. "Ethertwin: Blockchain-based secure digital twin information management." *Information Processing & Management* 58(1) (2021): 102425.

[23] Yan, Mingyu, Wei Gan, Yue Zhou, Jianfeng Wen, and Wei Yao. "Projection method for blockchain-enabled non-iterative decentralized management in integrated natural gas-electric systems and its application in digital twin modelling." *Applied Energy* 311 (2022): 118645.

[24] Sadri, Habib, Ibrahim Yitmen, Lavinia Chiara Tagliabue, *et al.* "Integration of blockchain and digital twins in the smart built environment adopting disruptive technologies—A systematic review." *Sustainability* 15(4) (2023): 3713.

[25] Leng, Jiewu, Xiaofeng Zhu, Zhiqiang Huang, *et al.* "ManuChain II: Blockchained smart contract system as the digital twin of decentralized autonomous manufacturing toward resilience in Industry 5.0." *IEEE Transactions on Systems, Man, and Cybernetics: Systems* 53(8) (2023): 4715–4728.

[26] Tang, Lun, Yucong Du, Qinghai Liu, Jinyu Li, Shirui Li, and Qianbin Chen. "Digital twin assisted resource allocation for network slicing in Industry 4.0

and beyond using distributed deep reinforcement learning." *IEEE Internet of Things Journal* 10(19) (2023): 16989–17006.

[27] Huynh-The, Thien, Thippa Reddy Gadekallu, Weizheng Wang, *et al.* "Blockchain for the metaverse: A review." *Future Generation Computer Systems* 143 (2023): 401–419.

[28] Ali, Sikandar, Abdullah, Tagne Poupi Theodore Armand, *et al.* "Metaverse in healthcare integrated with explainable AI and blockchain: Enabling immersiveness, ensuring trust, and providing patient data security." *Sensors* 23(2) (2023): 565.

[29] Mezquita, Yeray, Blaž Podgorelec, Ana Belén Gil-González, and Juan Manuel Corchado. "Blockchain-based supply chain systems, interoperability model in a pharmaceutical case study." *Sensors* 23(4) (2023): 1962.

[30] Teisserenc, Benjamin, and Samad Sepasgozar. "Project data categorization, adoption factors, and non-functional requirements for blockchain based digital twins in the construction industry 4.0." *Buildings* 11(12) (2021): 626.

[31] Kamble, Sachin S., Angappa Gunasekaran, Harsh Parekh, Venkatesh Mani, Amine Belhadi, and Rohit Sharma. "Digital twin for sustainable manufacturing supply chains: Current trends, future perspectives, and an implementation framework." *Technological Forecasting and Social Change* 176 (2022): 121448.

[32] Deng, Tianhu, Keren Zhang, and Zuo-Jun Max Shen. "A systematic review of a digital twin city: A new pattern of urban governance toward smart cities." *Journal of Management Science and Engineering* 6(2) (2021): 125–134.

[33] Huang, Sihan, Guoxin Wang, Yan Yan, and Xiongbing Fang. "Blockchain-based data management for digital twin of product." *Journal of Manufacturing Systems* 54 (2020): 361–371.

[34] Li, Tian, Huaqun Wang, Debiao He, and Jia Yu. "Synchronized provable data possession based on blockchain for digital twin." *IEEE Transactions on Information Forensics and Security* 17 (2022): 472–485.

[35] Shen, Weidong, Tianliang Hu, Chengrui Zhang, and Songhua Ma. "Secure sharing of big digital twin data for smart manufacturing based on blockchain." *Journal of Manufacturing Systems* 61 (2021): 338–350.

[36] Akram, Junaid, Awais Akram, Rutvij H. Jhaveri, Mamoun Alazab, and Haoran Chi. "BC-IoDT: Blockchain-based framework for authentication in Internet of Drone Things." In *5th ACM International Workshop on Drone Assisted Wireless Communications for 5G and Beyond (DroneCom 2022 co-located with ACM MobiCom 2022)*, Sydney, Oct 2022.

[37] Sahal, Radhya, Saeed H. Alsamhi, Kenneth N. Brown, Donna O'Shea, and Bader Alouffi. "Blockchain-based digital twins collaboration for smart pandemic alerting: Decentralized COVID-19 pandemic alerting use case." *Computational Intelligence and Neuroscience* 2022 (2022): 7786441.

[38] Bhattacharya, S., N. Victor, R. Chengoden, *et al.* "Blockchain for internet-of-underwater-things: State-of-the-art, applications, challenges and future directions." *Sustainability* 14(23) (2022): 15659

[39] Pittaras, Iakovos, Nikos Fotiou, Christos Karapapas, Vasilios A. Siris, and George C. Polyzos. "Secure, mass web of things actuation using smart contracts-based digital twins." In *2022 IEEE Symposium on Computers and Communications (ISCC)*, pp. 1–6. IEEE, 2022.

[40] Liao, Siyi, Jun Wu, Ali Kashif Bashir, Wu Yang, Jianhua Li, and Usman Tariq. "Digital twin consensus for blockchain-enabled intelligent transportation systems in smart cities." *IEEE Transactions on Intelligent Transportation Systems* 23, no. 11 (2021): 22619–22629.

[41] Altun, Cankal, Bulent Tavli, and Halim Yanikomeroglu. "Liberalization of digital twins of IoT-enabled home appliances via blockchains and absolute ownership rights." *IEEE Communications Magazine* 57(12) (2019): 65–71.

[42] Bhardwaj, Rashmi, and Debabrata Datta. "Consensus algorithm." In *Decentralised Internet of Things: A Blockchain Perspective*, pp. 91–107. Cham: Springer, 2020.

[43] Pal, Kamalendu. "Security implications of IoT applications with cryptography and blockchain technology in healthcare digital twin design." In *Digital Twins and Healthcare: Trends, Techniques, and Challenges*, pp. 229–252. IGI Global, 2023.

[44] Qu, Youyang, Longxiang Gao, Yong Xiang, Shigen Shen, and Shui Yu. "FedTwin: Blockchain-enabled adaptive asynchronous federated learning for digital twin networks." *IEEE Network* 36(6) (2022): 183–190.

[45] Holmes, David, Maria Papathanasaki, Leandros Maglaras, Mohamed Amine Ferrag, Surya Nepal, and Helge Janicke. "Digital twins and cyber security—Solution or challenge?" In *2021 6th South-East Europe Design Automation, Computer Engineering, Computer Networks and Social Media Conference (SEEDA-CECNSM)*, pp. 1–8. IEEE, 2021.

[46] R. Durga, E. Poovammal, Kadiyala Ramana, Rutvij H. Jhaveri, Saurabh Singh, and Byungun Yoon. "CES blocks – A novel chaotic encryption schemes based blockchain system for an IoT environment." *IEEE Access* 10 (2022): 11354–11371.

[47] Kanak, Alper, Niyazi Ugur, and Salih Ergun. "A visionary model on blockchain-based accountability for secure and collaborative digital twin environments." In *2019 IEEE International Conference on Systems, Man and Cybernetics (SMC)*, pp. 3512–3517. IEEE, 2019.

[48] Ferrara, Giuseppe, and Corrado Santoro. "Digital twin through physical assets tokenization in blockchain." In *Security, Trust and Privacy Models, and Architectures in IoT Environments*, pp. 149–166. Cham: Springer International Publishing, 2022.

[49] Sadri, Habib, Ibrahim Yitmen, Lavinia Chiara Tagliabue, *et al.* "Integration of blockchain and digital twins in the smart built environment adopting disruptive technologies—A systematic review." *Sustainability* 15(4) (2023): 3713.

[50] Liu, Shimin, Yuqian Lu, Jie Li, Xingwang Shen, Xuemin Sun, and Jinsong Bao. "A blockchain-based interactive approach between digital twin-based

manufacturing systems." *Computers & Industrial Engineering* 175 (2023): 108827.

[51] Avantaggiato, Mirko, and Pierluigi Gallo. "Challenges and opportunities using multichain for real estate." In *2019 IEEE International Black Sea Conference on Communications and Networking (BlackSeaCom)*, pp. 1–5. IEEE, 2019.

[52] Wu, Yiwen, Ke Zhang, and Yan Zhang. "Digital twin networks: A survey." *IEEE Internet of Things Journal* 8(18) (2021): 13789–13804.

[53] Hasan, Haya R., Khaled Salah, Raja Jayaraman, *et al.* "A blockchain-based approach for the creation of digital twins." *IEEE Access* 8 (2020): 34113–34126.

[54] Raj, Pethuru. "Empowering digital twins with blockchain." *Advances in Computers* 121 (2021): 267–283, Elsevier.

[55] Wang, Keqi, Wei Xie, Bo Wang, *et al.* "Simulation-based digital twin development for blockchain enabled end-to-end industrial hemp supply chain risk management." In *2020 Winter Simulation Conference (WSC)*, pp. 3200–3211. IEEE, 2020.

[56] CitySCAPE: https://www.cityscape-project.eu/ (Accessed on 24 May 2023).

[57] SecureIoT: https://secureiot.eu/ (Accessed on 24 May 2023).

[58] BIMCHAIN: https://bimchain.io/ (Accessed on 24 May 2023).

[59] DIATOMIC: https://diatomic.eu/ (Accessed on 24 May 2023).

[60] IOTA: https://www.iota.org/ (Accessed on 24 May 2023).

[61] Yaqoob, Ibrar, Khaled Salah, Mueen Uddin, Raja Jayaraman, Mohammed Omar, and Muhammad Imran. "Blockchain for digital twins: Recent advances and future research challenges." *IEEE Network* 34(5) (2020): 290–298.

[62] Khan, Latif U., Zhu Han, Walid Saad, Ekram Hossain, Mohsen Guizani, and Choong Seon Hong. "Digital twin of wireless systems: Overview, taxonomy, challenges, and opportunities." *IEEE Communications Surveys & Tutorials* 24(4) (2022): 2230–2254.

[63] Liu, Kangde, Zheng Yan, Xueqin Liang, Raimo Kantola, and Chuangyue Hu. "A survey on blockchain-enabled federated learning and its prospects with digital twin." *Digital Communications and Networks* 10(2) 2024: 248–264.

[64] Pandya, Sharnil, Gautam Srivastava, Rutvij Jhaveri, *et al.* "Federated Learning for Smart Cities: A Comprehensive Survey." *Sustainable Energy Technologies and Assessments* 55 (2023): 102987.

[65] Bharany, Salil, Sumit Badotra, Sandeep Sharma, *et al.* "Energy efficient fault tolerance techniques in Green Cloud Computing: A systematic survey and taxonomy." *Sustainable Energy Technologies and Assessments* 53 (2022): 102613.

[66] Jhaveri, Rutvij, Sagar Ramani, Gautam Srivastava, Thippa Reddy Gadekallu, and Vaneet Aggarwal. "Fault-resilience for bandwidth management in industrial software-defined networks." *IEEE Transactions on Network Science and Engineering* 8(4) (2021): 3129–3139.

[67] Victor, Nancy, Sweta Bhattacharya, Praveen Kumar Reddy Maddikunta, Fasial Mohammed Alotaibi, Thippa Reddy Gadekallu, and Rutvij H. Jhaveri. "FL-PSO: A Federated Learning approach with Particle Swarm Optimization for Brain Stroke Prediction." In *6th IEEE Workshop on Security Trust Privacy for Cyber-Physical Systems (IEEE STP-CPS Co-located with IEEE CCGRID 2023)*, Bengaluru, 1–4 May 2023.

[68] Akram, Junaid, Awais Akram, Rutvij H. Jhaveri, Mamoun Alazab, and Haoran Chi. "BC-IoDT: Blockchain-based framework for authentication in Internet of Drone Things." In *5th ACM International Workshop on Drone Assisted Wireless Communications for 5G and Beyond (DroneCom 2022 Co-located with ACM MobiCom 2022)*, Sydney, Oct 2022.

Chapter 7

Blockchain-based federated learning for Industry 5.0 applications

Rukhsana Ruby[1], Zehua Wang[2] and Lu Wang[1]

Abstract

Industry 5.0 is the newly updated standard of Industry 4.0, the aim of which is to incorporate human intelligence with machine intelligence for increasing the production of the manufacturing industry. In order to achieve this objective, all components in the supply chain right from the supplier to production lines, and then to end users are transferred to Internet-of-Things (IoT). These IoT devices require to learn some machine learning (ML) model time to time from the data acquired by themselves owing to the charismatic ability of artificial intelligence (AI). Because of the inconvenience in centralized learning and data privacy, federated learning (FL) is considered as one of the promising decentralized learning techniques. Despite some controversy, this learning technique still suffers from many privacy and security issues. Meanwhile, blockchain is a well-known technique to handle the privacy and security issues of a network in a decentralized manner. To this end, in this chapter, we present two application-specific blockchain-enhanced FL architectures to satisfy the requirements of Industry 5.0. Then, we discuss some security attacks and the potential of the proposed two architectures to counter-measure these attacks. Through some preliminary experiment results, we justify the effectiveness of the proposed two architectures. Finally, we outline some Industry 5.0-specific open challenges in the context of FL and blockchain technologies.

Keywords: Federated learning (FL), Blockchain, Blockchain-based FL, Centralized server-based FL, Decentralized FL

7.1 Introduction

Invented by Google, federated learning (FL) [1] is a promising distributed machine learning mechanism without exchanging training data between the centralized

[1]College of Computer Science and Software Engineering, Shenzhen University, China
[2]Department of Electrical and Computer Engineering, The University of British Columbia, Canada

authority and data-generating devices. Because of not exchanging data over the communication media, various security attacks including the privacy of the user could be preserved. It is also established that under optimized communication and computation control and resources, FL outperforms conventional centralized and distributed machine learning techniques in terms of preservation of data privacy, optimized usage of bandwidth, and low latency. To this end, FL is remarkably used in numerous real-world applications, such as healthcare, finance, transportation, and smart cities.

Despite its promising nature, FL endures various limitations in terms of new types of security and privacy attacks. Owing to the necessity of model aggregation, the FL process relies on a centralized model aggregating server. The failure of such a centralized server leads to single point of failure (SPoF) and distributed denial of service (DDoS) attack. Now, one may perceive that peer-to-peer (P2P) decentralized architecture may be a feasible approach to solve the SPoF issue in the FL process. However, in this process, there is no transparent mechanism or concept to record the local model updates, and thus if a model is poisoned somehow, the integrity of the entire FL process could be jeopardized. In recent years, a few attempts have been undertaken to tighten the model poisoning attacks of the FL process. For example, based on statistical knowledge, some existing defense mechanisms are coordinate-wise trimmed mean [2], the coordinate-wise median [3], the geometric median [4], and distance-based methods Krum [5], BREA [6], Bulyan [7]. To make byzantine models more likely to be selected, attackers can learn to improve their attack methods or carry out the denial of service (DoS) by tweaking pre-defined "honest" models. Therefore, identification of attackers is essential to prevent worsening effects in the learning process. There are some detect-based defense mechanisms in this context, such as [8,9], and [10], which detect attackers based on sample size, autoencoder-based anomaly detection mechanism and accuracy improvement, respectively. Still, these methods suffer from either heavy computation load due to the verification process or trapping global model to local optima phenomenon. Consequently, an effective decentralized system is required to detect and prevent malicious updates and solve other inter-related security attacks.

Blockchain [11] is a well-known decentralized technology to cope with the security challenges of an FL process, and ensures decentralized storage of model updates with the traceability feature. Furthermore, blockchain follows the combination of chain, tree, and graph structure to make the blocks temper-proof through recording history. In a similar manner, participated clients and their model updates are verified to maintain the order of blocks consistent and immutable. With the addition of a digital currency, blockchain has great potential to attract participants in model training [12]. At the same time, blockchain ensures the immutability of records through consensus algorithms, such as proof of work (PoW). Therefore, consensus and incentive schemes are required to be wisely implemented to successfully motivate the model exchange in the FL process. The incentives or rewards are determined based on the contribution of the participating clients in the FL training process. Having these features, blockchain has great potential to tackle the security attacks that a conventional FL process encounters, and thus blockchain-based FL [13] is an emerging topic. Due to the promising features, this is also an effective architecture for various Industry 5.0 applications.

In recent years, to ensure the security and privacy of the FL process from various angles, blockchain has been employed. For example, [14] has proposed a blockchain-based FL (BCFL) architecture, namely BytoChain, based on the efficient model verification concept through the consensus strategy. The objective of this work is to have a defense against some security attacks, such as denial of service (DoS), reverse model poisoning, and free-riding attacks. In [15], the authors proposed an FL framework based on two layers of blockchains, which can effectively detect fake model updates and lazy clients. Based on the P2P communication concept, BLADE-FL [16] is a blockchain-assisted decentralized FL framework to prevent the model from malicious learning updates as well as SPoF attacks. Moreover, BLADE-FL deals with privacy, resource allocation, and lazy participation issues. Based on this P2P concept, two more works are [13] and [17]. Relying on the consortium blockchain and the proof of verifying (PoV) consensus algorithm, the authors in [18] introduced a blockchain-enabled federated edge learning (BFEL) method with a decentralized server. BFFL ensures the reduction of gradient leaks from inference attacks, model training flexibility, detection of malicious model updates, and reduction of computation overhead. The authors in [19] used a blockchain-based algorithm, which is implemented in smart contracts, to work against poisoning attacks. [20] presented the decentralized training for blockchain-enabled FL process based on the differential privacy (DP) and homomorphic encryption (HE) techniques. In order to motivate honest FL clients while punishing malicious clients, blockchain technology supports the reward and incentive concept, and there are some existing works in this context as well. For example, based on the Shapley value, FedCoin is introduced in [21] to incentivize FL participants in updating the model. In a similar manner, based on a class sampled validation-error scheme (CSVES) and reputation, reward or incentive schemes are implemented in [22] and [23], respectively. The proportion of deliverable incentives can be implemented in the smart contract as well, and [24] and [25] are such two works. Verification and accountability approaches are introduced to prevent the attackers from sending malicious model updates. To this end, in [26], the authors proposed a blockchain-based verifiable and auditable FL approach, named VFChain, based on the committee consensus concept facilitated by a dual skip chain (DSC) data structure. By tracking the model transactions, the trust and verification mechanism is provided in [27]. In another blockchain-based FL framework [28], named BlockFLA, attacks are detected through accountability with hybrid blockchain technology, such as public and private tools leading to ethereum and hyperlegdger fabric, respectively. Through the smart contract and a weighted fair data algorithm, the authors in [29] proposed a trustworthy learning framework empowered with blockchain to improve accountability and equality in FL systems. Unlike the centralized nature of this work, the authors in [30] ensure the accountability and privacy of FL systems in a decentralized manner.

It is clear from the existing literature that there are two types of architectures for the BCFL process: one is centralized server-based BCFL and another is decentralized P2P network-based BCFL. Despite the existence of many works on these two architectures in handling many security and privacy issues in the conventional FL process, there is no work that has done a systematic performance analysis and comparison between these two BCFL architectures, especially in the context of Industry 5.0 applications. To this end, we first provide a detailed description about the components of each architecture, and then outline the detailed workflow of each of the architectures in conducting an FL process. The centralized server-based architecture relies on the parallel verification concept of each local model update. Both architectures adopt the consensus protocol of the blockchain technology to finalize the aggregated model. We further conduct a thorough security analysis in handling various security attacks by each of the BCFL architectures. To summarize, the contributions of this chapter are listed as follows.

- We provide two types of BCFL architectures: centralized server-based and decentralized P2P network-based for Industry 5.0 applications. For the centralized server-based architecture, we adopt the parallel verification concept of local model updates and then apply one state-of-the-art consensus technique to finalize the aggregated model. For the decentralized architecture, although we do not verify each local model update, we apply the same consensus algorithm as in the centralized version to conclude the final model for each round. Following the detailed description of the components, we provide a detailed workflow of each of the architectures.
- We perform a thorough security analysis on the proposed two architectures under various security attacks. In each of the attack scenarios, we show how the proposed two architectures are effective in handling these security attacks.
- We conduct a reasonable simulation-based study to verify the effectiveness of the proposed two architectures under random poisoning attack. The results show that the centralized server-based BCFL architecture is more effective in taking preventive measures against random poisoning attacks compared to the decentralized approach.

The remaining chapter is organized as follows. In Section 7.2, we provide background and preliminary information in the context of this chapter, such as FL, blockchain, and security attacks in the conventional FL process. Following the detailed description of the components, we provide a detailed explanation of the workflow of each of the architectures in Section 7.3. We conduct a thorough security analysis of the proposed two architectures in handling various security attacks in Section 7.4. We conduct an extensive simulation to verify the effectiveness of the proposed two architectures in handling random poisoning attacks in Section 7.5. Following the open issues and challenges in Section 7.6, we draw a conclusion about this chapter in Section 7.7.

7.2 Background and preliminaries

In this section, we provide an overview of relevant topics in the context of this chapter, such as FL, widely known security attacks in traditional FL systems, as well as conventional blockchain technology.

7.2.1 Overview of federated learning

From the architectural point of view, the structure of FL systems can have many forms, such as centralized, hierarchical, and decentralized peer-to-peer network-based. In the centralized architecture, at each round t of the FL process, the server broadcasts the global model G_t to the selected FL participants (let denote the number of selected FL participants as M_t). Based on the global model and local data set $\mathcal{D}_m$, each FL client m trains the global model and obtains the updated local model g_t^m. Afterward, the FL server aggregates the local model updates and builds the global model for the next round. At this stage, the FL server can use different strategies for model aggregation, such as FedProx [31] and FedOpt [32]. For example, according to FedAvg, the FL server aggregates the local models obeying the following rule.

$$G_{t+1} = G_t + \frac{1}{M_t}\sum_{m=1}^{M_t} g_t^m \tag{7.1}$$

where G_{t+1} is the updated global model at the round $t + 1$. This process of interaction between the FL server and FL clients is continued until the convergence is achieved. On the other hand, in the P2P-based architecture, there is no centralized aggregator. Rather, FL participants act as both the client and server for the FL process. In this architecture, each FL client has connectivity with the other clients and can broadcast its training model to all the clients, and vice versa. In the beginning, all the FL clients obtain an initial training model from some third-party node in the network. Upon the reception of the initial global model, each P2P client trains the model based on its local data set and then broadcasts the constructed local model to the remaining clients. Since all FL clients broadcast their individual model to the rest of the clients, each client can have $M_t - 1$ model updates from the remaining $M_t - 1$ clients, and thus each client applies a typical model aggregation rule and constructs a new global model. If all clients are honest and there is no security attack in the middle, the aggregated model constructed by all the FL clients should be the same. However, for the other case, when the constructed models are different, a third-party node could be involved in the FL process to select the best model among the FL clients for the next round of learning.

7.2.2 Security attacks in conventional FL systems

In this section, we explain existing attacks in the conventional FL architecture. In Figure 7.1, we present different types of attacks that lead to the failure of the entire system, such as SPoF [33].

7.2.2.1 Single point of failure (SPoF) attack

The traditional FL structure is heavily dependent on a centralized server. The centralized server aggregates local model updates from participating devices into a fully trained global model and continues this process till the convergence. In various situations, the central server could be the bottleneck of the entire learning process, such as (1) instability of the central server leads to a system crash, (2) a compromised central server generates a false global model, and (3) maximum consumption of system

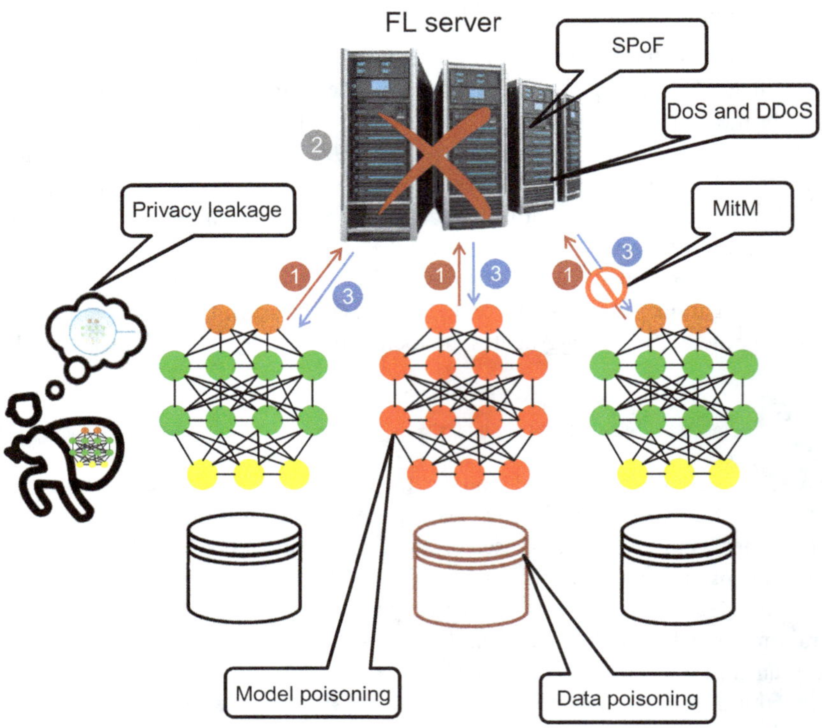

Figure 7.1 An illustration of possible security attacks in conventional FL systems

resources. Thus, this centralized server-oriented learning process could be vulnerable to a SPoF attack [34,35]. The FL process cannot progress much with this type of attack, and even if this continues, a fully convergent model with high accuracy is nearly impossible.

7.2.2.2 Denial of service (DoS) and distributed denial of service (DDoS) attack

Malicious participants in the FL training process could have evil intentions from different perspectives. For instance, by continuously propagating fake model updates, malicious devices can stress the system so much that this crashes, which is called a DoS attack. In a similar manner, if an FL server is compromised, this repeats the entire process and paralyzes the entire FL system, which is referred to as a DDoS attack. Furthermore, malicious FL servers or participants can add weak noise to the original global model for constructing a new model while ensuring an insignificant difference in accuracy.

7.2.2.3 Free-riding attack

The training of an ML model requires exhaustive system resources, such as CPU, network bandwidth, processing power, time and many others. In the training task, to avoid this high cost of model training, dishonest participants may want to gain incentives without contributing much to the training process. For instance, free riders can construct fake or noise-fortified valid model and then directly upload this untrained model. This situation in FL systems potentially leads to fairness and trustworthiness issues. Consequently, it is difficult to distinguish free-riders and honest clients as the model updates by both types of participants apparently look the same [36].

7.2.2.4 Poisoning attacks

The poisoning attacks can be categorized into two types, i.e., data poisoning and model poisoning. Through necessary changes to the training data, the data poisoning attack is launched and the resultant false model updates are propagated. Furthermore, malicious participants can flip the labels of data sets to implement a pre-defined poisoned local model, the propagation of which can degrade the performance of the global model aggregated by the centralized server. Therefore, data poisoning attacks ultimately lead to model poisoning attacks. Besides, reverse and random model poisoning attacks can also be generated in FL systems. In random and reverse poisoning attacks, the model is updated by arbitrarily generated gradients and the training model is updated in opposite directions [14].

7.2.2.5 Man-in-the-middle (MitM) attack

While communicating models between the FL server and clients, an MitM attack usually emerges. In this attack, the attacker pretends to be an FL server or client to send fake model updates and control the traffic. Session hijacking and Internet Protocol (IP) spoofing are common types of MitM attacks. In session hijacking, the attacker snatches a valid session between a trusted FL client and the FL server. On the other hand, through the IP spoofing attack, the FL server or clients are convinced to be in connection with a trusted entity; however, in reality, the attacker works on the other side.

7.2.2.6 Eavesdropping attacks

Although raw data is not passed through the communication media in the FL process, information (e.g., gender, profession, and location) can be inferred from a chain of communicating models between the FL participants and the server by high-skilled attackers [37]. In a similar manner, an adversary can delete, modify, corrupt, or intercept the broadcasted model between the FL server and participants. Till now, eavesdropping attacks are considered more harmful as these can be escalated to severe cyber-attacks (e.g., jamming and DoS). Owing to the jamming attack, the network communication between the server and clients is interrupted through collisions or interference.

7.2.3 Overview of blockchain technology

Blockchain technology is the decentralized ledger technology to keep an immutable record of transactions. It has a chain of blocks, in which a block contains the transaction record, timestamp, and hash value of the associated block. The transactions stored in the blockchain are digitally signed and the hash is stored to retrieve the information for future rounds. In this manner, the history of all transactions can be recorded in a tamper-proof manner. Furthermore, the blocks are connected through chains either in a centralized file system or in a P2P network to maintain the cloned version of the integral transactions logs [38]. Blockchain is broadly categorized into three types: public (i.e., permissionless) blockchain, private (i.e., authorized) blockchain, and consortium blockchain [39]. In a public blockchain, there is no dominant node, and all entities have equal power in the network. On the other hand, the centralized structure is the primary feature of a private blockchain, in which a single entity has full power to validate the transactions of the remaining others. Besides, with the consortium blockchain, different members have different levels of power or authority. A few members of the network are assigned with certain privileges to validate new blocks, and other members can also validate but require the consensus mechanism to finalize a vital task. A consensus algorithm is a collective decision made in a decentralized network. The basic properties of this concept include non-repudiation, authentication, decentralized control, transparency, and byzantine fault tolerance.

7.3 Proposed blockchain-based FL architecture

In the original setting, FL uses a centralized server to exchange updates and manage the global model. This centralized architecture has the risk of SPoF and single-point-of-attack (SPoA). Therefore, we introduce blockchain technology to achieve decentralized model exchange and management among widely distributed edge servers. We consider two types of architectures for the FL process: centralized server-based and decentralized P2P network-based. We know from previous works that verification of each local model is effective in detecting security vulnerabilities in a fine-grained manner. Knowing the high verification burden of every local model, we equip some verifiers for each centralized server in the first architecture to facilitate parallel verification. Although we do not consider the parallel verification concept of every detailed local model for the decentralized architecture, we employ an effective proof-of-accuracy (PoA) consensus technique to finalize the aggregated model in each training round for both types of architectures. In Table 7.1, we compare the characteristics of the two proposed architectures in this chapter with the light of the conventional FL process.

7.3.1 Centralized sever-based FL process

The system in this process consists of data holders in manufacturing environments, verifiers and miners at the network edge, and a task publisher in the blockchain network, as shown in Figure 7.2. The data holders are clients in the FL process, which can be industrial IoTs, robots, or sensors. The verifiers and miners are servers deployed at the edge of the network, with strong computing power and high bandwidth. The verifiers detect inferior local models submitted by malicious clients and generate transactions for miners. The miners mine legal global models and broadcast their blocks to reach an agreement. On the other hand, the task publisher is the leader

Table 7.1 Difference between FL and BCFL under the proposed two architectures

Attribute	FL	Centralized server-based BCFL	Decentralized BCFL
Decentralization	The responsible centralized server can be insecure and can mislead the training process	Multiple centralized servers can be involved in the training process and can apply a consensus algorithm to finalize an aggregated model	There is no any centralized server and FL participants play the role of the server and client. A consensus algorithm is applied here to reach a conclusion about the aggregated in each round
Traceability	FL only stores the latest model, and cannot trace historical models for offline audit	This architecture records all intermediate models in a centralized file system through blocks, which are connected by chains	Each individual FL participant records finalized aggregated model in its file system through a chain of blocks, and thus same data can be resided in multiple nodes
Immutability	The server can arbitrarily tamper with historical training records	Since the chain of blocks is stored in a centralized file system, any tampering with a block by any server can be easily detected by other servers	Model tampering by any FL participant can be detected by the other honest participants if the dishonest participant attempts to use the tampered or contaminated model for training
Incentives	FL does not have any digital currency concept to motivate inactive clients	BCFL has a crypto-currency concept to motivate clients in contributing to training	The same crypto-currency concept in the server-based BCFL is applicable to the decentralized BCFL
Integrity and Reliability	The entire training is coordinated by the centralized server, and thus the training could be misled by both the server and participants	Each block in the centralized file system contains an aggregated model verified by the consensus algorithm, which is immutable	The chain of blocks at each FL participant is also verified by the consensus algorithm
Trust	There is no trust concept in the FL process	Servers participating in the consensus algorithm are trustworthy and thus the verified model in each round is authentic	FL participants involved in the consensus algorithm are trustworthy as well, and thus the verified model held by them is authentic
Dynamic join and exit	The server must be online to continue the training process	Since there are multiple servers in the system, inactivity or failure of one server does not interrupt the training process	Similar to the server-based BCFL, leaving or dishonesty of one participant does not affect the training process

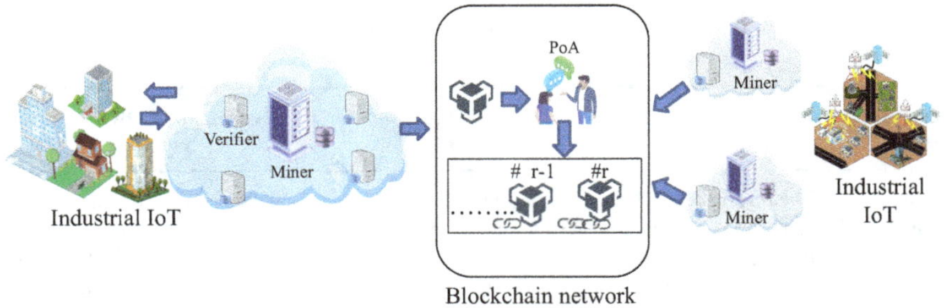

Figure 7.2 An illustration of centralized server-based BCFL systems for Industry 5.0 applications

node in the blockchain network, who creates the task initialization block (i.e., the first block) of a chain to publish the training task, and pays cryptocurrency to motivate clients to participate in the training process in a legitimate manner. We denote a miner and its nearby verifiers collectively as an edge cloud. The model exchange between the miner and the clients happens over wireless channels using the time-division-multiple-access (TDMA) or frequency-division-multiple-access (FDMA) communication protocol. For the verification task, the communication between the miner and verifier occurs through some secured private communication channels.

We consider a network environment, in which learning clients are arbitrary and can join and exit in a flexible manner. The verifier and miners are pre-defined, and selected by legitimate edge service providers in the network. In such an environment, the FL process encounters a severe security challenge due to the malicious activities of any of the nodes. Similar to the learning clients, both the verifiers and miners could be untrustworthy and can interrupt the FL process through some illegitimate activities. The overall workflow of this system is given as follows while pointing to Figure 7.3.

(a) System settings: We adopt a private authorized blockchain to control the scalability of the network as well as to authenticate the nodes entering the system. To construct this system, the authorized miners need to register with the system in advance. The newly added verifier should join the verifier group of the nearest edge cloud, and the clients randomly access a miner of the nearest edge cloud.

(b) Task initialization: Upon submitting a task to the system, the task publisher publishes the task initialization block. The miners download the initialization block and use the information in the block to build the training model, which is then sent to the corresponding clients for local training. To cope with the continuity of the latest training process, newly added miners are required to download the latest block to become up-to-date with the latest training process.

(c) Data preparation: The clients (i.e., industrial IoTs or sensors) collect training data from the environment and store in their local storage devices. The task publisher

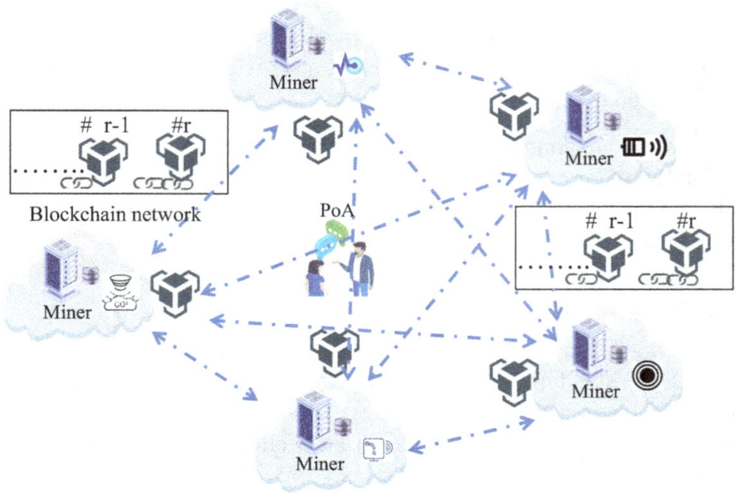

Figure 7.3 An illustration of decentralized BCFL systems for Industry 5.0 applications

is responsible to supply some legitimate validation data to the verifiers. The validation data sets for the edge clouds are randomly sampled such that no two edge clouds share the exact same validation data set.

1. Local training: At the beginning of each round, the clients pull the latest global model from the respective miners, and use local training data to train their local models. The trained local models are sent back to the corresponding miners for legitimate model aggregation.
2. Verification: To detect the most common malicious clients, a miner sends the collected local models to its verifiers for parallel verification. Each verifier uses its validation data set to calculate the accuracy of each local model. If the accuracy is $\geq \gamma$, each verifier passes the corresponding local model back to the miner, otherwise discards the accuracy-deviated model.
3. Mining: Upon receiving primarily verified local models from the verifiers, each miner competes to generate a legal global model from the collected local models. If the constructed global model passes the accuracy test based on the threshold γ, the miners construct a new block with all necessary information and broadcast to the blockchain network for the consensus test. The block which passes the consensus test is selected to be the winner block to be added to the chain. Other miners should give up mining blocks and download the latest global model to continue the next training round.
4. Reward dissemination: The winner miner obtains monetary rewards, and distributes this to its clients and verifiers. The reward amount is calculated based on the accuracy increment of the corresponding model, which can easily be verified by all miners, instead of training data size [6,10] or the Shapley value [9]

that can easily be falsified. As the training progresses, accuracy increases in a marginal manner, and hence the reward value is proportional to $\exp(\beta \text{ACC}_{t-1})$, where β is the compensation coefficient and ACC_{t-1} is the accuracy at $t-1$ training round.

The steps 1–4 are continued until the target round is reached. The task publisher can download stored models from the chain at any time for offline investigation. Otherwise, this node downloads only the finally converged global model and terminates the training task.

7.3.2 Decentralized FL process

There is no centralized server in this system, and the topology looks like the conventional P2P architecture. Different from the previous system, in which model aggregation occurs in a trusted community over the blockchain, a fully decentralized framework is realized here, in which each client must train ML models and mine blocks for publishing aggregated results. The considered network in this system is open, and hence any client joins and exits the FL process at any time. Because of this flexible deployment of the network, the FL process could be more vulnerable compared to that in the other architecture. Any client could be malicious and can jeopardize the entire learning process by applying any type of security attack. Obviously, there is a task publisher in the network to initiate an ML task by publishing the initializing block. Upon publishing the initialization block, the detailed workflow of this system is given as follows.

Initialization: Each client downloads the initialization block and stores this in the chain of its local storage for usage in the training process. With the information of the initial block, the training client builds a local model with its training data and then broadcasts this model over the P2P network.

Step 2: Upon receiving the local updates from other training nodes within a pre-defined time period, each client updates the global model according to the aggregating rule defined in the initial block. If the accuracy of the aggregated model is $\geq \gamma$, the corresponding client keeps this model for the following step and discards otherwise.

Step 3: Each training client changes roles from the trainer to the miner and begins mining until this can finalize an aggregated model verified by other miners. Each miner constructs a block using the aggregated model and other information, and then broadcasts the constructed block over the P2P network. Consequently, a consensus mechanism is initiated among all the miners in the network, and a block is finalized to be a winner. The information about the winner miner and the winner block is propagated over the P2P network. Having this information, other miners discard their failed blocks and consider the winner block to be added to its blockchain.

Step 4: The task publisher in the network provides a reward to the winner miner following the rule described in the previous architecture.

Step 5: Each client trains the model in the winner block with its data set and then broadcasts the trained local model over the P2P network. Thus, the operations in steps 2–5 are continued until the convergence is achieved on the target number of training rounds is reached.

7.3.3 Structure of block

We consider two types of blocks: task initialization block (#0) and model-equipped regular block ($\#t, t > 0$ and $t \leq T$), where t is the index of the current round and T is the total number of training rounds. Their detailed structure is provided in Figure 7.4. In the beginning, the task publisher encloses the initial system and training parameters in the header and body, respectively, and puts the initial parameters and validation accuracy of the global model in the initialization block #0. These parameters are used by the nodes in the blockchain network for the model training, verification, and mining. The regular block at round t contains n local models ($n \geq N$, N is the least number of local models). A Merkle tree is constructed by these local models, the root of which is stored in the header of the block, and so any interruption of local models can be detected. The regular block $\#t$ also contains the global model constructed from these local models. Consequently, historical blocks can be used for failure resolution and offline investigation. Only hash proofs are stored in blocks instead of raw models to keep them lightweight. Lightweight blocks consume affordable bandwidth while being exchanged among nodes in the system. We adopt the homomorphic hashing algorithm in [25] to verify that the global model is the average of the local models held by the corresponding block. According to the fundamental principle, the sum of homomorphic hash values of

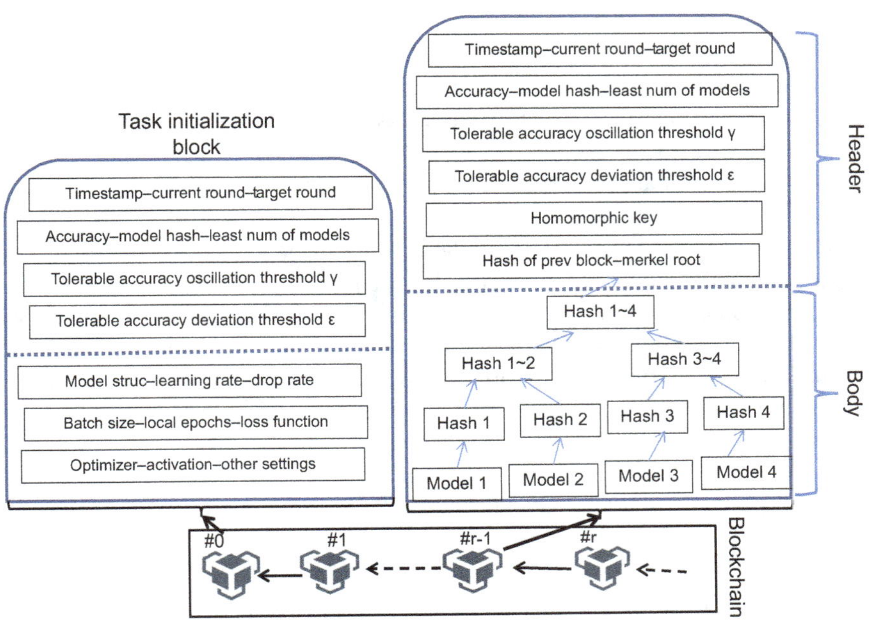

Figure 7.4 A sample structure of block in BCFL systems

the local models should be equal to the n times the homomorphic hash value of the global model. In this way, fast verification of the global model can be achieved, which avoids downloading heavy local models frequently. The accuracy oscillation threshold (AOT) and the accuracy deviation threshold (ADT) are two key thresholds of the proposed consensus algorithm. By AOT, we can determine the allowable reduction of the maximum accuracy of each received model, and we can set the maximum absolute difference in the validation accuracy of a model on different miners by ADT. AOT could be pre-defined, or it can be decayed dynamically as the training process progresses.

7.3.4 Idea of the adopted consensus algorithm

The structure of the constructed chain guarantees immutability and traceability, while an effective consensus mechanism ensures the addition of honest blocks to the chain. In both the proposed architectures, once a miner obtains enough local models from its clients and chooses the clients, the aggregated model of which has the highest accuracy and the resultant accuracy $\geq \gamma$. Here, accuracy is the key indicator of FL tasks, and thus choosing the clients in such a manner is quite effective in achieving security in the FL process. The successful miners (whose aggregated model accuracy $\geq \gamma$) construct a new block with the necessary information that contains the hash proof of the averaged model and broadcast the block for consensus verification. The new block should be verified by other miners to reach a consensus. Other miners download the parameters of the claimed averaged model to conduct the following checkup.

- The accuracy reduction is within the defined AOT threshold (i.e., γ).
- The accuracy deviation is within the defined ADT threshold (i.e., ε).
- The homomorphic hash values meet the additive homomorphism constraint.
- The actual number of selected local models is at least L.
- The Merkle root is correctly calculated from selected local models.

From the outcome of the checkup on these key points, the miners vote on a new block, and a block is finalized to be added to the chain if more than half of the miners approve. On the other hand, when most miners disapprove, the constructed block is considered to be invalid. The invalid blocks are rejected and the corresponding dishonest miners are punished. In order to avoid falling into local optima, the proposed consensus algorithm tolerates models with a certain accuracy drop as accuracy oscillations are common in the training process.

7.4 Security analysis

In this section, we discuss about a few security threats and the potential of the proposed two BCFL architectures to countermeasure those attacks.

7.4.1 Random and reverse poisoning detection

The random poisoning model is a training model that is generated through forged or falsified gradients, and when this becomes poisoned from the local models in the reverse direction, this is called the reverse poisoning model. Both the random and reverse poisoning models can be detected through the pre-defined accuracy threshold as the accuracy of any of the poisoning models is prone to fall under this threshold.

Centralized server-based BCFL architecture: All types of nodes in this architecture could be malicious in the context of this attack. However, under the honest nature of the verifier, if a training client forges its local model, most likely that forged models fail the verification test. On the other hand, although verifiers are authorized, a dishonest verifier can collude with a dishonest training client and help the verification test pass. In such circumstances, the constructed training model from the forged local model either by the verifier or the training client fails to have the accuracy above the ADT constraint. Finally, a miner or centralized aggregator could be malicious as well. If the miner intentionally does not perform its job in model aggregation fully or partially, the resultant accuracy of the aggregated model most likely fails the ADT constraint by the other miners. On the other hand, if the malicious miner deceitfully sets high accuracy for its constructed model, other miners may find that the forged aggregated model fails the AOT constraint.

Decentralized BCFL architecture: In this setting, any node can act in a malicious manner in its all roles: training client, model aggregator, and miner. In the first phase, if any node falsifies its local model, other nodes may find that the aggregated model constructed by that falsified model fails the ADT constraint. On the other hand, a malicious aggregator may perform its job fully or partially and can disseminate the block equipped with the accuracy-deviated model over the P2P network. In such a case, other miners may find that the accuracy-deviated block fails the ADT constraint, and hence the malicious aggregator most likely fails the consensus game. If a malicious miner sets high accuracy for its aggregated model, other miners may find that the constructed model may fail the AOT similar to the other architecture.

7.4.2 Overfitting poisoning

By this attack, the malicious miner somehow achieves high accuracy for its aggregated by using the same data set for the training. Although the malicious miner has high accuracy for its constructed model, other miners may not achieve the same accuracy, and thus the aggregated model of the malicious miner may fail the ADT constraint in the consensus algorithm.

Centralized server-based BCFL architecture: In this system, a malicious miner may share the validation data set with its training clients, and thus the accuracy of the constructed model becomes very high to a malicious miner. However, this falsely high accuracy may not be acceptable to other miners through the proposed consensus algorithm as the other miners easily find that this falsely high accuracy does not satisfy the ADT constraint.

Decentralized BCFL architecture: In this system, since a node plays both the roles of the training client and miner, a malicious node uses the same data set for both the training and verification, and thus the accuracy of the resultant model becomes very high. Similar to the other system, this falsely high accuracy may be detectable to other miners through the proposed consensus algorithm.

7.4.3 DoS attack

Besides destroying the training models, malicious may have other ways to jeopardize the FL system, such as continuously broadcasting a manipulated ML model over the blockchain network. In this case, a malicious miner adds a weak noise to the original ML model to generate an acceptable model. Although such a huge volume of broadcasted models satisfies the ADT and AOT constraints, these can paralyze the entire FL process.

The adopted consensus algorithm in either of the proposed systems can mitigate this attack through the homomorphic constraint. This constraint forces miners to use homomorphic hash values of local models to prove the validity of the claimed model. In this way, the consensus algorithm prevents miners from generating blocks over the air, and thus the generation rate of useless blocks is suppressed.

7.4.4 Free-riding attack

Training ML models are associated with high cost, such as CPU, memory, power, and time. Dishonest training clients may want to earn rewards while not contributing much to the training process. These clients may send the previously trained model without any change or adding some noise to the model. These free-riding clients suffer fairness issues and prevent other honest clients to contribute in the training process.

To disseminate the rewards in a fair manner, as described in the previous section, we use accuracy increment as the metric to quantify the reward value. Since the accuracy is tamper-proof in the blockchain network (either centralized or decentralized), all miners can verify its accuracy in an authorized manner. Since the accuracy increment of the free-riding clients is nearly zero, they soon lose motivation in this type of attack.

7.5 Performance evaluation

In this section, we conduct some preliminary simulations to evaluate the performance of the proposed BCFL architectures.

7.5.1 Simulation settings

To demonstrate the effectiveness of our proposed BCFL architectures, we consider a special network, in which there are 100 industrial IoTs, who have sensed data. For the centralized server-based system, we simulate 8 edge clouds, each of which consists of one miner and 8 verifiers. The deployed clients are randomly served by the deployed 8 edge clouds. We implement an abstract prototype of the blockchain network under both systems, with the consensus algorithm is implemented as described in Section 7.3.4. We use a lightweight convolutional network (e.g., Conv16 and FC10) suitable for industrial IoTs to train the famous data set MNIST. All the training clients hold the same volume of the data set, and the validation sets belonging to the verifiers and miners are randomly sampled and are not shared between any two entities. In the experiments, the stochastic gradient descent (SGD) optimizer is adopted by each training client with a learning rate of 0.001 and a batch size of 16. The total number of global rounds is 100, and each client trains the optimized for three epochs in each global round. The training, verification, and mining tasks are implemented on the MXNET engine and are executed in docker containers with Intel Xeon E5-2678 v3 CPUs and NVIDIA Geforce RTX 2080Ti GPUs.

Unless otherwise specified, we have 20 malicious training clients. Let the latest global model be G and the averaged model of honest data holders be G_h. The RandPA and RevPA models are randomly sampled from $G + \text{Uniform}(-p_1, p_1)$ and $G + p_2(G - G_h)$, respectively, where $p_1 = 0.1$ and $p_2 = 5$ hold. Furthermore, we set AOT and ADT to 0.003 and 0.05, respectively.

7.5.2 Simulation results

In Table 7.2, we compare the performance in terms of model accuracy (at the convergent point) between the proposed two architectures and the basic FL architecture with the growing number of attackers. This is clear from the results that the proposed two architectures outperform the basic FL system no matter the number of attackers is, which justifies the efficiency of the proposed two BCFL architectures. Obviously, the performance of the centralized system is better compared to the other one. This is due to the fact that in the centralized architecture, there is an extra level of model verification by the verifiers before the aggregation of local models.

In Figure 7.5, we compare the performance of the proposed two BCFL architectures as well as the basic FL one under reverse and random poisoning attacks with the increasing AOT. Similar to the results in Table II, the centralized BCFL

Table 7.2 Accuracy comparison among the proposed BCFL architectures and the basic FL one under different attack scenarios

Attack type	**Random poisoning attack $p_1 = 0.1$** **Reverse poisoning attack $p_2 = 5$**				
# Attacks	**1**	**5**	**10**	**15**	**20**
Basic FL	0.960	0.956	0.863	0.113	
	0.966	0.941	0.098	0.098	
Centralized BCFL	0.967	0.967	0.967	0.966	
	0.967	0.967	0.967	0.967	
Decentralized BCFL	0.923	0.898	0.827	0.766	
	0.923	0.895	0.825	0.764	

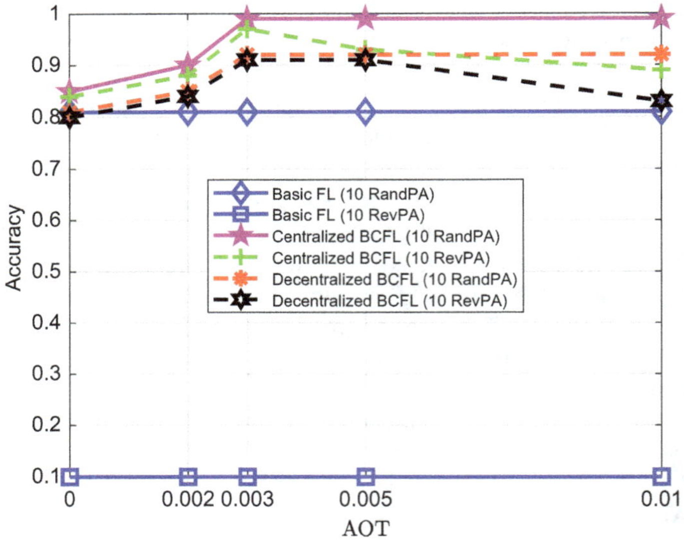

Figure 7.5 Accuracy comparison among the proposed BCFL architecture and the basic FL one with the increasing AOYT

system outperforms the decentralized one. Moreover, the results in this figure indicate that there is an optimal level of AOT architecture, in which the proposed BCFL architecture architectures have the best performance.

7.6 Open issues and challenges

In this section, we discuss some open issues in the context of the proposed two BCFL architectures.

7.6.1 Privacy of raw data

Curious nodes (e.g., verifiers and miners) can use generative models to reconstruct the raw data of training clients, which is called a privacy attack. Differential privacy (DP) is one of the mainstream technologies to protect data privacy. By this, training clients can add Laplace noise to their local models, which creates confusion among miners about the raw data.

7.6.2 Confidentiality of training model

The training model is an intellectual property that requires to be preserved. However, training clients can download the latest model to use this for their own purposes, leading to leakage and abuse of proprietary models. Trusted execution environment (TEE) is a hardware-level security technology that has been widely adopted on most mainstream CPUs, such as Intel SGX on x86 and TrustZone on ARM. TEE divides the storage space into a secure world and a normal world. The computation and storage of proprietary models are performed in the secure world, and thus training clients cannot access them from the normal world. However, the scheduling of the secure world needs careful investigation owing to its scarcity.

7.7 Conclusion

In this chapter, we proposed two BCFL architectures for Industry 5.0 applications, one of which is centralized server based and another one is based on the decentralized P2P architecture. Upon describing the components and mechanisms of these two systems, we illustrated a few security attack scenarios in basic FL systems and then discussed the potential of the proposed system to mitigate these attacks. We conducted some simulations to verify the effectiveness of the proposed BCFL architectures compared to the basic FL systems. The results further demonstrated that the centralized BCFL architecture outperforms the decentralized one owing to the extra layer of verification of local models. Finally, we discussed some open issues and challenges in the context of the proposed architectures.

References

[1] T. Li, A. K. Sahu, A. Talwalkar, and V. Smith, "Federated Learning: Challenges, Methods, and Future Directions," *IEEE Signal Processing Magazine*, vol. 37, no. 3, pp. 50–60, 2020.

[2] D. Yin, Y. Chen, R. Kannan, and P. Bartlett, "Byzantine-Robust Distributed Learning: Towards Optimal Statistical Rates," in *Proc. 35th International Conference on Machine Learning, ser. Proceedings of Machine Learning Research*, J. Dy and A. Krause, Eds., vol. 80, 10–15 2018, pp. 5650–5659.

[3] H. Yang, X. Zhang, M. Fang, and J. Liu, "Byzantine-Resilient Stochastic Gradient Descent for Distributed Learning: A Lipschitz-Inspired Coordinate-wise Median Approach," in *Proc. IEEE CDC*, 2019, pp. 5832–5837.

[4] K. Pillutla, S. M. Kakade, and Z. Harchaoui, "Robust Aggregation for Federated Learning," *IEEE Trans. Signal Processing*, vol. 70, pp. 1142–1154, 2022.

[5] P. Blanchard, E. M. El Mhamdi, R. Guerraoui, and J. Stainer, "Machine Learning with Adversaries: Byzantine Tolerant Gradient Descent," in *Proc. 31st International Conference on Neural Information Processing Systems*. Red Hook, NY, USA: Curran Associates Inc., 2017, p. 118–128.

[6] J. So, B. Güler, and A. S. Avestimehr, "Byzantine-Resilient Secure Federated Learning," *IEEE J. Sel. A. Commun.*, vol. 39, no. 7, pp. 2168–2181, 2021.

[7] E. M. El Mhamdi, R. Guerraoui, and S. L. A. Rouault, "The Hidden Vulnerability of Distributed Learning in Byzantium," in *Proc. International Conference on Machine Learning*, no. 80, 2018, pp. 3521–3530.

[8] H. Kim, J. Park, M. Bennis, and S.-L. Kim, "Blockchained On-Device Federated Learning," *IEEE Commun. Lett.*, vol. 24, no. 6, pp. 1279–1283, 2020.

[9] S. Zhou, H. Huang, W. Chen, P. Zhou, Z. Zheng, and S. Guo, "PIRATE: A Blockchain-Based Secure Framework of Distributed Machine Learning in 5G Networks," *IEEE Network*, vol. 34, no. 6, pp. 84–91, 2020.

[10] G. J. Mendis, Y. Wu, J. Wei, M. Sabounchi, and R. Roche, "A Blockchain-Powered Decentralized and Secure Computing Paradigm," *IEEE Trans. Emerging Topics Comput.*, vol. 9, no. 4, pp. 2201–2222, 2021.

[11] O. Ali, M. A. Ally, P. Clutterbuck, and Y. K. Dwivedi, "The State of Play of Blockchain Technology in the Financial Services Sector: A Systematic Literature Review," *Int. J. Inf. Manag.*, vol. 54, p. 102199, 2020.

[12] K. Toyoda and A. N. Zhang, "Mechanism Design for An Incentive-aware Blockchain-enabled Federated Learning Platform," in *Proc. IEEE Big Data*, 2019, pp. 395–403.

[13] M. Shayan, C. Fung, C. J. M. Yoon, and I. Beschastnikh, "Biscotti: A Blockchain System for Private and Secure Federated Learning," *IEEE Trans. Parallel Distribut. Sys.*, vol. 32, no. 7, pp. 1513–1525, 2021.

[14] Z. Li, H. Yu, T. Zhou, L. Luo, M. Fan, Z. Xu, and G. Sun, "Byzantine Resistant Secure Blockchained Federated Learning at the Edge," *IEEE Network*, vol. 35, no. 4, pp. 295–301, 2021.

[15] S. Yuan, B. Cao, M. Peng, and Y. Sun, "ChainsFL: Blockchain-driven Federated Learning from Design to Realization," in *Proc. IEEE WCNC*, 2021, pp. 1–6.

[16] C. Ma, J. Li, L. Shi, M. Ding, T. Wang, Z. Han, and H. V. Poor, "When Federated Learning Meets Blockchain: A New Distributed Learning Paradigm," *IEEE Computational Intelligence Magazine*, vol. 17, no. 3, pp. 26–33, 2022.

[17] X. Wu, Z. Wang, J. Zhao, Y. Zhang, and Y. Wu, "FedBC: Blockchain-based Decentralized Federated Learning," in *Proc. IEEE ICAICA*, 2020, pp. 217–221.

[18] J. Kang, Z. Xiong, D. Niyato, Y. Zou, Y. Zhang, and M. Guizani, "Reliable Federated Learning for Mobile Networks," *IEEE Wirel Commun.*, vol. 27, no. 2, pp. 72–80, 2020.

[19] A. R. Short, H. C. Leligou, M. Papoutsidakis, and E. Theocharis, "Using Blockchain Technologies to Improve Security in Federated Learning Systems," in *Proc. IEEE COMPSAC*, 2020, pp. 1183–1188.

[20] S. Kumar, S. Dutta, S. Chatturvedi, and M. Bhatia, "Strategies for Enhancing Training and Privacy in Blockchain Enabled Federated Learning," in *Proc. IEEE BigMM*, 2020, pp. 333–340.

[21] Y. Liu, Z. Ai, S. Sun, S. Zhang, Z. Liu, and H. Yu, *FedCoin: A Peer-to-Peer Payment System for Federated Learning*. Cham: Springer International Publishing, 2020, pp. 125–138.

[22] I. Martinez, S. Francis, and A. S. Hafid, "Record and Reward Federated Learning Contributions with Blockchain," in *Proc. IEEE CyberC*, 2019, pp. 50–57.

[23] J. Kang, Z. Xiong, D. Niyato, S. Xie, and J. Zhang, "Incentive Mechanism for Reliable Federated Learning: A Joint Optimization Approach to Combining

Reputation and Contract Theory," *IEEE Internet of Things Journal*, vol. 6, no. 6, pp. 10 700–10 714, 2019.

[24] M. R. Behera, S. Upadhyay, and S. Shetty, "Federated Learning using Smart Contracts on Blockchains, based on Reward Driven Approach," 2022.

[25] Z. Batool, K. Zhang, and M. Toews, "FL-MAB: Client Selection and Monetization for Blockchain-Based Federated Learning." New York, NY, USA: Association for Computing Machinery, 2022, p. 299–307.

[26] Z. Peng, J. Xu, X. Chu, *et al.*, "VFChain: Enabling Verifiable and Auditable Federated Learning via Blockchain Systems," *IEEE Trans. Network Science and Engineering*, vol. 9, no. 1, pp. 173–186, 2022.

[27] S. Awan, F. Li, B. Luo, and M. Liu, "Poster: A Reliable and Accountable Privacy-Preserving Federated Learning Framework Using the Blockchain," in *Proc. ACM SIGSAC Conference on Computer and Communications Security*. New York, NY, USA: Association for Computing Machinery, 2019, p. 2561–2563.

[28] H. B. Desai, M. S. Ozdayi, and M. Kantarcioglu, "BlockFLA: Accountable Federated Learning via Hybrid Blockchain Architecture," in *Proc. the Eleventh ACM Conference on Data and Application Security and Privacy*. New York, NY, USA: Association for Computing Machinery, 2021, p. 101–112.

[29] S. K. Lo, Y. Liu, Q. Lu, *et al.*, "Toward Trustworthy AI: Blockchain-Based Architecture Design for Accountability and Fairness of Federated Learning Systems," *IEEE Internet of Things Journal*, vol. 10, no. 4, pp. 3276–3284, 2023.

[30] V. Mugunthan, R. Rahman, and L. Kagal, "BlockFLow: An Accountable and Privacy-Preserving Solution for Federated Learning," *CoRR*, vol. abs/2007.03856, 2020. [Online]. Available: https://arxiv.org/abs/2007.03856

[31] A. K. Sahu, T. Li, M. Sanjabi, M. Zaheer, A. Talwalkar, and V. Smith, "On the Convergence of Federated Optimization in Heterogeneous Networks," *CoRR*, vol. abs/1812.06127, 2020. [Online]. Available: http://arxiv.org/abs/1812.06127

[32] H. Wang, M. Yurochkin, Y. Sun, D. Papailiopoulos, and Y. Khazaeni, "Federated Learning with Matched Averaging," ArXiv, vol. abs/2002.06440, 2020.

[33] A. Qammar, A. Karim, H. Ning, and J. Ding, "Securing Federated Learning with Blockchain: A Systematic Literature Review," *Artificial Intelligence Review*, vol. 56, no. 5, pp. 3951–3985, 2023.

[34] L. Feng, Y. Zhao, S. Guo, X. Qiu, W. Li, and P. Yu, "BAFL: A Blockchain-Based Asynchronous Federated Learning Framework," *IEEE Trans. Comput.*, vol. 71, no. 5, pp. 1092–1103, 2022.

[35] Y. Li, C. Chen, N. Liu, H. Huang, Z. Zheng, and Q. Yan, "A Blockchain-Based Decentralized Federated Learning Framework with Committee Consensus," *IEEE Network*, vol. 35, no. 1, pp. 234–241, 2021.

[36] Y. Fraboni, R. Vidal, and M. Lorenzi, "Free-rider Attacks on Model Aggregation in Federated Learning," in *Proc. 24th International Conference on Artificial Intelligence and Statistics*, ser. Proceedings of Machine Learning

Research, A. Banerjee and K. Fukumizu, Eds., vol. 130, 13–15 2021, pp. 1846–1854.

[37] L. Wang, S. Xu, X. Wang, and Q. Zhu, "Eavesdrop the Composition Proportion of Training Labels in Federated Learning," ArXiv, vol. abs/1910.06044, 2019.

[38] Z. Zheng, S. Xie, H. Dai, X. Chen, and H. Wang, "An Overview of Blockchain Technology: Architecture, Consensus, and Future Trends," in *Proc. IEEE BigData Congress*, 2017, pp. 557–564.

[39] M. Niranjanamurthy, B. Nithya, and S. Jagannatha, "Analysis of Blockchain technology: pros, cons and SWOT," *Cluster Computing*, pp. 1–15, 2018.

Chapter 8

Blockchain implementation of public key infrastructure for Industry 5.0 applications

Rukhsana Ruby[1], Salabat Khan[1], Zehua Wang[2] and Lu Wang[1]

Abstract

Cyberattacks are quite prevalent in Industry 5.0 applications owing to the growing necessity of online communication in our day-to-day activities. X.509 Public-key Infrastructure (PKIX) is the most prominent concept to safeguard our online tasks. However, this concept is vulnerable to various security attacks, by which attackers adopt various policies to ruin the primary objective of this system in online communication. Consequently, focusing on PKIX vulnerabilities, numerous projects (e.g., Let's Encrypt and Google certificate transparency) have been initiated to safeguard online communication, which in turn assists Internet users against cyberattacks. On the other hand, blockchain is one of the key enabling technologies for Industry 5.0 applications from the perspective of ensuring security and privacy in a decentralized manner. In this chapter, we first provide a taxonomy of PKIX proposals in the context of blockchain technology while making a comparative study with other conventional PKIX proposals. Second, we define a list of evaluation metrics against some well-known cyberattacks and then compare different blockchain-based PKIX implementations in terms of these evaluation metrics and cyberattacks. Finally, we present some open challenges and future works in the context of Industry 5.0 applications.

Keywords: X.509 Public-key Infrastructure (PKIX), Blockchain, Blockchain-based PKIX, Industry 5.0

8.1 Introduction

Owing to the industrial revolution with the emerging Industry 5.0 standard, usage of Internet has been increasing in an exponential manner. Almost all sectors in urban and rural areas (e.g., manufacturing and medical) are getting sophisticated, where

[1]College of Computer Science and Software Engineering, Shenzhen University, China
[2]Department of Electrical and Computer Engineering, The University of British Columbia, Canada

a huge number of Internet of Things (IoT) devices are adopted to make things life easier. Various platforms, such as online banking, mailing, and e-commerce, have become a unified and imperative part of our daily lives owing to their crucial services. A recent news reported that the number of Internet users has increased by 4.1% (around 200 million) over the last year. These Internet users significantly count on Web 3.0 technology to connect as well as write and own information in different entities to a great extent. With the increasing dependency on online smart applications and services, Internet users, WWW applications, intelligent services, and devices are getting more sensitive to cyberattacks. According to Skybox Security report, 20,175 vulnerabilities were found in 2021, which is an increase of almost 24% [1] compared to the former year.

More specifically, the privacy and security of Internet users are getting interrupted by different government agencies as well as hackers. Accordingly, numerous endeavors have been initiated to defend cyberattacks in Internet traffic using cryptographic algorithms, such as Google invented certificate transparency (CT) [2] and Let's Encrypt [3] project declared by Internet Engineering Task Force (IETF). Cryptographic algorithms can be classified into two primary categories: symmetric and asymmetric. In the first category, a sole key is adopted to encrypt/decrypt information although the distribution and management of this single key in an open communication environment (e.g., Internet) is a matter of concern. To solve the key management problem in this algorithm, PKC was invented in 1976, which uses public key (PK) to encrypt information and secret key (SK) to decrypt information. The key management problem in this method is tackled through a public registry that has mapping information between PK and domain name. To solve its evolved identity authentication problem, Public-Key Infrastructure (PKI) has been introduced. Among many PKI standards, X.509 standard PKI (PKIX), namely PKI/Web PKI has received widespread popularity in web communications. However, the design of PKIX has many drawbacks, which could be utilized by intelligent hackers [4,5] to conduct various cybercrimes.

Over the last decade, many proposals and endeavors have been introduced to resolve the flaws and vulnerabilities in conventional PKIX architecture. In [6], Rueppel *et al.* pointed out legal and technical challenges experienced while designing and operating a PKI framework. In [7], Holz *et al.* analyzed TLS/SSL certificates and key length of those certificates and provided explanation on various cipher suits adopted in PKIX. Grant [8] evaluated various PKIX proposals, such as convergence [9], perspectives [10], DNS-based Authentication of Named Entities (DANE) [11–13], Certification Authority Authorization (CAA) [14], Mutually Endorsed Certification Authority Infrastructure (MECAI) [15], PK Pinning (PKP) [16], Sovereign Keys Infrastructure (SKI) [17], and Google certificate transparency (CT) [2] and made a comparative analysis among them. Amann *et al.* [18] kept a record of TLS/SSL certificates over a year and inferred that detection of malicious certificates from structural changes is not practical. Albarqi *et al.* [19] studied the PKI framework at the operational level and made a comparative analysis between PKIX and Pretty Good Privacy (PGP) in terms of features and performance. The authors in [20] investigated man-in-the-middle (MitM) attacks on Facebook using TLS/SSL certificates. To set a standard for an ideal PKI framework, Vandersloot *et al.* [21] collected certificate-centric information from various platforms, such as Google CT logs. Upon discussing modeling and simulation of certificate validation cost, the authors in [22] illustrated a high-level summary of the PKIX framework. The authors in [23] wrote a chapter on conventional and log-based PKIX proposals while setting a set of evaluation metrics for performance. Amann *et al.* [24] studied new security attributes of some protocols, such as Google CT, DNSSEC [25], and HSTS-embedded HTTPS. The authors in [26] investigated the features of practically issued certificates to see whether these meet the base foundation of the PKIX system. The authors in [27] made a comparative study among blockchain-based PKI schemes to provide advice on the design of a better scheme. Albogam *et al.* The authors in [28] made a comparative study between conventional and blockchain-based PKI schemes.

Despite numerous available survey articles on conventional, log-based, and blockchain-based PKI proposals, there is no complete work that made a complete comparative study among all these PKI proposals. Moreover, we set a list of performance metrics to evaluate the security, privacy, and system performance of all these PKI proposals. To summarize, the contributions of this chapter are listed as follows.

- Before presenting the state-of-the-art of PKIX proposals, we provide a thorough review of the PKIX architecture, the certificate issuance process, and some well-known cyberattacks in such a system.
- We provide a taxonomy of PKIX proposals that includes defense policy and solution scheme, as well as the strengths and weaknesses of each proposal.
- Followed by defining a set of performance metrics, we evaluate the performance of the surveyed PKIX schemes based on these metrics in terms of security, privacy, and system-oriented features.
- Finally, we present some challenges and future works in the context of PKIX proposals.

The remainder of the chapter is organized as follows. In Section 8.2, we provide background information in the context of this work. Followed by the description of the state-of-the-art conventional PKIX proposals in Section 8.3, we present a detailed description of the state-of-the-art blockchain-based PKIX schemes in Section 8.4. We evaluate the performance of the discussed PKIX schemes in Section 8.5. Open challenges are studied in Section 8.6. Finally, we draw the conclusion of this chapter in Section 8.7.

8.2 Background and preliminaries

In this section, we provide some background information relevant to the topic of this work, such as the conventional PKIX framework, DV-certificate issuance process, and traditional cyberattacks on the PKIX architecture.

8.2.1 PKIX

Since the introduction of PKI, the Internet has been reigned by its well-known ITU-T X.509 standard [29], namely PKIX. Primary protocols of the Internet, such as TLS/SSL, HTTPS, POP, SMTP, IMAP, XMPP, and LDAP, natively depend on

PKIX for establishing secure connections [29]. PKIX has a typical layout for a certificate, known as X.509 certificate signed by certification authorities (CAs), and methods for registration, initialization, certification, cross-certification, key pair generation, its update, certificate expiry, and certificate revocation. Figure 8.1 presents a conventional PKIX framework, which consists of five main components [30] as follows.

- Certification authority (CA): This entity is liable to grant and revoke X.509 certificates. This can transfer certificate issuance authority to subordinate CAs (sub-CAs) and other executive tasks, such as identity authentication to registration authorities (RA).
- Server: A CA issues a certificate for this entity, whose identity is stored on the subject portion of the corresponding X.509 certificate. The server (e.g., www.a.com in Figure 8.1) considers the granted certificate(s) for authentication of clients as well as encryption/decryption.
- Registration authority (RA): This is a supporting entity that performs identity authentication as well as server registration. The CA can assign many other administrative tasks to this entity.
- Client: An entity authenticates web servers through certificate verification to use services offered by them.
- Repository: An entity holds certificate revocation lists (CRLs) to verify the revocation condition of X.509 certificates.

For the purpose of establishing secure communication with clients, a server first sends a certificate signing request (CSR) through RA with CA. With this request, a certificate is granted that consists of basic information (e.g., common name, IP address, and domain name) after thorough investigation of identity and provided

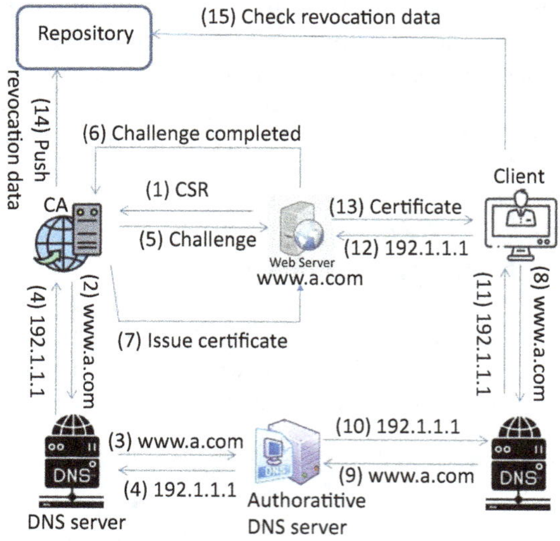

Figure 8.1 An illustration of PKIX framework

information. During the initialization process, the browsers of clients are installed with necessary materials, such as PKs of root CAs, that facilitate them in verifying a CA-signed domain certificate. Intending to establish secure communication with a server, a CA-signed certificate is received by the client. The client verifies whether the received certificate is signed by its trusted CAs, not expired and revoked through the revocation status resided in CRLs. In PKIX standard, CAs are considered totally trusted that handle certificate issuance and revocation issues for clients. However, such a design of PKIX standard has several drawbacks, such as single point of failure (SPoF), and global trust issue by a single compromised CA [18].

8.2.2 DV-certificate issuance procedure

The automated certificate management protocol (ACME) [31] is a well-known certificate-based domain authentication procedure adopted by Let's Encrypt and other CAs. This protocol consists of three principal steps: (1) upon submitting a CSR to an ACME-based CA by a domain owner, this receives a number of queries for identity authentication by the CA, (2) the owner encounters the set of challenges through appropriate responses, and (3) the CA issues DV-certificate to the domain owner upon satisfying the thrown queries. The core theme of the ACME protocol is identity validation to verify control over a domain using the following conventional mechanisms.

1. Email-based validation: According to this mechanism, after obtaining the email address of the designated domain stored in the Whois database, the CA sends an email to the registrar of that domain. The email contains necessary queries for domain identity verification. Upon satisfying the queries in the email by the applicant, CA grants a certificate for that domain.
2. HTTP-based validation: On obtaining the CSR, the CA sets forth a number of queries to the root of the web server. Through HTTP request, the CA accesses necessary files and issues a certificate upon successful verification.
3. Whois-based validation: Email is the sole means of validation in this method. However, unlike the email-based validation technique, where an email address is chosen by the domain, through this mechanism, the CA uses a random email address residing in the Whois database for that domain.
4. DNS-based validation: In this mechanism, a domain server is requested by the CA to set forth a challenge as a DNS Canonical NAME (CNAME) Resource Record (RR) in the respective zone file. For example, if the CA domain is ca-domain.com, the CNAME record for the a.com domain should be: challenge1.www.a.com CNAME challenge2.ca-dmoain.com. The CA adopts the DNS resolver to check the record and issues a certificate if the record is found.

8.2.3 Illustration of cyberattacks

In this section, we illustrate a few possible cyberattacks in the context of PKIX protocol that can happen in the real world.

8.2.3.1 MitM attacks

Typically, a cyberattack is targeted on PKIX clients through mischievous certificates. An attacker can hijack the Internet traffic of victims using fake/malicious certificates. A sample illustration of a cyberattack on a PKIX client is presented in Figure 6, in which an adversary omits the CA validation process. While diverting the CA validation process, in the steps between 1 and 4, the adversary grabs a malicious certificate for a victim domain using the spoofing of a DNS record. The adversary adopts the malicious certificate to pursue a cyberattack against the victim domain as well as its clients. After obtaining the IP address of the victim domain in the steps between 5 and 6, a client tends to establish the TLS connection with the victim server through a hello message in step 7. Consequently, the adversary initiates a MitM attack against the victims by taking control over the communication between the victim client and server as depicted in the steps between 8 and 10 of Figure 8.2.

8.2.3.2 CA compromise

A trusted CA could be corrupted by a sudden attacker issuing malicious certificates to domain owners. An intelligent attacker can take down any CA to grab all its certificates and pursue cyber-criminal activities against the web server and their clients associated with that CA. For instance, two famous CAs: Comodo and DigiNotar, were compromised, and the certificates of top sites were fraudulently acquired, and various cyberattacks were conducted against the top websites through maliciously acquired certificates.

8.2.3.3 Border gateway protocol (BGP) route hijacking

By maliciously tampering routing tables maintained and managed by BGP, this type of attack controls the routing path of a group of IP addresses. This is similar to an application layer DDoS attack, which is usually conducted by Internet Service

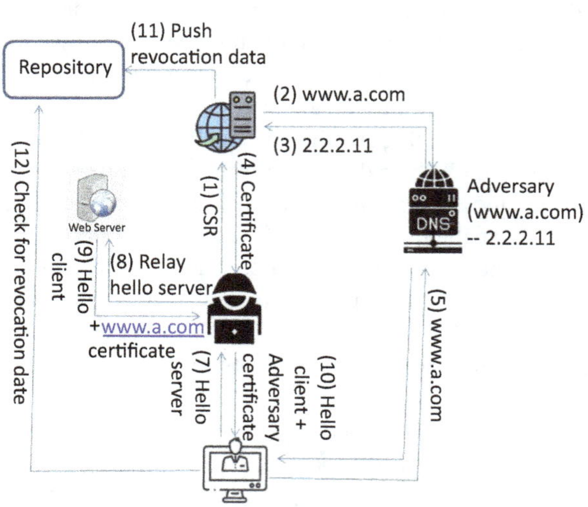

Figure 8.2 An illustration of MitM attack to PKIX framework

Providers (ISPs) when they do not properly monitor the network prefix announcements obtained from their neighboring ISPs before forwarding the advertisements to others. Through these attacks, an adversary impersonates a network maliciously while adopting the prefix of a legitimate network. Consequently, the adversary convinces other networks to accept the advertised network prefix, and thus Internet traffic is unintentionally forwarded to the adversary instead of its original destination. In the PKIX context, through this attack, domain control validation can be masqueraded and malicious certificates can be obtained. The common BGP hijacks used for the takeover of domain control are sub-prefix hijacks, equally specific hijacks, and autonomous systems (AS) path poisoning attacks [4]. A sample illustration of this attack is presented in Figure 8.3. In the first and second types of hijacking, an attacker announces a sub-prefix that includes the IP address of the targeted domain and a prefix of the same length as the victim domain server, respectively (shown in red color in Figure 8.3b). In the last scenario, an adversary announces a sub-prefix of equal length to the domain prefix of the victim appended with forwarding path to the victim domain (showing in magenta color in Figure 8.3b).

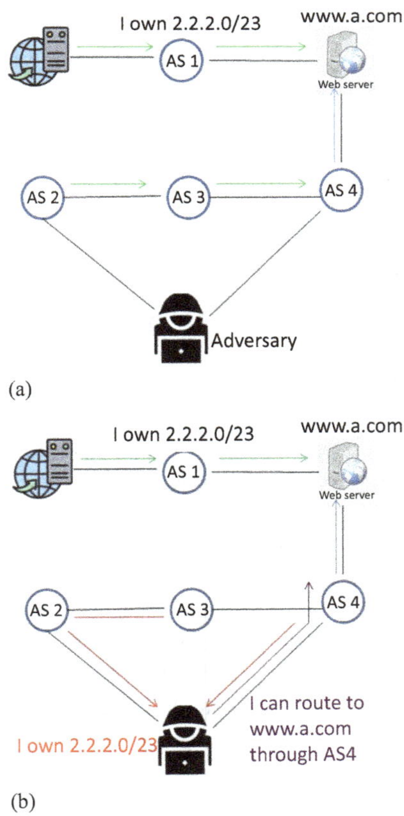

Figure 8.3 A sample illustration of path poisoning attack. (a) No attack and (b) attack.

(a)

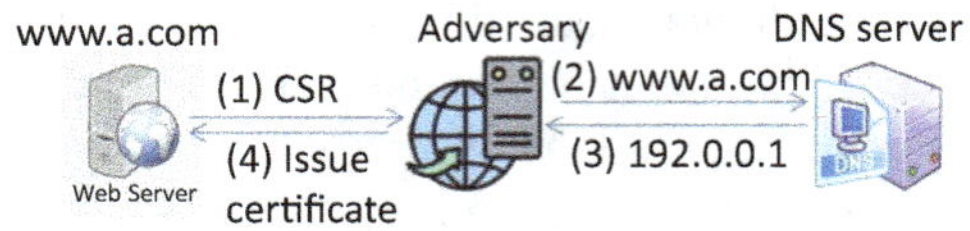

(b)

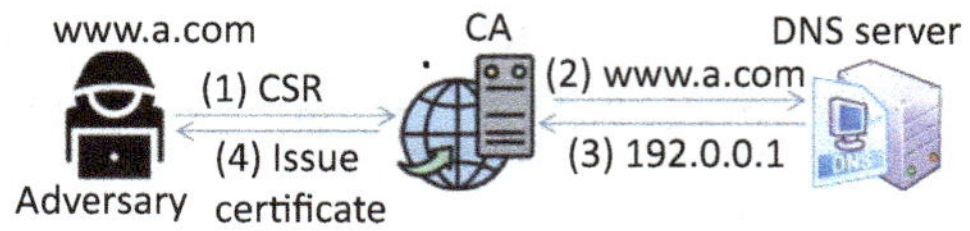

(c)

Figure 8.4 A sample illustration of subdomain takeover attack via dangling DNS record. (a) Dangling DNS record attack, (b) normal operation, and (c) subdomain takeover attack.

8.2.3.4 Dangling DNS record attack

Dangling DNS records imply the IP addresses pointing to an expired service or resource in the topmost DNS server. Antiquated DNS records directed toward unused IP addresses are adopted in this attack to conduct domain takeover attacks as illustrated in Figure 8.4. The dangling DNS records are categorized into the expired domain, discontinued services, and deprovisioned cloud instance.

8.2.3.5 DNS spoofing attack

The CA could be tricked into granting malicious certificates for certain domains through the manipulation of DNS records in DNS servers. With this objective, an adversary can administer a spoofed DNS record into the cache of DNS servers to falsify some victim domains so that communication traffic is forwarded to the adversary-owned domain server. MitM attack as well as the malicious interruption of the DNS server are the means of this attack. For the former method, the UDP source port and communication ID of the DNS handshake are required to be learned by the adversary. Upon learning these, the adversary introduces a spoofed DNS record to the response message of the DNS handshake such that the victim domain can accept it as an authentic reply. In the other case, a DNS server is required to be hacked for the desired modification.

8.2.3.6 Split-world attack

Through this attack, certain information in the PKIX system could be presented in a different manner to different entities. More specifically, the adversary illegitimately could administer a trusted entity (e.g., CA and transparency log server) to demonstrate different copies of signed records to legitimate users and victims. For example, message R1 in the third party server points that record m1 is invalid for member m1, and another message in the same server points that record m1 is valid for member m1.

8.2.3.7 DNS cache poisoning attack

Despite the ignorance about the DNS request, through this attack, an attacker inserts a spoof record into the DNS cache. Once the cache is poisoned, an intended site is resolved for the victim domain even if the storage of the DNS server is not tampered. In 2005, BGP hijacking was employed for poisoning DNS cache [32].

8.3 Conventional PKIX proposals

In this section, we provide the state-of-the-art of conventional PKIX proposals based on CA, client, domain, and log servers.

8.3.1 CA-centered proposals

In [33], it is proposed that only a few famous CAs have the authority to issue certificates for domain servers [34]. Having restrictions based on past behavior, a CA is restricted to endorse certificates for a designated pool of TLD. According to them, such a restriction in issuing or endorsing certificates can decrease the cyberattack in the PKIX system by 65–90%. Based on the browsing history of a client, in [35], a tool is developed that finds a set of preferred CAs. Trust issues are further studied based on a local user-centric knowledge base that computes trust decisions for different applicants in a dynamic manner. Based on the previously gathered knowledge of the trust level of users, the same authors in [36] confined the working regime of those users [37]. Classen *et al.* The concept of trust views is further extended in [38] by collecting the reputation data of CAs from their users through the peer-to-peer networking concept. However, Classen *et al.* [3] have shown that a newly added CA highly compatible with community requirements may obtain lower reputation grades compared to an older CA lesser compatible with community requirements. Moreover, reputation-based PKIX schemes [33,36,38] cannot prevent clients from malicious issuance of certificates from their authorized CA.

Domain validation++ (DV++) [39] is another recent PKIX system. DV++ improved MitM attack-prone traditional domain validation of CAs through protection from multi-vantage points. In this scheme, the identity of each domain server is verified from different holes to resist path-poisoning attacks as well as other on-path and off-path adversaries. In [40], the authors tackled the weakest-link issues of PKIX systems through the federation of all CAs based on the "Cothority" concept.

In [41], the authors made CAs oblivious by simultaneously validating identity and issuing a certificate to a domain owner without learning its true identity information. The Secure Channel Injection (SCI) protocol is adopted for identity verification of clients without knowing their original identities. The core concept of this protocol is the exchange of numerous encrypted messages by many entities for identity verification. Upon submitting a secured challenge message by the verifier, the prover uses a separate link to relay this back to the verifier to fulfill the identity verification challenges. Through this method, a conventional CA is initialized with an anonymous communication system without separating the tasks of identity verification and certificate issuance. Based on this concept, Let's Encrypt CA [3] project was started by IETF to make the certificate issuance, server configuration, and identity validation fast and automatic, which rely on the ACME protocol. However, the CA is still considered fully trusted [42]. By analyzing ZMAP [43], Perl *et al.* in [44] found 140 unused CA certificates that were never used in any web communication. They claimed that removing or restricting these unused certificates on the client truststore does not disallow any previously valid TLS/SSL certificates. In [45], the private key of a CA is among multiple entities to mitigate the risk of compromising the private key. The work in [45] adopts the same multi-party operation concept to sign certificates without exposing the real key.

8.3.2 Client-centered proposals

Perspective [10] is a Firefox browser-based tool designed in 2008 that aims to mitigate trust-on-first-use (TOFU)-prone PK cyberattacks by inquiring PK status in specialized notary servers. Being independent and distributed server entities, the notaries keep a record of all observed PKs including their timestamp and revocation status. Upon receiving a PK from a server, the end-user validates the PK through querying to multiple notaries. If the PK query results are consistent, the end-user accepts the PK, and rejects this otherwise, which in turn prevents MitM attacks. However, the assignment of multiple PKs to a server is not supported as these represent conflicting views of PKs to end-users. Moreover, a fresh PK could be diagnosed as invalid for a period of time until the notaries witness this.

DoubleCheck [46] solved the browsing history leakage and fresh PK invisibility problems of perspective by inquiring to a notary server two times. These inquiries are conducted through a Tor secure connection and an SSL/TLS secured connection. Similar to Perspective, DoubleCheck is independent of new infrastructural components compared to the traditional PKI scheme but preserves user privacy.

Marlinspike implemented a tool namely convergence in Firefox browser [9], that hides the browsing history of clients through adopting an onion routing-like technique, in which users randomly select one notary to forward the request to other notaries. The forwarding notary cannot know the details of the placed query, while the destination notaries cannot reveal the identity of the requester. Clients keep the verified certificates in their caches, and seek the help of notaries for newly encountered certificates. Similar to Perspective and DoubleCheck, the assignment of multiple PKs to a domain is not allowed in this scheme. CertLock [47] is the location-aware tool of CAs implemented in Firefox, which can observe the country of the certificate-granting CA. When more than one CA grant from different regions certificate for a certain domain, this can be identified by this tool, which in turn can detect MitM attacks conducted through maliciously granted certificates by different CAs located in different locations. However, this scheme cannot detect the attack when

CAs in the same region conduct. Relying on the notary servers, Crossbear [48] uses traceroutes to identify the MitM attacks. An add-on in the Mozilla Firefox browser and an independent hunter application are jointly responsible for finding traceroutes. With the assistance of the add-on that performs detection and localization tasks, the independent application can determine the attacks.

Through the Policy Engine [49], an end-user can make trust decisions about a certificate based on a policy of certificate sequence gathered from a web server. CERTSHIM [50] designed deployment-friendly shared entities in a dynamic manner to assist users against TLS/SSL attack risks. Through a policy engine, users can apply sophisticated certificate validation procedures tailored to certain applications or overall systems. However, this is not compatible with browsers and cannot protect against a local attacker. Moreover, its security policies can easily be bypassed by intelligent applications. Certificate Patrol [51] is monitoring-based another addon for Firefox, where a newly encountered certificate for a specific domain is diagnosed as suspicious to a client if it does not match with the previously saved certificates. Being lightweight, this tool can provide an extra layer of protection against cybersecurity attacks. However, it does not support multiple certificates for a specific domain.

8.3.3 DNS-centered proposals

HPKP [52,53] designed PK Pinning (PKP) for Chrome browser, where a list of authorized CAs is authorized for a domain server. Such a mapping of PKP between CA and domain is not scalable, which was cracked by caching the designated CA list in the HTTP extension [54]. Based on DNSSEC [25], Domain Name System (DNS)-based authentication of named entities (DANE) [11–13] attached a PK to a domain name, the mappings of which are stored in the extensions of domain DNS security. If the records are accurately declared according to DNSSEC [25], these are considered as legitimate. This concept is scalable as domain servers state trusted CAs on the DNSSEC record. In a similar manner, through CAA [14], domain servers persuade the authorized CAs to attest their PKs.

With the aim of mitigating the complete trust issues on CAs, trust asserts for certificate keys (TACK) [55] requires each domain to generate a TACK public/secret key pair and attest TLS key pair using the TACK key pair. After a thorough investigation of repeated PK to each domain, each user attaches the PK to the domain name and then stores it. This attachment is trusted for a certain duration of time and all the received PKs signed by the TACK key pair are accepted. In the case of leakage and losing issues of the TACK key pair, users are required to delete and refresh the attachment record of the key pairs. However, this is still vulnerable when clients visit domains for the first time.

Elapshurus [56] revisited initialization, TOFU, scalability, and update issues of the conventional PKP proposal. Under the recommendation of certificate with a false positive rate by multiple security schemes, PKP entries are usually initialized. In a similar manner, a pinned entry is updated when the certificate is signed by the same CA as the previous one and this is recommended by multiple security schemes. This proposal supports assignment of multiple certificates to a domain, unpinned certificates through the approval of security systems with tolerable false negative rate, and expiry issue of pinned entries. However, the domain certificate is not supported to be updated if the CA is changed by the domain compared to the previous one. The authors in [5] pointed out that stale DNS information associated with discontinued service could be the means of cyberattack. Consequently, they proposed a domain validation method that suggests domain owners and cloud operators to monitor their stale DNS records for preventing domain takeover attacks.

8.3.4 Log-based proposals

To defend against corrupted CAs, in SKI [17], domain owners are given governing power over their PKs. Each domain server has two sets of key pairs named as SKI and TLS, in which TLS PK is signed by SKI PK. The SKI PKs are stored on timeline servers, which are sufficiently cloned. A client accepts the certificate received from the server if the corresponding SKI PK is found on timeline servers, and the CA-signed certificate is attested by SKI PK. Although this first log-based proposal is less concerned about trust issues of CAs, this incurs extra latency due to protocol negotiation and has privacy issues.

Google invented CT [2] that holds a non-editable record of all CA-signed certificates in terms of opaque logs. CT has the following extra entities to improve the security of conventional.

- Transparency log server: Based on a Chronological Merkle Hash Tree (CMHT), this an expandable ledger, in which all CA-signed certificates along with their signed certificate timestamp (SCT) are stored.
- Monitor: Under the assumption that the stored logs are transparent and complete, this entity monitors for dubious entries through investigation and verification.
- Auditor: Update operations of the transparency logs are examined by this entity, which can be independent or an add-on of web clients or monitors.

Being public, transparency logs force CAs liable to their users for their operations. The logs are added in chronological left-to-right increasing order to MHT, which results in logarithmic computational and communication costs for any operation on the log server. Although CT can detect malicious certificates and resultant cyberattacks through them, this is oblivious about the revocation of certificates. A conventional PKIX system equipped with the Google CT log extension is presented in Figure 8.5.

Accountable Key Infrastructure (AKI) [57] proposed the idea of signing a certificate using multiple CAs with the assistance of a transparency log to mitigate the SPoF issue in a conventional PKIX scheme. Domain owners in this scheme define a list of CAs that can attest to their certificates. Moreover, a certificate is considered to be authentic if a threshold number of CAs attest to this. After the successful registration of a multi-CA-signed certificate to the transparency log, each domain receives membership proof (e.g., validity status) for its certificate and attests the proof with the certificate. The certificates are stored in binary hash tree-based transparency logs so that the revocation operation achieves logarithmic complexity. Different entities in the system check with each other about their operations to detect and prevent MitM attacks.

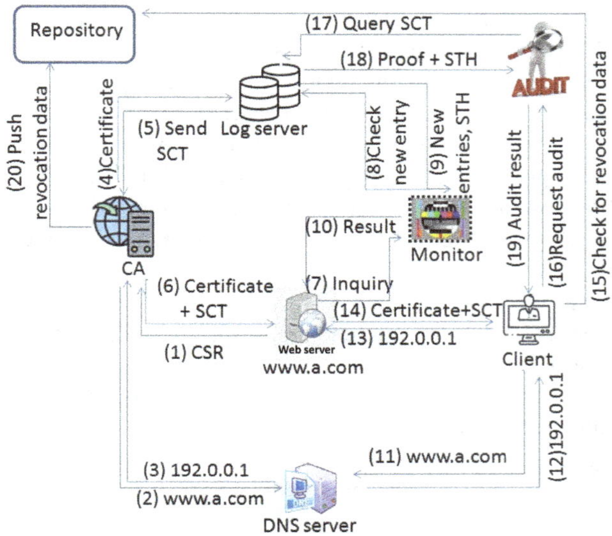

Figure 8.5 An illustration of Google CT framework

ARPKI [58,59] identified drawbacks in AKI and countered those by assigning m entities (e.g., transparency log and CAs) to a domain server while issuing and managing certificates. One designated CA in the transparency log is responsible for conducting the registration procedure. Similar to AKI, each certificate is attested by a threshold number of CAs, and the MitM attack can be thwarted even under the dishonesty of $m - 1$ entities. This process does not need a separate and more resilient compared to AKI. However, the enrollment of all entities in the issuing and management of certificates incurs latency.

Although Policert [60] uses the multi-signature certificate concept of AKI, domain owners are required to demonstrate their detailed policy in terms of certificate management. This protocol consists of policy enrollment, certificate signing by multiple CAs, certificate verification, and auditing of the transparency log through setting up a secure connection. The defined policy of each domain is attested by the PKs from multiple CAs and registered on the transparency log along with the certificate. Clients check and balance between policy parameters and signing of certificates by multiple CAs. Various authentication operations are required to ensure the functionalities of the log server in the audit phase.

DTKI [61] leverages the domain-specific master key concept, that is used to attest TLS certificate. Clients only accept CA-issued certificates that are attested by the master key. Both the master and TLS key pairs are added to the transparency log in the form of MHT. DTKI has two layers: certificate log maintainer (CLM) and mapping log maintainer (MLM). While CLM is responsible for storing, the domain-to-CLM mapping information is managed by the MLM. Mapping information from MLM is required to establish connections to a domain server. Despite its resiliency, the loss of the master key is not recoverable.

TripPKI [62] introduces a new type of entity, DNS, along with the entities in AKI/ARPKI protocol for thorough checks-and-balances among different parties, to detect malicious activities by any single entity in the system. The process consists of initialization, certificate management, update, and revocation. The certificate issuance period is further enhanced by the involvement of a threshold number of CAs in the signing process and their synchronization. Detailed protocol negotiation among all entities by this scheme during the certification process may incur extra latency while setting up a connection to a domain server. Moreover, evolved version attacks by this scheme cannot be easily identified.

The authors in [63] pointed out that MitM attacks are possible in Policert protocol and mitigated the attacks by intelligent negotiation among different parties and renovated data structure. By using the improved data structure, this protocol supports CA hierarchy and sub-CA revocation. Note that ATCM incurs extra latency while establishing a connection and is vulnerable to versioning attacks.

In ARCT [64], a collaborative effort of multiple entities in the system is required for certificate issuing and logging into the transparency log servers. The root CA plays the role of a transparency log server and sub-CAs comply with this. The collaborative effort of identity verification strengthens the security of the certification process. Versioning attacks by transparency log servers are further mitigated by this collaborative effort. However, root CAs in this scheme may suffer from denial of service attacks if the log server could be hijacked.

In SCM [65], domain owners participate in the certification process in addition to CAs and transparency log servers. In addition to the regular certification process including the logging and auditing activities of log servers, this proposal includes publishing fingerprints of log servers and revoked CAs to the blockchain platform, and proof generation. No provision of multi-domain certificates as well as inaccessible domains owing to extra latency while issuing certificates are major drawbacks of this scheme.

In Domain PKI [66], TLS certificate is co-signed with the domain-owned master key. Unlike typical log-based PKIX schemes, separate log servers are maintained for domain owners to hold their master key and TLS certificates. Retrieval of certificate logging information as well as master key are required for a client to establish a connection with the domain server. Consequently, only CA is not sufficient in the verification of the certificate (i.e., PK) until the domain-owned master key is available to the client. However, an additional connection to the log server is required each time a client connects to the domain server. On the other hand, recovery of the master key is almost impossible in the case of loss.

Lessons learned: Log-based PKIX schemes can tackle various cyberattacks and, however, are vulnerable to split-world attack [67]. Additionally, these incur additional complexity, operational overhead, and privacy issues during certificate validation.

8.4 Blockchain-based PKIX proposals

Blockchain-based proposals are further categorized into CA-centered, client-centered, and domain-based schemes.

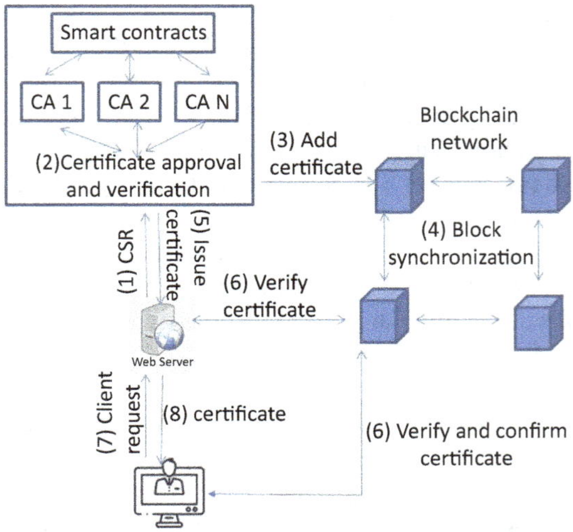

Figure 8.6 A sample illustration of CA-centered blockchain-based PKIX proposal

8.4.1 CA-centered proposals

In [68], Yakubov *et al.* conducted a certification process including its creation, update, and revocation, on a blockchain platform. Each CA along with its smart contract is initialized on the blockchain platform. The smart contract handles issuance of CA certificates along with their revocation status. Trust-related information except for the root CA certificate in terms of blockchain meta data are inserted in the extension field of a certificate, which in turn assists the verification of certificate path/chain in the authentication process of a client. Because of storing hash values of certificates to the blockchain platform, identity verification of root CA and detection of fake certificates are not rigorous. Korgan [69] identified privacy and security vulnerabilities of [68]. Unlike [68], Korgan is designed on the top of a public blockchain with an improved PBFT consensus method with threshold signature, in which external entities are not required for the verification of certificates. Moreover, this uses the maintenance concept of a part of the signing key by all nodes, by which a new transaction could be added by the designated leader after obtaining signatures from other consensus nodes.

In the framework of [70], a CA-issued certificate along with its revocation status is appended to the blockchain as a transaction with a pre-determined validity period. Two key pairs are maintained by a domain owner, such as the publishing key pair and TLS key pair. After the settlement of the publishing key pair, a set of web servers in the blockchain, the TLS certificate along with the revocation status is appended to the blockchain with the help of the publishing key pair. The process of inserting TLS certificate along with revocation status is repeated in a periodic manner as the transaction becomes invalid after a certain duration. The TLS key certificate is then used by a client for authentication with the respective domain server, which includes the revocation check-up as well. Although the revocation issue of a certificate is addressed in this proposal, this relies on a conventional CRL-based revocation method, and CAs can still be corrupted. Furthermore, this can tempt to bring MitM attack during the revocation process through key leaks with unexpired certificate transactions.

Based on a new data structure for blockchain transactions, CertChain [71] audits TLS certificates. The data structure, namely CertOper, keeps certificate-related information and operations, such as certificate registration, validation, update, and revocation. The bloom filter is adopted to tackle false positive rate while handling revocation issue, and a consensus algorithm called Ouroboros is that determines a leader through a CA or a bookkeeper dependability rank. However, communicating with a bookkeeper during certificate verification is a bottleneck for a client. Moreover, a dishonest bookkeeper may incur a fake certificate for a client, and bookkeeping process can hamper the user's privacy as well.

Taking the consent of domain owners, certificate transparency using blockchain (CTB) [72] utilizes the Hyperledger Fabric blockchain of IBM to issue certificates from CAs. Although CTB incorporates a revocation mechanism, this does not fulfill the main goal of CT because of using private blockchain, which cannot be inspected in detail by public. Moreover, detection of fraudulent certificates cannot be easily detected owing to the inherent nature of CTB and adopting the private blockchain.

Conifer [73] integrated CONIKS [74] and Catena log [75] to overcome the drawbacks of both log-based and blockchain-based PKI proposals. Two improved data structures are adopted in Conifer on the top of CONIKS [74], such as the transaction chain that links the name-to-key mapping to the Bitcoin blockchain and a tree forest for cost-effective and safe search operations over suspicious log servers. In Conifer, everyone can watch the name history, whereas this holds for the name owner. Moreover, owing to efficient data structure, Conifer has better communication cost.

In [67], Kubilay *et al.* conducted certificate management and revocation on a permissionless blockchain to make the operations transparent to the public. A group of authentic members is authorized to add a CA to the blockchain through a collaborative signing key if the CA meets the specified standards and security requirements. This scheme can defeat client truststore attacks as well as can mitigate the split-world attack issue of log-based proposals. However, manual intervention is required to manage the group members, and valid but malicious certificates can still be issued by CAs.

The authors in [76] introduced a semi-decentralized PKI framework that consists of four steps: request, clearing, examination, and verification. In the first step, interaction between users and CAs occurs through an enhanced proof of violation of cloud protocol. Second, the hash root of MHT including certificate-related information is uploaded to Interplanetary File System (IPFS) [77] in a periodic manner. In the third step, the operation of CAs is investigated by domains and fixed accordingly if there is any error. In the last step, upon receiving a certificate and MHT proof from a domain, certificate verification is conducted.

Based on the distributed trust concept among multiple parties, Meta-PKI [78] is a decentralized PKI approach that connects the parties through cross-certification. Based on the Hyberledger Fabric smart contracts, Meta-PKI consists of three layers from the perspective of the client, CA, and meta-CA. Upon the certificate request from end-entities, CAs from the second layer start working. The CAs at the second layer are constructed by CAs from the third layer connected to the blockchain.

Without the assistance of CAs, the authors in [79] brought a blockchain-based decentralized PKI framework, called DeTract, based on the DV-certificate issuance protocol. DeTract consists of three steps: (1) identity construction, (2) certification, and (3) revocation. In the first step, the identity of domains is created using uPort. Second, certificates of domain owners are spawned and managed, and their hash values are inserted into the blockchain along with the maintenance of off-chain storage. Finally, revocation issues are handled for the generated certificates. Upon the certificate issuing request by a client, the server offers a certificate including the hash value. If the hash value of the downloaded certificate matches that stored on the blockchain, the client accepts the certificate.

Lesson learned: Although blockchain is promising to mitigate conventional PKIX attacks, scalability is still an issue to be deployed on the Internet. An integrated approach combining a log-based PKIX solution and a blockchain-based proposal could be a good endeavor.

8.4.2 Client-centered proposals

In PADVA [80], notary servers [10] along with their transactions are maintained on a blockchain platform to reduce the trust issues of notary servers. In the initialization phase, a requester places a transaction to a notary server in terms of a domain name, a good set of keys, a payment, and a reference time (optional). Consequently, the notary server publishes the list of domain servers to the blockchain platform along with the time of the transaction. Similar to the traditional notary system, this protocol incurs additional latency owing to the extra latency clients experience while verifying the domain PK.

In [81], Tewari *et al.* considered a blockchain-based PKI framework in the cloud platform for authenticating users in different sectors (e.g., finance, medical and other businesses). The authentication of users as well as certificate granting procedure is conducted by the corporate sector acting as intermediate CAs. All the certificates are stored in the blockchain platform at local organizations for further usage to securely communicate over the Internet.

Lesson learned: Inquiring with blockchain-based platforms for verifying the encountered certificate similar to the conventional client-centered solution, which is computationally expensive as well as incurs additional latency.

8.4.3 DNS-centered proposals

Ethereum name service (ENS) [82] maps human-readable Ethereum names to machine-readable Ethereum addresses. Two smart contracts from two entities, such as registrars and resolvers, are adopted. The first type of smart contract holds TLDs and a record of all domains and subdomains in the Ethereum chain, whereas the latter one plays the role of a DNS resolver.

The authors in [83] proposed SSHTDNS to thwart vulnerabilities in DNS services. Consortium chains as well as linkable ring signatures are adopted for hiding

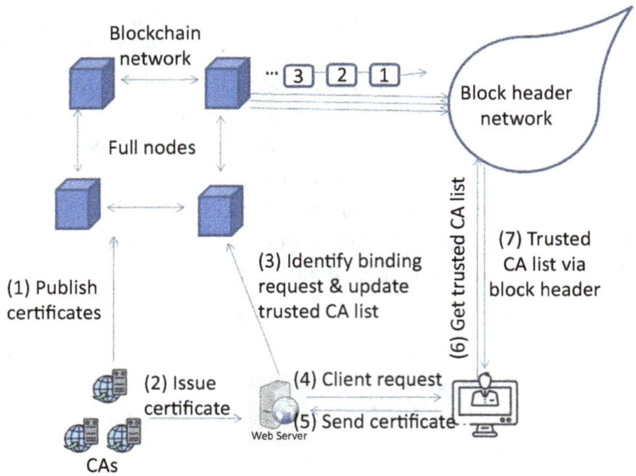

Figure 8.7 A sample illustration of domain-centered blockchain-based PKIX proposal

identity and ensuring fairness among consortium nodes. SSHTDNS stores information in multiple chains, where light information of each specific TLD is stored in the main chain while the complete ones are stored in subchains. Furthermore, the sharding approach is integrated with the multi-chain structure to ensure better quality. However, redundant storage issues and an inefficient ring signature are the major drawbacks of this scheme.

BB-PKI [84] handled cyberattacks in RAs of the PKI framework. In BB-PKI, identity verification of domains is conducted by several RAs. Afterward, upon submitting the CSR by one of the RAs to the blockchain platform, multiple CAs sign the certificate through some control channel. On the other hand, revocation can be performed by the designated CA or by the domain itself. By this scheme, clients can protect themselves from a powerful conspiracy capable of controlling $n - 1$ parties engaged in the certification process. However, the entire process is cumbersome and latency-prone, which is not affordable by some CAs (e.g., Let's Encrypt).

LightLedger [85] is an efficient and reliable blockchain-based domain authentication scheme without relying on an authentic third party. With the assistance of smart contracts, CAs are responsible for managing certificates in the blockchain platform. Moreover, the proposed scheme has a record of many authentic CAs connected to a certain blockchain platform. In other words, CAs must first justify themselves whether they can conduct the certificate-issuing process in a trustworthy manner. For low-constrained devices (e.g., IoTs), the proposed approach ensures robust and scalable domain authentication while preserving privacy on the client side. A similar type of domain authentic scheme is presented in [86], called AuthLedger, a scheme using Ethereum smart contracts. Owing to the public nature, the data size of the deployed blockchain grows in an exponential manner, which is one of the concerns for this type of proposal.

DNSBA [87] proposed a mechanism to map block labels in the chain to corresponding domain names alike IP-to-domain mappings. This provides resource records (RR) in two structures: the text RR and blockchain (BC) RR. The authors used BIND9 to deploy the BC RR and evaluated the performance of the proposed scheme for university students. Table 8.1 provides a comprehensive summary of the aforementioned discussed schemes.

Lesson learned: Similar to CA-centered proposals, scalability is an issue to be deployed on the Internet. Additional overhead is incorporated because of collaborative identity verification.

8.5 Performance evaluation

Followed by defining a set of performance metrics, in this section, we evaluate the performance of the blockchain-based PKIX proposals.

8.5.1 Evaluation metrics

Detection ability in issuing malicious certificate: This is the potential of a PKIX scheme to detect valid but malicious PK granted to users. Partial marks are provided for local detection of malicious certificates although the global detection is not robust.

Prevention ability in issuing malicious certificate: This feature of preventing entities from granting a valid but mischievous certificate is an enhanced level of security to PKIX systems.

Connection privacy: This feature preserves the certificate history of clients from third-party access.

Identity concealing ability: This feature allows a scheme to hide the identity of the domain server while issuing certificates.

Extra connection: This feature indicates whether extra supports from the server are required while validating the certificate.

Client-side changes: This metric depicts whether the amendment is required at client browsers/applications for nourishing the security suggested by a scheme.

Server-side changes: This metric shows the modification needed on the server side to utilize services offered by a scheme.

CA-side changes: This indicates the amendment required at the CA side to achieve the benefit by a designated proposal.

Limited trust: This feature indicates whether semi-trusted centralized servers are sufficient for the management of certificates.

Decentralized trust: This feature of the candidate PKI scheme ensures to distribute trust among various parties while issuing and verifying certificates.

No TOFU: The candidate schemes having this characteristic do not trust an unknown PK for the first time.

Table 8.1 Comparison among different PKIX proposals

Class	Proposal	Key Problem	Strength	Weakness
CA-centered	[33]	CA scope	Attack surface reduction	Locally trusted CA compromises cannot be prevented
	[35]	CA scope	Client-specific CA determination	Cannot preserve privacy of clients
	[36]	CA scope	Dynamic CA scope restriction	Locally trusted CA compromises cannot be prevented
	[37]	CA scope	Application-specific dynamic trust decision	Cannot preserve privacy of clients
	[38]	CA scope	Peer-to-peer CA reputation	Low compatibility of newly added CAs compared to older CAs
	[39]	Domain identity validation	Path poisoning as well as on-path and off-path attacks cannot be prevented	CA compromises cannot be prevented
	[40]	CA compromise	Decentralized trust among various parties	No detection and prevention mechanism in practice
	[41]	Identity privacy	Learning oblivious identity validation	Applicable to only email-based identity validation
	[44]	CA scope	Unused CA identification	Cannot prevent malicious certificate issuance by unused CAs
	[45]	CA key leakage	Trust distribution among several parties	Higher signing cost
Client-centered	[9]	TOFU	Privacy issue of Perspective resolution	No support for multiple PKs to a domain
	[10]	TOFU	Trust management at end-user level	Unavailability and privacy issues
	[46]	TOFU	Privacy and fresh PK unavailability problems of Perspective resolution	Extra latency
	[47]	CA change attack	Fake PK issuance detection by a outsider CA	Expose to same CA-issued malicious certificate attacks
	[48]	MitM attacks detection	Detection of attacked servers	Exposed privacy of attacked servers
	[49]	Trust decision	User-centered local trust support	Malicious certificate issuance cannot be protected
	[50]	TLS/SSL vulnerabilities	Transparent validation process	Security policies can be bypassed by guests
	[51]	Malicious certificate detection	Lightweight extra layer of security	Obliviousness to first connection and no support for multiple certificates to a domain

Domain-centered	[52]-[53]	CA scope	Assertion to a list of trusted CAs for certificate issuance	Malicious certificate can be issued by declared CAs
	[11]-[13]	Domain control via PK	Domain-related information visibility in their certificates	Reliant on DNS server security
	[14]	CA scope	CA authorization by domains for signing their certificates	Reliant on DNS servers security
	[55]	Trust model	Domains signed TLS certificates	No security on the first connection to a website
	[56]	TOFU	Update and multiple PK problems of PKP	No mechanism to update pinned entries in the case of CA change
Log-based	[17]	CA compromises	Defense against CA compromises	Client connection information information
	[2]	CA compromise	CA operation exposure to public	No support for certificate revocation
	[57]	CA compromise	CA compromise detection and trusted CA designation to domains	Downloading overhead a full copy of the transparency log
	[58]	CA compromise	Defense against collaborative $n-1$ trusted parties	Slower system performance in certificate management
	[60]	CA compromise	Empowers domains to define detailed policy for their certificate usage	Downloading overhead a full copy of the transparency log
	[61]	Oligopoly	Oligopoly elimination in log-based PKIX	Extra connection overhead to retrieve mapping information
	[62]	CA compromise	Denial of service attack resolution against CAs	Slower system performance in certificate management
	[63]	CA compromise	Eliminates attacks on Policert and enhances log structure	Vulnerable to versioning attacks
	[64]	Identity validation	Collaborative identity verification by a group of CAs	Exposure to denial of services attack
	[65]	CA compromise	Certificate storage cost reduction and versioning attack mitigation	Unavailability of domains due to additional latency during certificate issuance
	[66]	CA compromise	Domain controlled certificate issuance	No mechanism to recover the master key in case of loss

(continued)

Table 8.1 Comparison among different PKIX proposals (Continued)

Class	Proposal	Key Problem	Strength	Weakness
Blockchain-based	[68]	Trust model	Malicious CA insertion attack is eliminated via managing client truststore	
	[70]	CA compromise	Domain controlled certificate management	Old-fashioned revocation policy
	[81]	End-user certification	Lightweight certificate delivery to end-users	End-user privacy cannot be preserved from third party
	[71]	Certificate audit	Improved data structure for certificate audit	End-user privacy cannot be preserved due to bookkeeping
	[72]	MitM prevention	Malicious certificate issuance prevention by CAs	Difficult detection of malicious certificate once issued
	[73]	Auditing	Lightweight auditing of certificates	
	[67]	Split-world attack	Split-world attack elimination and truststore protection	Failure of CAs in malicious issuance
	[80]	TOFU	Transparent notary server-based trust management	Extra latency
	[83]	DNS attack	High throughput assurance	Redundant storage problem
	[84]	Identity validation	Defense against multiple compromised CAs	Longer and tedious validation process
	[76]	Certificate audit	Controlling CA operations by domains	Extra storage and computation overhead
	[82]	Mapping	Mapping Ethereum address to machine-readable address	Ineffective
	[86]	Domain validation	Client-based trust management	Practicality and performance issues
	[85]	Identity validation	Restricting scope of CAs	Intractable growth of ledger
	[87]	Mapping	Mapping blockchain address to domain name	Does not preserve of clients
	[69]	Privacy	Preserves privacy of clients	Extra latency in issuing certificates
	[78]	Privacy	Trust obliviousness to extra entities	Not fully transparent
	[72]	Mapping	Soft revocation policy	Additional latency

No extra burden on CA: This characteristic ensures that the candidate scheme does not require the participation of CA apart from the regular certificate management activities.

Scalability: This metric ensures whether the candidate scheme supports the certificate management burden owing to the expanded Internet.

No Infrastructural changes: The feature ensures that the candidate scheme does not require any infrastructural changes, such as the business model of CAs, servers, and clients, while offering its certificate management service.

8.5.2 Comparison through evaluation metrics

8.5.2.1 CA-centered proposals

This type of PKI scheme carry out identity verification before issuing certificates but cannot detect malicious ones once granted. Therefore, this category moderately bolsters this feature (e.g., [33] alerts users if a malicious DV certificate is issued by a compromised CA for a domain) except Lets' Encrypt and [41]. On the other hand, the schemes in [40] and [45] can identify and block the granting of malicious certificates because of not relying on a single entity for identity validation and certification. Except [40], clients and servers in these schemes are not required to change their architectural models. The business model of clients, servers, and CAs is substantially required to be altered as the clients and servers are required to manage a collaborative PK, and the responsibility of CA is divided among several entities. The other proposals require tiny amendments to the business model of CA. Except [40], all the schemes do not support limited and decentralized features as CAs are assumed fully liable and responsible for identity validation and certification. On the other hand, the scheme in [45] supports the limited trust feature. Furthermore, almost all schemes in this class fulfill No TOFU. Finally, except for the scheme in [40], these proposals are scalable and require amendment in the corresponding infrastructure owing to the enlarged Internet.

8.5.2.2 Client-centered PKIX proposals

In Perspective, DoubleCheck, and Convergence, users believe certificates are verified by authentic entities at the cost of extra connection with third-party servers. The other three schemes adopt the client-centric PK attachment concept to save clients from malicious certificates. Consequently, multipath probing-based schemes can identify malicious PKs using additional connections while the pioneer Perspective needs to learn browsing history. The business model at Server and CA sides does not require to be changed. However, as clients need to deploy additional tools, the schemes in this class partially fulfill the changes on the client side. This class assumes that servers are fully trusted while issuing and verifying certificates. The first three schemes consult auditors upon receiving a new certificate, while the latter three do not satisfy the No TOFU feature. Finally, in the context of no extra connection, scalability, and no Internet side changes, the performance of this class is satisfactory.

8.5.2.3 Domain-centered PKIX proposals

The server-based attachment proposals, i.e., PKP [52,53], and TACK [55] support blind TOFU. On the other hand, the DNS-based pinning proposal, i.e., DANE is designed based on DNSSEC, and Elaphurus [56] utilizes both the multi-path probing with server-based attachment concept. Consequently, server-based pinning schemes moderately can identify the malicious issuance of certificates, but cannot block in issuing of malicious certificates. All proposals can hide browsing history, and the extra connection is not required due to their local PK validation support. Although all the schemes need extra facilities from the server side, no special modifications are needed on the client and CA sides. In terms of trust, server-based pinning schemes satisfy the TOFU feature without endorsing limited and decentralized trust. Luckily, these proposals do not impose additional workload on the CA side and are highly scalable with the enlarged Internet. On the other hand, DNS-based pinning and multi-path probing schemes satisfy the No TOFU feature by extending the trust model. Pinning with multi-path probing has the advantage of successfully detecting the issuance of malicious certificates with the cost of additional connection and the leakage of browsing history.

8.5.2.4 Log-based PKIX proposals

Except CT, all schemes in this class can successfully detect and prevent the issuance of malicious certificates. CT can detect, but cannot prevent the issuance of malicious certificates. Multi-signed certification (e.g., ARPKI and AKI) or cross-signed certification (e.g., SK and DTKI) concepts of the schemes can prevent the issuance of malicious certificates. In a similar manner, this class fully supports connection privacy and no extra connection features except SK and DTKI, where users need to connect mirror servers and log maintainers while connecting to a domain server, which in turn leaks browsing history. The business model of client, server, and CA sides are required to be changed slightly in order to take advantage logging concept, which cultivates additional security benefits. The absolute trust held on CA is distributed among multiple entities. Consequently, they fully satisfy limited trust, partially satisfy decentralized trust, and entirely satisfy no TOFU feature. Besides certification, CAs are required to monitor malicious activities, and hence log-based schemes do not satisfy No Extra Burden on CA features except CT. Since certification in log-based schemes is managed in the log servers, these schemes satisfy the scalability feature to some extent.

8.5.2.5 Blockchain-based PKIX proposals

This class fully satisfies the detection of malicious certificates, and except [70], all the other schemes can prevent the issuance of malicious certificates relying on multi-CA signed certificates (e.g., BlockPKI) or cross-signed certificates (e.g., [70]). Since lightweight clients are required to communicate with full nodes for the verification of the certificate, this class does not satisfy Connection privacy and No extra connection features, as well as leaks the browsing history of light nodes. Because of adopting the blockchain technology in the certification process, the business model of the client, server, and CA sides are required to be changed substantially, which ultimately offers enhanced security benefits. Moreover, the trust placed on single CA is distributed among multiple entities. Thus, they entirely satisfy limited trust and have no TOFU features. However, they partially satisfy Decentralized trust since CAs are still responsible for issuing certificates. Unlike log-based proposals, no extra burden is imposed on CAs as they are ignorant of monitoring. Nonetheless, scalability is a big problem for this class as the size of the ledger grows proportionally with the enlarged Internet. Finally, with this class, substantial changes are required in online communication because of having blockchain technology, and hence they do not satisfy no Internet-side changes feature.

8.6 Open challenges and future research direction

In this section, we present strategies and directions to improve the security and performance of the PKIX schemes further.

8.6.1 Immature certificate revocation process

The existing revocation process is complicated and cannot ensure much defense in issuing malicious certificates. None of them actually solved the problem. Furthermore, the detection of revoked certificates by off-the-shelf browsers is quite low [88]. For example, according to a recent study, only 0.35–0.40% revoked certificates can be detected by browsers. The security of the Internet could be improved by integrating simplicity, security, and defense in revocation mechanisms.

8.6.2 Compatibility with Web 3.0 scenarios

Although blockchain is a core technology for Web 3.0 world, blockchain-based PKIX design still cannot meet the privacy and security requirements of Web 3.0 communications. Existing blockchain-based designs just make an attempt to solve the privacy and security vulnerabilities of conventional PKIX frameworks.

8.6.3 Client identity validation

Client authentication is still a big issue in web communication on the Internet. In the PKIX framework, existing works are ignorant of the identity validation mechanism of end-users, and these still rely on old mechanisms, such as password and two-factor authentications. Moreover, there are numerous vulnerabilities against the validation methods that could be exploited by adversaries in issuing malicious certificates. Incorporating the privacy preservation concept in identity validation is also a challenging task.

8.6.4 Elimination of certificate chaining

Certificate chain verification implies the requirement of at least two signature verification operations to authenticate a message, which induces an extra delay owing to the hierarchical CA model adopted by the conventional PKIX framework. Delay could be prolonged due to certificate chain depth, leaf certificate, revocation check-up, and occasional certificate path discovery. Consequently, certificate chain verification may not be suitable for resource-constrained IoT and real-time devices. Moreover, the security of the PKIX framework could be further hampered by certificate chaining. For example, invalid certificates could be accepted by browsers that violate constraints (e.g., NameConstraints and PathlenConstraint) [89]. Hence, redesigning truststore and authentication protocols, while taking care of certificate chaining as well as without compromising security, is essential for real-time and IoT services in the usage of the PKIX framework.

8.7 Conclusion

Blockchain is a core technology of Industry 5.0 applications and is suitable to ensure security and privacy for web communications in a decentralized manner. In this chapter, we presented the state-of-the-art of blockchain-based PKIX framework while making a comparative study with conventional PKIX proposals. To evaluate the security performance of the presented PKIX proposals, we define a set of evaluation metrics. Afterward, we made a thorough comparative study among the presented state-of-the-art PKIX proposals in terms of security, privacy, and system-oriented features. From the performance evaluation, we concluded that the blockchain-based PKIX proposal has better potential in securing web communications when compared with other PKIX proposals. Finally, we outline a few open challenges and future works in the context of blockchain-based PKIX implementation in the context of Industry 5.0 applications.

References

[1] "Vulnerability and threat trends report 2022," 2022. [Online]. Available: https://www.skyboxsecurity.com/resources/report/vulnerability-threat-trends-report-2022.

[2] R. S. Raman, L. Evdokimov, E. Wurstrow, J. A. Halderman, and R. Ensafi, "Investigating Large Scale HTTPS Interception in Kazakhstan," in *Proc. ACM IMC*, 2020, p. 125–132.

[3] J. Aas, R. Barnes, B. Case, *et al.*, "Let's Encrypt: An Automated Certificate Authority to Encrypt the Entire Web," in *Proc. ACM SIGSAC CCS*, 2019, p. 2473–2487.

[4] H. Birge-Lee, Y. Sun, A. Edmundson, J. Rexford, and P. Mittal, "Bamboozling Certificate Authorities with BGP," in *Proc. USENIX Security Symposium*, 2018, pp. 833–849.

[5] K. Borgolte, T. Fiebig, S. Hao, C. Kruegel, and G. Vigna, "Cloud Strife: Mitigating the Security Risks of Domain-Validated Certificates," in *Proc. Applied Networking Research Workshop*, 2018, p. 4.

[6] R. A. Rueppel and e. t. b. y. p. Wildhaber, Bruno.

[7] R. Holz, L. Braun, N. Kammenhuber, and G. Carle, "The SSL Landscape: A Thorough Analysis of the x.509 PKI Using Active and Passive Measurements," in *Proc. IMC*, 2011, p. 427–444.
[8] A. C. Grant, "Search for Trust: An Analysis and Comparison of CA System Alternatives and Enhancements," 2012.
[9] M. Marlinspike, "SSL and The Future of Authenticity," vol. 6, 2011.
[10] D. Wendlandt, D. G. Andersen, and A. Perrig, "Perspectives: Improving SSH-style Host Authentication with Multi-path Probing," in *Proc. USENIX Annual Technical Conference*, 2008, p. 321–334.
[11] M. Ford, "DANE: Taking TLS Authentication to the Next Level Using DNSSEC," 2011. [Online]. Available: https://api.semanticscholar.org/CorpusID:62449157
[12] R. Barnes, "Use Cases and Requirements for DNS-Based Authentication of Named Entities (DANE)," 2011.
[13] V. Dukhovni and W. Hardaker, "The DNS-Based Authentication of Named Entities (DANE) Protocol: Updates and Operational Guidance," 2015. [Online]. Available: https://www.rfc-editor.org/info/rfc7671
[14] P. Hallam-Baker and R. Stradling, "DNS Certification Authority Authorization (CAA) Resource Record," 2013. [Online]. Available: https://www.rfc-editor.org/info/rfc6844
[15] K. Engert, "MECAI - Mutually Endorsing CA Infrastructure," 2012. [Online]. Available: https://kuix.de/mecai/
[16] G. Toth and T. Vlieg, "Public Key Pinning for TLS using a Trust on First Use Model," 2013.
[17] P. Eckersley, "Sovereign Key Cryptography for Internet Domains," 2012. [Online]. Available: https://git.eff.org
[18] J. Amann, R. Sommer, M. Vallentin, and S. Hall, "No attack necessary: the surprising dynamics of SSL trust relationships," in *Proc ACM ACSAC*, 2013, p. 179–188.
[19] A. E. G. F. A. S. Albarqi, A. and J. Kar, "Public Key Infrastructure: A Survey," vol. 6, pp. 31–37, 2015.
[20] L. S. Huang, A. Rice, E. Ellingsen, and C. Jackson, "Analyzing Forged SSL Certificates in the Wild," in *Proc. IEEE Symposium on Security and Privacy*, 2014, pp. 83–97.
[21] B. VanderSloot, J. Amann, M. Bernhard, Z. Durumeric, M. Bailey, and J. A. Halderman, "Towards a Complete View of the Certificate Ecosystem," in *Proc. ACM IMC*, 2016, p. 543–549.
[22] R. W. Heiland, W. C. Garrison, Y. Qiao, A. J. Lee, and V. Welch, "The Web's PKI: An Expository Review and Certificate Validation Cost Simulation," 2016. [Online]. Available: https://api.semanticscholar.org/CorpusID:64446762
[23] J. Yu and M. Ryan, "Chapter 7 – Evaluating Web PKIs," pp. 105–126, 2017.
[24] J. Amann, O. Gasser, Q. Scheitle, L. Brent, G. Carle, and R. Holz, "Mission Accomplished? Https Security after Diginotar," in *Proc. IMC*, 2017, p. 325–340.

[25] S. Weiler and D. Blacka, "Clarifications and Implementation Notes for DNS Security (DNSSEC)," 2013. [Online]. Available: https://www.rfc-editor.org/info/rfc6840

[26] O. Gasser, B. Hof, M. Helm, M. Korczynski, R. Holz, and G. Carle, "In Log We Trust: Revealing Poor Security Practices with Certificate Transparency Logs and Internet Measurements," in *Passive and Active Measurement*, 2018, pp. 173–185.

[27] C. Brunner, F. Knirsch, A. Unterweger, and D. Engel, "A Comparison of Blockchain-based PKI Implementations," in *Proc. ICISSP*, 2020, pp. 333–340.

[28] K. A. O. Albogami, M. Alruqi and A. Aljahdali, "Public Key Infrastructure Traditional and Modern Implementation," vol. 23, no. 2, pp. 343–350, 2021.

[29] A. H. H. Leibowitz and E. Syta, "Provable Security for PKI Schemes," vol. 2019, pp. 807–817, 2019.

[30] S. Khan, F. Luo, Z. Zhang, *et al.*, "A Survey on X.509 Public-Key Infrastructure, Certificate Revocation, and Their Modern Implementation on Blockchain and Ledger Technologies," *IEEE Commun. Surv. Tutorials*, vol. 25, no. 4, pp. 2529–2568, 2023.

[31] R. Barnes, J. Hoffman-Andrews, D. McCarney, and J. Kasten, "Automatic Certificate Management Environment (ACME)," 2019. [Online]. Available: https://www.rfc-editor.org/info/rfc8555

[32] S. Goldberg, "The myetherwallet.com Hijack and Why It's Risky to Hold Cryptocurrency in a Webapp," pp. 105–126, 2018.

[33] J. Kasten, E. Wustrow, and J. A. Halderman, "Cage: Taming Certificate Authorities by Inferring Restricted Scopes," in *Financial Cryptography and Data Security*, A.-R. Sadeghi, Ed. Springer Berlin Heidelberg, 2013, pp. 329–337.

[34] N. Heninger, Z. Durumeric, E. Wustrow, and J. A. Halderman, "Mining Your ps and qs: Detection of Widespread Weak Keys in Network Devices," in *Proc. USENIX Conference on Security Symposium*, 2012, p. 35.

[35] J. Braun and G. Rynkowski, "The Potential of an Individualized Set of Trusted CAs: Defending against CA Failures in the Web PKI," in *Proc. IEEE SocialCom*, 2013, pp. 600–605.

[36] J. Braun, F. Volk, J. Classen, J. Buchmann, and M. Mühlhäuser, "CA Trust Management for the Web PKI," *J. Comput. Secur.*, vol. 22, no. 6, p. 91, 2014.

[37] J. Braun, F. Volk, J. Buchmann, and M. Mühlhäuser, "Trust Views for the Web PKI," in *Public Key Infrastructures, Services and Applications*, S. Katsikas and I. Agudo, Eds. Berlin, Heidelberg: Springer Berlin Heidelberg, 2014, pp. 134–151.

[38] J. Classen, J. Braun, F. Volk, M. Hollick, J. Buchmann, and M. Mühlhäuser, "A Distributed Reputation System for Certification Authority Trust Management," in *Proc. IEEE Trustcom/BigDataSE/ISPA*, vol. 1, 2015, pp. 1349–1356.

[39] M. Brandt, T. Dai, A. Klein, H. Shulman, and M. Waidner, "Domain Validation++ For MitM-Resilient PKI," in *Proceedings of the 2018 ACM SIGSAC Conference on Computer and Communications Security*, 2018, p. 2060–2076.

[40] E. Syta, I. Tamas, D. Visher, D. I. Wolinsky, and B. Ford, "Certificate Cothority: Towards Trustworthy Collective CAS," vol. 7, 2015.

[41] L. Wang, G. Asharov, R. Pass, T. Ristenpart, and Abhi Shelat, "Blind Certificate Authorities," Cryptology ePrint Archive, Paper 2018/1022, 2018. [Online]. Available: https://eprint.iacr.org/2018/1022

[42] E. F. Kfoury, D. Khoury, A. AlSabeh, J. Gomez, J. Crichigno, and E. Bou-Harb, "A Blockchain-based Method for Decentralizing the ACME Protocol to Enhance Trust in PKI," in *Proc. IEEE TSP*, 2020, pp. 461–465.

[43] Z. Durumeric, E. Wustrow, and J. A. Halderman, "ZMap: Fast Internet-wide Scanning and Its Security Applications," in *USENIX Security Symposium*, 2013, pp. 605–620.

[44] H. Perl, S. Fahl, and M. Smith, "You Won't Be Needing These Any More: On Removing Unused Certificates from Trust Stores," in *Proc. ACM FC*, N. Christin and R. Safavi-Naini, Eds., vol. 8437, 2014, pp. 307–315.

[45] B. Jayaraman, H. Li, and D. Evans, "Decentralized Certificate Authorities," *CoRR*, vol. abs/1706.03370, 2017. [Online]. Available: http://arxiv.org/abs/1706.03370

[46] M. Alicherry and A. D. Keromytis, "DoubleCheck: Multi-path Verification against Man-in-the-Middle Attacks," in *Proc. ISCC*, 2009, pp. 557–563.

[47] C. Soghoian and S. Stamm, "Certified Lies: Detecting and Defeating Government Interception Attacks against SSL (Short Paper)," in *Proc. ACM FC*, G. Danezis, Ed. Springer Berlin Heidelberg, 2012, pp. 250–259.

[48] R. Holz, T. Riedmaier, N. Kammenhuber, and G. Carle, "X.509 Forensics: Detecting and Localising the SSL/TLS Men-in-the-Middle," in *Computer Security – ESORICS 2012*, S. Foresti, M. Yung, and F. Martinelli, Eds. Springer Berlin Heidelberg, 2012, pp. 217–234.

[49] M. Abadi, A. Birrell, I. Mironov, T. Wobber, and Y. Xie, "Global Authentication in an Untrustworthy World," in *Proc. USENIX Workshop on Hot Topics in Operating Systems (HotOS XIV)*, 2013.

[50] A. Bates, J. Pletcher, T. Nichols, B. Hollembaek, D. Tian, K. R. Butler, and A. Alkhelaifi, "Securing SSL Certificate Verification through Dynamic Linking," in *Proc. ACM SIGSAC CCS*, 2014, p. 394–405.

[51] M. Modell, A. Barz, G. Toth, and C. Loesch, "Certificate Patrol," 2014. [Online]. Available: https://addons.mozilla.org/en-US/firefox/addon/certificate-patrol

[52] A. Langley, "Public Key Pinning," 2011. [Online]. Available: https://www.imperialviolet.org/2011/05/04/pinning.html

[53] C. Evans, C. Palmer, and R. Sleevi, "Public Key Pinning Extension for HTTP," 2015. [Online]. Available: https://www.rfc-editor.org/info/rfc7469

[54] Evans, C. Palmer, and R. Sleevi, "Public Key Pinning Extension for HTTP," 2015. [Online]. Available: https://www.rfc-editor.org/info/rfc7469

[55] M. Marlinspike, "Trust Assertions for Certificate Keys," Internet Engineering Task Force, Tech. Rep., 2013. [Online]. Available: https://datatracker.ietf.org/doc/draft-perrin-tls-tack/02/

[56] B. Li, W. Wang, L. Meng, J. Lin, X. Liu, and C. Wang, "Elaphurus: Ensemble Defense Against Fraudulent Certificates in TLS," in *Information Security*

and Cryptology, Z. Liu and M. Yung, Eds. Springer International Publishing, 2020, pp. 246–259.

[57] T. H.-J. Kim, L.-S. Huang, A. Perrig, C. Jackson, and V. Gligor, "Accountable Key Infrastructure (AKI): A Proposal for a Public-Key Validation Infrastructure," in *Proc. ACM WWW*, 2013, p. 679–690.

[58] D. Basin, C. Cremers, T. H.-J. Kim, A. Perrig, R. Sasse, and P. Szalachowski, "ARPKI: Attack Resilient Public-key Infrastructure," in *Proc. ACM CCS*, 2014, pp. 382–393.

[59] D. Basin, C. Cremers, T. H.-J. Kim, A. Perrig, R. Sasse, and P. Szalachowski, "Design, Analysis, and Implementation of ARPKI: An Attack-Resilient Public-Key Infrastructure," *IEEE Trans. Dependable and Secure Computing*, vol. 15, no. 3, pp. 393–408, 2018.

[60] P. Szalachowski, S. Matsumoto, and A. Perrig, "PoliCert: Secure and Flexible TLS Certificate Management," in *Proc. ACM SIGSAC CCS*, 2014, p. 406–417.

[61] J. Yu, V. Cheval, and M. Ryan, "DTKI: A New Formalized PKI with Verifiable Trusted Parties," *The Computer Journal*, vol. 59, no. 11, pp. 1695–1713, 2016.

[62] J. Chen, S. Yao, Q. Yuan, R. Du, and G. Xue, "Checks and Balances: A Tripartite Public Key Infrastructure for Secure Web-based Connections," in *Proc. IEEE INFOCOM*, 2017, pp. 1–9.

[63] S. Khan, Z. Zhang, L. Zhu, M. Li, Q. G. Khan Safi, X. Chen, and S. Zeadally, "Accountable and Transparent TLS Certificate Management: An Alternate Public-Key Infrastructure with Verifiable Trusted Parties," *Sec. Commun. Netw.*, vol. 2018, 2018.

[64] S. Khan, L. Zhu, Z. Zhang, M. A. Rahim, K. Khan, and M. Li, "Attack-Resilient TLS Certificate Transparency," *IEEE Access*, vol. 8, pp. 98 958–98 973, 2020.

[65] S. Khan, Z. Zhang, L. Zhu, M. Rahim, S. Ahmad, and R. Chen, "SCM: Secure and Accountable TLS Certificate Management," *International Journal of Communication Systems*, vol. 33, no. 15, 2020.

[66] X. Wang and M. El-Said, "DomainPKI: Domain Aware Certificate Management," in *Proc. SIGITE*, 2020, p. 419–425.

[67] M. Y. Kubilay, M. S. Kiraz, and H. A. Mantar, "CertLedger: A new PKI model with Certificate Transparency Based on blockchain," *Comput. Secur.*, vol. 85, no. C, p. 333–352, 2019.

[68] A. Yakubov, W. M. Shbair, A. Wallbom, D. Sanda, and R. State, "A Blockchain-based PKI Management Framework," in *Proc. IEEE/IFIP NOMS*, 2018, pp. 1–6.

[69] M. Y. Kubilay, M. S. Kiraz, and H. A. Mantar, "KORGAN: An Efficient PKI Architecture Based on PBFT Through Dynamic Threshold Signatures," *Comput. J.*, vol. 64, pp. 564–574, 2020.

[70] Z. Wang, J. Lin, Q. Cai, Q. Wang, D. Zha, and J. Jing, "Blockchain-Based Certificate Transparency and Revocation Transparency," *IEEE Trans. Dependable and Secure Computing*, vol. 19, no. 1, pp. 681–697, 2022.

[71] J. Chen, S. Yao, Q. Yuan, K. He, S. Ji, and R. Du, "CertChain: Public and Efficient Certificate Audit Based on Blockchain for TLS Connections," in *Proc. IEEE INFOCOM*, 2018, pp. 2060–2068.

[72] D. S. V. Madala, M. P. Jhanwar, and A. Chattopadhyay, "Certificate Transparency Using Blockchain," in *Proc. IEEE ICDMW*, 2018, pp. 71–80.

[73] Y. Dong, W. Kim, and R. Boutaba, "Conifer: Centrally-Managed PKI with Blockchain-Rooted Trust," in *Proc. IEEE iThings and GreenCom and CPSCom and SmartData*, 2018, pp. 1092–1099.

[74] M. S. Melara, A. Blankstein, J. Bonneau, E. W. Felten, and M. J. Freedman, "CONIKS: Bringing Key Transparency to End Users," in *Proc. USENIX SEC*, 2015, p. 383–398.

[75] A. Tomescu and S. Devadas, "Catena: Efficient Non-equivocation via Bitcoin," in *Proc. IEEE SP*, 2017, pp. 393–409.

[76] G.-H. Hwang, T.-K. Chang, H.-W. Chiang, and R. Amin, "A Semidecentralized PKI System Based on Public Blockchains with Automatic Indemnification Mechanism," *Sec. and Commun. Netw.*, vol. 2021, 2021.

[77] J. Benet, "IPFS-content Addressed, Versioned, p2p File System," *arXiv preprint arXiv:1407.3561*, p. 333–352, 2014.

[78] S. Kakei, Y. Shiraishi, M. Mohri, T. Nakamura, M. Hashimoto, and S. Saito, "Cross-Certification Towards Distributed Authentication Infrastructure: A Case of Hyperledger Fabric," *IEEE Access*, vol. 8, pp. 135 742–135 757, 2020.

[79] T. Sermpinis, G. Vlahavas, K. Karasavvas, and A. Vakali, "DeTRACT: A Decentralized, Transparent, Immutable and Open PKI Certificate Framework," *Int. J. Inf. Secur.*, vol. 20, no. 4, p. 553–570, 2021.

[80] P. Szalachowski, "PADVA: A Blockchain-Based TLS Notary Service," in *Proc. IEEE ICPADS*, 2019, pp. 836–843.

[81] H. Tewari, A. Hughes, S. Weber, and T. Barry, "X509Cloud — Framework for a ubiquitous PKI," in *Proc. IEEE MILCOM*, 2017, pp. 225–230.

[82] N. Johnson and V. Griffith, "Ethereum Name Service," 2018. [Online]. Available: https://docs.ens.domains

[83] Z. Xiong, Z. L. Jiang, S. Yang, X. Wang, and J. Fang, "SSHTDNS: A Secure, Scalable and High-Throughput Domain Name System via Blockchain Technique," in *Proc. IEEE NSS*, 2019, p. 272–287.

[84] A. Garba, Q. Hu, Z. Chen, and M. R. Asghar, "BB-PKI: Blockchain-Based Public Key Infrastructure Certificate Management," in *Proc. IEEE HPCC/SmartCity/DSS*, 2020, pp. 824–829.

[85] A. Garba, Z. Chen, Z. Guan, and G. Srivastava, "LightLedger: A Novel Blockchain-Based Domain Certificate Authentication and Validation Scheme," *IEEE Trans. Network Science and Engineering*, vol. 8, no. 2, pp. 1698–1710, 2021.

[86] Z. Guan, A. Garba, A. Li, Z. Chen, and N. Kaaniche, "AuthLedger: A Novel Blockchain-based Domain Name Authentication Scheme," in *International Conference on Information Systems Security and Privacy*, 2019.

[87] M. Caldeira and M. Correia, “Blockchain Address Transparency with DNS,” in *Proc. IEEE ISCC*, 2021, pp. 1–7.

[88] R. Li, X. Jia, Z. Zhang, J. Shao, R. Lu, J. Lin, X. Jia, and G. Wei, “A Longitudinal and Comprehensive Measurement of DNS Strict Privacy,” *IEEE/ACM Trans. Networking*, vol. 31, no. 6, pp. 2793–2808, 2023.

[89] M. Luo, B. Feng, L. Lu, E. Kirda, and K. Ren, “On the Complexity of the Web’s PKI: Evaluating Certificate Validation of Mobile Browsers,” *IEEE Trans. Dependable and Secure Computing*, vol. 21, no. 1, pp. 419–433, 2024.

Chapter 9

Federated learning for Supply Chain Management 5.0

Bushra Tahir[1] and Muhammad Tariq[1]

Abstract

This chapter explores the integration of federated learning (FL) in the evolution of supply chain management within the context of Industry 5.0. With the advancement of Industry 5.0, supply chain management has transitioned toward Supply Chain Management 5.0 (SCM 5.0), which incorporates emerging technologies like artificial intelligence (AI), automation, and the Internet of Things (IoT) to meet demands for mass personalization and efficiency. FL offers a decentralized approach to machine learning that enables different entities in the supply chain to collaboratively train models without sharing sensitive data, while enhancing privacy, optimizing resource utilization, and supporting real-time decision-making.

This chapter discusses the architecture of FL in SCM, detailing the roles of edge devices, federated servers, and machine learning models. Various applications, such as demand forecasting, logistics optimization, predictive maintenance, and risk management, demonstrate how FL can address the challenges associated with multimedia data in SCM 5.0. The chapter also highlights case studies across industries, illustrating how FL optimizes supply chain management in retail, manufacturing, and healthcare. Challenges such as data heterogeneity, trust, and system integration are examined, followed by future research directions to enhance the role of FL in secure, real-time, and sustainable SCM 5.0 solutions.

Keywords: Federated learning, Supply Chain Management 5.0, Data privacy, Industry 5.0, Real-time decision making, Logistics optimization, Resource utilization

9.1 Introduction

Supply Chain Management (SCM) is a critical function in any industry [1] as it ensures the efficient and effective flow of goods and services from suppliers to customers. It is the backbone of any business that enables the flow of products and

[1]Department of Electrical Engineering, National University of Computer and Emerging Sciences, Pakistan

services from the point of origin to the end customer. SCM is a complex process that involves multiple parties, as shown in Figure 9.1. The SCM process includes suppliers, manufacturers, warehousing [2], distributors [3], retailers, and customers including all links from raw material procurement [4], semi-finished product manufacturing, finished product manufacturing, product transportation, and product sales. It involves the coordination and integration of activities across the entire supply chain to ensure that the right products are delivered to the right place at the right time [5]. With the development of economic globalization and the continuous improvement of the technological level, enterprises have also begun to compete in the enterprise [6] supply chain and are committed to satisfying customers and providing suitable products to the market with the lowest cost and shortest logistics time.

With the advent of Industry 5.0 [5], the demands for mass personalization have grown, leading to the emergence of SCM 5.0. Industry 5.0 is characterized by the use of advanced technologies such as automation, robotics, artificial intelligence, and the Internet of Things (IoT) to improve efficiency, productivity, and customer satisfaction. SCM 5.0 builds on the foundation of traditional SCM by leveraging these advanced technologies to improve logistics and optimize resource utilization. However, the management of multimedia data, which includes sensitive and private information about customers, poses a significant challenge [5,7,8]. The introduction of artificial intelligence technology [9,10] has changed the organization, management, and tracking of the flow of goods and services in the supply chain. With the help of artificial intelligence technology, companies can develop more in-depth, predictive, and reliable observation methods to detect their business partners, and even allow competitors to merge into the same complex and huge supply chain. It enables enterprises to simplify activities in the process of supply chain management to achieve a more efficient and transparent cooperative relationship, and to improve the effectiveness and accuracy of logistics decision-making. Federated learning is a machine learning technique that allows multiple parties to train a model together without sharing their data [11–14]. It enables the development of models that can be used to improve logistics and optimize resource utilization while preserving customers'

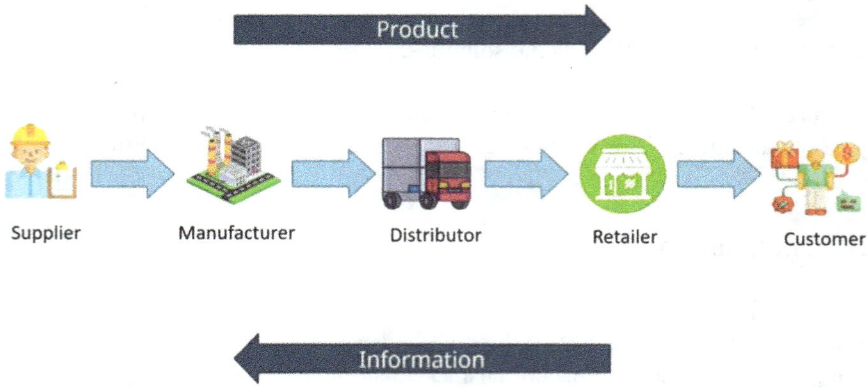

Figure 9.1 Supply chain management process

data privacy. The use of federated learning in SCM 5.0 can help unlock the full potential of this emerging technology and realize the benefits of mass personalization [15–17]. This chapter will delve into the challenges of multimedia data in SCM 5.0, the benefits of using federated learning, and real-time decision-making in SCM.

9.2 Architecture of federated learning in supply chain management

The architecture of federated learning in SCM 5.0 is shown in Figure 9.2. It consists of several key components that work together to ensure the efficient and secure handling of multimedia data [18]. These components are as follows:

9.2.1 Edge devices and data

Edge devices are the primary location where data is collected and processed in the architecture of federated learning in SCM. These devices may include sensors, cameras, and other IoT devices that are located at the edge of the network. These data sources in the architecture of federated learning in SCM include multimedia data such as images and videos, which are generated by various parties in the supply chain ecosystem. For example, a manufacturer might use cameras to capture images of products as they move through the production line, while a distributor might use sensors to track the temperature and humidity of products in transit. The edge devices collect and process the data locally, preserving customers' data privacy.

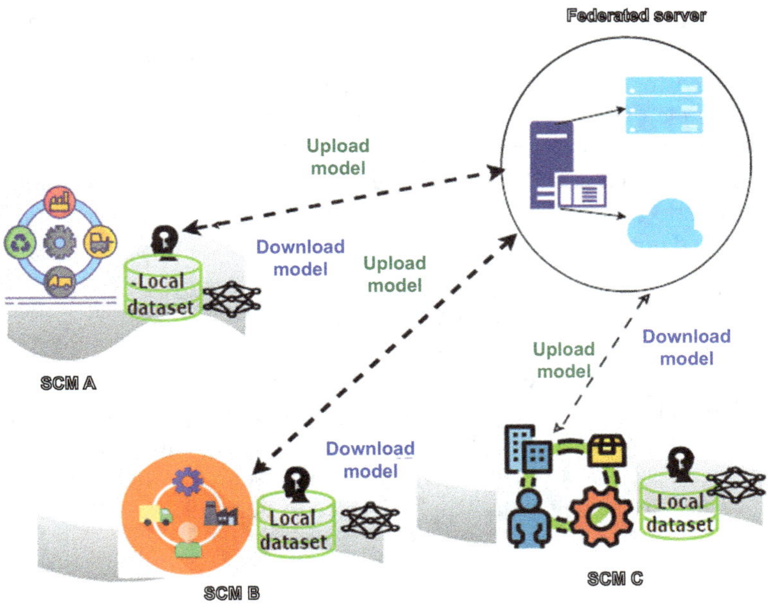

Figure 9.2 Architecture of federated learning in SCM 0.5

9.2.2 Federated server

The federated server acts as a central hub for coordinating the training of models in the architecture of federated learning in SCM. It is responsible for managing the communication between edge devices, aggregating model updates, and distributing the updated model to the participating parties. For example, the federated server might aggregate data from multiple manufacturers, distributors, and retailers to train a model that can predict demand for a particular product.

9.2.3 Model

The model is a machine learning algorithm trained using data from multiple parties in the supply chain ecosystem. The model is trained and updated locally on edge devices and then aggregated on the federated server. For example, a manufacturer might use a model trained on data from other manufacturers to predict demand for a particular product, while a distributor might use a model trained on data from retailers to predict shipping times.

9.2.4 Decision-making

The trained model is then used for decision-making by the participating parties in the supply chain ecosystem. These decisions include logistics, resource optimization, and other supply chain-related tasks. For example, a retailer might use the model to predict demand for a particular product and adjust inventory accordingly, while a manufacturer might use the model to optimize production schedules.

In summary, the architecture of federated learning in SCM involves coordinating multiple parties, including suppliers, manufacturers, distributors, retailers, and customers, all working together to train a model without sharing their data. Data is collected and processed on edge devices and then aggregated on a federated server, which is used for decision-making in the supply chain ecosystem. This architecture enables the preservation of customer data privacy and improves logistics and resource optimization while protecting sensitive information. Examples provided in this section illustrate how the architecture of federated learning can be applied in various scenarios, such as predicting demand for a product, optimizing production schedules, and improving logistics.

9.3 Applications of federated learning in SCM 5.0

In this section, we will delve deeper into the specific applications of federated learning in addressing the challenges of multimedia data in Supply Chain Management 5.0 (SCM 5.0). Federated learning is a powerful technique that can preserve customers' private and sensitive data while optimizing resource utilization and enabling real-time decision-making in the supply chain ecosystem [19].

9.3.1 Data privacy

One of the biggest challenges in SCM 5.0 is preserving customers' data privacy. With the increasing use of multimedia data such as images and videos, there is a growing concern about protecting customers' sensitive and private information. Federated learning allows data to remain on the device or system where it is generated, preserving customers' data privacy. Here are some possible applications of federated learning in SCM 5.0 that can be used to address some of the challenges that multimedia data present in a distributed and privacy-sensitive environment [20,21].

9.3.2 *Image and video annotation*

In a federated learning setup, suppliers can annotate images and videos of their products, without revealing the actual image/video data to the central server. The central server can use the annotated data to train a model that can recognize and categorize products across different suppliers [20,22].

9.3.3 *Quality control*

Federated learning can be used to train models for quality control in a privacy-sensitive manner. For example, manufacturers can take images of their products at different stages of production and send the annotated data to the central server, which can use to train a model for detecting defects [23].

9.3.4 *Inventory management*

Federated learning can be used to train models that can predict inventory levels and demand patterns across different suppliers and retailers. By keeping the inventory data on the local devices and only exchanging model parameters with the central server, the privacy of the suppliers and retailers can be protected [24].

9.3.5 *Logistics optimization*

Federated learning can be used to optimize logistics operations in a privacy-sensitive manner. For example, carriers can use GPS data and other sensor data to train models that can predict the arrival times of shipments and optimize delivery routes [25].

9.3.6 *Predictive maintenance*

Federated learning can be used to train models for predictive maintenance in a privacy-sensitive manner. For example, suppliers can use sensor data from their machines to train models that can predict when maintenance is needed, without revealing sensitive information about the machines or their operations to the central server [25].

9.3.7 *Resource utilization*

SCM 5.0 requires significant resources, including storage, processing power, and bandwidth. The large amount of multimedia data generated in SCM 5.0 increases communication costs, which can be a significant burden on the supply chain ecosystem. Federated learning optimizes resource utilization by training models on a distributed network of devices or systems, reducing the need for large central servers. This can help reduce costs and improve efficiency in the supply chain [25].

9.3.8 Real-time decision-making

Federated learning enables real-time decision-making by training and updating models locally on devices or systems. This allows for real-time predictions, which can be used to improve logistics and optimize resource utilization. For example, a distributor might use federated learning to train a model that predicts shipping times, using data from multiple retailers. This can help the distributor make real-time decisions about logistics and optimize resource utilization [25].

9.3.9 Supply chain optimization

Federated learning can be used to optimize the supply chain by improving logistics and resource utilization. By training models on data from multiple parties in the supply chain, federated learning can help identify patterns and trends that can be used to optimize logistics and resource utilization. This can help reduce costs, improve efficiency, and increase customer satisfaction [25]. In summary, Federated learning is a powerful technique that can be used to address the challenges of multimedia data in SCM 5.0. It enables the preservation of customers' data privacy, optimizes resource utilization, and enables real-time decision-making in the supply chain ecosystem. These applications of federated learning can help optimize the supply chain and improve logistics.

9.3.10 Demand forecasting

Federated learning can be used to forecast demand for products and services. This can help organizations to better plan their production and inventory levels. For example, a retailer could use federated learning to forecast demand for products from different suppliers. This would allow the retailer to optimize its inventory levels and reduce stockouts.

9.3.11 Risk management

Federated learning can be used to assess and manage risks in the supply chain. This can help organizations to prevent disruptions and losses. For example, a manufacturer could use federated learning to assess the risk of a supplier defaulting on a payment. This would allow the manufacturer to take steps to mitigate the risk, such as by diversifying its supplier base.

9.3.12 Sustainability

Federated learning can be used to improve the sustainability of the supply chain. This can help organizations to reduce their environmental impact. For example, a transportation company could use federated learning to optimize its routes. This would allow the company to reduce fuel consumption and emissions.

9.4 Federated learning in industry

In this section, we will delve deeper into the application of federated learning in various industries and provide more detailed examples of case studies. These case studies demonstrate how federated learning can be used to address the challenges of multimedia data in Supply Chain Management 5.0 (SCM 5.0) and optimize the supply chain.

9.4.1 Retail industry

In the retail industry [26], federated learning can be used to predict demand for particular products, optimize inventory, and improve logistics. For example, Walmart, one of the largest retailers in the world, which can use federated learning to train a model that predicts demand for a particular product, using data from multiple stores. This model is trained locally on edge devices at each store, preserving customers' data privacy. The model is then aggregated on a federated server, where it optimizes inventory and improves logistics. This helps Walmart optimize inventory and improve logistics, resulting in cost savings and increased customer satisfaction [27].

9.4.2 Manufacturing industry

In the manufacturing industry, federated learning can be used to optimize production schedules, reduce waste, and improve logistics. For example, Bosch, a leading manufacturer of automotive components, uses federated learning to train a model that predicts demand for a particular product, using data from multiple suppliers and distributors. The model is trained locally on edge devices at each supplier and distributor, preserving suppliers' and distributors' data privacy. The model is then aggregated on a federated server, where it is used to optimize production schedules and logistics. This helps Bosch optimize production schedules, reduce waste, and improve logistics, resulting in cost savings and increased efficiency [28].

9.4.3 Healthcare industry

In the healthcare industry, federated learning can be used to improve patient outcomes and reduce costs. For example, a hospital network can use federated learning to train a model that predicts patient outcomes, using data from multiple hospitals. The model is trained locally on edge devices at each hospital, preserving patients' data privacy. The model is then aggregated on a federated server, where it is used to optimize patient care and reduce costs. This helps the network optimize patient care and reduce costs, resulting in improved patient outcomes [29].

9.5 Federated learning for supply chain demand forecasting

Due to strong policy backing and the rapid advancement of internet technology, domestic consumption has been steadily rising, accompanied by significant changes in consumption patterns. However, the traditional retail sector faces challenges in adapting to these shifts due to concerns related to data security and privacy protection. Consequently, it struggles to make precise and timely adjustments to its sales strategies. The emergence of "new retail" signifies the need for a retail revolution. Within this context, accurate and timely supply chain demand forecasting becomes a crucial challenge in the realm of supply chain management.

Demand forecasting in the supply chain holds immense importance for both companies and consumers [30]. The outcomes of accurate forecasting enable companies to make critical adjustments to their operations, such as adapting production capacity (including hiring seasonal labor), subcontracting, managing inventory levels, and optimizing delivery schedules. This, in turn, facilitates effective supply management through strategies like short-term price discounts and promotional activities aimed at aligning with demand fluctuations. Failing to strike the right balance between inventory backlog and insufficient stock can result in significant cost losses for enterprises.

Accurate demand forecasting serves as a reliable guide for production decisions, helping to mitigate the challenges of overproduction and underproduction. Furthermore, within the realms of logistics and supply chains, products often fall into two categories: functional and innovative. However, these distinctions between the two product types are not always clear-cut.

Artificial intelligence technology, when applied with small-scale feature recognition and pre-training models tailored to various product types, has the capacity to anticipate and address the diverse product requirements effectively. This results in enhanced efficiency and interactivity across the entire supply chain, leading to holistic supply chain optimization.

For end-users, this translates into a solution to common issues such as product unavailability, sluggish logistics, or product deterioration caused by excess inventory or backlog. Anticipating potential customer needs in advance allows for timely fulfillment, ultimately enhancing customer satisfaction. Moreover, the ability to foresee these needs enables the strategic use of short-term price discounts and promotions to stimulate customer consumption, thereby encouraging increased purchasing activity from customers.

In [3], the authors proposed a new retail supply chain commodity demand forecasting framework based on vertical federal learning, which solves the problems of data security and privacy faced by new retail theoretically and empirically. In the experiments, they used data sets from different platforms such as social platforms, e-commerce platforms, and retailers in the same region for federated learning. They used a long- and short-term memory network based on federated learning to predict the future sales of goods in a region, integrated data between social networks, e-commerce platforms, and retailers, encrypted and aggregated the whole data on the basis of ensuring data nondisclosure, and could finally update the optimal model parameters after the training of the model. Experiments show that Fed-LSTM provides an effective sales prediction method and outperforms other Federated Learning-based machine learning methods in terms of privacy protection of commercial data.

9.6 A federated learning approach to data sharing in a food supply chain

The agri-food supply chain plays a pivotal role in the global economy, characterized by its complexity and immense value. Unfortunately, the competitive nature of this industry has often overshadowed the potential for collaboration and data sharing, which could prove advantageous for all stakeholders [31,32]. This lack of willingness to share data has hindered progress in addressing long-standing issues related to transparency and traceability, especially concerning the presence of adulterated or unsafe food throughout the supply chain [33]. Data sharing remains a major hindering factor when it comes to adopting emerging AI technologies in general, but particularly in the agri-food sector.

It's only natural for data owners to be protective of their data, as it represents a valuable asset that, when used effectively, can yield valuable insights into operations and processes, ultimately conferring a competitive advantage. Significant efforts have been invested in enhancing the traceability of food and beverages, driven by increasing consumer demands.

However, the challenge arises when novel AI technologies demand substantial volumes of training data, a requirement that often proves unfeasible in many scenarios. Fortunately, the emergence of federated learning and privacy-preserving technologies offers a promising solution to this dilemma [34]. These technologies provide the necessary infrastructure and underlying mechanisms to train models using data from various sources without the need to directly share the raw data itself.

In their study [18], the authors introduced a technical solution centered around federated learning. This approach leverages decentralized data, meaning data that remains under the ownership of its source without being directly exchanged or shared. The objective is to create a machine learning model that spans across different silos or entities, enabling data sharing across supply chains. Their primary focus was on proposing data sharing methods that could enhance production optimization, particularly in the context of soybean yield prediction. Additionally, they offered insights into potential applications of such techniques in other problem domains. It is important to note that their approach addressed horizontal data sharing across the supply chain. The intention was to support production optimization and facilitate regulatory reporting, aligning with the global commitments and sustainability goals that have become increasingly prominent in the agri-food supply chain [35].

To highlight the potential of federated learning (FL), ensembles of shared models, and the incorporation of differential privacy to establish trust in data sharing within the agri-food sector, the researchers utilized well-established open-source datasets for predicting crop yields. These datasets encompassed data from both imaging sources, such as remote sensing [36], and structured data sources, including weather and soil data [37].

The study's findings illustrated the performance of methods focused on data independence and privacy preservation when compared to traditional machine learning approaches. The primary objective was to empirically demonstrate that, even when operating under constrained conditions of data independence and the application of differential privacy, these training methods could generate competitive models.

The study employed specific use cases relevant to the agri-food sector to assess the potential benefits of data sharing and collaborative training. These use cases were identified as practical scenarios that could facilitate more effective data sharing and cooperative model training within the industry.

- Soft fruit production optimization for collaborative federations: Enhancing the performance of data-driven technologies is greatly facilitated by incorporating a broader range of data sources from multiple farms. In the agri-food sector, especially among soft fruit growers, there are instances where limitations exist in terms of data collection resources. However, these growers have a strong interest in utilizing data analytics not only to increase their profits but also to align with sustainability objectives, including the pursuit of net-zero targets. Another critical aspect to consider pertains to contractual agreements between growers and major retail supermarket chains. The accurate estimation of produce quantities is paramount, as both overestimation and underestimation can result in issues such as fruit wastage or shortages. These issues carry both financial and environmental consequences, affecting not only individual growers but also the entire sector. The concept of federations, similar to what was explored in [18], and facilitated through our proposed federated learning procedure, empowers multiple growers to collaborate and share their data in a reliable and secure manner. This collaborative approach aims to enhance the efficiency of their respective production systems.
- Analysis of client production from a distribution source—fresh food distribution center: In many instances, conducting statistical analysis on products distributed to clients can be advantageous for the supplier. This, in turn, benefits all parties involved, as data-driven analytical methods can lead to product enhancements tailored to meet the specific needs of clients. Much like the concept of production optimization, a federated learning framework can enable the central server (i.e., the distribution source) to orchestrate training processes aimed at creating a comprehensive statistical model encompassing all their clients. This holistic perspective on the data offers valuable insights. In the context of the fresh food industry, such an approach has the potential to optimize food availability, reduce transportation costs, minimize food wastage, and contribute to the overall financial well-being of all stakeholders within the supply chain

9.7 Federated learning for supply chain risk prediction

Our economy relies significantly on complex, international supply chains, which provide critical support to vital sectors like food, defense, aerospace, and automotive industries. However, these supply chains are becoming increasingly susceptible to disruptions from both high-impact, low-frequency events and low-impact, high-frequency events. This vulnerability is a result of growing complexity and interdependence among supply chain components. Supply chain disruptions have emerged as a prominent business risk factor across various industrial sectors and have garnered the attention of multiple governments [38]. Recent research underscores the inadequacy of efficiency-oriented management paradigms, as they traditionally assume a continuous and uninterrupted supply of resources. This prompts a critical question about the need for new paradigms capable of operating effectively in an environment characterized by long-term resource shortages [39–41].

Supply Chain Risk Management (SCRM) is a field dedicated to exploring risk management techniques with the goal of minimizing risk exposure within supply chains. Proactive strategies primarily aim at risk mitigation and involve measures like increasing safety stock, diversifying sourcing, sharing information, fostering collaboration, and establishing contingency plans for rerouting. Most of the existing research in this domain primarily centers on assessing the trade-offs between bolstering resilience and the associated costs of introducing redundancies or flexibility in supply sources or in-house production. On the other hand, reactive strategies come into play after a disruption has occurred and encompass tactics such as dynamic pricing adjustments to manage demand fluctuations, reconfiguring supply chains, and operational rerouting [42]. However, it is worth noting that predicting supply chain risks in advance remains an unresolved challenge that has not received adequate attention in the literature.

The utilization of AI technology for predicting supply chain risks has gained significant traction. However, most proposed approaches are built upon the assumption that organizations operate in isolation rather than collaboratively, despite the interconnected nature of supply chains. This leads to a fundamental challenge: organizations with limited or inadequate datasets struggle to predict risks effectively. While data-sharing has been suggested as a means to coordinate risk assessment efforts, practical implementation is hindered by privacy concerns. Typically, AI advancements are geared toward constructing predictive models using data exclusively from a single company. Given that AI-driven approaches rely on extensive datasets, their adoption becomes restricted to those companies with sufficient data for risk prediction. This can be problematic for companies at the initial stages of a supplier relationship or when subtle changes in the relationship occur, such as procuring a new product or ordering from a new location. In such cases, existing datasets may become less relevant for predicting new ordering patterns. Scholars in the field of Supply Chain Risk Management (SCRM) have long argued that data-sharing could lead to more accurate forecasts and mitigate the risks of stockouts or overproduction. However, organizations often refrain from sharing data due to apprehensions that others in the network might misuse the information to gain a competitive edge. [43].

FL originally developed as a privacy-preserving machine learning technique in the realm of mobile devices, offers a means to facilitate collective learning within supply chains. In this problem setting, multiple buyers each possess historical datasets comprising past transactions with their respective suppliers. These buyers may have exclusive suppliers and also share certain suppliers with one another. FL is employed to create a shared predictive model aimed at estimating whether a particular order will experience delays beyond the planned schedule, which constitutes a "classification" problem [44]. The FL model is grounded in a case study that originates from the maritime sector, where intricate engineering assets are manufactured. In this scenario, three buyers collaboratively engage with 70 suppliers, which collectively account for 47.54%, 39.04%, and 53.13% of their individual supply chains. Each buyer seeks to construct a predictive model to anticipate order delays, which can aid in production and inventory planning as well as facilitate what-if scenario analyses. While each buyer can develop a localized predictive model using their available historical data, they are interested in exploring whether a shared predictive model for their common suppliers could yield improved predictive performance. The dataset used spans orders delivered between 2015 and 2022. Recognizing the challenges brought about by the COVID-19 pandemic on global supply chains [45], the data is divided into two phases for each buyer: post-COVID-19 and pre-COVID-19. This division aims to investigate how the results obtained from the FL approach are influenced by the extensive disruptions caused by the pandemic. It is important to note that all the buyers are situated in the United Kingdom, where the first national lockdown was initiated in March 2020.

A comprehensive cross-comparison of federated learning (FL) approaches to local learning was conducted, with a focus on how buyers develop models using their own data versus centralized learning, where buyers aggregate their data resources. The study investigated various factors influencing the performance of FL, including local dataset size, the extent of disruptions experienced by companies during the COVID-19 pandemic, and the types of machine learning algorithms employed. The findings revealed that FL's performance closely aligns with both local and centralized learning methodologies. However, it offers a distinct advantage over centralized learning by prioritizing data privacy preservation. Additionally, FL may outperform local learning in scenarios where local datasets are insufficient. Notably, the study revealed that supply chain members with ample and well-balanced datasets can significantly support those with limited and skewed datasets by sharing predictive model parameters. This collaborative approach can enhance overall model performance and decision-making within the supply chain. Interestingly, the research contradicts previous studies on supply chain data-sharing, demonstrating that pooling datasets may not universally benefit all network members. Specifically, for companies with extensive historical datasets and long-standing relationships with suppliers, sharing data can introduce noise into the local learning process and lead to the loss of specialized supplier information, thereby diminishing the accuracy of inferences. However, such companies can still derive benefits from participating in a federated approach, particularly when changes occur within the supply chain, such as the introduction of a new product from an existing supplier. In these cases, federated approaches provide a balanced trade-off where local and federated models can be flexibly interchanged or weighted differentially as needed to improve overall performance.

9.8 Optimizing resource utilization, communication costs, and real-time decision-making with federated learning

In this section, we will explore how federated learning can be used to optimize resource utilization, and communication costs, and realize real-time decisions that benefit customers in Supply Chain Management 5.0 (SCM 5.0) [46].

9.8.1 Resource utilization

Federated learning optimizes resource utilization by training models on a distributed network of devices or systems, reducing the need for large central servers. This can help reduce costs and improve efficiency in the supply chain. For example, a manufacturer might use federated learning to train a model that predicts demand for a particular product, using data from multiple distributors and retailers. By training the model locally on edge devices at each distributor and retailer, the manufacturer can reduce the need for large central servers, which can help save costs and improve efficiency [46].

9.8.2 Communication cost

The large amount of multimedia data generated in SCM 5.0 increases communication costs, which can be a significant burden on the supply chain ecosystem. Federated learning can help reduce communication costs by training models on a distributed network of devices or systems, reducing the need for data to be transferred between parties in the supply chain. For example, a distributor might use federated learning to train a model that predicts shipping times, using data from multiple retailers. By training the model locally on edge devices at each retailer, the distributor can reduce the need for data to be transferred between parties, which can help save costs and improve efficiency [46].

9.8.3 Real-time decision-making

Federated learning enables real-time decision-making by training and updating models locally on devices or systems. This allows for real-time predictions, which can be used to improve logistics and optimize resource utilization. For example, a distributor might use federated learning to train a model that predicts shipping times, using data from multiple retailers. This can help the distributor make real-time decisions about logistics and optimize resource utilization, which can help improve customer satisfaction [46].

In summary, federated learning can be used to optimize resource utilization, and communication costs, and realize real-time decisions that benefit customers in SCM 5.0. By training models on a distributed network of devices or systems, federated learning can help reduce costs and improve efficiency in the supply chain. This can help improve customer satisfaction and bring significant benefits to the supply chain ecosystem.

9.9 Challenges of federated learning in SCM 5.0

While federated learning offers many benefits for addressing the challenges of multimedia data management in SCM 5.0, there are also several challenges that need to be considered.

9.9.1 *Heterogeneity of data and devices*

In SCM 5.0, the data and devices used by different participants can vary greatly in terms of quality, quantity, and processing capabilities. Supply chains involve various entities, including suppliers, manufacturers, distributors, and retailers, each with their own data formats, structures, and quality levels. Integrating and harmonizing these heterogeneous datasets for federated learning can be complex and time-consuming. This heterogeneity can make it difficult to train models that are effective for all participants and can also increase the complexity of the federated learning process.

9.9.2 *Trust and security*

Ensuring the security and privacy of sensitive multimedia data is a major concern in SCM 5.0. Federated learning requires a high degree of trust between participants to ensure that data is protected and models are trained securely.

9.9.3 *Data quality*

The quality of the data used for federated learning can have a significant impact on the quality of the models generated. In SCM 5.0, there may be a lack of standardization or quality control in the data collected and used by participants, which can make it difficult to ensure that models are accurate and effective.

9.9.4 *Latency and data transmission*

Federated learning requires a large amount of data transmission between participants, which can lead to increased latency and slow down the model training process. In SCM 5.0, this can be particularly challenging in scenarios where bandwidth constraints or other network limitations exist.

9.9.5 *Integration with existing systems*

Integrating federated learning into existing SCM 5.0 systems can be a challenge, as it may require significant changes to existing processes and systems. This can also increase the cost and complexity of implementing federated learning in SCM 5.0.

9.9.6 *Model aggregation*

Aggregating models from different nodes to create a global model is a non-trivial task. Ensuring that models converge correctly and that the aggregated model maintains accuracy and performance can be challenging, particularly when dealing with noisy or unreliable data sources.

9.9.7 Regulatory compliance

SCM 5.0 involves handling sensitive data related to logistics, inventory, and financial transactions. Adhering to data protection regulations like GDPR, HIPAA, or industry-specific compliance standards is essential. Federated learning systems must be designed to support these compliance requirements.

9.9.8 Scalability

As supply chains grow and evolve, the federated learning system needs to scale accordingly to accommodate an increasing number of participants, data sources, and data volume. Ensuring that the system remains efficient and responsive as it scales up can be a challenge.

9.9.9 Data imbalance

Some nodes in the supply chain may have more data than others, leading to data imbalance issues during model training. Handling this imbalance and ensuring that all nodes contribute meaningfully to the federated model is crucial for fairness and accuracy.

9.9.10 Reliability

The reliability and quality of data from different sources can vary significantly. Noisy or inaccurate data can negatively impact the performance of the federated model. Data cleaning and validation processes may be needed to address this challenge.

9.9.11 Interoperability

Integrating federated learning systems with existing SCM technologies and infrastructure may require interoperability standards and interfaces to ensure seamless data exchange and compatibility.

9.9.12 Change management

Implementing federated learning in SCM 5.0 may require a cultural shift within organizations and supply chain partners. Stakeholders need to understand and embrace the new collaborative and data-sharing approach.

To overcome these challenges, organizations should invest in robust infrastructure, data governance frameworks, security measures, and communication protocols tailored to the unique requirements of federated learning in SCM 5.0. Additionally, collaboration among stakeholders, regulatory compliance, and ongoing monitoring and adaptation of the federated learning system are essential for successful implementation in modern supply chain management.

Despite these challenges, federated learning has the potential to provide significant benefits for SCM 5.0 by enabling the optimization of resource utilization and improving the management of multimedia data. To fully realize the potential of federated learning in SCM 5.0, these challenges need to be carefully considered and addressed.

9.10 Future research directions

There are several potential future research directions in the field of Federated Learning in Supply Chain Management:

9.10.1 Secure federated learning

As more sensitive data is shared across the supply chain, research is needed to develop secure and privacy-preserving methods for federated learning. This could include developing secure aggregation methods, secure multiparty computation, and homomorphic encryption techniques.

9.10.2 Real-time federated learning

Real-time decision-making is becoming increasingly important in the supply chain. Research is needed to develop methods for real-time federated learning to enable near-instant predictions and improve logistics.

9.10.3 Resource constrained federated learning

Federated learning is often used in resource-constrained environments such as edge devices. Research is needed to develop methods for federated learning that can handle limited resources such as limited storage, computing power, and communication bandwidth.

9.10.4 Federated learning for autonomous systems

Autonomous systems are becoming increasingly prevalent in the supply chain. Research is needed to develop methods for federated learning that can be used to train and update models on autonomous systems such as drones and robots.

9.10.5 Multi-stakeholder federated learning

As supply chains become more complex, research is needed to develop methods for federated learning that can handle multiple stakeholders with different data and privacy requirements.

9.10.6 Federated learning in the context of Industry 5.0

As Industry 5.0 is emerging, research is needed to investigate how Federated learning can cater to the mass personalization needs of customers or clients in Industry 5.0.

9.10.7 Domain-specific federated learning

Tailor federated learning algorithms and techniques to specific SCM subdomains, such as demand forecasting, inventory optimization, or logistics routing. Domain-specific knowledge can lead to more effective federated learning models.

9.10.8 Supply chain risk prediction

Investigate how federated learning can be used to predict and mitigate supply chain risks, such as disruptions due to natural disasters, geopolitical events, or economic fluctuations. Federated learning can be a valuable tool for risk assessment and management.

9.10.9 Interoperability and standards

Develop standards and protocols for federated learning in SCM to promote interoperability between different supply chain partners and systems. Standardization can facilitate the adoption of federated learning in the industry.

9.10.10 Cross-organizational collaboration

Study methods for incentivizing and promoting cross-organizational collaboration in federated learning setups. Addressing challenges related to data sharing, trust, and incentives is essential for successful SCM applications.

9.10.11 Real-time and streaming data

Extend federated learning to handle real-time and streaming data in supply chains. This could involve developing online federated learning techniques that can adapt to rapidly changing data.

9.10.12 Ethical and legal considerations

Investigate the ethical and legal implications of federated learning in SCM, especially concerning data ownership, consent, and liability. Develop guidelines and frameworks for responsible federated learning practices.

9.10.13 Explainability and transparency

Work on making federated learning models more interpretable and transparent, especially in SCM scenarios where decision-makers require insights into the reasoning behind predictions and recommendations.

9.10.14 Benchmarking and evaluation

Create standardized benchmarks and evaluation metrics for federated learning in SCM. This can help compare different algorithms and approaches and advance the state-of-the-art.

9.10.15 Energy efficiency

Optimize federated learning algorithms and implementations for energy efficiency, considering the environmental impact of training large models in decentralized environments.

9.11 Conclusion

In this chapter, we have explored the application of federated learning in Supply Chain Management 5.0 (SCM 5.0) to address the challenges of multimedia data and preserve customers' private and sensitive data. We have discussed how federated learning can be used to optimize resource utilization, and communication costs, and realize real-time decisions that benefit customers. We have also provided examples and case studies of how federated learning has been applied in various industries to optimize the supply chain and improve customer satisfaction.

Federated learning is a powerful technique that enables the preservation of customers' data privacy, optimizes resource utilization, and enables real-time decision-making in the supply chain ecosystem. By training models on a distributed network of devices or systems, federated learning can help reduce costs and improve efficiency in the supply chain. These applications of federated learning can help optimize the supply chain and improve logistics, which can bring significant benefits to various industries and improve customer satisfaction.

In conclusion, as SCM 5.0 evolves, federated learning is likely to play an increasingly important role in optimizing the supply chain and addressing the challenges of multimedia data. As companies look for ways to improve logistics and reduce costs, federated learning will be a valuable tool for improving efficiency and customer satisfaction.

References

[1] Tahir B, Jolfaei A, and Tariq M. Experience-driven attack design and federated-learning-based intrusion detection in Industry 4.0. *IEEE Transactions on Industrial Informatics*. 2021;18(9):6398–6405.

[2] Zhang Y and Wen L. A multi-index pricing model for emergency material procurement based on constraint theory. In: *2020 2nd International conference on economic management and model engineering (ICEMME)*. IEEE; 2020. p. 556–559.

[3] Wang H, Xie F, Duan Q, *et al*. Federated learning for supply chain demand forecasting. *Mathematical Problems in Engineering*. 2022;2022.

[4] McCollough D, Santhoshkumar A, Das S, *et al*. Adaptive predictive modeling for supply chains. In: *2019 IEEE AUTOTESTCON*. IEEE; 2019. p. 1–4.

[5] Maddikunta PKR, Pham QV, Prabadevi B, *et al*. Industry 5.0: A survey on enabling technologies and potential applications. *Journal of Industrial Information Integration*. 2022;26:100257.

[6] Lee HS and Lee J. Applying artificial intelligence in physical education and future perspectives. *Sustainability*. 2021;13(1):351.

[7] Majid M, Habib S, Javed AR, *et al.* Applications of wireless sensor networks and internet of things frameworks in the Industry Revolution 4.0: A systematic literature review. *Sensors*. 2022;22(6). Available from: https://www.mdpi.com/1424-8220/22/6/2087.

[8] Tariq M, Ali M, Naeem F, *et al.* Vulnerability assessment of 6G-enabled smart grid cyber–physical systems. *IEEE Internet of Things Journal*. 2021;8(7):5468–5475.

[9] Zhang C. Intelligent Internet of things service based on artificial intelligence technology. In: *2021 IEEE 2nd International Conference on Big Data, Artificial Intelligence and Internet of Things Engineering (ICBAIE)*. IEEE; 2021. p. 731–734.

[10] Kodaira D and Kondoh J. Probabilistic forecasting model for non-normally distributed EV charging demand. In: *2020 International conference on smart grids and energy systems (SGES)*. IEEE; 2020. p. 623–626.

[11] Ali M, Karimipour H,and Tariq M. Integration of blockchain and federated learning for Internet of Things: Recent advances and future challenges. *Computers & Security*. 2021;108:102355. Available from: https://www.sciencedirect.com/science/article/pii/S0167404821001796.

[12] Ali M, Naeem F, Tariq M, *et al.* Federated learning for privacy preservation in smart healthcare systems: A comprehensive survey. *IEEE Journal of Biomedical and Health Informatics*. 2023;27(2):778–789.

[13] Srivastava G, K DRR, Yenduri G, *et al.* Federated learning enabled edge computing security for Internet of Medical Things: Concepts, challenges and open issues. In: *Security and Risk Analysis for Intelligent Edge Computing*. Springer; 2023. p. 67–89.

[14] Tariq M, Tahir B, and Zhou Z. Secure and enhanced online recommendations: A federated intelligence. *IEEE Transactions on Consumer Electronics*. 2023.

[15] Boobalan P, Ramu SP, Pham QV, *et al.* Fusion of federated learning and industrial Internet of Things: A survey. *Computer Networks*. 2022;212:109048.

[16] Alazab M, RM SP, M P, *et al.* Federated learning for cybersecurity: Concepts, challenges, and future directions. *IEEE Transactions on Industrial Informatics*. 2022;18(5):3501–3509.

[17] Pan C, Wang Z, Liao H, *et al.* Asynchronous federated deep reinforcement learning-based URLLC-aware computation offloading in space-assisted vehicular networks. *IEEE Transactions on Intelligent Transportation Systems*. 2022;1–13.

[18] Durrant A, Markovic M, Matthews D, *et al.* The role of cross-silo federated learning in facilitating data sharing in the agri-food sector. *Computers and Electronics in Agriculture*. 2022;193:106648.

[19] Zheng G, Kong L, and Brintrup A. Federated machine learning for privacy preserving, collective supply chain risk prediction. *International Journal of Production Research*. 2023;1–18.

[20] Issa W, Moustafa N, Turnbull B, *et al.* Blockchain-based federated learning for securing internet of things: A comprehensive survey. *ACM Computing Surveys*. 2023;55(9):1–43.

[21] Pandya S, Srivastava G, Jhaveri R, *et al.* Federated learning for smart cities: A comprehensive survey. *Sustainable Energy Technologies and Assessments*. 2023;55:102987.

[22] Teng L, Qiao Y, Shafiq M, *et al.* FLPK-BiSeNet: Federated learning based on priori knowledge and bilateral segmentation network for image edge extraction. *IEEE Transactions on Network and Service Management*. 2023;.

[23] Zhang W, Li Z, and Chen X. Quality-aware user recruitment based on federated learning in mobile crowd sensing. *Tsinghua Science and Technology*. 2021;26(6):869–877.

[24] Lau H, Tsang YP, Nakandala D, *et al.* Risk quantification in cold chain management: A federated learning-enabled multi-criteria decision-making methodology. *Industrial Management & Data Systems*. 2021;121(7):1684–1703.

[25] Nguyen DC, Ding M, Pathirana PN, *et al.* Federated learning for industrial internet of things in future industries. *IEEE Wireless Communications*. 2021;28(6):192–199.

[26] Tahir B and Tariq M. Vulnerability assessment and federated intrusion detection of Air Taxi enabled smart cities. *Sustainable Energy Technologies and Assessments*. 2022;53:102686.

[27] WSF Walmart Sales Forecast. Accessed on February, 2023. Available from: https://medium.com/analytics-vidhya/walmart-sales-forecast-41c6dc1028b8/.

[28] Witt L, Heyer M, Toyoda K, *et al.* Decentral and incentivized federated learning frameworks: A systematic literature review. *IEEE Internet of Things Journal*. 2022;.

[29] Tahir B, Jolfaei A, and Tariq M. A novel experience-driven and federated intelligent threat-defense framework in IoMT. *IEEE Journal of Biomedical and Health Informatics*. 2023;.

[30] Černe G, Dovžan D, and Škrjanc I. Short-term load forecasting by separating daily profiles and using a single fuzzy model across the entire domain. *IEEE Transactions on Industrial Electronics*. 2018;65(9):7406–7415.

[31] Markovic M, Leontidis G, Matthews D, *et al. Data sharing and interoperability for data trusts workshop: Summary report*. 2020.

[32] Durrant A, Markovic M, Matthews D, *et al.* How might technology rise to the challenge of data sharing in agri-food? *Global Food Security*. 2021;28:100493.

[33] Sarpong S. Traceability and supply chain complexity: Confronting the issues and concerns. *European Business Review*. 2014;26(3):271–284.

[34] Pearson S, May D, Leontidis G, *et al.* Are distributed ledger technologies the panacea for food traceability? *Global Food Security*. 2019;20:145–149.

[35] European Union, Sustainable agriculture in the cap. 2020. Available from: https://ec.europa.eu/info/food-farming-fisheries/sustainability/sustainable-cap_en.

[36] You J, Li X, Low M, *et al.* Deep Gaussian process for crop yield prediction based on remote sensing data. In: *Proceedings of the AAAI conference on artificial intelligence*. vol. 31; 2017.

[37] Khaki S, Wang L, and Archontoulis SV. A cnn-rnn framework for crop yield prediction. *Frontiers in Plant Science*. 2020;10:1750.

[38] Sweeney E. The big challenges for supply chains in 2022. *Logistics and Transport Focus*. 2022;24(2):48–49.

[39] Ivanov D. The Industry 5.0 framework: Viability-based integration of the resilience, sustainability, and human-centricity perspectives. *International Journal of Production Research*. 2023;61(5):1683–1695.

[40] Ivanov D and Dolgui A. Viability of intertwined supply networks: Extending the supply chain resilience angles towards survivability. A position paper motivated by COVID-19 outbreak. *International Journal of Production Research*. 2020;58(10):2904–2915.

[41] Ivanov D and Dolgui A. The shortage economy and its implications for supply chain and operations management. *International Journal of Production Research*. 2022;60(24):7141–7154.

[42] Baryannis G, Validi S, Dani S, *et al.* Supply chain risk management and artificial intelligence: State of the art and future research directions. *International Journal of Production Research*. 2019;57(7):2179–2202.

[43] Parashar S, Sood G, and Agrawal N. Modelling the enablers of food supply chain for reduction in carbon footprint. *Journal of Cleaner Production*. 2020;275:122932.

[44] Brintrup A, Pak J, Ratiney D, *et al.* Supply chain data analytics for predicting supplier disruptions: A case study in complex asset manufacturing. *International Journal of Production Research*. 2020;58(11):3330–3341.

[45] Guan D, Wang D, Hallegatte S, *et al.* Global supply-chain effects of COVID-19 control measures. *Nature Human Behaviour*. 2020;4(6):577–587.

[46] Yu S, Chen X, Zhou Z, *et al.* When deep reinforcement learning meets federated learning: Intelligent multi timescale resource management for multiaccess edge computing in 5G ultradense network. *IEEE Internet of Things Journal*. 2020;8(4):2238–2251.

Chapter 10

Federated learning for cobots in Industry 5.0

Pawan Hegde[1], Gokul Yenduri[1], Praveen Kumar Reddy Maddikunta[1], Ben Othman Soufiene[2] and Thippa Reddy Gadekallu[3,4]

Abstract

The transition of Industry 4.0 to Industry 5.0 has employed the integration of artificial intelligence, robots, and modern technologies to strengthen the traditional process in various domains by establishing a harmony between the robots and humans. Industry 5.0 requires an effective, seamless collaboration between the human and robots. The recent advancement in the AI-based distributed learning mechanism, i.e., federated learning (FL) enables the integration of data from multiple devices or components irrespective of their location by ensuring privacy. Thus to strengthen the capabilities of collaborative robots and to establish an effective, heterogeneous, safe production ecosystem, we have proposed a fusion of FL with collaborative robots in Industry 5.0 perspective. This research article presents the significance and impact of integrating federated learning in cobots considering the Industry 5.0 scenario on various aspects such as strengths challenges and applications. First, we present a detailed discussion on the federated learning architecture and existing FL-based solutions for robots. Next, we highlight the strengths of the FL-based cobots and their applications in various domains such as healthcare, production and manufacturing, education, supply-chain management, and disaster management. Finally, the challenges and future directions are discussed to improve the activities and operations of the FL-based cobots in an Industry 5.0 ecosystem.

Keywords: Collaborative robot (cobot), Federated learning (FL), Industry 5.0, Privacy

[1]School of Computer Science Engineering and Information Systems, Vellore Institute of Technology, India
[2]PRINCE Laboratory Research, ISITcom, Hammam Sousse, University of Sousse, Tunisia
[3]Division of Research and Development, Lovely Professional University, Phagwara, India
[4]Zhongda Group, Haiyan County, Jiaxing City, Zhejiang Province, China

10.1 Introduction

The evolution of technology has changed the human approach to perform a specific task, developing new services, or fulfilling their personal needs and desires by adopting the technologies and their features. Along with that, the modern technology-enabled devices, gadgets, equipment, tools, and machinery are effective in performing assigned tasks with minimal or no errors. With the aid of new technologies and ideas, the manufacturing and production industries could be able to increase their business interns of production quantity and quality without any issues leading to revolutionary growth. Basically, technology revolutions have transformed the industry's perspective by introducing novel procedures, techniques, materials, and machinery [1]. In the 18th century, industries started to replace old raw materials and procedures with contemporary methodologies to develop products or services. So in Industry 1.0, humans are replaced with water and steam-powered machinery. During the period of Industry 2.0 in 1870, electrical systems were introduced with an aim to increase business growth and economic growth by encouraging innovative ideas. Similarly, in 1969, Industry 3.0 introduced automation through programmable control systems and computers. The main aim is to carry mass production using electronic and digital systems, hence transforming the traditional mode of operations and procedures of developing products in digital mode. Later in 2011, Industry 4.0 introduced digital manufacturing with advanced technologies such as AI, IoT robots, 3D printing, and cloud computing. Even though every phase of the revolution is aimed to improve efficiency, productivity, and quality through technology and automation, it has also created many challenges, such as the displacement of workers, increase of cyber threats, lack of adaptability due to high specialization, and investment required to produce more complex and specialized products. To over the existing issues, Industry 5.0 emerged in the year 2020 and aimed to improve productivity and efficiency along with improving the quality of life for workers and society as a whole. Industry 5.0 is built on three major principles: human-centric, resilience, and sustainable (Figure 10.1) [2].

Collaborative robots (cobots) are the major enables of Industry 5.0. Every Cobot is a universal robot, equipped with sensors and vision technologies to work along with humans and machines. Cobots can be trained to work along with humans and reprogrammed to perform a wider range of tasks [3]. However, Industry 5.0 is a human-centered ecosystem, which blends people's creativity and craftsmanship with the speed, productivity, and consistency of robots, and explores to make use of all the potentials to create unimaginable economic and social growth. Even though Industry 5.0 exhibits several unique features such as faster processing with intelligent edge computing, optimized production using real-time data analytics, flexible and customizable production using adaptive manufacturing technique, efficient communication between devices, and intelligent decision-making also suffer from challenges such as security, privacy, lack of skilled workers, time-consuming process, and the need for a large budget. Adoption of Industry 5.0 requires well-defined industrial laws and regulations that will help to work together with smart machines and cobots [4].

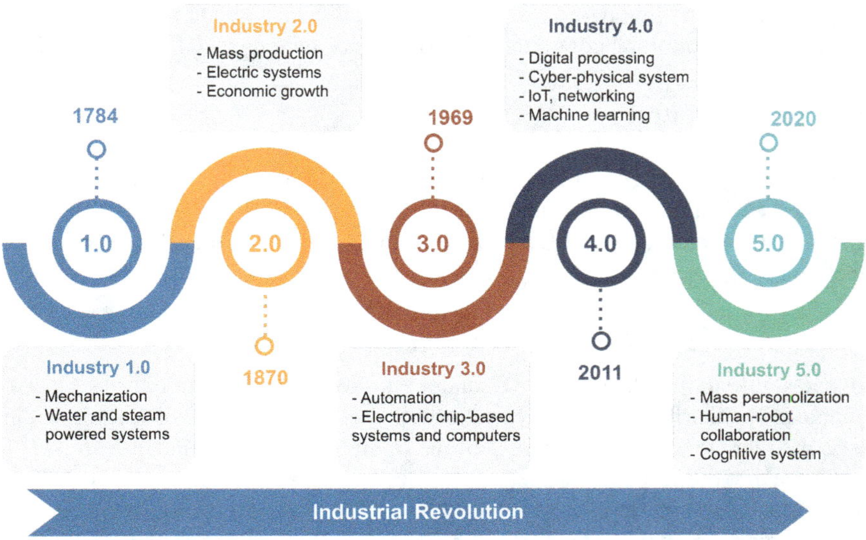

Figure 10.1 Stages of industrial revolution

Cobots will work in collaboration with humans in a shared working space, and to respond quickly and effectively in any situation, cobots should be able to detect objects, obstacles, and dangers. Although it is feasible to create rules-based models to direct an autonomous system, doing so has proven challenging a task in complex cobot-based application. However, the use of AI and ML in robots will strengthen their ability to recognize objects in the surrounding working space. With this knowledge and pattern-matching techniques, robots could be able to learn the appropriate behavior from past experience [5]. Similarly, deep neural network models [6] and mixed convolutional LSTM network [7] will help cobots to detect the collision and its occurrence; to ensure the safe and collaborative working environment, the cobots are trained with convolutional neural network models to detect the human interactions more efficiently [8].

Even though the machine learning and deep learning models improve the learning ability of cobots, they are still having major challenges such as requirement of high quality and diverse data for learning process, central data collection, and model training on third-party cloud, which induces security and privacy concerns; the complex deep learning models require huge computational resources, face scalability issues, and are difficult to adapt to dynamic industrial environment [9].

The recent advancement in AI has developed a privacy-preserving distributed learning mechanism to address the challenges of traditional machine learning and deep learning in cobots. The FL enables multiple clients to train a shared model by keeping the actual data on their devices. In this decentralized learning process, the clients only share model parameters with the server in various iterations; hence, FL consumes minimal communication cost and bandwidth, and the privacy of data is maintained. Thus, merging FL in cobots may result in several advantages such as data privacy and security, improved performance and efficiency due to real-time learning and adaptability, minimal communication overhead, and enhanced scalability [10].

10.2 Background

In this section, we discuss the fundamentals of FL which includes the history and use cases of FL, FL architecture, and advantages of FL. We also highlight the existing implementations of FL in various aspects of optimizing the operations or functionalities of robots.

10.2.1 Federated learning paradigm

Advanced research in the field of ML and AI has led to the innovations of FL (FL) a collaborative, distributed and decentralized, privacy-preserving, ML technique aiming to resolve the weakness or issues of the traditional ML. McMahan *et al.* [11] in 2016 have first proposed FL as a learning procedure allowing users to gain the advantages of shared model training without the necessity of central storage by identifying a general global model by combining the local models generated by the clients using their local data [12,13]. In FL, clients are associated to perform the training on their local systems without sharing the data; instead, only the parameters are shared with the central server. Hence, FL reduces the communication cost and ensures improved data privacy and security compared to the traditional models.

The large-scale deployment of FL was introduced in Google predictive keyboard (Gboard) on Android smartphones by Google where the users typing inputs and smartphone processing power are used for training the local models [14]. These locally trained models from several clients collaboratively contribute to optimizing the general word prediction model in Google's central server [15]. Hence, FL enables the integration of global user behaviors and features of local models for an efficient prediction of words in Gboard by ensuring the privacy concerns [16].

FL is an iterative process, where the global models are optimized in several iterations in the server using the local models of the several clients participating in the network. The major role of the central server is to manage the clients, aggregate the local models, and update the global models [17]. However, the FL consists of three major steps such as the following:

Model initialization: The central server initializes the weights based on the pre-training steps. Later, these model training parameters are distributed across the network among the various clients.

Local model training: Based on the global models and weights received from the servers, clients train their data locally using the local computing resources to generate the updated local models in several epochs. Finally the newly generated updated local model weights are transferred back to the server for further optimization of the model through an encrypted communication channel.

Aggregation: The central server aggregates all the updated local model weights sent by the clients. Later aggregated parameters of the local models are used to update the global model. Hence, the global model is further optimized with a new set of weights (Figure 10.2).

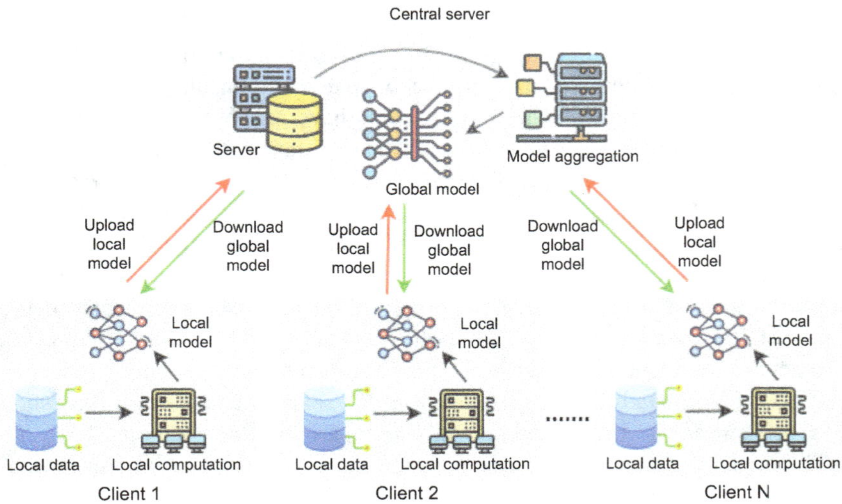

Figure 10.2 FL architecture

The Step 2 and Step 3 along with the model evaluation are repeated until satisfactory levels of accuracy are attained or the predefined numbers of iterations are satisfied.

The FL exhibits several benefits over the traditional, centralized ML techniques such as follows:

- Enhanced data privacy and security: FL allows the clients to keep the training data on their local machines thus avoiding the data sharing and exchange of information with third-party vendors. Instead, only the model parameters are shared during the learning process. Hence, FL protects the privacy if raw data and reduces the risk of data leakage [18].
- Increased scalability and cost-efficiency: FL allows the distribution of data among the multiple devices located in different places and also allows the local training on those data simultaneously without the need for central authority. Hence, it accelerated the model deployment and also improved the scalability. Similarly, in the FL model only the model parameters are transferred to a central server from the clients, hence, it reduces the cost of data transfer, computing, and storage [18].
- Higher adaptability: Since the FL models can learn from past events and build predictions on them, they can typically be applied to new scenarios without the need for retraining. Hence, the model's knowledge and improvements gained from one field can be applied to another to improve efficiency, reduce costs, and accelerate the process [18].
- Improved data accuracy and diversity: In FL, the models are trained in a distributed, decentralized and heterogeneous data from a diverse source, which results in improved models' ability to handle the various situations without any bias [18].

10.2.2 FL-based solutions for robots

Traditionally, reinforcement learning is widely used in autonomous vehicles but to improve the performance as well as the knowledge base considering the actions of other vehicles, the authors Magdum *et al.* [19] have proposed an FL model with V2X communication technology and collision avoidance mechanism. The model was aimed to reduce collision and improve reliability. The proposed model was tested in a SUMO, Veins, and Flow simulation environment; however, the results have shown that FL-based models are more efficient in reducing the accidents of vehicles. Hence, the overall performance is better compared to the non-FL-based model. Similarly, Na *et al.* [20] have proposed an FL-based deep reinforcement learning (DRL) training strategy for robotic applications. The model was proposed to protect the confidentiality of collected data and also reduce the robot's reliance on high-fidelity, high-bandwidth communications. The experimental results have shown higher robustness and better generalization compared to the traditional DRL models. The model is more suitable for environments with limited communication like underground or underwater.

To investigate and improve the user's privacy aspects of the autonomous driving policy from sensory data, the authors, Nguyen *et al.* [21], have introduced a deep FL technique to train deep architecture in a distributed environment. The proposed model also introduces a federated autonomous driving network for the federated training process. Even though the model was deployed and tested by considering limited mobile robots in an indoor environment, the model outperforms the existing schemes. Recently, the authors Kou *et al.* [22] have proposed an optimization-based Communication Resource Constrained Hierarchical Federated Learning (CRCHFL) framework aimed to reduce the generalization error of the autonomous driving models using hybrid data and model aggregation. The model was tested in a simulated environment. However, the results have shown a better convergence rate under constrained communication resources. The framework requires further analysis by considering several other parameters.

Majcherczyk *et al.* [23] have proposed an FL-based framework by enabling an effective learning process on distributed data from a set of robots. The proposed Flow-FL, a multi-robot setting performs model updates considering quota and quorum parameters. However, the experiment was conducted by considering the traditional FL-based approach where the server aggregates the local models and the Flow FL-based approach where gossip-based shared data structure is used for aggregation instead of the server. The existing AI-based techniques require a huge amount of data to infer the knowledge, however considering the various aspects of Industry 5.0, the authors Jabrane *et al.* [24] have proposed a new approach to training cobots with a small amount of data. The main aim of the model is to establish an effective and safe collaboration between humans and machines. The model consists of three deep learning neural networks such as zero-shot learning (ZSL), few-shot learning (FSL), and multi-task deep reinforcement learning (MTDRL). The authors have demonstrated the theoretical aspects only; hence, the model requires proper implementation and analysis.

Imteaj *et al.* [25] have proposed a trust and resource-aware FL model to deal with untrusted, resource-constrained IoT environments. The authors considered mobile robots as clients. The proposed model also verifies the clients' resource capacity and previous training performance and assigns the trust score for every robot client. Similarly, the authors Yu *et al.* [26] have done a detailed investigation on the effectiveness of FL for distributed mobile robots. The proposed vision-based deep obstacle avoidance in mobile robots was tested in both central learning as well as FL aggregation schemes. However, the results of the FL-based approach offer benefits in terms of communication optimization, data privacy preserving, and enabling collaboration among the users or organizations. Montero *et al.* [27] have proposed an asynchronous FL-based human–robot touch system with a multiuser, multi-robot, distributed, and scalable learning approach. To achieve high accuracy and avoid overfitting, the proposed framework incorporates a combination of incremental learning and a weight correction method during the FL aggregation phase. The experimental results have shown improved performance of the model. The authors, Huang *et al.* [28], introduced Fed-HANet an FL framework for human–robot handovers. The model utilizes an end-to-end control system for the visual grasping of unseen objects with six degrees of freedom. The proposed approach ensures the privacy of the users.

10.3 Strengths of FL-based cobots

10.3.1 Enhanced learning and adaptability

Basically, the cobots will be working in close interactions with the humans during the development of any product or while performing a specific task and often operate in a resource-constrained environment with limited reliable network, computational power [29]. The incorporation of FL allows cobots to train models directly on their local device resulting in reduced dependency on third-party infrastructures and also enables cobots to leverage their computational capabilities at the edge. However, each cobots are allowed to learn based on their own experience and interactions with the specific environment. Hence, the domain-specific knowledge will help cobots to make efficient, faster, and responsive decisions during the process.

FL enables continuous training and updating of local models based on the data collected during the process [30]. Thus, encourages incremental learning and adaption by ensuring the cobots to work with the latest information. Hence, FL enables personalized and context-specific model development, ensuring adaptability to the unique needs and challenges of different industrial environments [31].

10.3.2 Privacy-preserving and secure data sharing

Industry 5.0 involves collection, processing, and analysis of enormous amounts of sensitive data collected by the cobots by interacting with humans and the surrounding environment. Unlike the traditional central server-based model processing systems where during the transfer the sensitive data may be external nodes raising privacy and security concerns, the FL enables a decentralized data collaborative model training process, without the need of actual data being shared among other nodes [32].

Hence, the privacy of the data is preserved, reducing the risk of data exposure or unauthorized access of data [33].

During the process, only model parameters are shared among the server or the cobots, thus federated scheme will minimize the overall data transfer rate and reduce the privacy concerns associated with transferring a large amount of data among the server or cobots. To strengthen the privacy aspects in cobots, FL also introduces the implementation of Differential privacy techniques, by applying a random noise to the data or to the model parameters thus making it harder to identify the actual data [34].

Since the data remains on the cobots' devices, users have more control over their data and can decide whether to participate in the FL process [35]. Users can also set privacy preferences and specify the types of data they are comfortable sharing, ensuring transparency and giving individuals greater control over their data.

10.3.3 Collaborative knowledge sharing and real-time decision-making

Cobots are designed to physically interact with humans in a shared working environment without any barrier or protection as in traditional robots. To create an efficient and harmonious working environment, it is necessary to train the robot to make decisions and interact with the human. FL approach allows cobots to gain domain-specific knowledge by allowing local training and exchanging local and global model parameters with the server or other cobots, thereby enhancing their decision-making capabilities of cobots through knowledge sharing [10].

FL allows cobots to update the models based on the human interactions and dynamic changes in the working environment, thus encouraging continuous iterative learning and gaining contextualized knowledge based on the current status of the environment. During the iterative learning process, cobots will share gained insights and expertise with others resulting in collaborative knowledge sharing thus improving the real-time responsiveness of the cobots [24,36]. However, sharing only the model parameters among cobots will also reduce the burden of communication and synchronization overhead; hence, the overall performance of the system will be improved.

10.3.4 Robust and fault tolerance

FL is a distributed collaborative learning approach, where the cobots are allowed to train their models on a wide variety of data that are being collected from various sources, resulting in a robust model that can resist and adopt the changes in the environment. FL allows multiple cobots to train and share their models simultaneously with redundant and parallel processing mechanisms. Similarly, FL also introduces the robust model aggregation and fault detection mechanism to ensure the shared models are reliable and accurate. Hence, cobots are given the privilege to monitor their own performance and identify anomalies in their model updates. When the faults or errors are detected the cobots can invoke an error recovery procedure or they can retrain the model as a corrective measure. However, with the current collaborative knowledge, cobots are able to take proactive measures to improve the fault tolerance of the system before the significant impact on the overall performance [37].

10.3.5 Customization and personalization

The traditional ML-based approach requires a huge amount of data to be stored in a central server for the model training and analysis but the FL-based schemes are more flexible and secure since they allow cobots to share only the model parameters during the training process. In the local training process, cobots are given the opportunity to customize their local model by gaining knowledge from different environments [38]. For instance, FL-based robotic assembly, where the robots are trained to customize the assembly process based on the preferences of the customers [39].

Personalization can be achieved by customizing the model during iterative learning by considering the requirements of a specific task. FL enables fine-grained control over the learning process and customization options. Cobots and their human operators can have direct control over the model training and sharing parameters, allowing them to specify preferences, criteria, or constraints. This level of customization ensures that the learning process aligns with specific requirements and objectives, enabling tailored outcomes [40].

10.4 Applications of FL-based cobots

Fl-based cobots have several applications in Industry 5.0 where human–machine cobots will use the strengths of AI, robotics, and decentralized data processing to transform several industries [41]. In our discussion, we have considered three major industry applications such as healthcare, supply chain management, manufacturing, and production. Figure 10.3 represents the applications of FL-based cobots.

10.4.1 Healthcare

FL is a decentralized collaborative approach that allows multiple devices to train a model on their local systems without actually sharing the data with others. The FL overcomes the privacy and communication overhead of traditional ML models. In an Industry 5.0 ecosystem, the cobots are associated with FL-based approach to learn from and interact with the collaborative ecosystem. FL-based cobots will transform healthcare by improving human capabilities and patients care by combining AI-based technologies and human skills [42].

FL-based cobots can work together with healthcare providers to suggest personalized patient care by extracting insights from patients' medical histories. Cobots will fetch the real-time data of patients by interacting with wearable devices However, the cobots would be able to provide treatment plans and monitor continuously [39]. Based on the real-time health parameters, the cobots could be able to analyze the present status as well as predict the disease progression by making proper decisions regarding the treatment adjustment. FL-based cobots can also be used for disease diagnosis based on the proper analysis of healthcare data, collected from multiple medical sources without revealing the patient's sensitive information. Cobots will continuously interact and exchange model updates to improve the accuracy [43].

Similarly, the FL-based cobots can work along with the surgeons, in human–robot surgical collaboration aimed to enhance the precision and reduce human errors with an improved patient's safety [44]. Cobots can assist in various aspects of

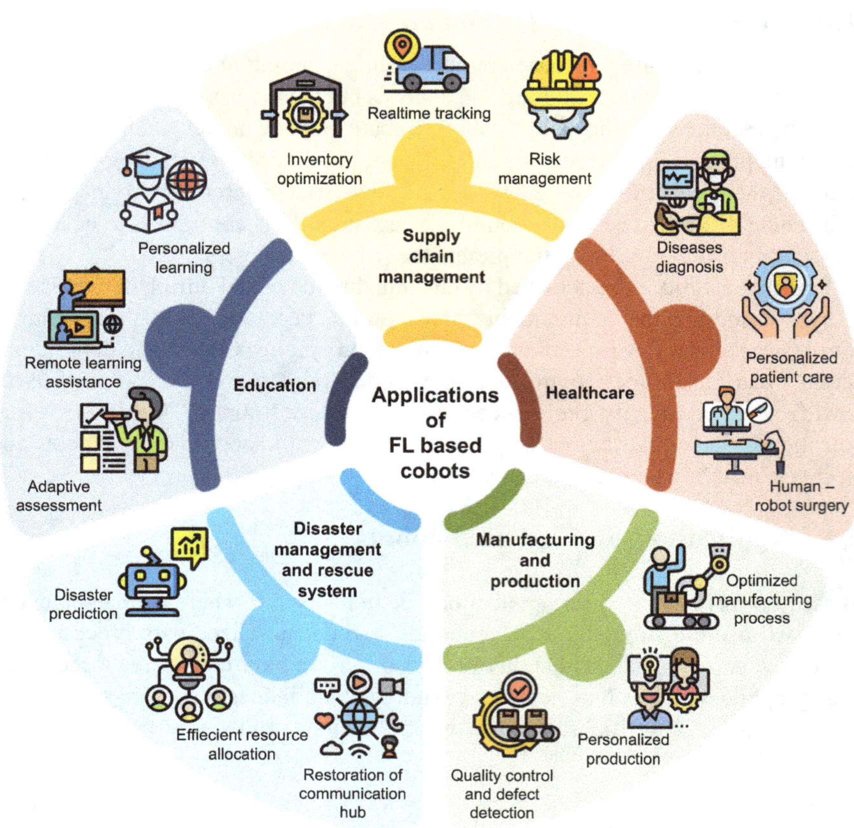

Figure 10.3 Applications of FL-based cobots

surgery such as preoperative planning—where the cobots can acquire knowledge based on past and current medical records collected from various sources, intraoperative guidance—during the surgery cobots can provide instructions to the doctors and track the monitoring parameters and instruments to personalize the strategies, and postoperative analysis—where the cobots can analyze the patient's recovery based on the surgery procedure. Hence, the cobots can optimize surgical procedures and also improve the patient's outcomes.

10.4.2 Production and manufacturing

The introduction of cobots in manufacturing is a game changer for all small and large industries. Cobots resolve the major issues of manufacturing and assembly by allowing the collaboration of humans and robots, thus resulting in increased productivity with minimal production cost [45]. With the aid of AI, robotics, and decentralized data processing, cobots can revolutionize manufacturing and production by ensuring the privacy of data collection as well as data usage. Hence, FL-based cobots can enhance efficiency, quality, safety, and product design by ensuring the security and privacy of data [46]. FL-based cobots can assist in the manufacturing and production industries in various tasks such as Quality Control and Defect Detection, Personalized Production and Customization, Workforce Safety and Compliance, Optimization of Manufacturing Processes, Resource Allocation and Capacity Planning, Energy Efficiency, and Sustainability.

FL-based cobots can be used in Quality control during the manufacturing process where the cobots will analyze the data collected from the various sensors using FL-based algorithms which helps to inspect the device and identify the defects in real time. Cabots can continuously improve the quality check process by collaborating with other production lines; hence, the defect detection accuracy will be increased with minimal manufacturing errors. FL-based cobots can also identify the process inefficiencies and recommend improvements in order to improve the production by analyzing the data from different manufacturing units. FL-based cobots can also customize the products by identifying customer preferences using the feedback across the market [47].

10.4.3 Education

The advancement in AI technology has increased the opportunities of AI robots for learning designs in schools or professional training. Several studies have proved that, AI robots as a powerful tool in Education by providing an efficient, cost-effective, and safe way to teach and learn a variety of skills [48]. Since the cobots are designed to work along with humans, they are programmed in such a way that cobots can be used to teach students various topics, used to improve the problem-solving, self-efficacy, creativity, collaboration/cooperative skills, and computational thinking of the students. Hence, the incorporation of cobots in education will not only improve the understanding capabilities and critical thinking of students but also provide a hands-on experience with the cutting edge technology thus resolving the gap between theoretical knowledge and practical application [49].

FL-based cobots will collect information based on students' interactions, behavior, learning choices, and performance on student problem-solving ability and learning pace. FL enables cobots to analyze the student's information and generates personalized learning schemes for the students based on their individual performance and understanding capabilities. FL-based cobots can also provide a separate learning scheme for the specially challenged students by analyzing their learning patterns and unique requirements [50].

Apart from the learning process, the FL-based cobots will also assist teachers in administrative works, students grading activities, and managing classroom tasks. Hence, the FL-based cobots reduce the additional burden of the teachers, thus allowing teachers to spend more time on meaningful interactions with the student [50].

Finally, the FL-based cobots can transform the traditional teaching and learning system by providing collaborative personalized learning methods, efficient remote learning assistance, implementing interactive content delivery methods for the skill and language development of the students, providing special learning methods for challenged students, and adaptive assessment systems for diverse students.

10.4.4 Disaster management and rescue systems

Disaster management is a process of efficiently anticipating and responding to calamities. It is a systematic process of planning, organizing, and harmonizing the resources and efforts to reduce the impact of natural or man-made disasters. Many researchers and decision-makers and strategic planners have proposed proactive measures/activities considering the various phases of disaster management such as pre-disaster activities, current, and post-disaster activities. The adoption of modern technologies such as AI in robotics, drones, machine learning, deep learning, sensors, and optimized algorithms for disaster prediction, to assist rescue process and relief delivery activities have shown positive results in disaster management [51].

An efficient collaborative interaction with the external environment and other devices, the FL-based cobots would be able to collect real-time data by adopting the changes in the environment. Using FL-based predictive models, the cobots can predict and detect the early signs of disasters in an effective manner [52]. Similarly, an efficient FL technique enables cobots to identify the signs of life, obstacles, and hazards. Thus, FL-based cobots can be used for real-time situation awareness and predictions.

With effective and optimized search patterns, FL-based cobots can identify the disaster-stricken areas, and using different inspection scenarios, cobots could be able to assess the damages accurately, thus increasing the changes of successful rescues from the affected areas [52]. FL-based cobots can also perform an effective allocation of resources such as manpower, equipment, and other supplies as per the need and also contribute to the restoring of communication hubs for the proper network connectivity. Hence, the FL-based cobots will enhance the response capabilities by accelerating decision-making in critical situations.

10.4.5 Supply-chain management

In Industry 5.0, the supply management system is extremely connected and data-driven where a huge amount of data is being generated by various sensors, machines, and other connected devices. FL-based cobots will transform the existing supply chain management systems by allowing data collaboration, improving the decision-making capability, and enhancing overall efficiency. FL-based cobots can analyze the real-time inventory data across the various warehouses and distribution centers thus contributing to optimizing inventory levels considering several aspects such as demands, reducing excess inventory, and enhancing working capital efficiency. Similarly, FL-based cobots can be used in several aspects of supply-chain management such as risk management, real-time tracking of products, and demand prediction [53].

10.5 Challenges and future directions

FL and cobots have shown several benefits in resolving the issues of Industry 5.0. However, FL-based cobots have a few challenges that need to be addressed

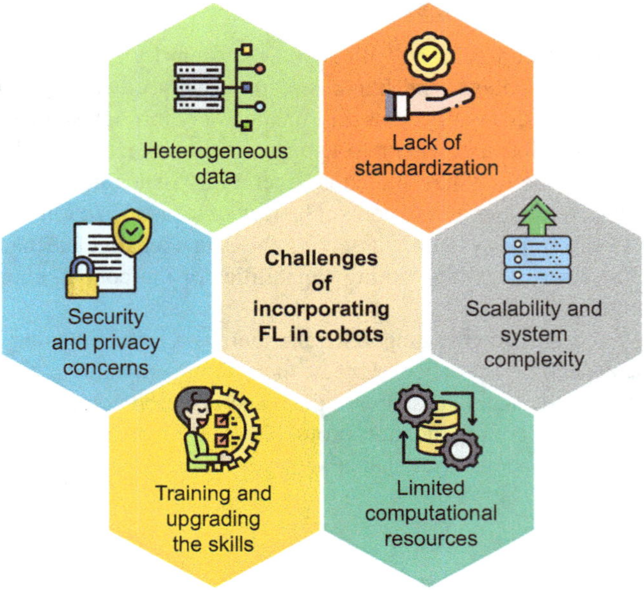

Figure 10.4 Challenges

to improve the productivity of Industry 5.0 applications. The major challenges of incorporating FL-based cobots in Industry 5.0-based applications are represented in Figure 10.4.

10.5.1 Security and privacy concerns

Industry 5.0 enforces the collaboration of humans and robots to perform a specific task. During the interaction process, cobots may collect sensitive data such as employee information, production details, process details, and trading secrets. Even though the FL guarantees the privacy of data by not allowing cobots to share the original data with the central server, but FL does not take care of malicious data being stored and collected by the faulty sensors and does not provide a security mechanism for model parameters. Similarly, the attacker can manipulate the model updates or tamper the sensitive data through model parameters by compromising the cobots or through insecure communication channels between the cobots and the server leading to disruption in production.

The implementation of data validation, anomaly detection, and data encryption techniques will strengthen the existing system. However, the traditional security and privacy techniques are not sufficient to build a resilient and trustworthy ecosystem. Hence, the adoption of blockchain-based solutions with strict security mechanisms [54] and quantum computing-based threat identification and mitigation techniques [39] will improve the privacy and security aspects of Industry 5.0.

10.5.2 Lack of standardization

Industry 5.0 aimed to create a collaborative ecosystem by interacting with cyber-physical systems, AI, robots, and humans to improve productivity. The seamless interaction among the diverse systems will happen only through standard communication protocols, data formats, and interfacing technologies. However, the absence of standard rules and policies will result in interoperability issues and inefficient interaction among the technologies and systems. The lack of standardization will imbalance the harmony of the entire system by affecting the data exchange mechanism among the cobots and server, decision-making capabilities of the cobots, coordination of cobots, and humans.

Industry 5.0 is still an emerging field, and there is a lack of standardized frameworks, protocols, and best practices. Hence, there should be collaborative initiatives from the stakeholders, standardization bodies, and research communities to design and develop common communication protocols, data formats, and security guidelines to improve interoperability, enhance security, and accelerate the adoption of FL in Industry 5.0 [4].

10.5.3 Heterogeneous data

In Industry 5.0, the cobots are mainly responsible for the collection of data. Since cobots are deployed in various locations or working environments, based on the interactions with the surroundings and task, cobots will collect heterogeneous data with varying distributions, formats, and characteristics, representations [55]. Hence, the integration of these heterogeneous data to extract meaningful insights using FL techniques is a challenging task. Hence, ensuring the seamless integration of model updates from different cobots will be troublesome, especially when they have different hyper-parameters resulting in model synchronization issues, affecting the efficiency and convergence of the collaborative learning process [56].

Implementing techniques to standardize data formats and preprocessing, sampling, and balancing methods, will minimize the heterogeneity across the cobots. Along with that, the use of data quality control mechanisms to identify and filter out noisy data from the FL learning process.

10.5.4 Communication bandwidth

FL enables a distributed learning mechanism, where the cobots will continuously interact with the servers and environment using a secure dedicated communication channel. Cobots train machine learning models locally and share only model updates with a central server. The exchange of model updates and gradients between cobots and the central server relies on communication channels, making communication bandwidth a crucial consideration. During the entire process, a stable, efficient, and reliable communication network will result in effective collaborative learning. However, poor network connectivity will result in delays in transmitting model updates or parameters leading to slow convergence; hence, low bandwidth and high latency connections can lead to reduced efficiency and safety risks.

Use of several techniques such as asynchronous communication mechanism to avoid strict synchronization requirements by allowing cobots to exchange updates at their convenience. Similarly, adaptive communication to dynamically adjust the data transfer rate, Edge computing [57], and 6G technologies will also strengthen the communication network; hence, the overall performance will be improved [58].

10.5.5 Scalability and system complexity

Industry 5.0 is a collaborative ecosystem where human, machine, robots, AI, and IoT work together in real life, thus creating a complex collaborative environment. However, as the number of cobots and participants increases, managing the scalability and system complexity of FL becomes a challenge, i.e., an increase in the number of cobots, the data sources will increase the amount of data that needs to be processed and managed by the FL systems, and model updates sent to the central server will also increase resulting in increasing the computation and communication complexity. Different computational capabilities and communication latencies will induce synchronization issues during the collaborative learning process. Similarly, coordinating model aggregation, handling failures, and ensuring consistent model versions in all the cobots and participants require robust system architectures and protocols.

Implementing distributed computational techniques such as edge computing, design of scalable model aggregation techniques, load balancing strategies, design of scalable data analytics, and AI algorithms capable of handling massive data streams will address the scalability and system complexity issues to some extent [59].

10.5.6 Limited computational resources

Cobots are designed to be lightweight, small, and equipped with sensors and often have limited processing power, memory, and energy capacity compared to the central server. The FL algorithm performs model training with a complex optimization process which requires huge computational resources and model aggregation with a continuous exchange of model updates with the server. Hence, the resource-constrained cobots may not be able to handle the complex iterative training process or may take longer time to train their local models. Thus the delayed training will result in jammed responses and affect the overall efficiency of collaborative learning. Similarly, during the aggregation process, the cobots cannot withstand the communication overhead caused by continuous exchange of model updates [60].

Use of lightweight and efficient machine learning models will reduce the computational cost of training; design of adaptive learning mechanism to dynamically adjust the learning process based on the resource availability of cobots [61]. Similarly, cloud–edge collaboration will improve the computing capabilities of cobots by offloading the task to cloud.

10.5.7 Training and upgrading the skills

Industry 5.0 is envisioned to develop an intelligent ecosystem where humans and machines collaborate to improve productivity. Since Industry 5.0 combines multiple advanced technologies, a lack of skilled laborers will increase the time required to complete the assigned task; however, it is necessary that the workers should be equipped with basic understanding of the technologies such as AI, ML, IoT, and automation to interact with the smart systems. Upskilling the workers through training programs, hands-on experience, certificate programs, and collaborative programs with AI experts will not only improve their knowledge, but also change their perspective on data analysis, understanding, and interaction with the safety of cobots. Hence, the overall productivity will be improved [4].

10.6 Conclusion

Industry 5.0 has evolved based on the principles of Industry 4.0, focusing mainly on the integration of technologies such as IoT, AI, Big Data, and automation to establish a collaborative working environment between humans and cobots. However, to strengthen the cobots and to establish harmony in Industry 5.0, we have introduced a distributed data processing mechanism. The privacy-preserving, distributed FL will not only improve the capabilities of cobots, but it help to enhance the overall performance and efficiency system. Considering the various advantages and applications of FL and cobots, we have presented an analysis focused on aspects of Industry 5.0. At the beginning of the chapter, we have given a brief introduction to the evolution of Industry 5.0, cobots, and motivation for integrating FL in cobots. Later, a detailed discussion on FL architecture, advantages, and various implementations of FL in robots for different applications. Following by, we have presented the strengths of FL-based cobots and also highlighted the role of FL-based cobots in healthcare, supply-chain management, and manufacturing and production applications. Finally, we have identified the challenges of FL-based cobots and also suggested possible future directions.

References

[1] S. Nahavandi, "Industry 5.0—a human-centric solution," *Sustainability*, vol. 11, no. 16, p. 4371, 2019.

[2] A. Aslandziya. Industry 5.0: What to Expect in the New Era. [Accessed on 23.07.2023]. [Online]. Available: https://www.jakarobotics.com/industry-5-0/

[3] E. H. Østergaard. (2020) Collaborative Robots Ushering in Industry 5.0 - UR Cobots. [Accessed on 23.07.2023]. [Online]. Available: https://www.universal-robots.com/blog/collaborative-robots-ushering-in-industry-50/

[4] A. Adel, "Future of industry 5.0 in society: Human-centric solutions, challenges and prospective research areas," *Journal of Cloud Computing*, vol. 11, no. 1, pp. 1–15, 2022.

[5] RoboticsBiz. (2020) AI in Robotics: How Machine Learning Works in Collaborative Robots. [Accessed on 23.07.2023]. [Online]. Available:

https://roboticsbiz.com/ai-in-robotics-how-machine-learning-works-in-collaborative-robots/

[6] Y. J. Heo, D. Kim, W. Lee, H. Kim, J. Park, and W. K. Chung, "Collision detection for industrial collaborative robots: A deep learning approach," *IEEE Robotics and Automation Letters*, vol. 4, no. 2, pp. 740–746, 2019.

[7] M. Czubenko and Z. Kowalczuk, "A simple neural network for collision detection of collaborative robots," *Sensors*, vol. 21, no. 12, p. 4235, 2021.

[8] J. Male and U. Martinez-Hernandez, "Deep learning based robot cognitive architecture for collaborative assembly tasks," *Robotics and Computer-Integrated Manufacturing*, vol. 83, p. 102572, 2023.

[9] M. Soori, B. Arezoo, and R. Dastres, "Artificial intelligence, machine learning and deep learning in advanced robotics, a review," *Cognitive Robotics*, 2023.

[10] S. Savazzi, M. Nicoli, M. Bennis, S. Kianoush, and L. Barbieri, "Opportunities of federated learning in connected, cooperative, and automated industrial systems," *IEEE Communications Magazine*, vol. 59, no. 2, pp. 16–21, 2021.

[11] J. Konečný, H. B. McMahan, F. X. Yu, P. Richtárik, A. T. Suresh, and D. Bacon, "Federated learning: Strategies for improving communication efficiency," *arXiv preprint arXiv:1610.05492*, 2016.

[12] S. AbdulRahman, H. Tout, H. Ould-Slimane, A. Mourad, C. Talhi, and M. Guizani, "A survey on federated learning: The journey from centralized to distributed on-site learning and beyond," *IEEE Internet of Things Journal*, vol. 8, no. 7, pp. 5476–5497, 2020.

[13] A. Hammoud, H. Otrok, A. Mourad, and Z. Dziong, "On demand fog federations for horizontal federated learning in iov," *IEEE Transactions on Network and Service Management*, vol. 19, no. 3, pp. 3062–3075, 2022.

[14] H.-V. Tran, G. Kaddoum, H. Elgala, C. Abou-Rjeily, and H. Kaushal, "Lightwave power transfer for federated learning-based wireless networks," *IEEE Communications Letters*, vol. 24, no. 7, pp. 1472–1476, 2020.

[15] S. A. Rahman, H. Tout, C. Talhi, and A. Mourad, "Internet of things intrusion detection: Centralized, on-device, or federated learning?" *IEEE Network*, vol. 34, no. 6, pp. 310–317, 2020.

[16] A. Hard, K. Rao, R. Mathews, *et al.*, "Federated learning for mobile keyboard prediction," *arXiv preprint arXiv:1811.03604*, 2018.

[17] Q.-V. Pham, K. Dev, P. K. R. Maddikunta, *et al.*, "Fusion of federated learning and industrial internet of things: A survey," *arXiv preprint arXiv:2101.00798*, 2021.

[18] t-dab.ai. Benefits of Federated Learning Explained. [Accessed on 23.07. 2023]. [Online]. Available: https://t-dab.ai/benefits-of-federated-learning-explained/

[19] S. S. Magdum, A. Franklin, and B. R. Tamma, "A cooperative federated learning mechanism for collision avoidance using cellular and 802.11 p based radios opportunistically," in *2021 IEEE International Conference on*

Advanced Networks and Telecommunications Systems (ANTS). IEEE, 2021, pp. 284–289.

[20] S. Na, T. Rouček, J. Ulrich, J. Pikman, T. s Krajník, B. Lennox, and F. Arvin, "Federated reinforcement learning for collective navigation of robotic swarms," *IEEE Transactions on Cognitive and Developmental Systems*, 2023.

[21] A. Nguyen, T. Do, M. Tran, *et al.*, "Deep federated learning for autonomous driving," in *2022 IEEE Intelligent Vehicles Symposium (IV)*. IEEE, 2022, pp. 1824–1830.

[22] W.-B. Kou, S. Wang, G. Zhu, *et al.*, "Communication resources constrained hierarchical federated learning for end-to-end autonomous driving," *arXiv preprint arXiv:2306.16169*, 2023.

[23] N. Majcherczyk, N. Srishankar, and C. Pinciroli, "Flow-fl: Data-driven federated learning for spatio-temporal predictions in multi-robot systems," in *2021 IEEE International Conference on Robotics and Automation (ICRA)*. IEEE, 2021, pp. 8836–8842.

[24] K. Jabrane and M. Bousmah, "A new approach for training cobots from small amount of data in industry 5.0," *International Journal of Advanced Computer Science and Applications*, vol. 12, no. 10, 2021.

[25] A. Imteaj and M. H. Amini, "Fedar: Activity and resource-aware federated learning model for distributed mobile robots," in *2020 19th IEEE International Conference on Machine Learning and Applications (ICMLA)*. IEEE, 2020, pp. 1153–1160.

[26] X. Yu, J. P. Queralta, and T. Westerlund, "Federated learning for vision-based obstacle avoidance in the internet of robotic things," in *2022 Seventh International Conference on Fog and Mobile Edge Computing (FMEC)*. IEEE, 2022, pp. 1–6.

[27] J. J. Gamboa-Montero, F. Alonso-Martin, S. Marques-Villarroya, J. Sequeira, and M. A. Salichs, "Asynchronous federated learning system for human–robot touch interaction," *Expert Systems with Applications*, vol. 211, p. 118510, 2023.

[28] C.-I. Huang, Y.-Y. Huang, J.-X. Liu, *et al.*, "Fed-hanet: Federated visual grasping learning for human robot handovers," *IEEE Robotics and Automation Letters*, 2023.

[29] G. Srivastava, D. R. R. K, G. Yenduri, *et al.*, "Federated learning enabled edge computing security for internet of medical things: Concepts, challenges and open issues," in *Security and Risk Analysis for Intelligent Edge Computing*. Springer, 2023, pp. 67–89.

[30] S. P. Ramu, G. Srivastava, R. Chengoden, N. Victor, P. K. R. Maddikunta, and T. R. Gadekallu, "The metaverse for cognitive health: A paradigm shift," *IEEE Consumer Electronics Magazine*, 2023.

[31] K. D. Stergiou and K. E. Psannis, "Federated learning approach decouples clients from training a local model and with the communication with the server," *IEEE Transactions on Network and Service Management*, vol. 19, no. 4, pp. 4213–4218, 2022.

[32] S. Pandya, G. Srivastava, R. Jhaveri, *et al.*, "Federated learning for smart cities: A comprehensive survey," *Sustainable Energy Technologies and Assessments*, vol. 55, p. 102987, 2023.

[33] A. K. Bashir, N. Victor, S. Bhattacharya, *et al.*, "A survey on federated learning for the healthcare metaverse: Concepts, applications, challenges, and future directions," *arXiv preprint arXiv:2304.00524*, 2023.

[34] A. El Ouadrhiri and A. Abdelhadi, "Differential privacy for deep and federated learning: A survey," *IEEE Access*, vol. 10, pp. 22 359–22 380, 2022.

[35] O. A. Wahab, A. Mourad, H. Otrok, and T. Taleb, "Federated machine learning: Survey, multi-level classification, desirable criteria and future directions in communication and networking systems," *IEEE Communications Surveys & Tutorials*, vol. 23, no. 2, pp. 1342–1397, 2021.

[36] J. M. Rožanec, I. Novalija, P. Zajec, *et al.*, "Human-centric artificial intelligence architecture for industry 5.0 applications," *International Journal of Production Research*, pp. 1–26, 2022.

[37] G. Manogaran, N. E. M. Khalifa, M. Loey, and M. H. N. Taha, *Cyber-physical Systems for Industrial Transformation: Fundamentals, Standards, and Protocols*. CRC Press, 2023.

[38] G. Srivastava, R. H. Jhaveri, S. Bhattacharya, *et al.*, "Xai for cybersecurity: state of the art, challenges, open issues and future directions," *arXiv preprint arXiv:2206.03585*, 2022.

[39] P. K. R. Maddikunta, Q.-V. Pham, B. Prabadevi, *et al.*, "Industry 5.0: A survey on enabling technologies and potential applications," *Journal of Industrial Information Integration*, vol. 26, p. 100257, 2022.

[40] L. Chen, P. Chen, and Z. Lin, "Artificial intelligence in education: A review," *IEEE Access*, vol. 8, pp. 75 264–75 278, 2020.

[41] G. Yenduri, G. Srivastava, P. K. R. Maddikunta, *et al.*, "Generative pre-trained transformer: A comprehensive review on enabling technologies, potential applications, emerging challenges, and future directions," *arXiv preprint arXiv:2305.10435*, 2023.

[42] K. Dasaradharami Reddy and T. R. Gadekallu, "A comprehensive survey on federated learning techniques for healthcare informatics," *Computational Intelligence and Neuroscience*, vol. 2023, 2023.

[43] G. Yang, Z. Pang, M. J. Deen, *et al.*, "Homecare robotic systems for healthcare 4.0: Visions and enabling technologies," *IEEE Journal of Biomedical and Health Informatics*, vol. 24, no. 9, pp. 2535–2549, 2020.

[44] M. Y. Gürce, Y. Wang, and Y. E. Zheng, "Artificial intelligence and collaborative robots in healthcare: The perspective of healthcare professionals," in *Transformation for Sustainable Business and Management Practices: Exploring the Spectrum of Industry 5.0*. Emerald Publishing Limited, 2023, pp. 309–325.

[45] E. Matheson, R. Minto, E. G. Zampieri, M. Faccio, and G. Rosati, "Human–robot collaboration in manufacturing applications: A review," *Robotics*, vol. 8, no. 4, p. 100, 2019.

[46] H. D. Nguyen and K. P. Tran, "Artificial intelligence for smart manufacturing in industry 5.0: Methods, applications, and challenges," *Artificial Intelligence for Smart Manufacturing: Methods, Applications, and Challenges*, pp. 5–33, 2023.

[47] A. Borboni, K. V. V. Reddy, I. Elamvazuthi, M. S. AL-Quraishi, E. Natarajan, and S. S. Azhar Ali, "The expanding role of artificial intelligence in collaborative robots for industrial applications: A systematic review of recent works," *Machines*, vol. 11, no. 1, p. 111, 2023.

[48] M. J. Timms, "Letting artificial intelligence in education out of the box: Educational cobots and smart classrooms," *International Journal of Artificial Intelligence in Education*, vol. 26, pp. 701–712, 2016.

[49] S.-T. Chu, G.-J. Hwang, and Y.-F. Tu, "Artificial intelligence-based robots in education: A systematic review of selected ssci publications," *Computers and Education: Artificial Intelligence*, p. 100091, 2022.

[50] M. Frackiewicz. (2023) The Role of Collaborative Robots in Education and Learning. [Accessed on 13.08.2023]. [Online]. Available: https://ts2.space

[51] S. K. Abid, N. Sulaiman, S. W. Chan, *et al.*, "Toward an integrated disaster management approach: How artificial intelligence can boost disaster management," *Sustainability*, vol. 13, no. 22, p. 12560, 2021.

[52] M. Frackiewicz. (2023) The Role of Collaborative Robots (Cobots) in Disaster Response and Recovery. [Accessed on 13.08.2023]. [Online]. Available: https://ts2.space/en/the-role-of-collaborative- robots-cobots-in-disaster-response-and-recovery/

[53] N. Jafari, M. Azarian, and H. Yu, "Moving from industry 4.0 to industry 5.0: what are the implications for smart logistics?" *Logistics*, vol. 6, no. 2, p. 26, 2022.

[54] N. Deepa, Q.-V. Pham, D. C. Nguyen, *et al.*, "A survey on blockchain for big data: Approaches, opportunities, and future directions," *Future Generation Computer Systems*, vol. 131, pp. 209–226, 2022.

[55] V. V. Martynov, D. N. Shavaleeva, and A. A. Zaytseva, "Information technology as the basis for transformation into a digital society and industry 5.0," in *2019 International Conference "Quality Management, Transport and Information Security, Information Technologies" (IT&QM&IS)*. IEEE, 2019, pp. 539–543.

[56] M. Borchardt, G. M. Pereira, G. S. Milan, A. R. Scavarda, E. O. Nogueira, and L. C. Poltosi, "Industry 5.0 beyond technology: An analysis through the lens of business and operations management literature," *Organizacija*, vol. 55, no. 4, pp. 305–321, 2022.

[57] G. Nain, K. Pattanaik, and G. Sharma, "Towards edge computing in intelligent manufacturing: Past, present and future," *Journal of Manufacturing Systems*, vol. 62, pp. 588–611, 2022.

[58] C. De Alwis, A. Kalla, Q.-V. Pham, *et al.*, "Survey on 6g frontiers: Trends, applications, requirements, technologies and future research," *IEEE Open Journal of the Communications Society*, vol. 2, pp. 836–886, 2021.

[59] B. Chander, S. Pal, D. De, and R. Buyya, "Artificial intelligence-based internet of things for Industry 5.0," *Artificial Intelligence-Based Internet of Things Systems*, pp. 3–45, 2022.

[60] S. Bharti and A. McGibney, "Corol: A reliable framework for computation offloading in collaborative robots," *IEEE Internet of Things Journal*, vol. 9, no. 19, pp. 18 195–18 207, 2022.

[61] M. Calzavara, M. Faccio, and I. Granata, "Multi-objective task allocation for collaborative robot systems with an industry 5.0 human-centered perspective," *The International Journal of Advanced Manufacturing Technology*, pp. 1–18, 2023.

Chapter 11

Federated learning in medical education in Industry 5.0

Y. Supriya[1], Dasari Bhulakshmi[1], Sweta Bhattacharya[1], Thippa Reddy Gadekallu[2], Rajesh Kaluri[1], S. Sumathy[1], Srinivas Koppu[1], Pratik Vyas[3], David J. Brown[3] and Mufti Mahmud[3]

Abstract

The integration of Federated Learning (FL) into medical education within the context of Industry 5.0 offers transformative potential for addressing key challenges such as data privacy, scalability, and personalization. Medical education, a cornerstone of healthcare development, is undergoing significant evolution driven by technological advancements. Industry 5.0 emphasizes human-centric and collaborative solutions, making it a natural fit for the integration of FL, which allows the decentralized training of machine learning models without compromising sensitive medical data. This chapter explores the interplay between FL and Industry 5.0 in medical education, detailing how technologies like Digital Twins, Blockchain, and Augmented Reality can foster personalized, secure, and efficient learning environments. Additionally, it highlights applications such as personalized simulators, collaborative case studies, and real-time curriculum updates, offering a framework for training competent healthcare professionals in a privacy-preserving, collaborative, and adaptive environment. Challenges and future directions are discussed to guide the adoption of FL in medical education for the Industry 5.0 era.

Keywords: Industry 5.0, Data privacy and security, Collaborative learning, Personalized training simulators

[1]School of Information Technology and Engineering, Vellore Institute of Technology, India
[2]Division of Research and Development, Lovely Professional University, India
[3]Department of Computer Science, School of Science and Technology, Nottingham Trent University, UK

11.1 Introduction

Education is the process of acquiring knowledge, skills, values, and attitudes through several means. It plays a crucial role in personal, social, and economic development. Education can take place in different platforms like schools, colleges, universities, vocational training centers, and even through self-study [51]. It involves a structured curriculum, trained teachers, and standardized assessments. The education system varies from one country to another.

Education is needed for every person to acquire knowledge and skills. It equips individuals with the knowledge and skills that are required to understand the world, solve several problems, and engage in productive activities. It also helps in developing literacy, numeracy, critical thinking, communication, and technological skills. Education is also needed for the personal development of an individual. It plays a key role in personal growth and character development. It fosters intellectual curiosity, creativity, ethical values, and social-emotional skills. Education also prepares individuals to participate actively in society and helps in developing social skills, cultural understanding, and respect for diversity [33]. Education is also closely related to economic development and opportunities and also has the potential to promote social mobility by providing every individual with opportunities to enhance their socio-economic status. It allows individuals to pursue their passions, interests, and intellectual pursuits. Lifelong learning through education promotes personal growth and enrichment throughout one's life [41].

The advent of Industry 5.0 marks a shift toward human-centric technologies across various sectors. In the context of a rapidly evolving healthcare environment, medical education has long been a cornerstone for training future professionals [9].

Medical education is referred to as the training and educational programs that are designed to prepare individuals for careers in the field of medicine [32]. It covers the knowledge, skills, and competencies that are required to become a qualified healthcare professional like a doctor, surgeon, nurse, or any other medical specialist.

Medical education plays a critical role in producing competent and compassionate healthcare professionals who can provide quality care, contribute to medical research, and improve the health and well-being of individuals and communities.

With the digital revolution, we are witnessing an influx of technologies that could reshape how medical education is delivered and received [20]. Industry 4.0 initially provided us with connected systems and data-driven approaches. Now, Industry 5.0 takes it a step further by focusing on human-centric collaborative environments. Meanwhile, FL, an advanced Machine Learning(ML) approach, allows for a decentralized, privacy-conscious method of data analysis, particularly suitable for sensitive medical data.

Medical education is at the threshold of a transformation, influenced by the unprecedented advancements in information technology. Industry 5.0 offers promising frameworks that prioritize human–machine collaboration, making it more relevant in healthcare, where the human element cannot be ignored. FL addresses significant concerns about data privacy and security, critical in medical settings [34]. Therefore, the intersection of FL and Industry 5.0 in medical education is not just timely but also imperative to explore.

Despite the promise, medical education faces numerous challenges such as scalability, privacy concerns, and the dire need for personalization to cater to individual learning curves. While Industry 5.0 offers advanced, human-centric systems, its full potential in medical education remains underexplored. Furthermore, there is a paucity of studies that integrate FL into medical education in an Industry 5.0 context, creating a gap in our understanding of how these technologies can collectively address the existing challenges [25,63].

11.1.1 Contributions

The major contributions of this book chapter are discussed in this subsection.

- Provides a comprehensive understanding of FL and Industry 5.0 individually.
- Explores the existing literature on the topics of FL and medical education, and Industry 5.0 and medical education.
- Assess the benefits of integrating FL and Industry 5.0 in medical education.
- Identify challenges in implementing FL in medical education.
- Highlight gaps in current research and suggest directions for future work.

11.2 Background

The interconnected trajectories of medical education, ML, and industrial technology have shaped the course of modern healthcare and opened the doors for unprecedented advancements. The concept of medical education dates back to ancient civilizations but has gone through revolutionary changes in the past few decades due to technological interventions. From chalk and board to sophisticated simulation environments, medical training has adopted various tools to enhance educational outcomes.

11.2.1 Medical education

Traditional medical education follows a hierarchical structure. It begins with foundational knowledge in medical school which is followed by hands-on experience in medical residencies and fellowships [70]. The learning model is mostly built on experience and cases, with a lot of time spent working with real patients under the watchful eye of more experienced professionals.

Medical education faces several challenges the problem of adapting to the rapidly evolving nature of medical knowledge, the increasing need for interdisciplinary skills, and limitations posed by geographic location [3]. In addition, to these, medical students and professionals also have limited access to patient data due to privacy concerns and data regulations.

With the advent of new technologies, medical education has begun to incorporate digital tools like Electronic Health Records (EHR), simulation-based training, and online educational resources. These digital tools not only provide opportunities for data-driven, personalized learning but also come with their own set of challenges, primarily concerning data privacy and the standardization of educational content [61].

In the context of Industry 5.0, which emphasizes human-centric technological advancements, there's a growing need to implement innovative solutions like FL to address these challenges [35].

Understanding the traditional structure and contemporary challenges of medical education is essential for appreciating the potential impact of FL in this field, especially within the Industry 5.0 framework.

11.2.2 Federated learning

FL is an ML paradigm that enables a model to be trained across multiple decentralized devices or servers, without centralizing the data [22–24]. This is especially important in medical contexts where data is often sensitive, regulated, and distributed across various healthcare institutions [37,53,60,64]. FL allows for the development of robust, generalized models without violating privacy norms or regulations such as HIPAA in the United States or GDPR in Europe.

In medical education, FL could revolutionize how medical students and professionals are trained. Traditionally, medical training relies heavily on case studies, simulations, and direct clinical experience. FL enables the creation of predictive models that can be tested and improved upon continuously by medical students and professionals alike, offering real-time insights drawn from a wide array of medical data [26]. This would not only enhance educational outcomes but also enable more personalized, effective patient care.

Within the broader context of Industry 5.0, which emphasizes human-centric technological progress, FL offers a balanced approach [2]. It combines cutting-edge ML techniques with a framework that prioritizes data security and individual privacy.

In summary, the FL subsection would outline the importance of this innovative method for decentralized, privacy-preserving data analysis, particularly in the advancement of medical education and practice in an Industry 5.0 environment.

11.2.3 Industry 5.0

Industry 5.0 is the fifth industrial revolution, building on the Industry 4.0 framework that primarily focused on the use of modern smart technology in manufacturing environments [48]. While Industry 4.0 emphasizes automation and data exchange, Industry 5.0 aims to bring a more human-centric approach back to industrial processes, integrating human intuition with technological advancements for optimized, personalized outcomes.

In medical education, Industry 5.0 could represent a shift, which prioritizes human skills like decision-making and emotional intelligence alongside technological proficiency. Here, FL can play a pivotal role [50]. It allows medical professionals and students to benefit from ML models trained on a diverse range of data sources, without compromising patient confidentiality. This creates a learning environment that is both technologically advanced and ethical.

In summary, Industry 5.0 serves as a backdrop for the application of FL in medical education, offering a framework that values both technological innovation and human-centric approaches. Understanding Industry 5.0 can help readers appreciate the significance and timeliness of applying FL in this context.

11.2.4 Key principles and terminologies

Before discussing the dependencies between these domains, it is important to discuss some key principles [30] and terminologies [7].

- Human-centric Technology: Explain the core principle of Industry 5.0 that emphasizes human intuition and creativity alongside technological advancements.
- Decentralization: Discuss how FL involves training ML models across multiple devices or servers without centralizing the data.
- Data Privacy: Highlight the importance of maintaining data privacy, especially in healthcare where sensitive data is involved.
- Interdisciplinary Learning: In the context of medical education, discuss the increasing need for healthcare professionals to be versed in both medical and technological disciplines.

The following list explains the key terminologies that are to be dealt in the above book chapter:

1. Federated Learning: Define the term and its significance in the context of Industry 5.0 and medical education.
2. Industry 5.0: Provide a definition and how it builds upon Industry 4.0's focus on automation.
3. EHR (Electronic Health Records): Explain what EHR are and their role in modern medical practice and education.
4. Non-IID Data: Briefly discuss what non-independently and Identically Distributed data means and why it's a challenge in FL.
5. HIPAA & GDPR: Define these regulations that are critical for data privacy in healthcare.
6. Secure Aggregation: Describe the method used to securely aggregate data in FL without compromising privacy.
7. Synchronous and Asynchronous Updates: Explain these terms in the context of FL models being updated either simultaneously or at different times across devices.

Understanding these principles and terminologies is much needed to know the potential of FL in medical education in the realm of Industry 5.0.

11.3 Related work

The integration of FL, medical education, and Industry 5.0 is a relatively novel undertaking that intersects various research domains. In this section, we review literature and studies that have made significant contributions to each of these areas, as well as works that hint at their convergence.

Table 11.1 Summary of literature on FL, medical education, and Industry 5.0

Reference	Objectives	Key Contributions	Limitations
[12]	Healthcare Informatics	Reviews FL applications, needs, and main uses in healthcare.	Unresolved concerns and obstacles
[8]	Internet of Healthcare Things	Discusses FL in IoHT, focusing on data security and privacy.	Focus on educational objectives
[47]	FL, AI, XAI in Healthcare	Comprehensive analysis of FL using AI for smart healthcare.	–
[59]	Deep Learning in Healthcare	Discusses FL's role in enhancing data security and privacy in healthcare.	Focuses on established FL standards
[42]	Smart Healthcare	Proposes layered healthcare informatics architecture using FL.	Benefits not fully explored
[39]	Internet-of-Medical-Things	Reviews FL's role in addressing data privacy in IOMT.	–
[47]	FL, AI, XAI in Healthcare	Discusses integration of FL, AI, and XAI in healthcare, focusing on security, privacy, and reliability.	–

The authors in [12] state that healthcare is essential for global physical and mental well-being. Healthcare systems create a lot of data, making maintenance difficult. This data is handled by ML, although privacy issues limit its importance. Especially for medical data. FL, a new ML concept, might be applicable. This research reviews FL applications in healthcare informatics, discusses their needs, and reviews current review papers. It explains FL and its main healthcare uses. The author also discusses FL applications in various healthcare sectors, lessons learned, unresolved concerns and obstacles, and future possibilities for academics (Table 11.1).

The authors in [8] explain that the ML-based approaches are promising in the Internet of Healthcare Things (IoHT), despite the fact that typical solutions need centralized data gathering and processing. FL secures IoHT data. This survey reviews emerging FL data security and privacy applications in IoHT networks, providing a background overview of FL's basic concepts, evaluating the main solutions to IoHT data security and privacy issues, categorizing relevant publications, listing IoHT network datasets for model training, and highlighting key lessons. The article also discusses FL-based IoHT data security and privacy problems, along with educational objectives.

The author in [47] discusses the integration of FL, Artificial Intelligence (AI), and Explainable Artificial Intelligence (XAI) in the healthcare field. The paper presents a complete analysis of FL using AI for smart healthcare applications. The authors in [59] explain that data-driven insights from deep learning (DL) can improve patient quality of life in smart healthcare applications. DL requires more data and variety for accurate systems. FL improves data security and access without transmitting data to the server. This literature analysis and in-depth investigation on FL's responsibilities in healthcare, the effectiveness of existing issues dealing with established standardized FL, and open research challenges and recommendations for future FL for telemedicine and distant healthcare applications are used [40]. An exhaustive data-centric FL literature study offered novel crossover matching across techniques that address or reduce all sorts of incorrect information.

The authors in [42] propose that the smart healthcare system improves patient quality of life by remotely analyzing records from scattered stakeholders. Open communication channels place data privacy at risk and impact model training at centralized servers. FL is a promising option. FL trains nodes associated with clients and combines findings to train the global model, protecting patient data. FL offers several benefits in healthcare, but they have not been fully explored. The survey recommends a FL-based, layered healthcare informatics architecture to improve patient quality of life and data privacy. The study examines developing FL models and statistical and security issues in medical FL adoption.

The authors in [39] explain that communication technologies and the Internet-of-Medical-Things (IOMT) have revolutionized smart healthcare with AI. AI's excellent scalability and developing data privacy issues may make centralized data collection and processing problematic in healthcare. FL, a distributed collaborative AI paradigm, organizes several clients to train AI without sharing raw data, making it useful for smart healthcare. The authors in [47] say that FL, AI, and XAI are developing intelligent healthcare solutions. Traditional healthcare systems use centralized agents to share raw data, causing risks and obstacles. Integrating AI with FL enables numerous agents to interact immediately while FL maintains a preferred model without sending raw data. Combining the FL, AI, and XAI to reduce these restrictions and obstacles The study analyses FL using AI for smart healthcare applications, discusses current concepts, integrates and classifies FL-AI with healthcare technologies, addresses security, privacy, stability, and reliability, and guides readers through FL and AI healthcare strategies [42]. It also examines FL-based AI studies in healthcare management systems and their possibilities.

By understanding the contributions and limitations of these works, this chapter aims to fill a gap in the literature, offering a comprehensive view of how FL can revolutionize medical education in the context of Industry 5.0.

11.4 Integration of technologies with FL to foster medical education

The integration of several technologies like digital twins (DT), blockchain (BC), edge computing (EC), and Internet of things (IoT), explainable AI (XAI), virtual reality (VR), augmented reality (AR), and cobots with FL can significantly enhance medical education [20].

These technologies can provide a more immersive and interactive learning experience, fostering a deeper understanding of medical concepts and terminology. They also ensure data privacy and security, enable collaborative learning, allow for real-time updates, and facilitate personalized education [68].

11.4.1 Digital twins

A DT is a replication of a physical system. In the field of medical education, DTs replicate human physiology to create a real environment for medical research and simulation [16].

The integration of DTs and FL transforms the approach to medical education. The integration enables personalized, scalable, and secure learning environments [38]. DTs enable real-time, simulated human physiology which is very valuable for training, while FL allows for the decentralized, collaborative refinement of these models without compromising data privacy. This combination of technologies allows medical students and institutions to make real-time decisions based on realistic simulations while complying with strict data protection rules. These technologies can make medical education more flexible, ethical, and relevant to real-world medical situations [46].

Combining DT and FL in medical education is an innovative and promising idea, but also a difficult one. It faces many obstacles, such as protecting data privacy, managing computational resources, and ensuring compatibility [38].

11.4.2 Blockchain

BC is a distributed, decentralized digital ledger technology used to record transactions across multiple computers in a way that ensures security, transparency, and immutability [19].

FL systems are susceptible to accountability and privacy threats, such as model poisoning attacks. FL and BC techniques are promising in health data analytics and management. BC is a secure and transparent way of recording data transactions, while FL is a collaborative way of training ML models without sharing data [27]. The four advantages of integrating BC and FL for medical education: are data privacy and security, collaborative learning, real-time updates, and personalized education [21].

The integration of BC with FL to enhance medical education is an interesting and complex test. The integration challenges range from ensuring data privacy and regulatory compliance to grappling with the inherent scalability and computational demands of both technologies [52]. Figure 11.1 indicates the integration of technologies with FL for medical education.

11.4.3 Edge computing

EC is a distributed computing paradigm that gets data storage and computation closer to the location where it is required. It can improve response times and save bandwidth [54].

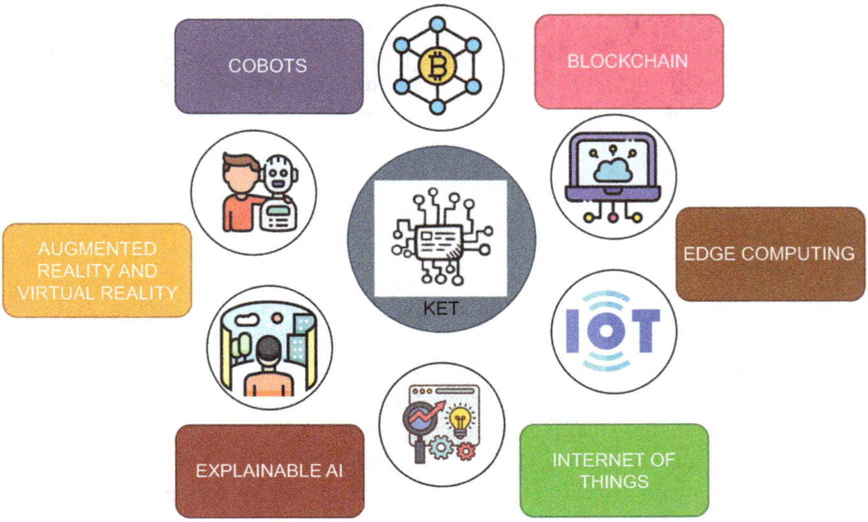

Figure 11.1 KET for FL in medical education

The integration of EC and FL has the potential to enable remote patient monitoring, medical image analysis, medical simulation, and training. As a part of patient monitoring, EC and FL can enable advanced monitoring by processing data from medical devices such as glucose monitors and blood pressure cuffs and then alerting clinicians to problematic readings [1]. EC and FL can facilitate medical image analysis by allowing local devices to train models using their own data and then aggregating the model updates at the edge server. EC and FL can support medical simulation and training by creating realistic and interactive environments for medical students and professionals [58].

However, challenges such as security concerns, infrastructure development, data consistency, and the complexity of model aggregation pose significant hurdles [55].

11.4.4 IoT

The Internet of Things (IoT) is a network of devices or vehicles or any other buildings, and other items embedded with sensors, software, and other technologies. This enables connecting and exchanging data with other devices and systems over the Internet [31].

The integration of the IoT with FL enables revolutionizing medical education by offering real-time data analysis, advanced simulation training, and personalized educational experiences. IoT devices can gather diverse healthcare data, which can then be securely analyzed by FL algorithms, enhancing both research and educational content. This integration facilitates a more dynamic, data-driven approach to medical training, allowing for real-time updates to curricula and multi-institutional research collaborations.

Though the integration of IoT and FL acts as a savior for medical education, there are a few challenges like data security and the need for standardization, which must be addressed even before their successful implementation. The lack of standardization across both domains hampers interoperability, while the variable quality of data from diverse IoT devices can compromise the training models. Additionally, network latency, resource constraints on IoT devices, and scalability issues complicate real-time data processing and model training.

11.4.5 XAI

XAI is used to describe AI systems that are designed to be understandable by humans. This can be either in terms of how they arrive at a decision or how they work [15].

Integration of XAI and FL can help in enhancing medical education by creating a framework that is privacy-preserving and transparent [5]. FL allows for the development of ML models that can learn from different medical institutions without compromising patient privacy. When integrated with XAI, these models become more interpretable and also help in building trust, and allow students and clinicians to understand the logic behind medical predictions. This amalgamation also enables real-world, interactive learning experiences and also provides good lessons on data privacy and ethics to students [69].

Integrating FL and XAI into medical education presents multiple challenges across technical, ethical, regulatory, and educational domains.

11.4.6 VR and AR

VR gives users a completely artificial environment where they can interact with their surroundings. AR adds digital elements to the real world, typically through smartphones, tablets, or AR glasses [6].

The integration of AR and VR with FL has the capacity to transform the approach to medical education. AR and VR can simulate a range of medical scenarios, from basic anatomy lessons to complex surgical procedures, offering medical students a rich, interactive, and immersive learning environment. FL, on the other hand, allows the decentralized training of ML models across multiple institutions while keeping data localized [29].

Combining these technologies could lead to a more personalized, efficient, and secure educational experience. For example, FL can be used to continually update and refine the educational content and simulations in AR/VR based on real-world data from multiple institutions. This makes it possible to have a dynamic, up-to-date educational platform that adapts to new medical findings and techniques. Furthermore, because FL allows for data to be kept locally, it addresses potential privacy concerns that are often associated with the sharing of sensitive medical information.

Integration of AR, VR, and FL into medical education presents several sets of challenges. It faces several issues such as data management, and computational complexity. Scalability is also a major hurdle. Additionally, optimizing user experience and curriculum standardization within an educational framework that combines immersive and adaptive technologies is a complex task.

11.4.7 Cobots

Cobots are designed to work along with human workers in a shared workspace. Unlike industrial robots, which are often isolated from human workers for safety reasons, cobots are intended to interact with humans in a way that is safe and efficient [65].

The integration of cobots and FL in medical education has the capability to improve the training facilities by offering a personalized, dynamic, and up-to-date educational experience. Cobots, designed to work safely alongside humans, can facilitate hands-on training in areas such as surgical procedures and diagnostics [13]. When combined with FL, it allows for decentralized data processing, the cobots can adapt their training protocols based on real-world data from various medical institutions while maintaining data privacy. This integration could optimize resource use, extend the accessibility of advanced training tools to remote locations, and offer a more interdisciplinary educational approach [50].

However, challenges such as data security, content standardization, and ethical considerations would need to be addressed to fully realize the benefits of this integration [4].

The integration of several technologies like DT, BC, EC, IoT, XAI, VR, AR, and cobots with FL holds great potential to transform medical education in Industry 5.0. This integration majorly aims at creating immersive, interactive, and secure learning environments.

11.5 Applications of federated learning in medical education

Industry 5.0, often referred to as the era of human–machine collaboration, envisions a world where automation and humans coexist harmoniously, with machines enhancing human capabilities rather than replacing them. FL, which is an emerging paradigm in the ML domain, has been significantly influencing various sectors in Industry 5.0, including healthcare. The decentralized approach of FL helps several medical institutions to collaboratively utilize the data without compromising patient privacy. In the realm of medical education, this approach changes the landscape by introducing efficiencies, enhancing research capabilities, and fostering collaborative learning environments [71]. As medical data remains sensitive and highly regulated, the framework of FL keeps the data localized which is well suited to medical education applications. This section delves into the various applications of FL in medical education and also illustrates the potential to revolutionize the way medical professionals learn, research, and collaborate.

11.5.1 Personalized medical training simulators

The integration of several technologies and advancements in Industry 5.0, FL can help the creation of medical simulators that are tailored to specific patient data. These simulators allow the medical students to practice several procedures on virtual patients which mimic real-life cases without compromising the patient privacy [2].

By leveraging FL's decentralized approach to model training, medical institutions can collaboratively train these simulators using distributed data sources without the need for centralized data sharing. This not only enhances the realism and effectiveness of medical education but also addresses the ethical and legal concerns associated with handling sensitive patient data. The application of FL in medical simulators represents a groundbreaking paradigm shift in medical education, empowering future healthcare professionals to acquire practical skills in a secure and privacy-preserving environment [10].

11.5.2 Collaborative case studies

Medical students and professionals across the world use FL to collaborate on complex case studies in real time. FL enables fetching data from different sources without compromising on data privacy. By keeping data localized, FL helps several medical professionals to work together seamlessly, sharing knowledge and expertise across borders without compromising patient privacy [11]. This approach helps medical practitioners to learn from each other's experiences, contribute to research, and collectively advance medical knowledge.

Several FL algorithms identify gaps in knowledge and recommend targeted educational resources, which enables medical students to acquire the skills and knowledge necessary for their professional growth.

11.5.3 Augmented reality assistance

In Industry 5.0, AR plays a major role in hands-on training, particularly in the field of medicine. With the integration of FL and AR tools, medical institutions can update these tools in real time using data from various institutions [43]. The dynamic integration ensures that medical students have access to the latest information and techniques during procedures or dissections, enhancing their learning experience and practical skills.

The combination of AR and FL holds immense potential for revolutionizing medical education in Industry 5.0. It enables medical students to acquire practical skills and knowledge in a secure and privacy-preserving manner. This also ensures that the medical students learn and practice procedures with cutting-edge techniques, thereby paving the way for a more immersive and effective learning environment. Figure 11.2 depicts the applications of FL for medical education.

11.5.4 Curriculum updates

With data coming from multiple healthcare institutions, medical education curriculums can be continuously updated. By using FL, medical institutions can collectively analyze data from diverse sources while preserving data privacy and security.

The continuous updating of medical education curriculums through FL has several benefits. It enables educators to incorporate the latest research findings and clinical guidelines. New treatment methods can also be incorporated into their study material [44]. Medical students can stay updated on emerging medical trends and

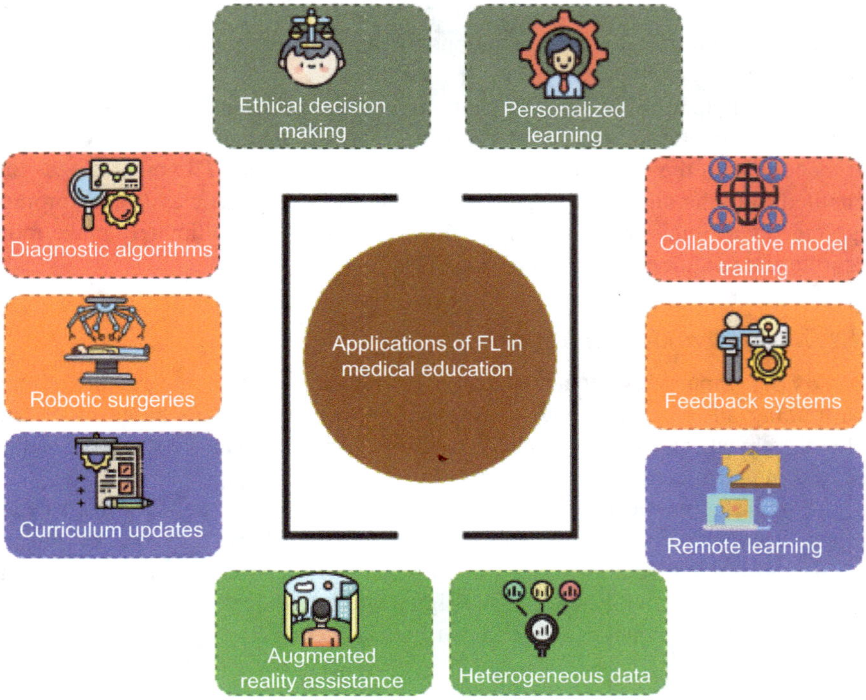

Figure 11.2 Applications of FL in medical education

breakthroughs. This enhances their knowledge and skills in parallel with current best practices. This approach fosters a culture of lifelong learning among healthcare professionals and contributes to improved patient care worldwide.

11.5.5 Remote robotic surgeries

Remote robotic surgeries have heralded a new era in the field of medical procedures. However, the safety, correctness, and effectiveness of these surgeries are questioned every time by the professional. This is where FL can play a transformative role. FL can enhance the capabilities of robotic surgical tools used in remote surgeries. As surgeons from around the world use these tools, FL can aggregate this data to improve the performance, accuracy, and safety of the tool [28].

11.5.6 Diagnostic algorithms

In the field of medical education, the introduction of FL gives a vast opportunity to train future physicians. The conventional methods of teaching diagnosis primarily depend on textbooks, lectures, and limited interaction with patients. Through FL, medical students can now use diagnostic algorithms that undergo continuous refinement using the vast amount of data from various healthcare institutions worldwide.

These algorithms possess the ability to assimilate and represent a more comprehensive spectrum of patient presentations, unique disease manifestations, and rare anomalies [56].

Each participating healthcare institution retains control and ownership of its data, ensuring no direct data transfer or exposure. Yet, the algorithms, updated through FL, benefit from the collective intelligence of these datasets. The medical students benefited from the diagnostic algorithms which act as diagnostic assistants, prompting students to think critically, ask pertinent questions, and ultimately make more accurate and confident diagnostic decisions [17].

11.5.7 Ethical decision-making

Industry 5.0 emphasizes human values, and medical ethics is an integral part of medical training. FL can help in developing decision-making models based on diverse cultural, ethical, and social inputs from medical professionals worldwide, aiding students in understanding and resolving ethical dilemmas [18].

For budding medical professionals, these FL-augmented models serve as comprehensive tools to dive deep into the world of medical ethics. They expose students to real-world ethical dilemmas faced by clinicians across different cultural and social contexts. More importantly, they offer insights into resolving these dilemmas in ways that align with the human-centric ethos of Industry 5.0 [47].

11.5.8 Feedback systems

With wearable devices and sensors becoming an integral part of Industry 5.0, FL can be applied to gather feedback on medical student performance during hands-on training, allowing for real-time adjustments and improvements. In summary, as Industry 5.0 emphasizes the integration of humans and machines, FL stands as a keystone in the advancement of medical education, offering a fusion of privacy-preserving technology with collaborative human-centric learning and research.

11.6 Benefits of federated learning in medical education

FL, particularly within the context of Industry 5.0, can significantly transform the landscape of medical education. By allowing for data analysis without direct data sharing, it provides an innovative means to enhance medical training, research, and collaboration.

1. Data Privacy and Security: FL allows medical institutions to train models without sharing raw patient data, thus adhering to strict data protection regulations and ensuring patient confidentiality.
2. Global Collaboration: FL breaks down geographical barriers. Medical schools and institutions worldwide can collaborate on research and training without compromising on data security, leading to more robust and diverse models and insights.
3. Real-time Updates: With the interconnected nature of Industry 5.0, FL enables real-time updates to medical models and algorithms. As new data emerges

across different institutions, models can be updated continuously, ensuring that medical students and professionals have access to the latest insights.

4. Personalized Medical Education: Drawing from diverse datasets, FL can help in developing customized training programs. This can ensure that medical students receive training tailored to specific trends, demographics, or challenges pertinent to their region or institution.
5. Optimized Clinical Decision Support: FL can improve the performance and accuracy of clinical decision support systems by integrating insights from diverse healthcare ecosystems. This offers medical students advanced tools that reflect global medical knowledge.
6. Enhanced Research Quality: FL fosters a new era of collaborative research without raw data exchange. This allows for diverse inputs in medical research, leading to more comprehensive studies and potentially groundbreaking discoveries.
7. Scalability: With the decentralized nature of FL, it's easier to scale up research and training endeavors. As more institutions participate, the richness and depth of insights grow, all without the need for a centralized data repository.
8. Reduction in Data Transfer Costs: By processing data locally and only sharing model updates, FL can significantly reduce the costs and time associated with transferring large datasets.
9. Ethical and Cultural Sensitivity: FL ensures that insights are drawn from a wide range of populations, leading to models and training that respect diverse cultural, ethical, and social perspectives, which is crucial in medical practice.
10. Interdisciplinary Collaboration: Industry 5.0's emphasis on human–machine collaboration can be actualized in medical education as well. FL can facilitate interdisciplinary studies, where medical education can integrate insights from fields like sociology, psychology, or even economics, fostering a holistic training approach.
11. Continuous Learning Environment: With the capabilities of Industry 5.0 technologies and FL combined, it's possible to create an environment where learning is continuous, adaptive, and responsive to global medical trends.

In essence, FL in the realm of Industry 5.0 stands to revolutionize medical education by making it more collaborative, data-driven, and adaptive while ensuring the utmost standards of data privacy and ethical considerations.

11.7 Challenges of implementing federated learning in medical education

FL is an emerging paradigm that allows for decentralized ML models to be trained across multiple devices or servers holding local data samples and without exchanging them. This approach is particularly appealing in medical education where sensitive health data is involved. However, implementing federated learning in this field comes with several challenges.

11.7.1 Data heterogeneity

Data heterogeneity is the variation in the data distribution, format, scales, and feature representations across different devices or locations.

The data concerned with medical education is generated from various sources like online learning platforms, electronic health records, assessments, and educational resources. Every source will have its own data format, structure, and semantics, which leads to data heterogeneity [14]. The heterogeneity in the data can impact the performance of the FL process in medical education.

11.7.2 Ensuring regulatory compliance and ethical considerations

FL in medical education must adhere to legal and regulatory requirements, including data protection laws and medical research regulations [45]. Institutions and researchers need to ensure that the collection, storage, and processing of data comply with relevant laws and regulations, such as obtaining informed consent from patients and maintaining data anonymization.

11.7.3 Data privacy and confidentiality concerns

Data privacy and confidentiality are significant concerns in various fields, including medical education. In the context of medical education, there are several areas where these concerns arise.

Several medical institutions that participate in the process of FL collect and store personal information about their students, including their academic records, health information, and sometimes even genetic data. It is very important to preserve and protect this sensitive data to ensure the privacy and confidentiality of students [67]. The student also interacts with patients and can access their medical records. Strict safeguards must be enacted to prevent unauthorized access, and use of patient data. The institutes also conduct research studies on human subjects. The data that is collected when this study happens, should be kept secret and private. The increasing use of digital platforms in medical education has led to the leakage of sensitive data [66]. These platforms must have robust security measures. Medical education involves the creation and distribution of educational materials which include lectures, case studies, and simulations. When using real patient data it is crucial to re-identify the data to ensure privacy.

11.7.4 Governance and coordination among multiple institutions

Implementing FL in medical education across multiple institutions poses complex challenges in governance and coordination. These challenges range from establishing a unified regulatory framework that accommodates varying legal jurisdictions to ensuring data harmonization and technical standardization across diverse systems [62]. The involvement of multiple stakeholders complicates decision-making processes and raises ethical concerns, including differing standards for data privacy and intellectual property rights. Additionally, the potential for conflicts among collaborating entities necessitates robust mechanisms for conflict resolution [43]. Therefore, effective governance and coordination are critical for the successful adoption of FL in multi-institutional medical education settings.

11.8 Future directions and recommendations

This section delves into the future directions and recommendations for FL in medical education in the context of Industry 5.0.

Medical data is sensitive. When leveraging FL, there is a need to ensure that this data isn't misused or exposed. Additionally, biases in training data from one institution could affect the learning outcomes [57]. Ethical use is ensured through constant vigilance and understanding of the data from multiple sources. FL when combined with quantum computing fulfills the need for heavy computational power required to process the data from several sources. Quantum computing could make real-time data analysis across institutions a reality. Medical research often requires vast amounts of data. Institutions can use FL to collaborate without sharing raw data, ensuring patient privacy. This collaboration can lead to breakthroughs as it allows pooling of diverse data sets. FL utilizes varied patient data, which leads to more realistic diagnostic scenarios for training [36]. Students can get a broader exposure to potential cases, enhancing their diagnostic capabilities without directly accessing sensitive patient information. Standardized protocols ensure interoperability between different institutions' systems, making the process of FL more efficient. Institutions can be encouraged to work together to create a richer data pool, improving the quality of outcome [49].

11.9 Conclusion

As the world needs to adapt to the complexities of Industry 5.0, there is an increasing need to combine human-centered approaches with cutting-edge technological advances. In this scenario, the sector of medical education, which is crucial for generating competent healthcare professionals, must come up with innovative solutions. The idea of FL shines like a star in this context.

The decentralized nature of FL enables the training of ML models across various devices or institutions. The collaboration between several devices or institutions without compromising the privacy of sensitive data, finds unique applicability in medical education. The enormous repositories of patient data across healthcare institutions, though immensely valuable for education and research, are often underutilized due to legitimate concerns about privacy and regulatory compliance. FL bridges this gap, unlocking the potential of distributed datasets while ensuring stringent adherence to data privacy norms.

Leveraging FL in medical curriculums helps future healthcare professionals with the ability to harness real-time and different patient data in their journey of learning. This not only amplifies the practical skills but also ensures that they remain ahead in medical knowledge. Furthermore, Industry 5.0 which emphasizes human values, FL enhances the principles of Industry 5.0, and fosters the collaborative environment while also prioritizing patient confidentiality.

References

[1] Haftay Gebreslasie Abreha, Mohammad Hayajneh, and Mohamed Adel Serhani. Federated learning in edge computing: A systematic survey. *Sensors*, 22(2), 2022.

[2] Amr Adel. Future of Industry 5.0 in society: Human-centric solutions, challenges and prospective research areas. *Journal of Cloud Computing*, 11(1):1–15, 2022.

[3] Ahmed Alsoufi, Ali Alsuyihili, Ahmed Msherghi, *et al.* Impact of the covid-19 pandemic on medical education: Medical students' knowledge, attitudes, and practices regarding electronic learning. *PLOS One*, 15(11):e0242905, 2020.

[4] Keith Bonawitz, Hubert Eichner, Wolfgang Grieskamp, *et al.* Towards federated learning at scale: System design. *Proceedings of Machine Learning and Systems*, 1:374–388, 2019.

[5] Theodora S Brisimi, Ruidi Chen, Theofanie Mela, Alex Olshevsky, Ioannis Ch Paschalidis, and Wei Shi. Federated learning of predictive models from federated electronic health records. *International Journal of Medical Informatics*, 112:59–67, 2018.

[6] Ferran Calabuig-Moreno, María Huertas González-Serrano, Javier Fombona, and Marta Garcia-Tascon. The emergence of technology in physical education: A general bibliometric analysis with a focus on virtual and augmented reality. *Sustainability*, 12(7):2728, 2020.

[7] Zheng Chai, Yujing Chen, Ali Anwar, Liang Zhao, Yue Cheng, and Huzefa Rangwala. Fedat: A high-performance and communication-efficient federated learning system with asynchronous tiers. In *Proceedings of the International Conference for High Performance Computing, Networking, Storage and Analysis*, pages 1–16, 2021.

[8] Kristtopher K Coelho, Michele Nogueira, Alex B Vieira, Edelberto F Silva, and José AM Nacif. A survey on federated learning for security and privacy in healthcare applications. *Computer Communications*, 2023.

[9] Pedro Coelho, Catarina Bessa, Jorge Landeck, and Cristovão Silva. Industry 5.0: The arising of a concept. *Procedia Computer Science*, 217:1137–1144, 2023.

[10] Jelena Crnobrnja, Darko Stefanovic, David Romero, Selver Softic, and Ugljesa Marjanovic. Digital transformation towards Industry 5.0: A systematic literature review. In *IFIP International Conference on Advances in Production Management Systems*, pages 269–281. Springer, 2023.

[11] MG Crowson, D Moukheiber, AR Arévalo, *et al.* A systematic review of federated learning applications for biomedical data. *PLOS Digit Health* 1(5):e0000033, 2022.

[12] K Dasaradharami Reddy and Thippa Reddy Gadekallu, A comprehensive survey on federated learning techniques for healthcare informatics. *Computational Intelligence and Neuroscience*, 2023:8393990, 2023.

[13] Daniela D'Auria and Fabio Persia. A collaborative robotic cyber physical system for surgery applications. In *2017 IEEE International Conference on Information Reuse and Integration (IRI)*, pages 79–83. IEEE, 2017.

[14] Artur Back de Luca, Guojun Zhang, Xi Chen, and Yaoliang Yu. Mitigating data heterogeneity in federated learning with data augmentation. *arXiv preprint arXiv:2206.09979*, 2022.

[15] Finale Doshi-Velez and Been Kim. Towards a rigorous science of interpretable machine learning. *arXiv preprint arXiv:1702.08608*, 2017.

[16] Safa Elkefi and Onur Asan. Digital twins for managing health care systems: Rapid literature review. *Journal of Medical Internet Research*, 24(8):e37641, 2022.

[17] Louise Forsetlund, Mary Ann O'Brien, Lisa Forsen, *et al.* Continuing education meetings and workshops: Effects on professional practice and healthcare outcomes. *Cochrane Database of Systematic Reviews*, (9), 2021.

[18] PK Garg. The future healthcare technologies: A roadmap to society 5.0. In *Geospatial Data Science in Healthcare for Society 5.0*, pages 305–318. Springer, 2022.

[19] Lorenzo Ghiro, Francesco Restuccia, Salvatore D'Oro, *et al.* What is a blockchain? A definition to clarify the role of the blockchain in the internet of things, 2021.

[20] L Gomathi, Anand Kumar Mishra, and Amit Kumar Tyagi. Industry 5.0 for healthcare 5.0: Opportunities, challenges and future research possibilities. In *2023 7th International Conference on Trends in Electronics and Informatics (ICOEI)*, pages 204–213. IEEE, 2023.

[21] Tao Hai, Jincheng Zhou, SR Srividhya, Sanjiv Kumar Jain, Praise Young, and Shweta Agrawal. Bvflemr: An integrated federated learning and blockchain technology for cloud-based medical records recommendation system. *Journal of Cloud Computing*, 11(1):22, 2022.

[22] Ahmad Hammoud, Hadi Otrok, Azzam Mourad, and Zbigniew Dziong. Stable federated fog formation: An evolutionary game theoretical approach. *Future Generation Computer Systems*, 124:21–32, 2021.

[23] Ahmad Hammoud, Hadi Otrok, Azzam Mourad, and Zbigniew Dziong. On demand fog federations for horizontal federated learning in iov. *IEEE Transactions on Network and Service Management*, 19(3):3062–3075, 2022.

[24] Omar Hashash, Sanaa Sharafeddine, and Zaher Dawy. Mec-based energy-aware distributed feature extraction for mhealth applications with strict latency requirements. In *2021 IEEE International Conference on Communications Workshops (ICC Workshops)*, pages 1–6. IEEE, 2021.

[25] Ali Asghar Hayat, Mohmmad Hasan Keshavarzi, Soolmaz Zare, *et al.* Challenges and opportunities from the covid-19 pandemic in medical education: a qualitative study. *BMC Medical Education*, 21(1):247, 2021.

[26] Eduardo Herrera-Aliaga and Lisbell D Estrada. Trends and innovations of simulation for twenty first century medical education. *Frontiers in Public Health*, 10:619769, 2022.

[27] Madhuri Hiwale, Rahee Walambe, Vidyasagar Potdar, and Ketan Kotecha. A systematic review of privacy-preserving methods deployed with blockchain and federated learning for the telemedicine. *Healthcare Analytics*, 3:100192, 2023.

[28] Julian Klodmann, Christopher Schlenk, Anja Hellings-Kuß, *et al.* An introduction to robotically assisted surgical systems: Current developments and focus areas of research. *Current Robotics Reports*, 2(3):321–332, 2021.

[29] Bhone Myint Kyaw, Nakul Saxena, Pawel Posadzki, *et al.* Virtual reality for health professions education: Systematic review and meta-analysis by the digital health education collaboration. *Journal of Medical Internet Research*, 21(1):e12959, 2019.

[30] Johannes Lang and Holger Repp. Artificial intelligence in medical education and the meaning of interaction with natural intelligence–an interdisciplinary approach. *GMS Journal for Medical Education*, 37(6), 2020.

[31] Theo Lynn, Patricia Takako Endo, Andrea Maria N. C. Ribeiro, Gibson B. N. Barbosa, and Pierangelo Rosati. *The Internet of Things: Definitions, Key Concepts, and Reference Architectures*, pages 1–22. Springer International Publishing, Cham, 2020.

[32] Praveen Kumar Reddy Maddikunta, Quoc-Viet Pham, B Prabadevi, *et al.* Industry 5.0: A survey on enabling technologies and potential applications. *Journal of Industrial Information Integration*, 26:100257, 2022.

[33] Katarzyna Maj-Waśniowska, J Stanienda, and J Wyrobek. Challenges for the education system in the era of the fourth industrial revolution. In *Public Goods and the Fourth Industrial Revolution*. Taylor & Francis, 2023.

[34] Amir Mehdiabadi, Vahid Shahabi, Saeed Shamsinejad, Mohammad Amiri, Cristi Spulbar, and Ramona Birau. Investigating Industry 5.0 and its impact on the banking industry: Requirements, approaches and communications. *Applied Sciences*, 12(10):5126, 2022.

[35] Stewart Mennin. Ten global challenges in medical education: Wicked issues and options for action. *Medical Science Educator*, 31(Suppl 1):17–20, 2021.

[36] Devin B Morris, Philip A Gruppuso, Heather A McGee, Anarina L Murillo, Atul Grover, and Eli Y Adashi. Diversity of the national medical student body—four decades of inequities. *New England Journal of Medicine*, 384(17):1661–1668, 2021.

[37] Azzam Mourad, Hanine Tout, Omar Abdel Wahab, Hadi Otrok, and Toufic Dbouk. Ad hoc vehicular fog enabling cooperative low-latency intrusion detection. *IEEE Internet of Things Journal*, 8(2):829–843, 2020.

[38] Divya Nagaraj, Priya Khandelwal, Sandra Steyaert, and Olivier Gevaert. Augmenting digital twins with federated learning in medicine. *The Lancet Digital Health*, 5(5):e251–e253, 2023.

[39] Dinh C Nguyen, Quoc-Viet Pham, Pubudu N Pathirana, *et al.* Federated learning for smart healthcare: A survey. *ACM Computing Surveys (CSUR)*, 55(3):1–37, 2022.

[40] Sharnil Pandya, Gautam Srivastava, Rutvij Jhaveri, *et al.* Federated learning for smart cities: A comprehensive survey. *Sustainable Energy Technologies and Assessments*, 55:102987, 2023.

[41] Nicholas Parkin. Pacifism and educational violence. *Journal of Peace Education*, pages 1–20, 2023.

[42] Vishwa Amitkumar Patel, Pronaya Bhattacharya, Sudeep Tanwar, Rajesh Gupta, Gulshan Sharma, Pitshou N Bokoro, and Ravi Sharma. Adoption of federated learning for healthcare informatics: Emerging applications and future directions. *IEEE Access*, 2022.

[43] Bjarne Pfitzner, Nico Steckhan, and Bert Arnrich. Federated learning in a medical context: A systematic literature review. *ACM Transactions on Internet Technology (TOIT)*, 21(2):1–31, 2021.

[44] Prayitno, Chi-Ren Shyu, Karisma Trinanda Putra, Hsing-Chung Chen, Yuan-Yu Tsai, KSM Tozammel Hossain, Wei Jiang, and Zon-Yin Shae. A systematic review of federated learning in the healthcare area: From the perspective of data properties and applications. *Applied Sciences*, 11(23):11191, 2021.

[45] Liangqiong Qu, Niranjan Balachandar, and Daniel L Rubin. An experimental study of data heterogeneity in federated learning methods for medical imaging. *arXiv preprint arXiv:2107.08371*, 2021.

[46] Zhiguo Qu, Yang Li, Bo Liu, Deepak Gupta, and Prayag Tiwari. Dtqfl: A digital twin-assisted quantum federated learning algorithm for intelligent diagnosis in 5g mobile network. *IEEE Journal of Biomedical and Health Informatics*, pages 1–10, 2023.

[47] Anichur Rahman, Md Sazzad Hossain, Ghulam Muhammad, *et al.* Federated learning-based ai approaches in smart healthcare: Concepts, taxonomies, challenges and open issues. *Cluster Computing*, 26(4):2271–2311, 2023.

[48] Abirami Raja Santhi and Padmakumar Muthuswamy. Industry 5.0 or Industry 4.0 s? Introduction to Industry 4.0 and a peek into the prospective Industry 5.0 technologies. *International Journal on Interactive Design and Manufacturing (IJIDeM)*, 17(2):947–979, 2023.

[49] Suraj Rajendran, Zhenxing Xu, Weishen Pan, Arnab Ghosh, and Fei Wang. Data heterogeneity in federated learning with electronic health records: Case studies of risk prediction for acute kidney injury and sepsis diseases in critical care. *PLOS Digital Health*, 2(3):e0000117, 2023.

[50] Nicola Rieke, Jonny Hancox, Wenqi Li, *et al.* The future of digital health with federated learning. *NPJ Digital Medicine*, 3(1):119, 2020.

[51] Ebrahim Navid Sadjadi. Challenges and opportunities for education systems with the current movement toward digitalization at the time of covid-19. *Mathematics*, 11(2):259, 2023.

[52] Nishant K Shah, Neil K Taunk, Russell Maxwell, *et al.* Comparison of virtual reality platforms to enhance medical education for procedures. *Frontiers in Virtual Reality*, 3:1000035, 2022.

[53] Hala Shamseddine, Jana Nizam, Ahmad Hammoud, *et al.* A novel federated fog architecture embedding intelligent formation. *IEEE Network*, 35(3): 198–204, 2020.

[54] Weisong Shi, Jie Cao, Quan Zhang, Youhuizi Li, and Lanyu Xu. Edge computing: Vision and challenges. *IEEE Internet of Things Journal*, 3(5): 637–646, 2016.

[55] Weisong Shi, Jie Cao, Quan Zhang, Youhuizi Li, and Lanyu Xu. Edge computing: Vision and challenges. *IEEE Internet of Things Journal*, 3(5): 637–646, 2016.

[56] Carlos R Sierra-Fernández, Huipe-Dimas Alejandra, Sergio A Trevethan-Cravioto, *et al.* Flipped learning as an educational model in a cardiology residency program. *BMC Medical Education*, 23(1):1–6, 2023.

[57] Md Fahimuzzman Sohan and Anas Basalamah. A systematic review on federated learning in medical image analysis. *IEEE Access*, 11:28628–28644, 2023.

[58] Lanfang Sun, Xin Jiang, Huixia Ren, and Yi Guo. Edge-cloud computing and artificial intelligence in internet of medical things: Architecture, technology and application. *IEEE Access*, 8:101079–101092, 2020.

[59] Zahraa Khduair Taha, Chong Tak Yaw, Siaw Paw Koh, *et al.* A survey of federated learning from data perspective in the healthcare domain: Challenges, methods, and future directions. *IEEE Access*, 2023.

[60] Yue Tan, Guodong Long, Jie Ma, Lu Liu, Tianyi Zhou, and Jing Jiang. Federated learning from pre-trained models: A contrastive learning approach. *Advances in Neural Information Processing Systems*, 35:19332–19344, 2022.

[61] Stella Timotheou, Ourania Miliou, Yiannis Dimitriadis, *et al.* Impacts of digital technologies on education and factors influencing schools' digital capacity and transformation: A literature review. *Education and Information Technologies*, 28(6):6695–6726, 2023.

[62] Mustafa Y Topaloglu, Elisabeth M Morrell, Suraj Rajendran, and Umit Topaloglu. In the pursuit of privacy: The promises and predicaments of federated learning in healthcare. *Frontiers in Artificial Intelligence*, 4:746497, 2021.

[63] Mario Gabriel Torres-Calixto. Trends and challenges of medical education. *Revista de la Facultad de Medicina*, 69(3):e84330–e84330, 2021.

[64] Ha-Vu Tran, Georges Kaddoum, Hany Elgala, Chadi Abou-Rjeily, and Hemani Kaushal. Lightwave power transfer for federated learning-based wireless networks. *IEEE Communications Letters*, 24(7):1472–1476, 2020.

[65] Federico Vicentini. Collaborative robotics: A survey. *Journal of Mechanical Design*, 143(4):040802, 2021.

[66] Lin Wei, Zhang Yu, and Zhang Qinge. Medical college education data analysis method based on improved deep learning algorithm. *Mobile Information Systems*, 2022, 2022.

[67] Jeffrey A Wilhite, Lisa Altshuler, Sondra Zabar, Colleen Gillespie, and Adina Kalet. Development and maintenance of a medical education research registry. *BMC Medical Education*, 20(1):1–12, 2020.

[68] He Xue, Dajiang Chen, Ning Zhang, Hong-Ning Dai, and Keping Yu. Integration of blockchain and edge computing in internet of things: A survey, 2022.

[69] Qiang Yang, Yang Liu, Tianjian Chen, and Yongxin Tong. Federated machine learning: Concept and applications. *ACM Transactions on Intelligent Systems and Technology (TIST)*, 10(2):1–19, 2019.

[70] Doris George Yohannan, Aswathy Maria Oommen, Kannanvilakom Govindapillai Umesan, *et al*. Overcoming barriers in a traditional medical education system by the stepwise, evidence-based introduction of a modern learning technology. *Medical Science Educator*, 29:803–817, 2019.

[71] Joo Hun Yoo, Hyejun Jeong, Jaehyeok Lee, and Tai-Myoung Chung. Federated learning: Issues in medical application. In *Future Data and Security Engineering: 8th International Conference, FDSE 2021, Virtual Event, November 24–26, 2021, Proceedings 8*, pages 3–22. Springer, 2021.

Chapter 12

A comprehensive survey on enhanced privacy techniques for federated learning in healthcare systems

Dasaradharami Reddy Kandati[1] and Thippa Reddy Gadekallu[2,3]

Abstract

Federated learning (FL) is a decentralised approach to machine learning (ML) in which individuals build models utilising their own information without sharing it with a central server. This is particularly beneficial in healthcare systems, where devices like Medical Internet of Things (MIoT) and electronic health records (EHRs) can be educated remotely while maintaining patient privacy. FL enables collaboration and decision-making based on datasets from multiple participants, improving healthcare processes. However, FL faces privacy challenges as the algorithmic changes exchanged between the client and server might potentially reveal the personal information of the client, violating confidentiality laws, especially in sensitive fields such as medical care. To tackle these challenges, researchers have proposed various techniques to strengthen safety and privacy in FL in medical systems. This chapter presents a literature review that examines existing techniques in this area. The review analysed eight primary methods used to enhance privacy in healthcare FL systems. These techniques include Hierarchical Methods, Peer-to-Peer Sharing, Differential Privacy, Homomorphic Encryption, Edge Device Intelligence, Blockchain, Hybrid, and Diverse Methods, and Industry 5.0. The review analysed the advantages, disadvantages, and compromises of each method while also highlighting possible future paths for improving privacy in healthcare federated learning systems.

Keywords: Federated learning, Enhanced privacy, Peer-to-peer sharing, Differential privacy, Homomorphic encryption, Edge device, Blockchain, Industry 5.0

[1]Department of Computer Science and Engineering, NBKR Institute of Science and Technology, Vidyanagar, India
[2]Division of Research and Development, Lovely Professional University, Phagwara, India
[3]Zhongda Group, Haiyan County, Jiaxing City, Zhejiang Province, China

12.1 Introduction

FL continues to gain significant prominence in both scientific studies and real-life applications. It differs from traditional ML systems by offering a distributed ML approach. In FL, participants build their personal models using their personal information, eliminating the requirement of sharing information [1]. Instead of exchanging data, users simply communicate the inputs and outputs of their learned models with a central FL database. The FL database then combines these model weights and returns the updated weights to the users. Through this iterative learning process, participants collaboratively construct a global model without the need to share their data with others [2].

The healthcare industry has seen a rise in the adoption of FL due to its decentralised training and learning model structure. This method allows different medical organisations to work together and build ML algorithms using their own information without threatening the safety of patient information. As a result, FL has gained popularity and is being used in practical medical situations, going beyond just being a theoretical concept.

Google and Stanford Medicine collaborated on a research project that employed FL to create a prediction algorithm for readmission to the hospital. The medical information collected from different institutions was kept regionally, and the distributed ML model was trained on this data without disclosing any sensitive information. The result was a personalised model for assessing the risk of readmission, which placed a high priority on protecting patient privacy.

Kyung Hee University has created a clinical decision support system that utilises deep learning (DL) techniques in an FL framework. This system enables the extensive analysis of clinical data, aiming to help the medical community come up with treatment decisions and timely diagnoses.

A recent advancement in drug discovery involves the use of FL. A group of ten organisations, including industrial companies, startups, pharmaceutical companies, and academic research labs, joined forces to create a significant FL model for accelerating the process of discovering and developing drugs. Importantly, this model was constructed without the need to share confidential datasets [4]. By training on diverse patient data, FL models have the potential to identify potential drug targets, predict drug effectiveness, and optimise treatment protocols, all while ensuring the confidentiality of patient data is maintained.

Collaborative disease detection and diagnosis, particularly for diabetic retinal disease using retinal images [5], has been made easier with the use of FL. Various hospitals have provided individually developed algorithms for identifying diabetic retinal disease, and these algorithms have been combined using FL to create a highly efficient and broadly applicable algorithm for identifying retinal damage from retinal images.

The field of managing public health is currently being thoroughly researched, especially in the context of FL, with a focus on predicting clinical outcomes for individuals impacted by COVID-19 [6]. By using FL, proactive measures can be taken to intervene, allocate resources effectively, and prevent diseases, all while maintaining confidentiality and complying with restrictions on the use of personal information.

12.2 Recent studies

In the past three years, there have been several reviews and surveys conducted on the topic of FL in the healthcare field, taking into account the significant progress made in this area. Here, we will present a concise summary of several recently published surveys and evaluations.

Different review studies have examined and evaluated FL from various perspectives. These perspectives include traceability and accountability [1], data-centric perspectives [8], privacy and security [1, 7], system challenges [7], data heterogeneity [1], statistical challenges [7], system architecture [1], and its suitability for private medical records [9]. Rieke *et al.* [1] provided a summary of the key factors of FL and its potential as a solution in the field of digital health for the future. They also emphasised the challenges and important factors to consider in FL systems, including traceability and accountability, system architecture, privacy and security concerns, and data heterogeneity. Xu *et al.* [7] conducted a research study that investigated the use of FL technologies in the biomedical field. The studies specifically examined privacy-related concerns such as differential privacy and secure multi-party computation. Shyu *et al.* [8] conducted a comprehensive analysis of 24 research papers that focused on the use of FL in medical applications. They examined various challenges associated with data, including benchmark datasets, data protection mechanisms, data distributions, and characteristics of data partitioning. Pfitzner *et al.* [9] conducted a comprehensive analysis of 80 research articles that focused on the use of FL in confidential healthcare datasets. Their review specifically excluded studies that explored decentralised learning methods involving peer-to-peer approaches or blockchain.

Several review studies have been carried out on FL in relation to EHRs. Kumar *et al.* [10] focused on FL medical approaches in the areas of disease prediction systems, drug growth, and EHR systems. The researchers assessed and compared several FL methods using metrics including precision, accuracy, recall, and F-score. Nguyen *et al.* [11] conducted a study on the usage of FL in innovative medical care. This study analysed 16 articles and presented an overview of FL-based solutions for the medical industry, like COVID-19 detection, remote health monitoring, EHR data management, and medical imaging. Antunes *et al.* [12] conducted a systematic literature review based on 44 articles, exploring FL-based medical solutions specifically in the broader setting of EHR data. This study also covered the broader structure that enables the seamless incorporation of FL into algorithms combined with ML.

Several review studies have been conducted in specific areas, such as oncology-based applications [13], security threats [14], and IoMT-related FL [15]. In their comprehensive assessment of 63 articles, Chowdhury *et al.* [13] addressed FL techniques in cancer. The identification and analysis of privacy issues and prevention approaches in FL were carried out, as well as an evaluation of potential risks in FL. Mothukuri *et al.* [14] specifically examined privacy-related issues related to FL, comparing them to safety concerns. Ali *et al.* [15] performed a privacy-focused study on FL in intelligent IoMT medical centres. Their study explored the FL in IoMT and the security and privacy aspects of IoMT, as well as different FL architectures, including privacy-enabled FL, incentive-enabled FL for IoMT, and FL-enabled digital twin for IoMT.

Table 12.1 presents a summary of the main subjects and notable findings discussed in these review studies.

Table 12.1 Main subjects and notable findings of the existing review studies

Reference	Main Subject	Notable Findings
[1]	FL design	Discuss various aspects of FL systems, including traceability and accountability, privacy and security, system architecture, and data heterogeneity.
[7]	FL design	Provide a solution for the privacy issues, system challenges, and statistical challenges associated with FL systems, including differential privacy and secure multi-party computation.
[8]	FL design	Consider the partitioning, distribution, safety methods, and reference data sets used in FL systems and rate their qualities.
[9]	FL design	Investigation of FL and its suitability for maintaining the confidentiality of healthcare datasets, excluding decentralised learning methods such as blockchain or direct peer-to-peer networks.
[10]	FL in EHR	Recall, precision, accuracy, and F-score are the parameters that may be compared across a range of FL algorithms in the healthcare industry.
[12]	FL for EHR	Studies of EHR's practical uses, including further talk of FL's fundamental design and its compatibility with ML-powered systems.
[13]	FL in cancer treatment	FL algorithms and their potential uses in the field of cancer treatment are discussed.
[14]	Protective Measures of FL	Exposure of personal information in FL systems: a comparative analysis. Protections against security flaws, as well as privacy invasions, are discussed.
[15]	FL in IoMT	Privacy aspects related to the IoMT network include discussions on architectures such as privacy-enabled FL, FL-enabled digital twins for IoMT, and incentive-enabled FL for IoMT.
[16]	FL for EHR	All aspects of FL structure are discussed, including security, privacy, incentives, resource-awareness, and individualisation.
This chapter	Enhanced confidentiality for FL	Evaluate the improved privacy methods for using FL in healthcare.

The previous research examined various facets of FL in healthcare systems, encompassing topics such as data, system, statistical hurdles, practicality, as well as privacy and security concerns.

Although FL architecture offers some level of privacy by not sharing raw data, it does not guarantee complete protection against privacy preservation. It is critical to emphasise the significance of safeguarding medical information, such as computerised medical records, as they frequently include extremely sensitive, crucial, and secret information. The characteristics of medical records pose notable concerns regarding patient confidentiality.

Numerous recent experiments have highlighted the potential risk of patient privacy being compromised in FL systems, as the shared model parameters could inadvertently reveal sensitive data [17,18]. In addition, it is important to note that the privacy guarantee for the FL process has not been formally proven [19]. This lack of formal proof leaves FL vulnerable to security attacks that are inherent in distributed systems. As a result, it becomes necessary to implement additional measures to enhance confidentiality and address safety issues, especially when FL is used in the medical field. The major goal of this chapter is to improve privacy protection by tackling the issue of private information leakage through modelling variations in FL applications, with a few limitations [20].

We aim to address the limited research on privacy enhancement methods used in medical centres that employ FL. Our main goal is to examine and analyse the different privacy-enhancing approaches applied in FL within medical centres. To accomplish this, we have developed the following research questions:

RQ. 1: What privacy enhancement methods are currently used in healthcare systems to ensure the security of data in FL?

RQ. 2: What is the current status of privacy-enhancing measures in healthcare systems in FL? Can you provide information about their benefits, limitations, and trade-offs?

RQ. 3: What does the future hold for enhanced privacy techniques in healthcare systems using FL?

This article provides an overview of the most recent techniques designed to enhance privacy in FL within the medical industry. The review concentrates on scholarly works published from 2020 to 2023, with a particular emphasis on methods that strive to safeguard FL systems and ensure security measures for extremely personal health information.

Section 12.3 of the document offers a detailed explanation of the approach employed for the review. The outcomes of the review, along with the related responses to each of the questionnaires, are presented in Section 12.4. Section 12.5 provides a concise overview of the results and includes a discussion on the potential prospects for improving privacy in FL within healthcare systems. Additionally, it offers suggestions for future research in this area.

12.3 Methodology

To accomplish our study goals, we collected significant studies using Scopus, a highly regarded bibliographic database renowned for its comprehensive coverage of peer-reviewed journals and printed materials [21–23]. For more information about the search process, including the origin of the bibliographical data and the searching criteria used, please refer to Table 12.2.

To achieve the goals of this review, three main criteria were considered in the search query. The first criterion was to prioritise published work that specifically pertained to FL. The second requirement was that the studies had to be carried out within the healthcare sector. Last, the chosen publications needed to cover subjects such as confidentiality, safety, or credibility in FL. These search elements are outlined in Table 12.3.

The constructed Boolean search Component string is based on the identified search themes in the three features: TITLE-ABS-KEY ("Federated learning" AND ("Healthcare") AND ("privacy" or "security" or "trust")).

After conducting a Scopus search, a total of 216 records were obtained. These records were then screened, mapped, and extracted for further analysis. A comprehensive review was conducted to assess the relevance of these papers based on three search features: FL, healthcare, and confidentiality/security/credibility. Ultimately, a subset of 39 papers was considered as being related to the topic.

Through the examination of reference lists, a pertinent article related to intelligence on edge devices was discovered and subsequently incorporated into this review. As a result, a comprehensive review was conducted, encompassing a total of 40 relevant papers that were considered and included.

Table 12.2 The sources of the bibliography data and the parameters used for the search

Search criteria	Target
Citation information	Scopus
Style of article	Technical papers, conference papers, journal articles, book chapters
Search for	Title of the paper, abstract, keywords
Ranking based on receipts	Outcome-based sorting
Duration of publication	Infinite
Date of search	27 July 2023

Table 12.3 Search keywords

Index of components	Themes
Feature 1	"Federated learning"
Feature 2	"Healthcare"
Feature 3	"Privacy" or "security" or "trust"

12.4 Results

This section presents the findings of the review conducted on 40 featured articles.

12.4.1 RQ 1

The first research question is "What privacy enhancement methods are currently used in healthcare systems to ensure the security of data in FL?"

To categorise the selected papers for addressing this research inquiry, we can classify them into different groups based on the primary approaches used to improve safety and confidentiality in FL systems.

- Hierarchical Methods
- Peer-to-Peer Sharing
- Differential Privacy
- Homomorphic Encryption
- Edge Device Intelligence
- Blockchain
- Hybrid and Diverse Methods
- Industry 5.0

The recommended paper begins by providing a concise overview of the fundamental concept, followed by an assessment and explanation of its implications for improving FL safety.

12.4.1.1 Hierarchical methods

Despite the fact that FL can address privacy concerns associated with central cloud system-based visualisation of data, the conventional FL technique has limitations when it comes to data aggregation on a single server. As a result, researchers have focused on developing a structured FL strategy that allows aggregation towards different stages, allowing numerous parties to collaborate [24–26].

Gupta *et al.* [24] introduced a structured FL method designed specifically for the IoMT application. This approach enables secure collaboration among multiple healthcare organisations by allowing data aggregation at various levels. The authors also proposed a unique grouping technique that categorises data with regard to illness groupings. Additionally, they created a new anomaly detection model training approach called Federation Time Distribution (FEDTIMEDIS) Long Short-Term Memory (LSTM).

Singh *et al.* [25] developed a structured FL method using the Dew-Cloud technique to improve data confidentiality in IoMT applications. They also implemented a hierarchical long-short-term memory (HLSTM) model on distributed Dew servers to detect intrusions in incoming traffic. The researchers assert that their proposed model has the potential to instill trust among users across the IoMT environment.

Abdellatif *et al.* [26] introduced a structured FL method designed to improve confidentiality in medical devices. Their identified framework consists of three stages: the edge node layer, the centralised server layer, and the end user (EU) layer.

In this method, EU members work together to develop a DL model without revealing all of their data. Instead, they establish connections with nearby edges of the network, which reside across their transmission reach. These little nodes are then linked together to form a single central server. Researchers emphasise that their strategy focuses on efficiency by taking into account the various data allocations across EU members in addition to the digital environment's features.

12.4.1.2 Peer-to-peer sharing

In FL, achieving high efficiency is crucial. One way to accomplish this is through the use of peer-to-peer sharing (P2PS). P2PS enables participating devices to exchange model updates, thereby reducing the computational load on centralised servers and enhancing the learning process's efficiency. Moreover, P2PS has the added benefit of improving user privacy since sensitive data doesn't need to be stored or processed by a central intermediary.

Gandhi *et al.* [27] introduced an FL system aimed at preserving the confidentiality of sensitive medical information. They utilised a set of DL models for classifying cancer-related text. The outcomes of their study demonstrated the effectiveness of their framework in tackling privacy concerns associated with sensitive medical data in the context of cancer text classification.

Chen *et al.* [28] introduced a privacy-preserving system called PFL-IU, designed to handle the growing number of EHRs obtained from smartphones and wearable devices. This system efficiently manages irrelevant updates while ensuring privacy. The study demonstrated that PFL-IU performs well in the areas of confidentiality, precision, integration, and performance.

12.4.1.3 Differential privacy

In healthcare systems, the future of enhanced privacy techniques in FL looks promising. One such method is differential privacy (DP), which allows for the secure sharing of aggregated information from datasets while protecting the privacy of individual data subjects. This is especially important in AI applications that rely on large datasets for training models, as privacy concerns can arise when sensitive information is involved. The utilisation of DP in the context of FL involves incorporating a framework that enables the development of intelligent algorithms capable of analysing privacy concerns while still retaining an appropriate level of reliability [29]. This is achieved by adding sound to the variables that are shared among users prior to the modelling compilation taking place on the hosting platform, thereby preventing any potential information leakage [30].

To strengthen privacy in medical centres using FL, it is crucial to focus on resolving vulnerabilities associated with collecting data from fluctuations transmitted by users. DP offers a solution by quantifying the disclosure of personal information when ML models utilise user data. By introducing uncertainty into the model, privacy can be safeguarded. Finding a middle ground between the accuracy of a model and the desired level of privacy is crucial [31].

The vulnerability of privacy attacks in FL arises from the centralised server performing global model aggregation. To tackle the security risks associated with patient data in the healthcare sector, a potential solution is to incorporate an edge aggregator. This aggregator would introduce fake sound to the client's variables in the model in three distinct stages [32]. By implementing this approach, it becomes possible to maintain a high level of model accuracy while ensuring privacy. This solution aligns with the group of options outlined in Section 4.1.6.

To tackle the issue of privacy concerns regarding patients' data, there is a security obstacle when feeding data into ML models. To overcome this obstacle, DP and statistical feature selection techniques are employed [33]. These approaches aim to decrease data transfer while also adding sound to regions of interest before they are sent back to the FL servers for consolidation. These findings demonstrate promising reliability while upholding a certain degree of anonymity for the estimation of variables.

When using FL to identify COVID-19 by analysing manifestations and chest X-ray data from several health centres, it is crucial to prioritise additional privacy measures. This is necessary to safeguard the data from potential malicious attacks. To increase both the reliability of the model and privacy protection, a technique called differential privacy stochastic gradient descent (DP-SGD) is employed [31]. DP-SGD allows participants in the FL system to introduce perturbations in the form of variations after learning an algorithm on the actual data. Privacy is preserved through the application of random Gaussian fluctuations as part of the regional variations, while model accuracy suffers slightly. The study examined this tradeoff and discovered that expanding the variety of users in the FL method could result in an improvement in the degree of DP assurance while minimising the impact on model accuracy [31].

The Internet of Health Things (IoHT) faces the risk of privacy breaches, as the network traffic it exchanges can be vulnerable to attacks. To address this issue, a proposed anomaly detection system utilises FL and DP to ensure privacy for data owners. Additionally, ML techniques are employed to enhance the security of network traffic [34]. Another proposed solution involves a collaborative FL architecture enabled by blockchain technology (BT). This architecture utilises DP to protect user data and employs blockchain for secure data sharing [35]. Theoretical analysis has demonstrated that this system effectively safeguards data sharing processes.

DP is a technique that ensures privacy while sacrificing some prediction accuracy in ML models. To address this, a proposed end-to-end pipeline for health data streams incorporates FL and DP mechanisms. The pipeline incorporates an optimisation technique to decrease the time required for generating the models, all while preserving a high level of accuracy [36]. By implementing DP, the system ensures secure data sharing, and the findings reveal that the modification only leads to a 2% decrease in the prediction accuracy of the trained model. Furthermore, DP is utilised in a collaborative setting during FL training for the classification of medical images [37]. The outcomes demonstrate that the decentralised federated training approach, with safeguards provided by DP, achieves performance that is comparable to the traditional training system.

Maintaining privacy is crucial in an intelligent house setting where various IoT gadgets capture your medical history and other types of information. A detector has been created to identify Alzheimer's disease by analysing user audio gathered from different IoT devices. To ensure privacy, the detector utilises a novel differentially personal-based sequential secure integration approach. This framework guarantees confidentiality while also proposing an encryption approach to protect the anonymity of the mean during each cycle of the algorithm. The method relies on the assumption that solving a discrete algorithm problem is difficult. The results show that the disease detection module performs effectively while maintaining a high level of security.

12.4.1.4 Homomorphic encryption

Homomorphic encryption (HE) represents a unique form of password protection that permits mathematical operations over cypher text without the need for decryption [38]. This makes it particularly useful for encrypting model updates in FL systems, as the updates can be aggregated without the need for decryption.

HE is utilised in the context of analysing diabetes data using FL to ensure privacy. In this process, an outside contributor was involved to produce accessible and private password combinations. An open password is then shared with the participants [39], who use it to encrypt their modelling changes prior to submitting them to the platform. The FL server might collect these encrypted changes without decrypting them before transmitting back the weights that have been modified. This approach, known as the federated forest algorithm, has demonstrated promising results in terms of both the security of data and predictability. Precisely, another application of FL involves a cancer text classification system, which also employs homomorphic encryption to secure the communication of variables in the model between FL participants and the server [27].

One possible solution to tackle the problem of data islands is to employ a hybrid ML model. This model incorporates HE to safely deliver the necessary information to train ML models [40]. Furthermore, a vertical FL system has been created to compress and decompress elements while transmitting them, thereby enhancing the security of the data. The outcomes of this approach demonstrate the feasibility of multi-modal learning and show improved accuracy compared to using only a single modality.

A proposed solution has been introduced to defend against data island-level contamination assaults in clinical evaluation. This secure FL system utilises multikey computation and a reduced-optimised strategy to protect against different types of data island-level contamination assaults. Additionally, to ensure the security of personal information, a portable diagnostic technique that uses various keys using HE has been suggested [41].

A collaborative learning protocol has been suggested for situations where saving resources is important and privacy is a concern. This protocol involves transferring the main learning part of a neural network model to cloud servers, which helps save resources for participants. To maintain privacy while transmitting data and updating the model between participants and hosts, minimal information tampering and compressed partly HE techniques are used [42].

12.4.1.5 Edge device intelligence

Edge intelligent computing is widely considered suitable for utilisation in the healthcare field, particularly in conjunction with FL, due to its ability to minimise the transmission of customer's personal information towards the clouds [43]. In this approach, the basic version is collected by border gateways from the cloud, and subsequently, the model is trained using data gathered from edge-intelligent devices. To ensure the security of model parameters after training at the gateways, a virtual signature and mask will be employed. A cloud-based aggregator includes a standard filter array before transmitting the modified version to its entry points. Since no distortion is introduced to the system's variables, this system demonstrates higher accuracy compared to systems that rely on DP for protecting client data.

To enhance knowledge at the boundary, one approach is to integrate a data analytics framework on the edge. This framework can assist the FL module in retraining local ML models using personalised insights from users [44]. Hakak *et al.* [44] have presented a structure that incorporates cloud, edge, and application modules to ensure data privacy. By enabling the collection of information at both the personal product and global database levels, the confidentiality of information is preserved. The local controller saves the data based on application requirements, and the newly created secured remote values are collected remotely through a remote aggregation. The aggregated results are then sent to the cloud aggregator, which changes the global structure. HE is utilised, allowing calculations to be performed on sensitive information rather than the requirement for decryption.

Wang *et al.* [45] introduced a new approach to address variable aggressiveness in FL and its implementation on low-capacity peripheral gadgets. The objective was to enhance safety by minimising transmission and processing burdens. The researchers have put forward a unique method called orthogonal gradient aggregation (OGA), which safeguards previously acquired information even if relevant training samples are eliminated, thereby ensuring data privacy.

Wang *et al.* [43] introduce a privacy protection scheme for federated learning (PPFLEC) in the context of edge computing. The scheme utilises a novel security mechanism that relies on a common secret and electronic masking. The technique employs the stochastic masking method for encryption and emphasises minimal characteristics, making it well-suited for IoMT at the edge. Additionally, the proposed approach incorporates a hashing algorithm and a private key to guarantee message authenticity and safeguard it against replay attacks.

Edge computing involves performing computations on the margins with secret keys, which can lead to significant resource overhead for IoT devices with limited capabilities. To address this issue and improve data privacy while keeping complexity low, Akter *et al.* [32] suggested the use of an edge aggregator. This aggregator adds variation to the parameter values for the model of clients and incorporates DP techniques while managing the security cost. The findings of their study demonstrated that this approach resulted in excellent precision in modelling.

12.4.1.6 Blockchain

FL is a technique that enables numerous participants to collectively train a shared model rather than disclosing their individual information in its raw form. Although one of the main challenges in FL is ensuring the trustworthiness of participating devices and preventing malicious behaviour. If a participant intentionally provides corrupted data, it can significantly impact the accuracy of the model. Additionally, there is a need for fairness and transparency in rewarding participants for their contributions.

To address these challenges, BT can be utilised in managing the FL method, avoiding the need for middlemen. A blockchain is a distributed database that maintains transactions safely and publicly. In the realm of FL, blockchain has the potential to establish an unchangeable and easily accessible log of the data provided by every participant, ensuring transparency. This helps to maintain the quality of the information and allows for a fair distribution of rewards. By leveraging BT, FL can overcome privacy concerns and enhance trust among participants [11, 46].

The FL-chain system utilises BT to identify and verify participating devices through a shared key [47]. It guarantees that only reliable gadgets are permitted to take part in the process of development. Moreover, gadgets might be motivated to engage in the process of development by receiving credentials as rewards that can subsequently be traded for products or activities.

BT has the potential to revolutionise the model selection and ML processes by introducing transparency and decentralisation [48]. Through the conventional FL method, decision-making is often handled by a central webserver. On the other hand, within an FL-chain system, the method of choice can be distributed, which guarantees fairness and transparency in decision-making. Similarly, in traditional ML, model owners must trust a centralised platform to handle transactions. But with FL-chain, transactions might be controlled in a distributed and visible manner, establishing fairness and trustworthiness. This decentralised approach can be totally distributed, partly distributed, or in a mixed mode, depending on the specific requirements.

Chang, Fang, and Sun *et al.* [49] introduced an FL-chain mechanism that incorporates an adaptable DP method. This method dynamically manages the level of sound by incorporating a threshold, aiming to strike a balance between confidentiality and efficiency in a Mobile Internet of Things (MIoT) setting. One notable advantage of this FL-chain mechanism is its implementation of a consensus protocol based on gradient verification, which effectively safeguards against malicious attacks and the risk of a single perspective of loss.

Passerat-Palmbach *et al.* [50] introduced a framework called FL-chain, which consists of six components. This framework aims to enhance the security and durability of electronic health data while ensuring privacy. Computational assurances, confidentiality assurances, discoverable data and computational method, created value, and reliability of data are the six factors.

Salim and Park *et al.* [51] introduced a safe EHR technique in a clinic that utilised BT and FL. In this system, private data is stored in the Inter Planetary File System (IPFS). The IPFS keeps track of the hashed addresses of all EHRs using a network based on the Consortium blockchain. Individual patients are given access to their EHR through innovative agreements. The EHR information is evaluated either at a local level or on a global scale.

Lakhan *et al.* [52] developed a rule-based blockchain system for fraud detection using the IoMT FL technology. Their research introduced the FL-chain-enabled task scheduling (FL-BETS) structure, which utilises adaptive strategies to address security and information theft problems across multiple domains.

12.4.1.7 Hybrid and diverse methods

In this section, we will explore various approaches that aim to enhance data privacy while minimising computational and communication overhead. One such approach is the combination of BT with HE. This hybrid solution offers a decentralised and transparent privacy-preserving solution for smart parking, ensuring strong privacy protection with minimal resource requirements [2].

- Various approaches have been utilised to ensure privacy in federated learning (FL) systems.
- The unique nature of edge computing sets it apart from other categories, making it difficult to classify it in a separate category.

To address the privacy concerns in FL systems, a novel approach called the syntactic anonymity approach has been proposed [53]. Unlike the traditional differential privacy approach, this approach offers interpretable universal privacy guarantees while maintaining good model accuracy. The training process is tailored to fulfil the constraints of the semantic protection approach. In a healthcare context, this approach was applied to forecast negative medication responses and death rates using sensitive data, and its performance was compared to that of a centralised model.

A solution is proposed in [28] to address the problem of irrelevant updates in privacy-preserving FL. The method utilises a non-interactive password generation mechanism to securely aggregate model changes on the FL system. The orientation of the structure variable, which represents the gradient's guidance, dictates how the system is revised, and the impact of each regional change is decided accordingly. The findings demonstrate that this approach can expedite modelling convergence while maintaining strong predicted reliability in a safe way.

Innovative methods aim to enhance the reliability of FL approaches by combining the advantages of multiple approaches. These approaches help to accelerate the convergence speed of FL designs but also improve their accuracy by enhancing the quality of the data. Furthermore, incorporating domain-specific knowledge during training can enhance the robustness of the models.

In the field of radiology, researchers [54] utilised FL to address the challenges imposed by confidentiality and information exchange standards. They proposed an anomaly detection system [55] to maintain user data privacy, and their findings show that this post-quantised FL approach efficiently identifies harmful activities with significant precision while ensuring confidentiality. To tackle secure evaluation using dynamically split information, [56] suggested establishing numerous algorithms across various categories.

In the domain of securing medical devices, Otoum *et al.* [57] proposed a federated system that employs transfer learning and neural networks. Their model outperformed other models in central training programmes. Chamikara *et al.* [58] introduced a secure approach for symmetrical FL networks that demonstrated superior behaviour on the basis of scalability, precision, effectiveness, and threat tolerance. Nguyen *et al.* [59] presented a distributed FL approach that relies on knowledge distillation focused on the security and confidentiality of data. Their model exhibited high performance even with poor-quality data. Luo *et al.* [60] presented a unique approach for fitting the generic regular hybrid simulation, which offered benefits such as seamless operation, security of data, and rapid convergence in healthcare profiles.

Ma *et al.* [61] suggested an enhanced distributed vector factoring method to minimise broadband transmission expenses. Additionally, these results demonstrated that the proposed model's rapid rate of convergence was not compromised even when aggressive communication compression techniques were employed. Wu *et al.* [62] proposed an FL approach that effectively reduced transmission expenses through the use of several strategies. The outcomes revealed a significant decrease in transmission expenses while maintaining comparative performance.

Paragliola [63] introduced a technique to enhance the efficiency of the FL procedure by finding a middle ground between the precision of the model and transmission expenses. This approach aims to minimise the total number of variables transmitted between clients and servers by improving efficiency without sacrificing performance.

To mitigate the resource constraints faced by IoT devices in edge computing, researchers have proposed various solutions. For instance, Han *et al.* [64] proposed an encryption technique to ensure the correctness of scientific information and demonstrated their resilience against traditional and mathematical assaults. Gong *et al.* [65] developed an FL framework for monitoring human interaction, incorporating LSTM to address this non-IID nature that characterises the dispersed information used to train the model. Their model outperformed other comparative models in terms of performance. In order to tackle the issue of unfairness through FL, Siniosoglou *et al.* [66] suggested an unstructured equality technique that effectively identified flawed designs, yielding positive outcomes. Recognising the vulnerability of existing distributed FL approaches to Byzantium assaults, Gouissem *et al.* [67] presented an adaptive serverless FL approach that employed simultaneous updates. This suggested paradigm demonstrated highly efficient transmission of error mitigation and interactive separation decisions for malevolent users.

12.4.1.8 Industry 5.0

To improve the safety of FL for Industry 5.0 in healthcare systems, several key implications need to be considered:

1. Data encryption: Implementing strong encryption techniques ensures that data remains secure during transmission and storage. Encryption algorithms like AES (advanced encryption standard) can be used to protect sensitive data.

2. Secure communication: Employing secure communication protocols, such as Transport Layer Security (TLS), helps safeguard data during transmission between devices or servers. This prevents unauthorised access and eavesdropping.

3. Access control: Implementing strict access control mechanisms ensures that only authorised personnel can access the FL system. This includes user authentication, role-based access control, and regular audits to monitor and manage access privileges.

4. Data anonymisation: Before participating in FL, patient data should be anonymised to remove personally identifiable information. This reduces the risk of data breaches and protects patient privacy.

5. Model aggregation: During the FL process, the aggregated model should be carefully validated and audited to ensure that it doesn't inadvertently leak sensitive information. This step helps maintain the integrity and privacy of the trained model.

6. Robust security measures: Implementing robust security measures, such as intrusion detection systems, firewalls, and regular security updates, helps protect the FL infrastructure from potential cyber threats.

By considering these implications, the safety of FL in healthcare systems can be significantly improved. It allows for collaborative model training while preserving data privacy and security, making it a suitable approach for Industry 5.0 in healthcare.

12.4.2 RQ 2

The next question of the study is "What is the current status of privacy-enhancing measures in healthcare systems in FL? Can you provide information about their benefits, limitations, and trade-offs?"

The next question of study is addressed by analysing each of the different process styles discussed in the analysis of the literature conducted for the first research question. Table 12.4 provides an in-depth discussion of some of the main advantages associated with each sort of privacy enhancement method.

Table 12.5 provides an in-depth discussion of the failures associated with each sort of privacy enhancement method.

12.4.2.1 Hierarchical methods

Layered structures offer advantages in the form of separation and openness by incorporating several remote servers and implementing a simple aggregation process.

Table 12.4 Significant advantages of enhanced confidentiality techniques in current evaluation surveys

Advantage	**HM**	**P2PS**	**DP**	**HE**	**EI**	**BC**	**HYM**
Confidentiality	True	True	True	True	True	True	True
Safety	True	True	Partial	Partial	True	True	True
Globalisation	True	True	Partial	Partial	True	True	True
Openness	True		True	True	True	True	True
Data administration	True	True		True	True	True	True
Cooperation	True	True	True	True	True	True	True
Flexibility	True	True	True	True	True		True
Computing power	True	True	True	True	True		True
Communication of information	True		True	True			True
Acceptance of faults		True		True	True	True	True
Renewable power		True			True		
Enhanced stability		True			True		True
Automation of smart contracts		True				True	Maybe
Geographic spread		True			True	True	True

Table 12.5 Significant failure of enhanced confidentiality techniques in current evaluation surveys

Failure	HM	P2PS	DP	HE	EI	BC	HYM
Flexibility		True	True	True	True	True	True
Computation cost	Maybe		True	True	True	True	True
Communication cost	True	True	True	True	True	True	True
Confidentiality issues	Partial	True	Partial	Partial	True	True	True
Creative difficulty	True	True	True	True	True	True	True
Utilisation of energy	Partial	True	True	True	No	True	True
Administration	True	True		True	True	True	True
Multidisciplinary systems		True			True		True
Conflict of information and systems		True			True		True

These features make hierarchical techniques well-suited for various FL purposes. The geographically dispersed structure of the network, along with interaction at different tiers, enhances privacy and security within the FL system. Hierarchical systems excel in governance and collaboration, as they serve as a structured framework for managing and controlling data as well as organising customers efficiently.

These approaches offer a significant advantage in terms of scalability. By adding more clients, demand and administration costs can be distributed among additional edge servers. Although the computing power and consumption of resources may increase at data centres and remote servers when more clients participate, the impact on the clients themselves is minimal. However, managing a significant amount of both clients and servers, as well as implementing effective consolidation techniques, can be complex and challenging, posing administration and technical difficulties as significant obstacles in these systems.

Hierarchical approaches in FL have been explored to address the distribution of network load and ensure balanced client grouping. However, a deeper understanding of the choices associated with these techniques is necessary to assess the safety risks associated with critical user data and potential risks from adversaries at distinct network stages. The inclusion of several remote servers exposes additional susceptible actors that require robust security measures to protect participant data. Moreover, the addition of many layers in the hierarchy may result in higher convergence times for the global model, which is an important consideration for systems that require actual job scheduling.

12.4.2.2 Peer-to-peer sharing

P2PS innovation has become increasingly popular in FL applications due to its numerous advantages. One key benefit is the improved privacy it offers. The sharing of innovations among participants allows for direct communication, which helps to minimise the risk of personal information being exposed by independent organisations and minimises the likelihood of privacy incidents. Furthermore, P2PS enhances the resilience of FL systems by reducing the impact of individual failures. Even if one participant becomes unavailable, the remaining members might proceed to collaborate and contribute to the development of their skills.

Another advantage of P2PS systems is the utilisation of computing resources among several actors. Each participant contributes its own computational resources, leading to a significant improvement in the total computing capacity of the FL system. As additional users join the P2PS, the number of computational resources grows, allowing the FL system to successfully handle enormous datasets or sophisticated models.

P2PS in FL also facilitates one-on-one interaction among consumers, eliminating the need for a primary server. This helps to ease network bottlenecks and reduces the average delay in the framework, resulting in a larger and faster FL system.

Last, P2PS might cover many geographic regions, allowing users diversified involvement within the FL system. This enables the generation of a predictive model using a wider range of input data, enhancing the system's effectiveness and adaptability.

While P2P FL systems offer several advantages in terms of privacy, they also have some limitations. One challenge is handling large-scale networks with an infinite number of users. Coordinating and synchronising model updates becomes difficult, and maintaining network connections and ensuring transmission dependability becomes more challenging as the number of users increases. Ensuring the reliability of all participants becomes challenging due to the absence of administrative leadership, while the close interaction among users can pose security risks like theft of information and illegal access.

The system can be exploited by malicious participants to access and manipulate sensitive user data. Moreover, decentralised resource discovery mechanisms make it challenging to find suitable participants with the desired computational resources. FL systems suffer from overall performance issues due to the difficulty of identifying capable and trustworthy participants.

Furthermore, transmission between users and variations in the model can result in latency and increased expenses for communication. Transmitting significant variations in the model across users increases the bandwidth requirements and transmission delay. These factors need to be considered when implementing P2P FL systems.

During the design of a P2P FL system, trade-offs must be considered. While distributed computing provides many advantages, it may also lead to resource imbalances due to the heterogeneity of capabilities. P2P sharing of model updates in FL raises concerns about privacy due to the fact that it keeps user data on local devices. Establishing trust among participants is crucial for maintaining data integrity and confidentiality. The lack of centralised control in P2P introduces security risks, which can be mitigated through encryption and authentication measures. While P2P allows for scalability by distributing computational tasks, coordinating and synchronising the learning process becomes challenging with a larger number of participants. Transferring large model parameters consumes significant bandwidth and increases latency, so it is essential to balance network efficiency and communication overhead.

The use of resources, the security of data, flexibility, and system effectiveness need to be balanced with these trade-offs.

12.4.2.3 Differential privacy

DP ensures a mathematical guarantee of privacy for information collected by users by ensuring that certain data points are able to be distinguished from the model parameters in a decentralised manner. This means that no centralised authority is necessary to handle the enhanced privacy, which improves the FL system's security. With the addition of randomness to the algorithm's variables prior to aggregation, it becomes more difficult for attackers to extract information through model inversion attacks.

DP operates on a quantifiable framework with defined privacy guarantees, confidentiality costs, and acoustic variation, fostering user confidence. While certain basic interactions with parameters might be necessary, real computation is performed by each user, making it a distributed method that aligns well with the FL systems architecture.

It is vital to note that DP does not directly contribute to the management of data in an FL environment. DP does not handle issues such as the integrity of information, information accessibility regulations, and knowledge administration. However, the usage of DP in FL fosters collaboration and offers a higher level of security with regard to personal sources of information, which aligns with the collaborative principles of FL systems.

The use of DP in large-scale systems can pose challenges in terms of scalability. As the number of clients increases, more noise is required to provide privacy guarantees, which can impact the performance of machine learning algorithms in federated learning systems. Additionally, clients must do more computations to introduce variation to the algorithm's variables, leading to increased computational overhead and design complexity. This is particularly problematic for resource-constrained IoT devices, as it also results in higher energy consumption. Furthermore, since governance is not inherently included in differential privacy approaches, it is necessary to implement relevant structures, regulations, and methodologies to ensure efficient information and resource allocation.

In the context of FL, the privacy of user information is protected by DP, which ensures that individual identities cannot be reconstructed from the shared data. However, the introduction of noise to the data in order to achieve privacy can negatively impact the accuracy of ML algorithms. Striking a compromise between confidentiality and precision is a key topic of focus for future research in DP, particularly in different domains where context awareness is important.

Precision is crucial in the medical profession for predictive techniques used in disease detection and related applications. Balancing high privacy guarantees with high accuracy in healthcare FL systems remains a significant challenge. Additional methods are needed to mitigate the impact of DP on system accuracy in order to meet the critical requirement of maintaining both privacy and accuracy in healthcare FL systems.

12.4.2.4 Homomorphic encryption

HE aligns with the decentralised design of FL by enabling encryption at the client level, necessitating a specific type of password administration. This cryptography technique enhances the confidentiality and trustworthiness of FL solutions by ensuring that information and parameters associated with the model stay private through the process of acquisition, movement, and aggregate processes. The use of the same encryption/decryption methods by all clients promotes transparency in the HE structure. Teamwork is facilitated in HE-based systems because users retain ownership over the data they share and can perform calculations based on protected common data for the model without compromising security. Although HE provides some support for governance, additional mechanisms are necessary to handle tasks like sharing encryption keys, managing data throughout its lifecycle, and handling consent.

In FL, HE-based techniques have certain drawbacks, particularly in the area of energy utilisation. Encoding adds complexity to the layout, leading to higher computational overhead and higher power usage, especially for limited-supply IoT applications. Scalability becomes an issue on FL platforms with a significant number of users since the processing needs increase dramatically owing to the extra difficulty of encrypting information calculations. While HE promotes confidentiality, it is not without its flaws. Vulnerabilities in information have the potential to possibly disclose secrets and expose important information and calculation specifics. Additionally, administration becomes a crucial aspect, as managing encryption keys poses a challenge.

In decentralised FL scenarios with distributed data and varying computational capacities among participants, it becomes necessary to develop new algorithms that efficiently utilise computational resources. This involves considering the specific computational requirements of different ML techniques and employing a collection of homomorphic techniques to optimise performance. As mentioned earlier, it is important to balance scalability and privacy-accuracy trade-offs when designing homomorphic algorithms tailored for FL applications.

12.4.2.5 Edge device intelligence

The primary advantage of incorporating information from cutting-edge technologies into FL networks is improved privacy. The distributed design guarantees that personal safety is maintained and that regulatory compatibility is upheld. Furthermore, this distributed approach enables scalability, enabling larger amounts of data and greater computational efficiency. By merely communicating new models and consolidated outcomes, transmission costs are decreased, system assets are conserved, and delay is reduced. Rapid computation and interpretation on mobile devices enable immediate responses while also improving system robustness and fault tolerance. Additionally, the consumption of energy is enhanced since this type of processing reduces the requirement for constant transfer across networks. Edge intelligence has various benefits that make it an excellent option for FL systems that prioritise confidentiality, minimised interaction, immediate response time, robustness, cost-effectiveness, and adaptability.

However, there are constraints when it comes to edge intelligence in FL systems. The computing power available on mobile phones is limited, which restricts model complexity and training capabilities. Device heterogeneity, resulting from differences in software and hardware, can make performance and scalability more challenging. Data imbalances among distributed datasets can impact model performance. Network bandwidth and latency can pose challenges for sharing data and updating models. The vulnerability of edge devices raises security concerns, necessitating robust security measures that are not provided by the edge devices themselves.

When incorporating edge intelligence in FL platforms, some alternatives must be considered. The computational capabilities of the devices may limit the complexity of the models that can be used. This limitation can potentially compromise the accuracy of the models. Additionally, since the availability and reliability of data can differ across equipment, safeguarding anonymity can have an impact on the quality and ability of models to generalise. While local processing on edge devices enhances energy efficiency, more complex models can consume higher amounts of energy. The wide range of edge technologies can also affect scalability, requiring additional efforts to ensure compatibility. To effectively harness edge intelligence in FL structures, it is crucial to strike a balance between predictive power, confidentiality, flexibility, processor speed, unified control, and cost-effectiveness.

12.4.2.6 Blockchain

BT offers several advantages when applied to FL systems, particularly with regard to confidentiality, safety, and transparency. Its decentralised nature, combined with its cryptographic algorithms and immutability, enhances the confidentiality and safety of data in FL. By storing information locally on individual devices and utilising blockchain's cryptographic features, sensitive information remains private through the development, movement, and aggregate processes.

Additionally, the apparent characteristic of blockchain allows all individuals involved in FL systems to have access to information regarding modifications and updates made to the collaborative model. This transparency promotes trust and ensures that all participants can verify the integrity of the model updates. Collaboration is further facilitated by the decentralised and secure characteristics of blockchain, as participants have increased confidence in the distributed paradigm and the accuracy of their revisions due to BT's agreement process and permanence.

Furthermore, the automation capabilities of smart contracts embedded in BT are particularly advantageous for FL systems. Data consumption policies can be defined and enforced using digital agreements in accordance with specified laws and guidelines. The FL systems with this feature are enhanced in terms of governance, consent management, and data lifecycle management.

While BT offers certain advantages in terms of privacy and decentralisation in FL structures, it also has restrictions. One limitation is that blockchain's transparency can expose sensitive information, which can be detrimental to the privacy of a distributed ledger system [49–52]. To address this, additional enhanced privacy techniques are often integrated into FL-chain systems to improve privacy protection.

Another limitation is the computational overhead associated with the decision procedures used in distributed ledger systems [49–52]. When multiple participants are involved, maintaining the blockchain requires significant computational resources. This can result in slower training speeds, reduced system efficiency, and scalability challenges. Additionally, the energy consumption required for computation in blockchain networks can be substantial.

Scalability is another concern when incorporating blockchain into FL systems. Blockchain networks often face limitations in terms of scalability, which can impact the processing time and reduce scalability. The integration of a distributed ledger into an FL structure requires careful planning and cooperation, including the development of smart necessitate contracts, the definition of collective decision-making processes, and the assurance of interoperability with current FL standards. This complexity can lengthen production duration and cost.

Achieving a unified position on system upgrades, protocol changes, or policy modifications in FL systems requires significant collaboration and cooperation across individuals, which can potentially impede the speed of decision-making processes. Therefore, careful consideration and coordination are necessary to ensure effective governance in FL systems incorporating BT.

When considering the use of BT in FL healthcare systems, it is critical to thoroughly assess the consequences involved. While its distributed design can enhance safety and openness, it may also pose challenges in terms of sustainability. The openness provided by cryptocurrency allows all participants to view actions, which can improve confidence and accountability but may conflict with confidentiality concerns in FL applications. Additionally, the encryption and collaborative approaches used in blockchain can enhance security but may introduce computational overhead, potentially impacting the efficiency of FL structures, particularly in development.

Implementing cryptocurrency in an FL environment necessitates extensive innovation and competence, including the implementation of intelligent agreements, negotiation methods, and compatibility with current FL technologies. This intricate design can increase the difficulties associated with future support for the system.

When it comes to governance and decision-making, time and cost are important considerations. The task of making decisions can be slowed down due to the need for substantial cooperation and consensus among parties when it comes to technology upgrades, shifts in policy, and procedural modifications.

Overall, it is crucial to carefully consider a variety of factors in designing an FL-chain healthcare system, including flexibility, restructuring, reliability, safety, insertion, administration, and accountability.

12.4.2.7 Hybrid and diverse methods

Hybrid and diverse methods of privacy protection for FL strive to integrate various techniques to establish effective and resilient security architecture. These methods enable precise control over privacy considerations at every stage of the FL method. They investigate methods that ensure robust confidentiality assurances at the expense of appropriate system precision and efficiency. Additionally, these approaches offer the ability to meet a wide range of privacy needs and operational restrictions. By incorporating different strategies, they enhance the security of FL systems against personal assaults. Moreover, they prioritise flexibility and connectivity with other FL mechanisms and facilities, fostering on-going advancements and inventions in safeguarding personal data. It is important to note that the effectiveness of these approaches depends on the selection, combination, and proper implementation of techniques. It is essential to consider individual privacy needs, dataset features, and technology limits when establishing the best strategy for an existing FL framework.

Using different privacy mechanisms in a combined method can make the FL system more complex. It can also create challenges related to scalability and reliability when integrating multiple privacy approaches. Technologies like encoding, safe multiparty computing, and DP might raise the system's capacity for processing and the need for interaction. Balancing the security of personal data and the effectiveness of the model might necessitate accepting decisions. Additionally, integrating several privacy mechanisms might lead to additional vulnerabilities or access paths, necessitating careful configuration and parameter tuning. Developing and maintaining an FL system that incorporates multiple privacy techniques requires additional effort. The use of security-enhancing technologies in FL is still developing, and regulation is restricted. To overcome such flaws, it is crucial to thoroughly investigate and implement mixed, hybrid, and diverse methods, considering the difficulty, productivity effect, and safety in mind. This will allow us to build on the advantages of these techniques while limiting their shortcomings in the overall framework of FL.

The integration of various techniques in HE and FL involves decisions that must be seriously considered. These decisions include complexity versus success, confidentiality versus usefulness, speed versus anonymity, adaptability versus modification, safety versus difficulty, and uniformity versus customisation. To address these decisions, it is important to conduct a thorough evaluation and study of the individual use case, taking into account the priorities, constraints, and goals of the federated learning system. Informed decisions about the implementation and use of hybrid and other privacy-improving techniques should be made by considering these factors.

12.4.2.8 Industry 5.0

In the context of FL for Industry 5.0, privacy-enhancing measures in healthcare systems are crucial to protect sensitive patient data while enabling collaborative ML. These measures aim to strike a balance between data privacy and the benefits of sharing data for improved healthcare outcomes.

Benefits of privacy-enhancing measures in healthcare systems include:

1. Data privacy: By implementing techniques like differential privacy, FL ensures that individual patient data remains private and secure. This is particularly important in healthcare, where patient confidentiality is of utmost importance.

2. Data access: FL allows healthcare organisations to collaborate and share insights without directly sharing raw patient data. This enables access to a larger and more diverse dataset, leading to improved models and better healthcare outcomes.

3. Regulatory compliance: Privacy-enhancing measures help healthcare systems comply with data protection regulations, such as the General Data Protection

Regulation (GDPR) and the Health Insurance Portability and Accountability Act (HIPAA). This ensures that patient data is handled in a legally compliant manner.

However, privacy-enhancing measures in healthcare systems also have limitations and trade-offs:

1. Computational overhead: Implementing privacy-enhancing techniques like encryption and differential privacy can introduce additional computational overhead. This may result in increased training time and resource requirements.

2. Model performance: Privacy-preserving techniques can impact the performance of ML models. By limiting access to raw data, FL may result in slightly lower model accuracy compared to traditional centralised approaches. However, advancements in FL techniques aim to minimise this performance gap.

3. Data heterogeneity: FL relies on collaboration between multiple healthcare organisations, which may have different data formats, quality, and distribution. Managing data heterogeneity can be challenging and may require additional preprocessing and standardisation efforts.

In summary, privacy-enhancing measures in healthcare systems for FL in Industry 5.0 offer significant benefits in terms of data privacy, access, and regulatory compliance. However, they also come with limitations such as computational overhead, potential impact on model performance, and the need to address data heterogeneity. Ongoing research and advancements in privacy-preserving techniques aim to mitigate these limitations and improve the overall effectiveness of FL in healthcare.

12.4.3 RQ 3

The next question of the study is "What does the future hold for enhanced privacy techniques in healthcare systems using FL?"

The answer to the next question of the study is derived from the analysis of the eight factors discussed within the scientific review conducted for the first research question.

12.4.3.1 Hierarchical methods

Previous FL research has primarily concentrated on hierarchical approaches. These approaches involve grouping clients or implementing a hierarchy of structures to evenly distribute the network load across connected devices. The goal is to minimise the impact of customer relocation or differences in capabilities. These techniques are valuable for improving the security of personal data in federated learning environments because they offer a further level of regulation for the transfer of information between customers, remote servers, and cloud-based servers. By utilising hierarchical architectures to establish servers and clients, it becomes easier to facilitate privacy-preserving collaboration [24–26].

To enhance the security of critical user data in order to mitigate the risks posed by attackers in cyberspace, further work is necessary. It is essential to establish secure communication mechanisms that prioritise privacy at every stage of the organisation in FL. Incorporating fine-grained privacy guarantees into these approaches will enable precise decision-making regarding the transmission of data and user interaction.

To instill trust in the system, a dynamic hierarchical structure can be implemented, allowing users to interact with servers that they are familiar with or confidence. Additionally, customised aggregation mechanisms should be developed to cater to the specific requirements of different applications while ensuring privacy preservation. Furthermore, effective workflow control is critical to ensuring compliance with privacy laws and preventing any potential data loss. By addressing these aspects, the overall privacy and security of the FL system can be significantly improved.

12.4.3.2 Peer-to-peer sharing

P2PS offers several advantages, including strong privacy assurances, enhanced availability of data, decentralised computational resources, geographical diversity, teaching and learning opportunities, improved flexibility, and enhanced fault resilience. However, there are numerous areas where P2PS can be further improved in the context of FL. One promising area for improvement is the development of novel methods and interfaces that address transmission overhead and alignment issues, with the goal of reducing transmission costs and ensuring effective synchronisation. Additionally, it is important to consider challenges related to safety and reliability, networking and transmission costs, management and oversight, as well as acceptance and scalability when enhancing P2PS in FL.

The implementation of P2PS technologies for FL brings forth numerous significant benefits, including the possibility of enhanced confidentiality, improved cooperation, and increased computational capacity through distributed systems. Although it is crucial to address security challenges, effectively manage network overhead, establish suitable governance models, and ensure compatibility to ensure the successful implementation of this technology.

Furthermore, while the distributed design of P2PS on FL is highly significant, optimising the basis of the structure continues to be a complicated and ongoing process. This optimisation is necessary to effectively address the resource-intensive nature of ML workloads. Additionally, enhancing P2PS is crucial for the development of privacy-preserving mechanisms, which serve a vital function in increasing confidentiality and security within the P2PS framework. Moreover, the majority of techniques offer a good option for members of the P2PS system to establish acceptance of information or concepts. However, in order to obtain consensus on massive quantities of data, new consensus mechanisms are required.

To summarise, the future endeavours of P2PS should prioritise the creation of novel methods and interfaces for transmission and alignment. It should also concentrate on enhancing the distributed design, devising novel secure methods and acceptance processes, and establishing assessment measures. Overall success using P2PS technologies in an FL network hinges on various factors such as execution, network attributes, privacy policies, and organisational structures. By ensuring a well-thought-out architecture and efficient operation of every aspect of the P2P facilities while also resolving possible problems, we can maximise the effectiveness of P2PS in FL circumstances.

12.4.3.3 Differential privacy

DP is widely embraced by major technology companies like Apple, Google, and Facebook as it offers a robust approach to quantifying privacy assurances in FL systems. The fundamental concept of differential privacy is that machine learning algorithms should produce similar results regardless of whether one individual's data is included or excluded from the dataset. By collecting and sharing data from multiple participants, differential privacy guarantees that the personal information of any individual cannot be reconstructed, thus safeguarding user privacy.

DP offers a robust solution for protecting the transmission of ML variables between users and FL or remote servers [32–34, 36]. It encompasses most of the necessary features to address the problems that arise from potential data loss throughout the exchange of modelling parameters [31, 35, 37]. DP ensures that confidential patient data cannot be reverse-engineered or inferred from health-related information by effectively controlling the level of variation introduced throughout the FL framework consolidation method.

Moving on to DP, this strategy safeguards the confidentiality of information by adding variation to the predictive ability of ML techniques employed by FL applications. To strike a compromise between confidentiality and precision, it is crucial to develop novel consolidation methods designed for DP in FL. While previous consolidating methods like the Federated Averaging (FedAvg) algorithm utilise stochastic methodologies to ensure DP, their rate of success may decrease when faced with malicious assaults. Therefore, it is necessary to design more sophisticated aggregation techniques that can survive such assaults while still maintaining robust privacy assurances. Given that FL frameworks typically include a significant number of users that interact without distributing the information they collect, scalability and the ability to deal with the technical difficulties associated with DP in FL are essential considerations for these new aggregation algorithms and techniques.

Furthermore, the evaluation of privacy guarantees in differential privacy involves assessing the currently available privacy assessment measures, which do not appear to be specifically tailored for networked systems, including FL. Consequently, it is imperative to develop appropriate and rigorous assessment measures that adjust for the particular features of FL technologies.

12.4.3.4 Homomorphic encryption

HE is a technique that ensures privacy in FL applications by enabling calculations that can be carried out on sensitive information while safeguarding its confidentiality. This approach proves highly effective in preserving privacy within FL systems, as it allows essential operations such as consolidation, refinement of models, and differential computations that can be done rather than access to the original information [39–43]. By employing this kind of authentication technology, FL systems can offer an accurate and adequate choice, so that remote or distant servers involved in the consolidation process are unable to access the information. Decentralised access to personal information is ensured by granting exclusive privileges with respect to basic information to customers. This decentralised control fosters client participation in FL structures, alleviating concerns regarding the loss of sensitive patient information in healthcare applications.

Performing computations on encrypted data using HE can be resource-intensive and computationally expensive. This poses an issue in FL situations because information is shared among participants with varying computational capacities. To address this, novel methodologies must be developed to optimise the utilisation of computing power among users. It is important to take into account the specific calculations needed by various ML strategies and develop a collection of homomorphic methods that can enhance computational efficiency for these models. Additionally, when designing FL-specific homomorphic algorithms, scalability and the trade-off between privacy and accuracy should be taken into account.

12.4.3.5 Edge device intelligence

As mentioned in Section 4.1, the existing literature has explored different approaches to enhancing data privacy in health systems. These approaches include utilising different AI and ML designs, introducing sound, employing techniques for encrypting data, and more. However, further research is necessary to develop a novel privacy protection scheme specifically tailored for FL, taking into account the portability needs of healthcare IoT gadgets deployed at the edge of the network. Additionally, there continues to be potential for advancement in secure measures, for instance, integrating DP, secure multi-party computation, noisy injections, and effective cryptography approaches, to achieve improved outcomes.

In summary, it is important to highlight the significant role that expertise in cutting-edge technologies might play in enhancing confidentiality and operational effectiveness in FL. However, there are notable issues that require additional focus, including the design of optimal infrastructure and the development of novel secure processes and tactics. By tackling all of these obstacles, we might come up with improved and streamlined techniques for safeguarding privacy in FL on the boundary.

Knowledge of cutting-edge technologies in FL networks offers numerous advantages across different contexts and domains. These benefits extend beyond privacy enhancement and include flexibility, rapid interpreting, network-optimised performance, cost-effectiveness, and remote functioning. By incorporating knowledge on the outermost layer of the network, FL technologies can achieve a higher level of privacy assurance, improved security of personal information, flexibility, decreased latency on the network, instantaneous analysis, reliability, and a reduction in resource consumption. This approach empowers quick and safe ML implementations in distributed structures, making knowledge on the front lines a powerful strategy. Enabling intelligence to be utilised at the edge of the network enables FL technology to facilitate ML implementations that are both effective and risk-free.

12.4.3.6 Blockchain

In FL, BT has been implemented to enhance privacy. By utilising a distributed circumstance, it ensures a safe and secure method of exchanging and processing data through secured shared keys. As a result, information gathered at the regional level is better safeguarded with improved privacy and security. The deployment of BT in FL intends to improve privacy by utilising a distributed ecosystem. This ensures a safe and secure method for transferring and processing data through secured private keys. As a result, users' personal information is better safeguarded with improved privacy and security. The previous research discussed various approaches, such as incorporating gradients [49], additional factors [50], encrypted EHR addresses [51], and supplementary criteria [52]. All of these strategies necessitate the use of a secondary enhanced privacy tool.

The reviewed clinical scenarios [49–52] demonstrate the relevance of BT to FL. By combining these technologies, confidentiality, safety, openness, cooperation, and administration are effectively improved. However, the main obstacle is the computational burden. To ensure optimal effectiveness, decisions must be taken on the implementation of electronic agreements and agreement methods, general system architecture, appropriate learning duration, extra privacy-enhancing approaches, rules, administration, and other related factors.

While BT offers a significant amount of safety, it is not immune to threats. However, there still exist problems regarding the possibility of adversaries connecting transactions to specific participants within the network. Further research is needed to explore alternative methods for preserving privacy, such as multi-party computation, within an FL-chain framework. These techniques aim to enhance both confidentiality and safety.

Furthermore, intelligent contracts, which are autonomous contracts recorded on a digital ledger, have the potential to automate specific functions within federated learning systems. These smart contracts can help enforce established guidelines, procedures, and promotions, ensuring compliance with information use restrictions, providing prizes, and controlling system-wide administration. By reducing the reliance on manual intervention, smart contracts can enhance efficiency. It is worth noting that while autonomous vehicles were briefly referenced in one of the evaluated publications [68], further investigation is needed to fully explore their potential in the future.

To encourage more cooperation and engagement in blockchain-driven FL medical systems, it is suggested that token-based economics or incentive methods be introduced. This concept, facilitated by the advancing BT, enables the allocation of community revenue to individuals who provide benefits to the technology [69]. However, one of the 4 FL-chain programmes reviewed in this study has implemented an incentive mechanism. Therefore, implementing such systems can foster greater engagement and cooperation among users.

12.4.3.7 Hybrid and diverse methods

Integrating multiple privacy techniques through hybrid and diverse methods provides greater privacy assurances than utilising any one strategy individually. By combining different mechanisms, the problems and restrictions of each technique can be reduced, leading to improved privacy preservation. These approaches enhance data security by protecting it or doing calculations without disclosing the original data [70]. This helps reduce the chances of information loss or illegal usage. Additionally, all of these methods have the advantage of adaptability, allowing data security to be tailored according to unique needs and limitations. Private protections can be customised to the nature of the information, the need to comply with laws, or the personal choices of the persons involved.

Combining various privacy techniques can lead to challenges in terms of high computational costs, connectivity, and standardised procedures. Moreover, establishing and administering such mixed strategies might be more intricate than employing one approach at the same time [71]. Assessing the efficacy and safety of each of these methods is difficult since it might necessitate professional assessment tools and standards to measure their influence on the confidentiality, usefulness, and performance of the system as a whole.

Such hybrid techniques proved to work well in FL by efficiently resolving the problems involved with safeguarding personal information [72]. These provide a number of advantages that add to the efficacy and feasibility of maintaining confidentiality in FL.

First, these approaches establish a complete foundation for safeguarding personal information in FL by combining several mechanisms. This ensures your critical information stays protected and secret during the FL method [73]. By combining different privacy techniques, organisations can create a robust and holistic privacy protection system.

Second, these approaches provide companies with the ability to tailor and adjust security mechanisms to suit their individual security needs. This allows companies to tailor their encryption strategies to their specific usage scenarios and regulatory obligations, all while ensuring the required degree of security for personal data [74].

Furthermore, these approaches enable the optimisation of the privacy-utility compromise in FL. They ensure that the confidentiality of the augmentation has no impact on the FL method's efficacy and value, striking a compromise between confidentiality and design correctness [75].

The use of different privacy approaches further improves the FL method's resistance to privacy threats. It aids in the prevention of various sorts of privacy threats, such as inferential threats, classification threats, and simulation inverting threats.

Companies have the opportunity to show that they are committed to preserving individuals' personal data by implementing a thorough privacy strategy. This is crucial in building trust with users and stakeholders.

Moreover, scientists are integrating various methodologies to explore innovative approaches to enhance privacy safeguards and tackle increasing privacy issues, leading to the implementation of novel technologies and procedures.

Additionally, these hybrid approaches encourage collaboration across different disciplines [76]. Researchers can benefit from the merits of multiple privacy measures, fostering knowledge exchange and accelerating the development of security-enhancing technology.

In summary, these diverse techniques in FL offer a comprehensive, flexible, and effective framework for privacy protection. They enhance privacy while maintaining utility, increase the FL system's resistance to privacy threats, and foster collaboration and innovation in privacy-enhancing technologies.

The performance of privacy enhancement technologies in an FL system can be influenced by various factors, such as the types of methods used, the variety of information concerned, and the intended purpose. While hybrid and diverse techniques have the potential to enhance the security of personal information, their effectiveness may differ. Evaluating these approaches on the basis of individual circumstances is critical, considering the unique specifications, material features, and potential threats of the FL framework. Effective execution, setup, and testing are essential to ensuring the success of these approaches in enhancing privacy in FL.

To enhance future work, there is potential for exploring novel distributed FL concepts that can decrease the cost of communication and assure effective coordination. It is crucial to consider the model architecture when integrating several ML designs, as this plays a key role. Additionally, designing an appropriate optimisation algorithm can further optimise the process.

Addressing privacy concerns in the current hybrid FL approach is important. One way to safeguard the confidentiality and security of data using encrypted data in FL. It entails securing the information prior to distributing it and carrying out calculations on the data that has been encrypted. To enhance privacy and security, a strategy can be developed by combining methods related to DP, HE, and secured multi-party computing.

Integrating different privacy-enhancing strategies into FL systems might be beneficial as well. This would provide an added layer of protection for sensitive data during the collaborative learning process.

Last, developing robust evaluation metrics is essential for determining the efficacy of P2P-sharing-based FL systems. These metrics would establish a consistent set of parameters for evaluating the performance and efficiency of hybrid FL approaches.

Overall, by exploring decentralised FL models, optimising model architecture, addressing privacy concerns, integrating privacy enhancement methods, and developing appropriate assessment measures, future work on composite FL can be significantly improved.

12.4.3.8 Industry 5.0

The future of enhanced privacy techniques in healthcare systems using FL for Industry 5.0 looks promising. FL is a decentralised approach that allows multiple healthcare institutions to collaborate and train ML models without sharing sensitive patient data.

In Industry 5.0, which focuses on human-machine collaboration, privacy will be a crucial aspect. Enhanced privacy techniques will ensure that patient data remains secure and confidential throughout the FL process. Here are a few developments we can expect:

1. Differential privacy: DP techniques will be employed to add noise or perturbations to the data before sharing it with the central server. This ensures that individual patient information cannot be extracted from the aggregated data, providing a higher level of privacy.

2. Secure multi-party computation: Secure Multi-Party Computation (MPC) protocols will be used to perform computations on encrypted data. This allows healthcare institutions to collaborate on training models without revealing the underlying data, thus preserving privacy.

3. Homomorphic encryption: HE enables computations to be performed on encrypted data without decrypting it. This technique will allow healthcare institutions to securely share encrypted patient data for FL, ensuring privacy is maintained throughout the process.

4. Federated transfer learning: Federated Transfer Learning techniques will be developed to leverage knowledge gained from multiple healthcare institutions while preserving privacy. Models trained on one institution's data can be fine-tuned on another institution's data without sharing the raw data, enabling better generalisation and improved performance.

5. Privacy-preserving aggregation: Advanced aggregation techniques will be employed to combine model updates from different institutions while preserving privacy. Aggregation algorithms will be designed to prevent the leakage of sensitive information during the model update process.

Overall, the future of enhanced privacy techniques in healthcare systems using FL for Industry 5.0 holds great potential. These techniques will enable healthcare institutions to collaborate and train robust ML models while ensuring the privacy and security of patient data.

12.5 Conclusions

DL, a subset of ML, has sparked numerous advancements in the field of digital healthcare. One such innovation is FL, which offers enhanced possibilities for both research and corporate operations by ensuring the safety and confidentiality of the information provided by users. FL enables multiple individuals, in the form of medical facilities, EHRs, or MIoT gadgets at different places within the medical sector, to take part in local training while transmitting information to a main server. A streamlined approach to medicine enhances decision-making or diagnostic capabilities.

Our review aims to address the current gap in comprehensive surveys of privacy-enhancing approaches for healthcare systems using FL. We provide in-depth research and debate on 7 key fields, such as DP, HE, blockchain, hierarchical methods, P2PS, edge device intelligence, hybrid, and diverse methods. Additionally, we identify and explore the potential for future study in these areas to further improve FL confidentiality in the medical field.

The use of novel FL technology in the medical field is currently in its infancy. As such, it is important that you carefully evaluate the precise specifications, limitations, and alternatives associated with incorporating further privacy-enhancing approaches into FL systems. By experimenting with various methods and creating innovative solutions that integrate numerous strategies, we can potentially overcome the constraints of every enhanced privacy strategy and improve the entire system's long-term efficiency.

Techniques such as HE and DP offer major privacy benefits but come with cognitive and regulatory costs. However, distributed methods such as peer-to-peer systems and blockchain offer stability, flexibility, and reliability, while their privacy assurances are somewhat limited. Therefore, it is necessary to consider the benefits and limits of various techniques and conduct further study to develop a comprehensive method that can be applied to all types of medical fields employing FL-based interactive ML.

P2PS technology is suitable for use with FL systems that require shared processing capacity, flexibility, secrecy, reliability, and geographic coverage. It can also be applied for FL systems that prioritise intelligence on edge devices, where critical factors include confidentiality, decreased interactions, processing speed, resilience, cost-effectiveness, and flexibility. Additionally, hybrid and diverse methods have the potential to be used in FL systems that require identical privacy methods, smooth privacy management, a balance between confidentiality and usefulness, adaptability and portability, strong assault defence, and integration.

Patient data is highly personal and must be treated with the utmost sensitivity, confidentiality, and privacy. Unauthorised access or disclosure of this data can pose significant risks. While FL design and privacy improvement approaches offer some protection, there are ethical challenges to consider. Throughout the aggregate and transfer stages, customer information is vulnerable to security risks such as illegal usage, fraud, and intentional alteration. Accessing customer information among various organisations involves explicit permission, and a partnership between medical organisations necessitates responsibility norms and control frameworks to guarantee moral behaviour through the FL system. Biased information can also impact FL test results, so frequent inspections and testing methods should be undertaken to identify and mitigate possible biases. Additionally, failures in data transfer or the results of training might undermine trust among users of the FL system. As a result, it is critical to establish an ethical and trustworthy environment for running FL-based healthcare systems.

We strongly believe the technical innovations originating in FL would greatly improve the medical industry worldwide. The privacy-enhancing strategies discussed in this article and all of those outside it should contribute to the further advancement of FL.

References

[1] Rieke, N., Hancox, J., Li, W., *et al.* The future of digital health with federated learning. *NPJ Digit. Med.* 2020, 3, 119.

[2] Haritha, T., and Anitha, A. Asymmetric consortium blockchain and homomorphically polynomial-based PIR for secured smart parking systems. *Comput. Mater. Contin.* 2023, 75, 3923–3939.

[3] Thwal, C.M., Thar, K., Tun, Y.L., and Hong, C.S. Attention on personalized clinical decision support system: Federated learning approach. In *Proceedings of the 2021 IEEE International Conference on Big Data and Smart Computing (BigComp), Jeju Island, Republic of Korea, 17–20 January 2021*; IEEE: Jeju Island, Republic of Korea, 2021; pp. 141–147.

[4] Oldenhof, M., Ács,G., Pejó, B., *et al.* Industry-Scale Orchestrated Federated Learning for Drug Discovery. arXiv 2022, arXiv:2210.08871

[5] Mohan, N.J., Murugan, R., Goel, T., and Roy, P. DRFL: Federated learning in diabetic retinopathy grading using fundus images. *IEEE Trans. Parallel Distrib. Syst.* 2023, in press.

[6] Dayan, I., Roth, H.R., Zhong, A., *et al.* Federated learning for predicting clinical outcomes in patients with COVID-19. *Nat. Med.* 2021, 27, 1735–1743.

[7] Xu, J., Glicksberg, B.S., Su, C., Walker, P., Bian, J., and Wang, F. Federated learning for healthcare informatics. *J. Healthc. Inform. Res.* 2021, 5, 1–19.

[8] Shyu, C.R., Putra, K.T., Chen, H.C., *et al.* A systematic review of federated learning in the healthcare area: From the perspective of data properties and applications. *Appl. Sci.* 2021, 11, 11191.

[9] Pfitzner, B., Steckhan, N., and Arnrich, B. Federated learning in a medical context: A systematic literature review. *ACM Trans. Internet Technol.* 2021, 21, 50.

[10] Kumar, Y., and Singla, R. Federated learning systems for healthcare: Perspective and recent progress. In *Federated Learning Systems: Towards Next-Generation AI*; Springer: Cham, 2021; pp. 141–156.

[11] Nguyen, D.C., Ding, M., Pham, Q.V., *et al.* Federated learning meets blockchain in edge computing: Opportunities and challenges. *IEEE Internet Things J.* 2021, 8, 12806–12825.

[12] Antunes, R.S., André da Costa, C., Küderle, A., Yari, I.A., and Eskofier, B. Federated learning for healthcare: Systematic review and architecture proposal. *ACM Trans. Intell. Syst. Technol.* 2022, 13, 54.

[13] Chowdhury, A., Kassem, H., Padoy, N., Umeton, R., and Karargyris, A. A review of medical federated learning: Applications in oncology and cancer research. In *Brainlesion: Glioma, Multiple Sclerosis, Stroke and Traumatic Brain Injuries: Proceedings of the 7th International Workshop, BrainLes 2021, Held in Conjunction with MICCAI 2021, Virtual Event, 27 September 2021; Revised Selected Papers, Part I*; Springer: Berlin, 2022; pp. 3–24.

[14] Mothukuri, V., Parizi, R.M., Pouriyeh, S., Huang, Y., Dehghantanha, A., and Srivastava, G. A survey on security and privacy of federated learning. *Future Gener. Comput. Syst.* 2021, 115, 619–640.

[15] Ali, M., Naeem, F., Tariq, M., and Kaddoum, G. Federated learning for privacy preservation in smart healthcare systems: A comprehensive survey. *IEEE J. Biomed. Health Inform.* 2022, in press.

[16] Nguyen, D.C., Pham, Q.V., Pathirana, P.N., *et al.* Federated learning for smart healthcare: A survey. *ACM Comput. Surv.* 2022, 55, 60.

[17] Xu, G., Li, H., Liu, S., Yang, K., and Lin, X. Verifynet: Secure and verifiable federated learning. *IEEE Trans. Inf. Forensics Secur.* 2019, 15, 911–926.

[18] Bouacida, N., and Mohapatra, P. Vulnerabilities in federated learning. *IEEE Access* 2021, 9, 63229–63249.

[19] Novikova, E., Fomichov, D., Kholod, I., and Filippov, E. Analysis of privacy-enhancing technologies in open-source federated learning frameworks for driver activity recognition. *Sensors* 2022, 22, 2983.

[20] Liu, P., Xu, X., and Wang, W. Threats, attacks and defenses to federated learning: Issues, taxonomy and perspectives. *Cybersecurity* 2022, 5, 4.

[21] Gu, X., and Blackmore, K. Characterisation of academic journals in the digital age. *Scientometrics* 2017, 110, 1333–1350.

[22] Jacsó, P. Google Scholar: The pros and the cons. *Online Inf. Rev. 2005*, 29, 208–214.
[23] Pranckute, R. Web of Science (WoS) and Scopus: The titans of bibliographic information in today's academic world. *Publications* 2021, 9, 12.
[24] Gupta, D., Kayode, O., Bhatt, S., Gupta, M., and Tosun, A.S. Hierarchical federated learning based anomaly detection using digital twins for smart healthcare. In *Proceedings of the 2021 IEEE 7th International Conference on Collaboration and Internet Computing (CIC)*, Atlanta, GA, 13–15 December 2021; pp. 16–25.
[25] Singh, P., Gaba, G.S., Kaur, A., Hedabou, M., and Gurtov, A. Dew-cloud-based hierarchical federated learning for intrusion detection in IoMT. *IEEE J. Biomed. Health Inform.* 2022, 27, 722–731.
[26] Abdellatif, A.A., Mhaisen, N., Mohamed, A., Erbad, A., Guizani, M., Dawy, Z., and Nasreddine, W. Communication-efficient hierarchical federated learning for IoT heterogeneous systems with imbalanced data. *Future Gener. Comput. Syst.* 2022, 128, 406–419.
[27] Gandhi, N., Mishra, S., Bharti, S.K., and Bhagat, K. Leveraging towards privacy-preserving using federated machine learning for healthcare systems. In *Proceedings of the 2021 IEEE International Conference on Electronics, Computing and Communication Technologies (CONECCT)*, Bangalore, India, 9–11 July 2021; IEEE: New York, NY, 2021; pp. 1–6.
[28] Chen, H., Li, H., Xu, G., Zhang, Y., and Luo, X. Achieving privacy-preserving federated learning with irrelevant updates over e-health applications. In *Proceedings of the ICC 2020–2020 IEEE International Conference on Communications (ICC)*, Dublin, Ireland, 20–23 October 2020; IEEE: New York, NY, 2020; pp. 1–6.
[29] Abadi, M., Chu, A., Goodfellow, I., *et al.* Deep learning with differential privacy. In *Proceedings of the 2016 ACM SIGSAC Conference on Computer and Communications Security*, Wien, Austria, 24–28 October 2016; pp. 308–318.
[30] Wei, K., Li, J., Ding, M., *et al.* Federated learning with differential privacy: Algorithms and performance analysis. *IEEE Trans. Inf. Forensics Secur.* 2020, 15, 3454–3469.
[31] Ho, T.T., Tran, K.D., and Huang, Y. FedSGDCOVID: Federated SGD COVID-19 detection under local differential privacy using chest X-ray images and symptom information. *Sensors* 2022, 22, 3728.
[32] Akter, M., Moustafa, N., Lynar, T., and Razzak, I. Edge intelligence: Federated learning-based privacy protection framework for smart healthcare systems. *IEEE J. Biomed. Health Inform.* 2022, 26, 5805–5816.
[33] Islam, T.U., Ghasemi, R., and Mohammed, N. Privacy-preserving federated learning model for healthcare data. In *Proceedings of the 2022 IEEE 12th Annual Computing and Communication Workshop and Conference (CCWC)*, Las Vegas, NV, 26–29 January 2022; pp. 0281–0287.
[34] Cholakoska, A., Pfitzner, B., Gjoreski, H., Rakovic, V., Arnrich, B., and Kalendar, M. Differentially private federated learning for anomaly detection

in eHealth networks. In *Proceedings of the 2021 ACM International Joint Conference on Pervasive and Ubiquitous Computing and Proceedings of the 2021 ACM International Symposium on Wearable Computers*, New York, NY, 21–26 September, 2021; pp. 514–518.

[35] Das, P., Singh, M., and Roy, D.G. A secure softwarized blockchain-based federated health alliance for next generation IoT networks. In *Proceedings of the 2021 IEEE Globecom Workshops (GC Wkshps)*, Madrid, Spain, 7–11 December 2021; IEEE: New York, NY, 2021; pp. 1–6.

[36] Imtiaz, S., Horchidan, S.F., Abbas, Z., Arsalan, M., Chaudhry, H.N., and Vlassov, V. Privacy preserving time-series forecasting of user health data streams. In *Proceedings of the 2020 IEEE International Conference on Big Data (Big Data)*, Atlanta, GA, 10–13 December 2020; IEEE: New York, NY, 2020; pp. 3428–3437.

[37] Adnan, M., Kalra, S., Cresswell, J.C., Taylor, G.W., and Tizhoosh, H.R. Federated learning and differential privacy for medical image analysis. *Sci. Rep.* 2022, 12, 1953.

[38] Acar, A., Aksu, H., Uluagac, A.S., and Conti, M. A survey on homomorphic encryption schemes: Theory and implementation. *ACM Comput. Surv.* 2018, 51, 79.

[39] Xie, Y., Li, P., Zhu, X., and Wu, Q. Federated diabetes mellitus analysis via homomorphic encryption. *Proc. J. Phys. Conf. Ser. IOP Publ.* 2020, 1684, 012033.

[40] Ji, J., Yan, D., and Mu, Z. Personnel status detection model suitable for vertical federated learning structure. In *Proceedings of the 2022 6th International Conference on Machine Learning and Soft Computing*, Haikou, China, 15–17 January 2022; pp. 98–104.

[41] Ma, Z., Ma, J., Miao, Y., Liu, X., Choo, K.K.R., and Deng, R.H. Pocket diagnosis: Secure federated learning against poisoning attack in the cloud. IEEE Trans. Serv. Comput. 2021, 15, 3429–3442.

[42] Hao, M., Li, H., Xu, G., Liu, Z., and Chen, Z. Privacy-aware and resource-saving collaborative learning for healthcare in cloud computing. In *Proceedings of the ICC 2020 IEEE International Conference on Communications (ICC)*, Dublin, Ireland, 7–11 June 2020; IEEE: New York, NY, 2020; pp. 1–6.

[43] Wang, R., Lai, J., Zhang, Z., Li, X., Vijayakumar, P., and Karuppiah, M. Privacy-preserving federated learning for internet of medical things under edge computing. *IEEE J. Biomed. Health Inform.* 2022, 3, 1882.

[44] Hakak, S., Ray, S., Khan, W.Z., and Scheme, E. A framework for edge-assisted healthcare data analytics using federated learning. In *Proceedings of the 2020 IEEE International Conference on Big Data (Big Data)*, Atlanta, GA, 10–13 December 2020; IEEE: New York, NY, 2020; pp. 3423–3427.

[45] Wang, X., Liang, Z., Koe, A.S.V., *et al.* Secure and efficient parameters aggregation protocol for federated incremental learning and its applications. *Int. J. Intell. Syst.* 2022, 37, 4471–4487.

[46] Shayan, M., Fung, C., Yoon, C.J., and Beschastnikh, I. Biscotti: A blockchain system for private and secure federated learning. *IEEE Trans. Parallel Distrib. Syst.* 2020, 32, 1513–1525.

[47] Ali, M., Karimipour, H., and Tariq, M. Integration of blockchain and federated learning for Internet of Things: Recent advances and future challenges. *Comput. Secur.* 2021, 108, 102355.

[48] Qu, Y., Uddin, M.P., Gan, C., Xiang, Y., Gao, L., and Yearwood, J. Blockchain-enabled federated learning: A survey. *ACM Comput. Surv.* 2022, 55, 70.

[49] Chang, Y., Fang, C., and Sun, W. A blockchain-based federated learning method for smart healthcare. *Comput. Intell. Neurosci.* 2021, 2021, 376418.

[50] Passerat-Palmbach, J., Farnan, T., McCoy, M., Harris, J.D., Manion, S.T., Flannery, H.L., and Gleim, B. Blockchain-orchestrated machine learning for privacy preserving federated learning in electronic health data. In *Proceedings of the 2020 IEEE International Conference on Blockchain (Blockchain)*, Toronto, ON, Canada, 3–6 2020; IEEE: New York, NY, 2020; pp. 550–555.

[51] Salim, M.M., and Park, J.H. Federated learning-based secure electronic health record sharing scheme in medical informatics. *IEEE J. Biomed. Health Inform.* 2022, 27, 617–624.

[52] Lakhan, A., Mohammed, M.A., Nedoma, J., *et al.* Federated-learning based privacy preservation and fraud-enabled blockchain IoMT system for healthcare. *IEEE J. Biomed. Health Inform.* 2022, 27, 664–672.

[53] Choudhury, O., Gkoulalas-Divanis, A., Salonidis, T., *et al.* A syntactic approach for privacy preserving federated learning. In *Proceedings of the 24th European Conference on Artificial Intelligence (ECAI 2020)*, Santiago de Compostela, Spain, 29 August–8 September 2020; IOS Press: Amsterdam, The Netherlands, 2020; pp. 1762–1769.

[54] Darzidehkalani, E., Ghasemi-Rad, M., and van Ooijen, P. Federated learning in medical imaging: Part I: Toward multicentral health care ecosystems. *J. Am. Coll. Radiol.* 2022, 19, 969–974.

[55] Astillo, P.V., Duguma, D.G., Park, H., Kim, J., Kim, B., and You, I. Federated intelligence of anomaly detection agent in IoTMD-enabled diabetes management control system. *Future Gener. Comput. Syst.* 2022, 128, 395–405.

[56] Cellamare, M., van Gestel, A.J., Alradhi, H., Martin, F., and Moncada-Torres, A. A federated generalized linear model for privacy-preserving analysis. *Algorithms* 2022, 15, 243.

[57] Otoum, Y., Wan, Y., and Nayak, A. Federated transfer learning-based ids for the internet of medical things (IoMT). In *Proceedings of the 2021 IEEE Globecom Workshops (GC Wkshps)*, Madrid, Spain, 7–11 December 2021; IEEE: New York, NY, 2021; pp. 1–6.

[58] Chamikara, M.A.P., Bertok, P., Khalil, I., Liu, D., and Camtepe, S. Privacy preserving distributed machine learning with federated learning. *Comput. Commun.* 2021, 171, 112–125.

[59] Nguyen, T., Dakka, M., Diakiw, S., *et al.* A novel decentralized federated learning approach to train on globally distributed, poor quality, and protected private medical data. *Sci. Rep.* 2022, 12, 8888.

[60] Luo, C., Islam, M.N., Sheils, N.E., *et al.* dPQL: A lossless distributed algorithm for generalized linear mixed model with application to

privacy-preserving hospital profiling. *J. Am. Med. Inform. Assoc.* 2022, 29, 1366–1371.

[61] Ma, J., Zhang, Q., Lou, J., Xiong, L., and Ho, J.C. Communication efficient federated generalized tensor factorization for collaborative health data analytics. In *Proceedings of the Web Conference 2021*, Ljubljana, Slovenia, 19–23 April 2021; ACM: New York, NY, 2021; pp. 171–182.

[62] Wu, C., Wu, F., Lyu, L., Huang, Y., and Xie, X. Communication-efficient federated learning via knowledge distillation. *Nat. Commun.* 2022, 13, 2032.

[63] Paragliola, G. Evaluation of the trade-off between performance and communication costs in federated learning scenario. *Future Gener. Comput. Syst.* 2022, 136, 282–293.

[64] Han, B., Jhaveri, R., Wang, H., Qiao, D., and Du, J. Application of robust zero-watermarking scheme based on federated learning for securing the healthcare data. *IEEE J. Biomed. Health Inform.* 2021, 27, 2, 804–813.

[65] Gong, Q., Ruan, H., Chen, Y., and Su, X. CloudyFL: A cloudlet-based federated learning framework for sensing user behavior using wearable devices. In *Proceedings of the 6th International Workshop on Embedded and Mobile Deep Learning*, Portland, OR, 1–3 July 2022; ACM: New York, NY, 2022; pp. 13–18.

[66] Siniosoglou, I., Argyriou, V., Lagkas, T., Moscholios, I., Fragulis, G., and Sarigiannidis, P. Unsupervised Bias Evaluation of DNNs in non-IID Federated Learning Through Latent micro-Manifolds. In *Proceedings of the IEEE INFOCOM 2022—IEEE Conference on Computer Communications Workshops (INFOCOM WKSHPS)*, New York, NY, 2–5 May 2022; IEEE: New York, NY, 2022; pp. 1–6.

[67] Gouissem, A., Abualsaud, K., Yaacoub, E., Khattab, T., and Guizani, M. Robust decentralized federated learning using collaborative decisions. In *Proceedings of the 2022 International Wireless Communications and Mobile Computing (IWCMC)*, Dubrovnik, Croatia, 30 May–3 June 2022; IEEE: New York, NY, 2022; pp. 254–258.

[68] Durga, R., and Poovammal, E. Federated learning model for healthchain system. In *Proceedings of the 2021 6th IEEE International Conference on Recent Advances and Innovations in Engineering (ICRAIE)*, Kedah, Malaysia, 1–3 December 2021; IEEE: New York, NY, 2021; Volume 6, pp. 1–6.

[69] Lee, J.Y. A decentralized token economy: How blockchain and cryptocurrency can revolutionize business. *Bus. Horizons* 2019, 62, 773–784.

[70] Hammoud, A., Otrok, H., Mourad, A., and Dziong, Z. Stable federated fog formation: An evolutionary game theoretical approach. *Future Gener. Comput. Syst.* 2021, 124, 21–32.

[71] Hashash, O., Sharafeddine, S., and Dawy, Z. MEC-based energy-aware distributed feature extraction for mHealth applications with strict latency requirements. In *2021 IEEE International Conference on Communications Workshops (ICC Workshops)*. IEEE: New York, NY, 2021.

[72] Shamseddine, H., Nizam, J., Hammoud, A., *et al.* A novel federated fog architecture embedding intelligent formation. In *IEEE Netw.* 2020, 35.3, 198–204.

[73] Dasaradharami Reddy, K., and Thippa Reddy Gadekallu. A comprehensive survey on federated learning techniques for healthcare informatics. *Comput. Intel. Neurosci.* 2023.

[74] Lee, J.Y. A decentralized token economy: How blockchain and cryptocurrency can revolutionize business. *Bus. Horiz.* 2019, 62.6, 773–784.

[75] Tran, H.-V., Kaddoum, G., Elgala, H., Abou-Rjeily, C., and Kaushal, H. Lightwave power transfer for federated learning-based wireless networks. *IEEE Commun. Lett.* 2020, 24.7, 1472–1476.

[76] Mourad, A., Tout, H., Wahab, O.A., Otrok, H., and Dbouk, T. Ad hoc vehicular fog enabling cooperative low-latency intrusion detection. *IEEE Internet Things J.* 2020, 8.2, 829–843.

Chapter 13

FL for secured medical image analysis

Thien Huynh-The[1] *and Tan Do-Duy*[1]

Abstract

In recent years, federated learning (FL) has emerged as an innovative paradigm in the field of artificial intelligence (AI), garnering significant attention from both academic researchers and industrial practitioners. At the heart of FL lies its ability to handle data in a decentralized manner, ushering in a new era of privacy-preserving AI applications [1–3]. This aspect is particularly appealing in the context of medical data, which often contains sensitive and private information about patients, necessitating robust safeguards against unauthorized disclosure.

In this chapter, we delve into the fascinating realm of FL for Secure Medical Image Analysis. We meticulously survey and analyze the wealth of research articles dedicated to FL-based medical image analysis. Throughout the chapter, we emphasize the crucial aspects associated with the implementation of FL in medical imaging. By meticulously extracting core information from the selected articles, we offer a detailed exploration of the characteristics of federated data and models. Delving into the performance achieved by these models, we provide an in-depth comparison between FL models with traditional machine learning (ML) models, shedding light on the groundbreaking potential of FL in the medical domain. Moreover, we recognize the significance of addressing the open issues and challenges that arise when integrating FL in various applications and services for medical image analysis. Along with that, we put forth our recommendations for the future trajectory of this field, envisioning the promising advancements that lie ahead. Ultimately, this chapter encapsulates a state-of-the-art compilation of FL methods tailored for deep learning (DL)-based medical image analysis. Readers will gain valuable insights into the advancements, limitations, and transformative capabilities of FL in the realm of secure medical image analysis. It is our fervent hope that this chapter will serve as a guiding light for researchers, practitioners, and stakeholders, fostering further advancements in the quest to leverage AI for enhanced patient care and medical decision-making while safeguarding the privacy of sensitive medical data.

[1]Department of Computer and Communications Engineering, Ho Chi Minh City University of Technology and Education, Vietnam

Keywords: Convolutional neural networks, Deep learning, Federated learning, Image classification, Medical image analysis, Model aggregation, Semantic segmentation

13.1 Introduction

Image processing and analysis are two distinct interconnected tasks, particularly in terms of image data classification. Image processing has found applications in numerous research fields, including the domain of medical imaging [4,5]. An image essentially comprises 2D signals, both vertical and horizontal dimensions, along with a number of pixels [6]. These pixel parameters vary for different types of medical images and play a crucial role in extracting pertinent information during an analysis procedure.

On the other hand, the primary role of analysis tasks is to comprehend the processed images through various techniques, prominently ML, which encompasses a range of learning-oriented algorithms. Initially, traditional ML algorithms such as decision trees, random forests, support vector machine (SVM), and naive Bayes were widely employed in image processing research. Subsequently, the advent of DL revolutionized the field, leading to neural network-based models becoming integral to image analysis, including medical imaging. The adoption and development of medical imaging for diagnostics has been steadily increasing worldwide, encompassing various radiological images like X-rays, computed tomography (CT), magnetic resonance imaging (MRI), ophthalmology images, and others. Additionally, valuable data from diversified sources such as the eye, skin, and cells have made significant contributions to clinical decision-making, enabling disease detection, diagnosis, and treatment [7]. As the demand for medical imaging rapidly increases, the need arises to transmit medical images securely across different systems featured by various computing platforms, necessitating the use of computer networks. However, handling a large number of such images in a centralized manner raises many challenges in terms of data storage, processing, and analysis. In the traditional ML approach, models are trained at individual centralized locations, making collaboration between models cumbersome. Furthermore, the sensitivity of medical information, such as X-rays, CT scans, and MRI data, demands stringent protection to prevent unauthorized access. While data sharing might seem like a solution, it is complicated and unsustainable to implement in real-world medical applications and services, particularly when it comes to data encryption-decryption processes [8].

To address these challenges, an alternative approach emerges, instead of bringing data to the central location where an AI model is trained, why not bring the AI model to data? This approach, known as Federated Learning, enables collaborative learning without the requirement of data accumulation from multiple sources. FL was first introduced in 2016 and has gained significant traction, especially in the healthcare domain [9]. One of its primary benefits lies in its ability to address privacy and data protection concerns, critical factors in developing secure medical AI solutions. In FL, clients/participants can train models locally using their owned data, estimating different parameters for their respective models, which are then shared with a centralized server for aggregation. This way, the focus shifts from which data is used or what algorithms are employed to managing data in a privacy-preserving manner [10].

In this chapter, we delve into the realm of FL for Secure Medical Image Analysis, exploring its potential to safeguard patient privacy while fostering collaboration and advancements in AI-based medical imaging. By bringing the model to the data, FL presents a promising pathway toward responsible and effective AI deployment in healthcare. Through empirical studies and practical insights, we demonstrate the viability and reliability of FL in the medical imaging domain, paving the way for a more privacy-conscious and patient-centric future in AI-enabled healthcare.

13.2 Fundamentals of federated learning

Federated Learning is a revolutionary approach that overcomes the limitations of isolated data silos by enabling the use of data from diverse locations worldwide for global model learning while preserving the privacy of local data at distributed clients [11,12]. While it may seem intuitive to train each local model on its respective data and then aggregate their parameters to create a global model, this approach often results in poor overall performance across all datasets [13]. To achieve effective FL, the training processes of local and global models should be carried out repeatedly for multiple rounds, terminating once a performance threshold is reached [14].

The FL process begins with the acquisition of an initial model from the central server. Each local client then trains an AI model using its own data locally. Once trained, the trainable parameters or weights are shared with the central server, which waits for gradients from other participating clients. An aggregation algorithm, such as federated averaging algorithm (FedAvg) [15], then combines these gradients to create the updated global model. This aggregated global model is subsequently shared with all clients in a network, completing one round of the learning procedure. The iterative nature of FL allows for continuous improvement until the global model's accuracy meets the requirement. Throughout the learning and client-server communication procedures, both the clients and the central server reserve the models obtained from previous iterations, thus deciding whether to update the new model or revert to a previous version based on various evaluation factors.

Several considerations come into play when initiating the model training process, setting the training configurations/options, and defining the role of central server. For instance, when a certain number of clients have contributed their model updates, the model aggregation will be performed to optimize learning efficiency. A distinguishing aspect of FL is its focus on the ability of trained models to generalize unseen data rather than its performance achieved on the training or seen data. The availability of more diverse data in FL reduces biases stemming from demographics, equipment types, and other factors, leading to model generalization enhancement. Some studies have shown that FL models, such as those used to detect and classify breast density, can achieve a remarkable improvement of 45.8% approximately in model generalization [16]. In summary, FL offers a promising solution to the challenges posed by isolated data silos, facilitating collaboration while maintaining data

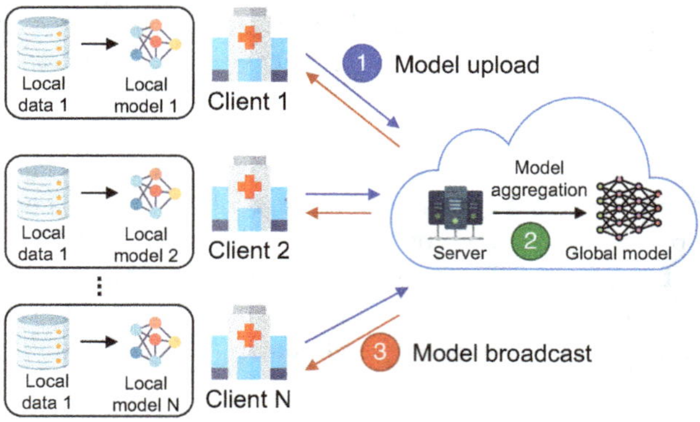

Figure 13.1 *Overview of FL applied in the domain of healthcare analysis and medical diagnosis, employing a server–client architecture. Multiple clients are involved, and each selected client independently trains an AI model using its local dataset. The server gathers the locally trained models and aggregates them to create a global model, which is then distributed back to all the selected clients for deployment.*

privacy. Through iterative model updates and global aggregation, FL empowers the development of robust and generalized AI models, fostering advancements across various domains, including healthcare, finance, and other data-rich industries.

In Figure 13.1, we present the typical process of FL, which operates within a client-server architecture and relies on the FedAvg serving as the foundation for many popular FL algorithms. This process is designed to facilitate collaborative model training while preserving the privacy of clients' data. The key components of the process are outlined as follows:

- *Client Selection*: The server is responsible for selecting a specific set of clients that meet certain requirements. For instance, in the context of medical data, a client may only participate in the federation and check in with the server if it can securely access the federation's intranet and has relatively good bandwidth.
- *Local Training*: Each selected client independently performs local model training using optimization techniques like stochastic gradient descent with momentum (SGDM) and adaptive moment estimation (Adam) based on its own private data. Initially, the trainable parameters (a.k.a., model weights) can be initialized either on each client or by the server.
- *Model Upload*: After local training, all the selected clients upload their trained models, including their respective weights, to the central server.
- *Model Aggregation*: The server aggregates the models received from all participating clients to update the global model. This aggregation process combines the knowledge learned from various local models while preserving privacy.
- *Broadcast*: The server then broadcasts the current shared global model, including its weights, to the selected clients. Upon receiving the updated global model,

each client downloads and deploys it for further local fine-tuning or updates using its private data.

This cyclical process continues iteratively until a predefined stopping criterion is met, ensuring that the global model is continuously refined based on contributions from various clients without requiring direct access to their private data. FL's distributed and privacy-preserving nature enables cooperative learning among diverse clients while fostering advancements in AI models across different domains, including healthcare and medical imaging.

13.3 FL for medical image analysis

In this section, we conduct a comprehensive survey of the latest research literature focused on the principal applications of FL techniques to medical image analysis and image-based healthcare diagnosis. Emphasizing the critical need for secure data handling in healthcare, we explore how FL addresses security challenges while enhancing the efficiency of the learning process. Furthermore, we present a diverse range of medical image modalities utilized for the diagnosis of different organs (such as brain, lung, chest, etc), estimating the intricate features that demand explicit description for accurate medical assessments.

13.3.1 Brain image analysis

13.3.1.1 Datasets

We highlight some significant datasets that have played a pivotal role in advanced medical image analysis, particularly in the domain of brain imaging.

- Alzheimer's Disease Neuroimaging Initiative (ADNI) stands as a prominent benchmark for Alzheimer's Disease research, offering a comprehensive collection of brain MRI, functional MRI, and positron emission tomography (PET) data from over 1,900 subjects across 59 centers.
- Autism Brain Imaging Data Exchange (ABIDE) initiative provides an essential database for Autism spectrum disorder research, encompassing both structural and functional brain images gathered independently from more than 24 imaging laboratories worldwide.
- Multimodal Brain Tumor Image Segmentation Benchmark (BraTS) is an instrumental dataset for brain image segmentation, offering brain MRIs acquired from around 19 independent institutions, continuously updated for the Brain Tumor Segmentation Challenge.
- Radiological Society of North America (RSNA) presents a large-scale multi-institutional dataset of CT images to detect and intracranial hemorrhage detection, comprising 874,035 images from three different institutions.

13.3.1.2 FL-based approaches

For the applications of brain tumor segmentation, the work [17] demonstrated the feasibility of using FL with U-Net architecture for brain tumor segmentation through different medical centers without sharing the raw patient data. Relying on the evaluation results of the BraTS dataset, the study verified the effectiveness of FL in preserving the privacy of patient data while achieving accurate and consistent segmentation results, thus making it a promising approach for collaborative medical image analysis. In another work [18], FL was exploited to address the challenges of protecting patient data privacy across multiple institutions. The key contribution was the development of a privacy-preserving FL framework that allowed multiple institutions and medical centers to collaboratively train a DL model for brain tumor segmentation without sharing raw patient data. Besides ensuring data privacy, the approach gained collective knowledge of distributed datasets and became an effective solution for multi-institutional medical image analysis in a privacy-conscious manner.

In [19], a multi-site 3D brain MRI images analysis framework, namely guide-weighted federated DL, was proposed to overcome the challenges of data privacy and heterogeneity across different sites by utilizing weighted aggregation and incorporating guide gradients to modernize the federated models. The study validated the framework using a publicly accessible multi-site brain MRI database of autism spectrum disorder (ASD) and demonstrated that the federated models outperform local models by an accuracy improvement of 0.92–4.02% on the ABIDE dataset. As the first FL framework for 3D MRI data, this approach had the potential to facilitate secure sharing of medical imaging data across multiple sites, leading to the formation of a robust federated model for future diagnostic classification tasks and assisting in the diagnosis and screening of neuropsychiatric disorders. As a novel privacy-preserving FL approach for multi-site fMRI classification, [20] addressed the challenges of gathering large fMRI datasets from multiple distributed health centers while safeguarding patient privacy. By employing a decentralized iterative optimization algorithm and incorporating domain adaptation methods, the proposed FL framework enabled the effective utilization of multi-site data without gathering the patient data in a centralized manner, thus leading to the performance enhancement of neuroimage analysis and the identification of reliable disease-related biomarkers. This approach is demonstrated as an effective AI-based solution to deal with privacy-sensitive medical data analysis problems through FL, and the suggested pipeline has potential applications in other domains.

FedNI [22], a learning framework adopting a graph generative adversarial network (GAN), was designed to federatively train missing node and edge predictors and a global graph convolutional neural network (GCN) node classifier across institutions, hence resulting in more accurate ML models for disease prediction (e.g., autism spectrum disorder and Alzheimer disease) on population graphs, particularly in the context of medical applications. Additionally, the proposed FedNI outperforms many local and baseline FL methods with significant margins on two public neuroimage datasets, thus making obvious its novelty and effectiveness.

For intracranial hemorrhage diagnosis, the work [21] improved upon traditional consistency regularization methods by introducing a new inter-client relation matching scheme that connected the learning across labeled and unlabeled clients (hospitals) in an FL setting, where the proposed matching scheme is illustrated in Figure 13.2. The method effectively leveraged data from both labeled and unlabeled

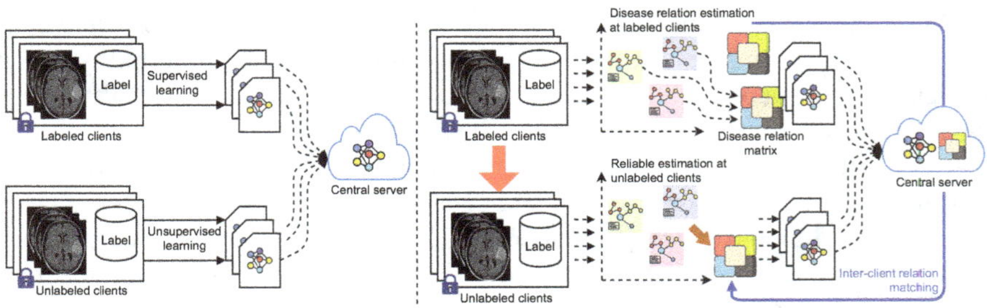

Figure 13.2 Left: The initial FSSL approach involves unsupervised learning (such as consistency regularization) at unmarked clients, which can lead to the local model forgetting the original task knowledge over the course of training. Right: By contrast, the proposed FedIRM [21] method explicitly leverages the knowledge from marked clients to assist the pattern-learning data of unmarked clients. By associating extracted disease correlations and relationships, FedIRM mitigates the loss of knowledgeable information at unlabeled clients and encourages the incorporation of discriminative information from the unlabeled data.

clients for medical image classification tasks, demonstrating clear improvements over state-of-the-art methods on large-scale medical image datasets like RSNA.

13.3.2 Chest image analysis

13.3.2.1 Datasets

We summarize some well-known chest image datasets that have been commonly used in healthcare and medical diagnosis:

- CheXpert [23] is a comprehensive collection of 224,316 chest radiographs obtained from 65,240 patients, sourced from Stanford University Medical Center.
- ChestX-ray (also known as ChestX-ray14) [24] is a publicly-available medical image dataset comprising 112,120 frontal-view X-ray images from 30,805 patients, annotated with 14 disease labels. It was expanded from the ChestX-ray8 dataset to include six additional thorax diseases, namely Edema, Emphysema, Fibrosis, Hernia, Pleural, and Thickening.
- COVID-19 Chest X-ray (also known as COVID-19 CXR) [25] is an openly accessible database of chest X-ray images, containing 3,616 cases of COVID-19 positivity, 10,192 normal controls, 6,012 cases of lung opacity (non-COVID infection), and 1,345 viral pneumonia cases.

13.3.2.2 FL-based approaches

Based on the combination of CNN and GNN, the work [26] addressed the challenges of multi-institutional collaborations to detect and diagnose cardio, thoracic, and pulmonary pathologies in chest radiographs. In particular, the combined CNN-GNN model was trained with a modified FedAvg algorithm, thus allowing the share of

CNN weights across all clients to extract meaningful and robust features while training GNN models separately at each client to capture the local co-morbidity dependencies for multi-label chest disease classification. The simulation results on the CheXpert dataset, partitioned across five sites regarding FL configurations, demonstrated the effectiveness of the FL approach, with no significant drop in performance compared to the centralized training strategy. Additionally, the site-specific GNN models showed their efficiency in modeling local disease co-occurrence statistics, thus conducting an average area under the ROC curve of 0.79 with an improvement of 1.74%. In summary, besides addressing the challenges of data privacy and variations in disease prevalence across different sites, the proposed approach introduced a promising solution for accurate and collaborative disease detection in medical image analysis. To protect byzantine clients from malicious attacks, the authors in [27] proposed a robust aggregation rule, called distance-based outlier suppression (DOS), for FL in chest image-based disease detection and analysis. The DOS method computed outlier scores for each client based on the distance between their local parameter updates using Copula-based outlier detection (COPOD). These outlier scores were then converted into normalized weights using the softmax function to obtain a locally weighted parameter averaging mechanism to upgrade the global model. The proposed DOS aggregation approach effectively suppressed the parameter update procedure from malignant clients without hyperparameter selection, even when data distributions were heterogeneous. Evaluation of some well-known medical imaging datasets (CheXpert and HAM10000) demonstrated the remarkable robustness of the DOS method compared to other state-of-the-art methods in counteracting various poisoning attacks.

In [28], a novel FL framework, called FedFew, was introduced to overcome the problem of extreme class imbalance in medical datasets with decentralized and partially labeled data. The FedFew framework consisted of three stages: federated self-supervised learning to learn class-agnostic representations, energy-based multi-label classification for common classes using decentralized partially labeled data, and a prototype-based nearest-neighbor model for few-shot matching of underrepresented classes. The evaluation results on the ChestX-ray dataset for multi-label thoracic disease classification tasks demonstrated that FedFew outperforms standard FL approaches by a significant margin, and is recommended as an effective solution for robust and accurate multi-label classification in federated medical data scenarios with class-wise data imbalance.

To prevent data leakage in a model training process, particularly in healthcare applications where patient and data privacy is crucial, the work [29] exploited FL to collaboratively train AI models without the demand of raw data sharing. The research demonstrated that existing FL attacks, involving the inversion of deep neural networks from model gradients, were impractical in scenarios where clients updated batch normalization (BN) statistics during the training process. The study introduced a new baseline attack that worked specifically for different FL setups. Additionally, the research presented some effective methods to measure and visualize potential data leakage in FL, contributing to the establishment of reproducible techniques for quantifying data privacy risks. This work provided valuable insights into determining the optimal trade-off between privacy-preserving techniques like differential privacy and model accuracy based on measurable metrics, thus enhancing the security and privacy considerations in FL implementations.

13.3.3 Lung image analysis

13.3.3.1 Datasets

Besides COVID-19 CXR [25], the COVIDx dataset has been exploited for several lung image-based analysis works. The COVIDx dataset [30] is a large-scale and fully accessible database comprising 13,975 chest X-ray images of 13,870 patients. COVIDx includes 358 chest X-ray images from 266 COVID-19 patient cases, 8,066 normal cases, and 5,538 non-COVID-19 pneumonia cases.

13.3.3.2 FL-based approaches

As an effort to address the challenges of privacy protection and data scarcity in automatic diagnosis of COVID-19 via DL models, the authors [31] proposed a new algorithm, called FL on medical datasets using partial networks (FLOP) which enabled different hospitals and medical centers to cooperatively train an effective DL model by only sharing a partial model between the server and clients instead of sharing raw data as an insecure regular strategy. Extensive experiments on benchmark data and real-world healthcare tasks, including the COVID-19 dataset, demonstrated that FLOP achieved comparable or even better performance while reducing privacy and security risks, thus allowing different hospitals to train a partially shared model collaboratively and effectively without sharing locally sensitive patients' data. This research contributed to the advancement of FL in medical applications, offering a promising solution for secure and privacy-preserving diagnosis of COVID-19 and other medical conditions.

Unlike the widely used FedAvg, MediSecFed [33], a secure framework for FL in hostile environments, employed knowledge distillation and model inversion techniques to ensure additional security and privacy features. This approach enabled knowledge exchange among different active medical centers without revealing model parameters, thereby protecting local data privacy, and significantly reducing communication costs. Evaluation of two chest X-ray datasets demonstrated that MediSecFed performed more effectively than FedAvg by 15% in a hostile environment, and it maintained good performance even with an increased number of malicious participating entities. Based on the robustness of MediSecFed in collaboratively learning in a malicious environment while preserving privacy and reducing communication costs, it is recognized that MediSecFed was a more desirable and efficient alternative to FedAvg for FL-based medical image analysis applications.

The authors in [32] developed a robust federated contrastive learning (FCL) framework in Figure 13.3, called FedMoCo, which was specifically designed for efficient use of decentralized unlabeled medical data in a federated computing environment. FedMoCo presented two innovative modules: metadata transformation for inter-node statistical data augmentation and self-adaptive aggregation for representational similarity measurement. As the first FCL approach applied to medical images, the experiments demonstrated that FedMoCo consistently outperformed FedAvg in extracting meaningful representations for downstream tasks. Furthermore, FedMoCo substantially reduced the amount of labeled data required for downstream tasks,

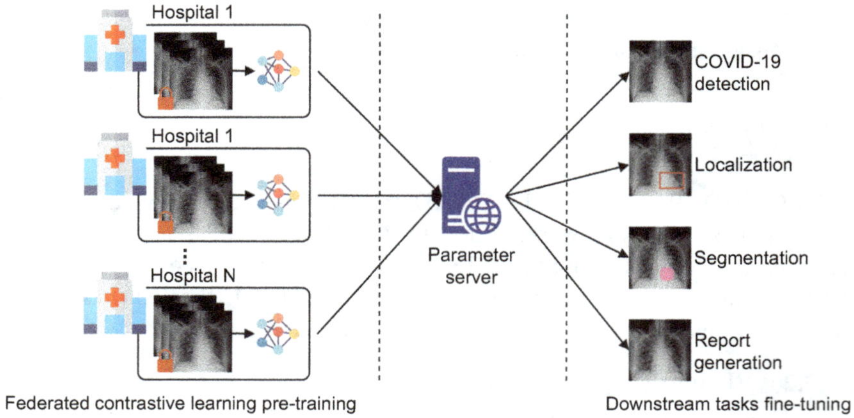

Figure 13.3 The FedMoCo framework in [32] enables training medical image models using decentralized unlabeled data from multiple hospitals. Remarkably, the framework facilitates pre-training on unlabeled data, followed by fine-tuning for various downstream tasks.

such as COVID-19 detection, while achieving reasonable performance, thus being more appropriate to label-efficient learning in the clinical domain using federated computing environments.

13.3.4 Skin image analysis

13.3.4.1 Datasets

There are two widely used image datasets for skin disease analysis and diagnosis:

- The HAM10000 dataset [34], also known as "Human Against Machine with 10000 training images," has gained significant popularity as a comprehensive collection of dermatoscopic images used for diagnosing pigmented skin lesions (Tschandl *et al.*, 2018). Comprising a total of 10,015 images from various sources, this extensive dataset encompasses a wide range of representative diagnostic categories for pigmented lesions.
- The ISIC challenge dataset [35], as introduced by Cassidy *et al.* (2022), is a substantial collection of data focused on skin lesion image analysis. It consists of various challenges designed for this purpose and has now become a widely accepted and standard benchmark dataset in the field of dermatoscopic image analysis.

13.3.4.2 FL-based approaches

For skin lesion classification, several recent methods have exploited FL to gain the high privacy and security of patient information and medical image data. The work [36] presented a personalized retrogress-resilient framework for FL in the field of computer-aided diagnosis, in which the framework addressed the challenges of privacy and ethical concerns in collecting large-scale medical data from multiple institutions. Especially, it introduced a Progressive Fourier Aggregation (PFA) approach at the server to enhance global knowledge gathering, along with a Deputy-Enhanced Transfer (DET) strategy for clients to improve the efficiency of locally trained models by transferring global knowledge smoothly. Extensive experiments on the ISIC challenge dataset demonstrated that the proposed framework outperformed state-of-the-art FL methods and exhibited excellent generalization on an out-of-distribution cohort. In [37], FedPerl, a semi-supervised FL method, for skin cancer classification leveraged peer learning from social sciences and ensemble averaging from committee machines to create communities of clients and encourage mutual learning, thus resulting in more accurate pseudo labels. The proposed peer anonymization (PA) technique ensured privacy preservation and reduced communication costs while maintaining performance without complexity increment. The validation on a large dataset demonstrated that FedPerl defeated several baseline methods and state-of-the-art semi-supervised FL (SSFL) by 15.8% and 1.8%, respectively, in terms of accuracy. In a reliable and label-efficient self-supervised FL framework as presented in Figure 13.4 for medical image analysis, a novel transformer-based self-supervised pre-training architecture was introduced to directly pre-trains models on decentralized target task datasets using masked image modeling [38]. This approach enhanced representation learning on heterogeneous data and enabled effective knowledge transfer to downstream models, thus significantly improving the test accuracy on retinal, dermatology, and chest X-ray classification compared to supervised baseline models with ImageNet pre-training. Moreover, the proposed federated self-supervised pre-training methods yielded better generalization to out-of-distribution data and improved performance when fine-tuning with limited labeled data, surpassing existing FL algorithms in these aspects.

To address the limitations of deep CNNs for medical image analysis in privacy-sensitive scenarios, a customized FL (CusFL) [39] enabled multiple healthcare and medical centers to collaboratively train their models with local datasets. Each client trained a client-specific CNN model guided by a federated global CNN model, which primarily contained multiple feature extraction layers for selective feature alignment. With this learning strategy, each client selectively learned useful information and knowledge from the federated global model, providing superior performance in

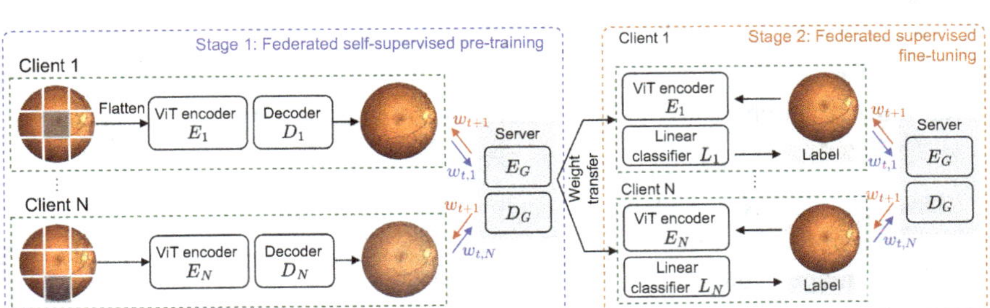

Figure 13.4 Overview of the federated self-supervised learning framework in [38]

detecting clinically significant prostate cancer and skin lesion classification in multi-source medical image datasets. In another work [27], DOS for FL was developed for learning skin lesion classification model. Unlike existing FL solutions, DOS overcame the vulnerability to poisoning attacks from malicious parties by computing the distance between local parameter updates of various clients and using Copula-based outlier detection (COPOD) to obtain outlier scores for each client. These scores were then transformed into normalized weights using a softmax function, allowing for a weighted average of the local parameters to update the global model. The novelty of DOS relied on the ability to effectively suppress parameter updates from malicious clients without the need of hyperparameter selection and while accommodating heterogeneous data distributions, as demonstrated in evaluations on CheXpert and HAM10000. For multi-center multi-sequence cardiac magnetic resonance (CMR) segmentation, an innovative cross-center cross-sequence medical image segmentation FL framework (FedCRLD) was proposed to overcome the challenges posed by the heterogeneity among CMR data in FL, specifically focusing on two main issues: (1) representation bias in model fusion, which was mitigated by the contrastive re-localization module (CRL) that leveraged a contrastive difference metric of reciprocal information in a cross-attention localization transformer to transfer client-correlated meaningful information from the federated global model without bias; (2) optimization stop in model replacing, which was resolved through the momentum distillation strategy (MD) that can optimize continuously by adopting self-training on a dynamically updated client momentum set to distill optimization with local historical optimization records. The validation of FedCRLD on 420 CMR images from 6 clients and 2 public datasets verified its effectiveness for multi-center multi-sequence CMR segmentation. The authors in [21] proposed a novel approach of the federated semi-supervised learning (FSSL) in the scenario of collaborating distributed medical centers to improve conventional consistency regularization mechanisms by encompassing a novel inter-client relation matching scheme. This learning scheme explicitly connected the labeled and unlabeled clients by aligning their extracted disease relationships, addressing the challenge of limited task knowledge at unlabeled clients, and effectively leveraging discriminative information from unlabeled samples. The validation on two large-scale medical image classification datasets demonstrated the method's effectiveness with clear improvements over state-of-the-art techniques, as well as thorough ablation analysis on both tasks.

13.3.5 Eye image analysis

13.3.5.1 Datasets

To serve the research in eye disease detection and analysis, two image datasets are usually utilized:

- The Retina dataset available on Kaggle is a substantial collection of color digital retinal fundus images used for diabetic retinopathy detection. Comprising 17,563 image pairs, each image in the dataset is assigned a label on a scale from 0 to 4, indicating the presence and severity of diabetic retinopathy. The labels range from 0 (no diabetic retinopathy) to 4 (proliferative diabetic retinopathy).

- The Messidor-2 dataset comprises Diabetic Retinopathy (DR) examinations, with each examination consisting of two macula-centered eye fundus images, one for each eye. In total, the dataset contains 874 examinations, corresponding to 1748 images. While the dataset includes a spreadsheet with image pairing information, it does not provide annotations such as diabetic retinopathy "ground truth." Some third-party sources have proposed annotations, but these annotations are separate from the official Messidor-2 database and are not managed by our services.

13.3.5.2 FL-based approaches

In [40], a novel Diabetic Retinopathy (DR) severity grading technique called DRFL, was proposed based on FL. DRFL addresses the challenges of automated DR detection while protecting patient data privacy by utilizing FL, which allows DL models to be collectively trained without disclosing clinical information. DRFL combined FedAvg with the median of the categorical cross-entropy loss, which was better suited for handling under-fitted or over-fitted clients. Additionally, the work introduced a novel central server that effectively extracted multi-scale features from fundus images to identify small lesions, thus enhancing the accuracy of the model. The proposed model was evaluated on five clients with different preprocessed fundus images from various publicly available databases and achieved superior accuracy, specificity, precision, and F1 scores compared to other existing works.

To address the challenge of data heterogeneity in collaborative learning methods for diabetic retinopathy classification, a novel generative replay strategy was introduced with generative adversarial learning to aggregate knowledge from all local institutions in a privacy-preserving manner [41]. The method presented a dual model architecture, consisting of a primary model for task performance and an auxiliary "generative replay model" to facilitate the aggregation of knowledge from heterogeneous clients. Experimental results demonstrated the effectiveness of the proposed method in handling highly heterogeneous data partitions, achieving significant improvements in prediction accuracy for diabetic retinopathy classification and mean absolute value reduction for bone age prediction compared to state-of-the-art collaborative learning methods.

In another work [42], the authors proposed an innovative regional IoT-enabled federated learning-based approach, called IoT-FHR, for the accurate classification of hypertensive retinopathy (HR) lesions. The approach incorporated both the global and local lesion attributes to overcome the limitations of traditional classification algorithms, which struggled with HR lesion detection and classification due to the lack of distinct characteristics. By combining a local feature arterial and venous nicking classification model with the overall IoT-FHR classification model, the developed approach effectively boosted the classification accuracy significantly. The adoption of a neural network and a sigmoid-based classifier further refined the final output to exhaustively yield the probability value of IoT-FHR in the fundus image. In a nutshell, this work presented a new intersection detection algorithm for HR lesions classification, which significantly increased the overall accuracy, sensitivity, and specificity compared to recent centralized methods, particularly in comparison to single-stage classification models.

13.4 Challenges and future research directions

13.4.1 Challenges of FL for medical image analysis

Data heterogeneity: The data heterogeneity among clients is a common challenge encountered in real-world medical image sites, stemming from various factors. First, medical images from different sites or datasets are often captured using different scanners or scanning protocols. Additionally, patients across different sites or hospitals exhibit distinct data distributions, leading to what is known as "domain shift" or "client shift." Such heterogeneity can significantly degrade the performance and introduce biases in a federated learning system focused on medical imaging. Addressing the negative impact of data heterogeneity becomes a vital and complex research problem in this domain.

Privacy leakage/poisoning threats/attacks: In traditional federated learning, privacy protection is primarily achieved by exchanging and updating only the model parameters, without sharing raw data. However, extensive research has revealed that federated learning still faces privacy and security risks, notably privacy leakage and poisoning attacks. These concerns can arise at both the server and client ends of the federated learning system. Given the intricate communication and interaction among various entities or parties within an FL system, safeguarding individual privacy and ensuring data security poses a highly challenging task.

13.4.2 Future research directions

Monitoring client shift: Addressing domain shift between client datasets, known as "client shift," has emerged as a significant concern in federated learning for medical image analysis. To tackle this issue, domain adaptation techniques have garnered substantial interest. However, traditional domain adaptation methods often require access to both source and target domains, which may compromise privacy protection [43]. Therefore, developing more efficient federated domain adaptation methods presents a promising avenue for research. Additionally, personalized federated learning techniques that leverage local data to optimize a trained global model offer another potential solution.

Multi-modality data fusion: While numerous imaging techniques and tools exist to create various visual representations of each subject, such as structural MRI, functional MRI, CT, and PET, most existing federated learning studies focus on images from a single modality within each client. Leveraging multi-modal imaging data in a federated learning system presents an intriguing problem with practical implications. Although a few works have taken early steps in this direction, further research is anticipated in this area.

AI model generalization for unseen clients: Most current federated learning studies concentrate on model training and testing within a fixed federation system, where a global model is trained on and adopted to the same datasets of a client.

However, the challenge arises when facing data from unseen sites outside the federation (outside clients). Ensuring the generalization of a federated learning model in such scenarios constitutes a domain generalization problem or test-time adaptation problem [43]. Some recent works have introduced domain generalization into federated learning, but analyzing and enhancing the generalization of a trained federated learning model to unseen sites or unseen classes remains a promising research direction.

Weakly-supervised learning: In the realm of medical imaging data, weakly-supervised learning shows promise as a technique to handle incomplete, inexact, and inaccurate labels. These challenges are widespread in medical imaging, and exploring how to address "imperfect" data, such as learning from noisy labels, in a federated learning system deserves further investigation.

FL security with attacking prediction for robust defense: attach prediction for defense: The robustness and data privacy of several existing federated learning systems have been found vulnerable to both inside and outside attacks. Therefore, exploring strong defense strategies is essential to enhance the security of federated learning systems. Moreover, a pertinent question arises: if an institution wants to withdraw from a federation, how can it ensure its data has been completely removed from the trained federated learning model? One viable solution lies in employing data auditing techniques, which can also be used to detect the presence of poisoned or suspicious datasets used in federated learning training.

Decentralization concern and blockchain: Many existing federated learning (FL) methods for medical tasks follow a centralized paradigm, necessitating a trustworthy central server. However, this approach exhibits several drawbacks, such as vulnerability to poisonous attacks and credibility issues. To address these concerns, blockchain technology has emerged as a potentially promising solution. By incorporating blockchain, the dependency on a central server, which often becomes a bottleneck for the entire federation, can be avoided. While some efforts have been made to apply blockchain or other decentralization methods in medical image analysis, this direction remains relatively unexplored, leaving ample room for future research.

Availability of large-scale medical image dataset for FL benchmark: Currently, numerous medical image databases for the performance benchmark consist of quite small datasets for clients. Some studies resort to dividing a single large dataset into separate parts, simulating different client datasets. Unfortunately, there is a scarcity of large-scale federations comprising diverse sites worldwide. Only a few works have successfully explored real-world datasets from multiple countries. For instance, chest X-ray images are collected from different cities for COVID-19 detection [44], healthcare and medical data are gathered from various clinical institutions worldwide to design an FL model for breast density classification [16], and a large-scale federation through international cooperation is acknowledged for FL benchmarks [45]. Constructing comprehensive large-scale benchmarks, encompassing publicly available medical image databases and state-of-the-art FL algorithms through extensive international collaboration, would be highly favorable for real-world FL applications.

13.5 Conclusion

In conclusion, FL offers a transformative approach to medical image analysis, enabling collaborative learning while preserving patient privacy and data security. Through various applications in brain, chest, lung, skin, and eye image analysis, FL demonstrates its capability to overcome existing challenges, including sensitive data management and privacy risks in centralized systems. The chapter highlights that while FL has shown considerable potential in achieving high diagnostic accuracy and robust model generalization across diverse data sources, several challenges remain, including data heterogeneity, privacy threats, and model robustness. Future research directions, such as multi-modal data fusion, personalized FL techniques, and integration with blockchain for decentralization, are decisive for further advancing the adoption and development of FL in medical imaging. The innovative framework of FL continues to extend to various sectors in healthcare, thus ensuring that sensitive medical data remains secure while promoting the development of efficient and accurate diagnostic tools for enhanced patient care.

References

[1] Pandya S, Srivastava G, Jhaveri R, *et al.* Federated learning for smart cities: A comprehensive survey. *Sustainable Energy Technologies and Assessments*. 2023;55:102987.

[2] Bashir AK, Victor N, Bhattacharya S, *et al.* A Survey on Federated Learning for the Healthcare Metaverse: Concepts, Applications, Challenges, and Future Directions. arXiv preprint arXiv:230400524. 2023.

[3] Ramu SP, Boopalan P, Pham QV, *et al.* Federated learning enabled digital twins for smart cities: Concepts, recent advances, and future directions. *Sustainable Cities and Society*. 2022;79:103663.

[4] Hua CH, Huynh-The T, and Lee S. Retinal vessel segmentation using round-wise features aggregation on bracket-shaped convolutional neural networks. In: *2019 41st Annual International Conference of the IEEE Engineering in Medicine and Biology Society (EMBC)*. IEEE; 2019. p. 36–39.

[5] Hua CH, Huynh-The T, and Lee S. DRAN: Densely reversed attention based convolutional network for diabetic retinopathy detection. In: *2020 42nd Annual International Conference of the IEEE Engineering in Medicine & Biology Society (EMBC)*. IEEE; 2020. p. 1992–1995.

[6] Maier A, Steidl S, Christlein V, *et al. Medical Imaging Systems: An Introductory Guide*. Springer Cham; 2018.

[7] Giger ML. Machine learning in medical imaging. *Journal of the American College of Radiology*. 2018;15(3):512–520.

[8] Yan Z, Wicaksana J, Wang Z, *et al.* Variation-aware federated learning with multi-source decentralized medical image data. *IEEE Journal of Biomedical and Health Informatics*. 2020;25(7):2615–2628.

[9] McMahan HB, Moore E, Ramage D, *et al.* Federated Learning of Deep Networks Using Model Averaging. arXiv preprint arXiv:160205629. 2016;2:2.

[10] Karimireddy SP, Kale S, Mohri M, *et al.* Scaffold: Stochastic controlled averaging for federated learning. In: *International Conference on Machine Learning*. PMLR; 2020. p. 5132–5143.

[11] Pham QV, Zeng M, Huynh-The T, *et al.* Aerial access networks for federated learning: Applications and challenges. *IEEE Network*. 2022;36(3):159–166.

[12] Ruby R, Yang H, de Figueiredo FA, *et al.* Energy-efficient multiprocessor-based computation and communication resource allocation in two-tier federated learning networks. *IEEE Internet of Things Journal*. 2022;10(7):5689–5703.

[13] Zhang C, Xie Y, Bai H, *et al.* A survey on federated learning. *Knowledge-Based Systems*. 2021;216:106775.

[14] Teng L, Qiao Y, Shafiq M, *et al.* FLPK-BiSeNet: Federated learning based on priori knowledge and bilateral segmentation network for image edge extraction. *IEEE Transactions on Network and Service Management*. 2023.

[15] McMahan B, Moore E, Ramage D, *et al.* Communication-efficient learning of deep networks from decentralized data. In: *Artificial Intelligence and Statistics*. PMLR; 2017. p. 1273–1282.

[16] Roth HR, Chang K, Singh P, *et al.* Federated learning for breast density classification: A real-world implementation. In: *Domain Adaptation and Representation Transfer, and Distributed and Collaborative Learning: Second MICCAI Workshop, DART 2020, and First MICCAI Workshop, DCL 2020, Held in Conjunction with MICCAI 2020, Lima, Peru, October 4–8, 2020, Proceedings* 2. Springer; 2020. p. 181–191.

[17] Sheller MJ, Reina GA, Edwards B, *et al.* Multi-institutional deep learning modeling without sharing patient data: A feasibility study on brain tumor segmentation. In: *Brainlesion: Glioma, Multiple Sclerosis, Stroke and Traumatic Brain Injuries: 4th International Workshop, BrainLes 2018, Held in Conjunction with MICCAI 2018, Granada, Spain, September 16, 2018, Revised Selected Papers, Part I* 4. Springer; 2019. p. 92–104.

[18] Li W, Milletarì F, Xu D, *et al.* Privacy-preserving federated brain tumour segmentation. In: *Machine Learning in Medical Imaging: 10th International Workshop, MLMI 2019, Held in Conjunction with MICCAI 2019, Shenzhen, China, October 13, 2019, Proceedings* 10. Springer; 2019. p. 133–141.

[19] Fan Z, Su J, Gao K, *et al.* A federated deep learning framework for 3D brain MRI images. In: *2021 International Joint Conference on Neural Networks (IJCNN)*; 2021. p. 1–6.

[20] Li X, Gu Y, Dvornek N, *et al.* Multi-site fMRI analysis using privacy-preserving federated learning and domain adaptation: ABIDE results. *Medical Image Analysis*. 2020;65:101765.

[21] Liu Q, Yang H, Dou Q, *et al.* Federated semi-supervised medical image classification via inter-client relation matching. In: *Medical Image Computing and Computer Assisted Intervention–MICCAI 2021: 24th International Conference, Strasbourg, France, September 27–October 1, 2021, Proceedings, Part III* 24. Springer; 2021. p. 325–335.

[22] Peng L, Wang N, Dvornek N, *et al.* FedNI: Federated graph learning with network in painting for population-based disease prediction. *IEEE Transactions on Medical Imaging*. 2023;42(7):2032–2043.

[23] Irvin J, Rajpurkar P, Ko M, *et al.* Chexpert: A large chest radiograph dataset with uncertainty labels and expert comparison. In: *Proceedings of the AAAI Conference on Artificial Intelligence* 33. 2019. p. 590–597.

[24] Wang X, Peng Y, Lu L, *et al.* Chestx-ray8: Hospital-scale chest x-ray database and benchmarks on weakly-supervised classification and localization of common thorax diseases. In: *Proceedings of the IEEE Conference on Computer Vision and Pattern Recognition*; 2017. p. 2097–2106.

[25] Chowdhury ME, Rahman T, Khandakar A, *et al.* Can AI help in screening viral and COVID-19 pneumonia? *IEEE Access*. 2020;8:132665–132676.

[26] Chakravarty A, Kar A, Sethuraman R, *et al.* Federated learning for site aware chest radiograph screening. In: *2021 IEEE 18th International Symposium on Biomedical Imaging (ISBI)*. IEEE; 2021. p. 1077–1081.

[27] Alkhunaizi N, Kamzolov D, Takáč M, *et al.* Suppressing poisoning attacks on federated learning for medical imaging. In: *International Conference on Medical Image Computing and Computer-Assisted Intervention*. Springer; 2022. p. 673–683.

[28] Dong N, Kampffmeyer M, and Voiculescu I. Learning underrepresented classes from decentralized partially labeled medical images. In: *International Conference on Medical Image Computing and Computer-Assisted Intervention*. Springer; 2022. p. 67–76.

[29] Hatamizadeh A, Yin H, Molchanov P, *et al.* Do gradient inversion attacks make federated learning unsafe? *IEEE Transactions on Medical Imaging*. 2023.

[30] Wang L, Lin ZQ, and Wong A. Covid-net: A tailored deep convolutional neural network design for detection of covid-19 cases from chest x-ray images. *Scientific Reports*. 2020;10(1):19549.

[31] Yang Q, Zhang J, Hao W, *et al.* Flop: Federated learning on medical datasets using partial networks. In: *Proceedings of the 27th ACM SIGKDD Conference on Knowledge Discovery & Data Mining*; 2021. p. 3845–3853.

[32] Dong N and Voiculescu I. Federated contrastive learning for decentralized unlabeled medical images. In: *Medical Image Computing and Computer Assisted Intervention–MICCAI 2021: 24th International Conference, Strasbourg, France, September 27–October 1, 2021, Proceedings, Part III* 24. Springer; 2021. p. 378–387.

[33] Kumar A, Purohit V, Bharti V, *et al.* Medisecfed: Private and secure medical image classification in the presence of malicious clients. *IEEE Transactions on Industrial Informatics*. 2021;18(8):5648–5657.

[34] Tschandl P, Rosendahl C, and Kittler H. The HAM10000 dataset, a large collection of multi-source dermatoscopic images of common pigmented skin lesions. *Scientific Data*. 2018;5(1):1–9.

[35] Cassidy B, Kendrick C, Brodzicki A, *et al.* Analysis of the ISIC image datasets: Usage, benchmarks and recommendations. *Medical Image Analysis*. 2022;75:102305.

[36] Chen Z, Zhu M, Yang C, *et al.* Personalized retrogress-resilient framework for real-world medical federated learning. In: *Medical Image Computing and Computer Assisted Intervention–MICCAI 2021: 24th International Conference, Strasbourg, France, September 27–October 1, 2021, Proceedings, Part III* 24. Springer; 2021. p. 347–356.

[37] Bdair T, Navab N, and Albarqouni S. FedPerl: Semi-supervised peer learning for skin lesion classification. In: *International Conference on Medical Image Computing and Computer-Assisted Intervention*. Springer; 2021. p. 336–346.

[38] Yan R, Qu L, Wei Q, *et al.* Label-efficient self-supervised federated learning for tackling data heterogeneity in medical imaging. *IEEE Transactions on Medical Imaging*. 2023.

[39] Wicaksana J, Yan Z, Yang X, *et al.* Customized federated learning for multi-source decentralized medical image classification. *IEEE Journal of Biomedical and Health Informatics*. 2022;26(11):5596–5607.

[40] Mohan NJ, Murugan R, Goel T, *et al.* DRFL: Federated learning in diabetic retinopathy grading using fundus images. *IEEE Transactions on Parallel and Distributed Systems*. 2023.

[41] Qu L, Balachandar N, Zhang M, *et al.* Handling data heterogeneity with generative replay in collaborative learning for medical imaging. *Medical Image Analysis*. 2022;78:102424.

[42] Soni M, Singh NK, Das P, *et al.* IoT-based federated learning model for hypertensive retinopathy lesions classification. *IEEE Transactions on Computational Social Systems*. 2022;p. 1–10.

[43] Guan H, Yap PT, Bozoki A, *et al.* Federated Learning for Medical Image Analysis: A Survey; 2024. Available from: https://arxiv.org/abs/2306.05980.

[44] Li Z, Xu X, Cao X, *et al.* Integrated CNN and federated learning for COVID-19 detection on chest X-ray images. *IEEE/ACM Transactions on Computational Biology and Bioinformatics*. 2022;p. 1–11.

[45] Dayan I, Roth HR, Zhong A, *et al.* Federated learning for predicting clinical outcomes in patients with COVID-19. *Nature Medicine*. 2021;27(10): 1735–1743.

Conclusion

Gautam Srivastava[1]

Industry 5.0 is expected to integrate sustainable, human-centric, and resilient technologies, management principles, and organizational concepts into operations, supply chains, and ecosystems across the industries. Industry 5.0 focuses on a circular economy, cross-sector collaboration, and a human-centric approach and uses technology aimed at a better future. Humans are expected to play a major role through their creativity and expertise to collaborate with cognitive systems, machines, and algorithms to perform tasks. Artificial intelligence and machine learning algorithms are expected to play a pivotal role in helping human experts make decisions in the era of Industry 5.0. However, preserving the privacy of data when training algorithms at edge devices or servers is of paramount importance. Federated learning can collaboratively train a shared model while keeping the training data locally without exchanging it with a central cloud or server. This ability of federated learning can help in the preserving privacy of the data that is generated by various devices, which is used to train the machine learning model in the applications of Industry 5.0. Apart from this, through federated learning, mass personalization, which is one of the major aims of Industry 5.0, can be realized. In this book, several researchers have contributed chapters to elucidate how federated learning helps in achieving the aforementioned goals in Industry 5.0. This book will help researchers from academia and industry gain insights into how federated learning can be helpful in several application domains of Industry 5.0.

[1]Department of Math and Computer Science, Brandon University, Brandon, Canada

Index

www.ingramcontent.com/pod-product-compliance
Lightning Source LLC
LaVergne TN
LVHW011845200926
848484LV00002B/399

9781839537578